Colección Támesis

SERIE A: MONOGRAFÍAS, 328

LOVE POETRY IN THE SPANISH GOLDEN AGE

EROS, ERIS AND EMPIRE

ISABEL TORRES

LOVE POETRY IN THE SPANISH GOLDEN AGE

EROS, ERIS AND EMPIRE

TAMESIS

First published 2013 by Tamesis, Woodbridge

ISBN 978 1 85566 265 0

Tamesis is an imprint of Boydell & Brewer Ltd
PO Box 9, Woodbridge, Suffolk IP12 3DF, UK
and of Boydell & Brewer Inc.
668 Mt Hope Avenue, Rochester, NY 14620–2731, USA
website: www.boydellandbrewer.com

A CIP catalogue record for this book is available
from the British Library

The publisher has no responsibility for the continued existence or
accuracy of URLs for external or third-party internet websites referred to
in this book, and does not guarantee that any content on such websites is,
or will remain, accurate or appropriate

Papers used by Boydell & Brewer Ltd are natural, recyclable products
made from wood grown in sustainable forests

MIX
Paper from
responsible sources
FSC
www.fsc.org   FSC® C013604

Printed and bound in Great Britain by
CPI Antony Rowe, Chippenham and Eastbourne

Contents

Acknowledgements

A few years back, Ellie Ferguson, the former commissioning editor for Tamesis, suggested that I should author a Companion volume to Golden Age love poetry. It seemed like a good idea to both of us at the time. I realised some way into the project, however, that I was writing a different book. I hope that Ellie will forgive me (her idea is still a good one and pending!), and I thank her for her faith in me, her friendship and her support. My thanks also to the present editorial team at Tamesis for accommodating my change in direction, and to them and the production team for their guidance in bringing this project to fruition. I would also like to take this opportunity to acknowledge the support of Golden Age scholars whose intellectual generosity and friendship have been a source of inspiration and encouragement throughout my career, notably Professors Trevor Dadson, Terence O'Reilly and Anne Cruz.

I am grateful to the Arts and Humanities Research Council for funding a period of research leave which gave me the time and space to read, think and write, and to the School of Modern Languages at Queen's University, Belfast, for financial support that facilitated the publication of the book and dissemination of related research. Early versions of parts of the study were presented as papers at various conferences and symposia (including the AHGBI, SRBHP, and UCC Research Seminar) and my thanks to all those colleagues whose constructive engagement has informed and shaped my readings. Versions of parts of chapters 1, 2 and 4 have appeared as articles: 'Neo-Parkerism: An Approach to Reading Garcilaso de la Vega, Eclogue 1', *Bulletin of Spanish Studies,* LXXXV: 6 (2008), 93–105; 'Sites of Speculation: Water/Mirror Poetics in Garcilaso de la Vega, Eclogue II', *Bulletin of Hispanic Studies*, 86.6 (2009), 877–92 and 'Broaching the Void: Reconsidering Góngora's Indeterminate Poetics', *Bulletin of Spanish Studies*, 90.1 (2013), 107–29. I thank the editors of both journals for their permission to reprint. Special thanks are also due to those friends and colleagues who offered (often vital) moral support and assisted in various ways in the book's preparation (especially Eamon, Melanie, Anne and Jill), to Maeve for reading so positively beyond the border and to Janice for reminding us that it is still possible to deliver creative, academic leadership with honesty and integrity.

During this process I have been fuelled by caffeine and friendship in equally liberal measures by, and with, friends who are too numerous to mention and who heard more and knew more about this book than they ever wanted. My warmest thanks to you all for staying the distance, and to my parents and sister Gina for enduring support. Finally, the completion of this book, like so much else, would have been impossible without the unconditional love of Elena, Ana and Wence. It doesn't go without saying. Thank you.

Isabel Torres 2013

Eros, Eris and Empire

Preface

For over twenty years I have been delivering courses related to the amorous lyric of imperial Spain, one of the most significant bodies of verse in European literature. During that time I have fielded questions across the whole range of the 'frequently asked' and, on occasions, I have risen and fallen to the more idiosyncratic intervention. One query, however, stands out for the complexity at the core of its very obviousness, and because it has dogged me ever since. Simply put: 'what has love got to do with it?' This book takes that nagging question as its starting point and revolves around it.

The intelligibility of the question is secured, as Charnes has observed, by our awareness of the 'love story', or story of love, as an authoritative and authorising epistemology; a coercive ideological apparatus behind which a range of other narratives find cover: 'one of the most effective smokescreens available in the politics of cultural production.'[1] It would seem appropriate, therefore, that we should consider the lyric utterances of Renaissance love poetry, the foremost genre of European literature in the period, within the larger arena of the cultural politics in which they were conceived. Roland Greene set a persuasive precedent for just such an approach over a decade ago, in a study that established the significance of unrequited love (as framed within the Petrarchist tradition), as a 'staging area' for a variety of problems that beset the lived history of European imperialism. Greene located Petrarchism's 'discourse of differences', in 'the space where Renaissance love poetry encountered early modern empire at the inception of the Americas'.[2] The space of the present study is smaller than Greene's, its perspective less panoramic and without the detailed biographical, historical and social contexts which, I believe, by now, have been fully covered elsewhere. My focus is on the imperial 'home' space, where Golden Age Spanish love poetry meets early modern empire at the inception of a very conflicted national consciousness within Spain itself; and where the vernacular language, specifically Castilian, emerges in this encounter as a strategic locus of national

---

[1] See 'What's Love Got To Do With it? Reading the Liberal Humanist Romance in Antony and Cleopatra', in *Shakespearean Tragedy and Gender*, eds Shirley Nelson Garner and Madelon Springnether (Bloomington and Indianapolis: Indiana University Press, 1996), pp. 268–86 (p. 269).

[2] See Roland Greene, *Unrequited Conquests: Love and Empire in the Colonial Americas* (Chicago: University of Chicago Press, 2000). Quotations are cited from pp. 11, 6 and 1 respectively.

and imperial identity. The imperial 'home' is conceptualised, therefore, against the conventional anthropological paradigm which assumes, paradoxically, a relationship between identity and fixity, and which depends upon accepting self-centredness as a stable point of perspective that emanates outwards.[3] When the characteristic 'self-texturing crisis' of Spanish post-Petrarchan love poetry is re-evaluated as an aesthetic response to the contradictory currents of its provenance (in time and space),[4] a less homogeneous lyric emerges. Indeed, as the poetic voices of this volume will demonstrate, Petrarchan 'norms' were subject to a continuous process of reformulation before, and during, their encounter with transatlantic 'otherness'.

Responsiveness to the socio-cultural and political discourses that inform Spanish love poetry of the period marks out a growing body of scholarship. This has been accompanied, on occasions, by a tendency to forget that if imaginative literature matters at all, then, as Bongie reminds us, 'it matters first and foremost as literature'.[5] To over-historicise is to miss the point of lyric, to underestimate the fractal dimension that allows poetry to converse critically with its historical moment of origin, but also to transcend it and to open out to infinite reappropriations. For it is lyric's illusion of individuation that allows for the undoing and re-making of the lyric subject over space and time. The primary commitment of this book, then, is to lyric poetry, and to poets, individually, but also in terms of their dynamic interconnectedness. The political is a pervasive background presence, nonetheless, teased out where relevant in recognition of the lyric poet's sensitivity to the political architecture and ideology within which writing comes into being; and to the poet's awareness of how societal transformations impact upon the individual consciousness. I recognise, as will the reader, the influence of the new historicism in my own thinking, but have tried to construct the past as 'delicately' as possible, bearing in mind O'Brien's advice that if we pay due regard to 'the specificity and singularity' of the textual products of the past, '*their* reflections, if sensitively used, may help forge a way ahead for us'.[6] This has involved a respectful disengagement with the Foucauldian theory of unique sets of epistemes, whose 'breaks' are

---

[3] For a summary of this position, see Andrew Rapport and Nigel Dawson, 'Home and Movement: A Polemic', in *Migrants of Identity. Perceptions of Home in a World of Movement*, eds Andrew Rapport and Nigel Dawson (Oxford and New York: Berg, 1998), pp. 3–38.

[4] See Mariann Sanders Regan, who addresses the issue of self-texturing in her study *Love Words: The Self and the Text in Medieval and Renaissance Poetry* (Ithaca: Cornell University Press, 1982).

[5] See Chris Bongie's review essay of *Postcolonialism: An Historical Introduction* by Robert J.C. Young (Oxford: Blackwell, 2001), entitled 'What's Literature Got To Do With It?', *Comparative Literature*, 54.3 (2002), 256–67 (267).

[6] See John O'Brien's summation of Terence Cave's stance on the issue of how to avoid a teleological imposition of theory on to early modern texts: 'Critical Distance', *Paragraph*, 29.1 (2006), 108–19 (117).

not always easily reconciled with specific historical conditions or with the individual texts that are 'imprisoned' within them.[7] Within the particular frame of this study, I have renegotiated the concept of the epistemic break (onto-logical and political) that is often associated with the anti-mimetic impulses of seventeenth-century Baroque poets, such as Góngora, and with the breakdown of a Renaissance world view based on absolutes. This more flexible model accommodates the multiperspectivism and subjective self-fashioning that inter-rogated imperial ideology even in an early sixteenth-century poet like Gar-cilaso de la Vega. It also allows for the exploration of new horizons in the in-terpretation of four major poets of the period: Garcilaso de la Vega, Fernando de Herrera, Luis de Góngora and Francisco de Quevedo.

There are still those who misread 'what love has to do with it' in recognis-ably post-Romantic terms – who continue to search for traces of Isabel Freire in Garcilaso or for the Countess of Gelves in Herrera. I have also disengaged critically with this body of biographical research, which has survived (though not entirely unscathed) the shift from New Critical assumptions to the newer methodologies that are contextually informed. The challenge in reading the high rhetorical poetry of the Golden Age, as I have experienced it, is to recognise what is productive about the affective power of love as an elaborately crafted master metaphor; to appreciate that when poet and reader co-operate in cogni-tion and recognition, love's unreciprocated conditioning can open out beyond the private and, as Greene has demonstrated, 'serve as a template' for other collective experiences of unrequitedness and frustration.[8] Reading Golden Age love poetry as poetry, but produced in response to a very concrete socio-polit-ical context – that is, the need to provide a polity in the throes of centralisation and imperial expansion with a literary 'tradition' as proof of its national make-up – can help us understand what goes on at 'the critical juncture of personal psychological processes with larger cultural forces'.[9] The autonomous world of values constructed in and through the language of the lyric poem, its referencing of a world fashioned for itself, not only facilitates reflection upon the language which expresses unrequited love's contradictory desires, but also articulates new models of individualistic thinking that engage with, challenge and/or undermine

7   See Chapter 4, below, for a more detailed discussion of how this impacts upon our reading of Spanish poetry of the Baroque period. See also Terence Cave's article in which he identifies Foucault (along with Marx and others) as 'prophetic heroes' for the essentialisation of the 'modern' ('Locating the Early Modern', *Paragraph*, 29.1 [2006], 12–26 [14]).

8   See Greene, *Unrequited Conquests*, p. 11.

9   I have adapted the comments of Anthony Low whose broad allegiances I share (to writers, individual texts, relationships between texts, and to the facts and forces of social history insofar as we can reasonably know or infer them), but whose analysis of 'ways of loving' takes more ac-count of biography in its appeal to individual psychologies than I am inclined to do in the present study. See *The Reinvention of Love: Poetry, Politics and Culture from Sidney to Milton* (Cambridge: Cambridge University Press, 1993), p. 9.

the idealism of an emerging national self-consciousness. As I have come to realise, it is not enough to ask 'what has love got to do with it?'; much more interesting is what love, as a complex and contestatory signifier, actually does.

The six chapters that follow function as discrete studies, but have also been designed to be read in order, offering arguments that unfold conceptually as they advance chronologically. I have deliberately chosen to include poets who, to a greater or lesser extent, are deemed 'canonical'. This should not be understood as a gesture of defiance against those 'deconstructionalists' who would open the canon to forgotten writers of the past (usually women),[10] or against those who would reject the whole idea of the canon *per se* as inevitably elitist. On the contrary, I am invested in an assumption that is shared by both positions – that is, that canonical writers serve the interests of the dominant ideology. I would wish, however, to question the extent to which the poetry under consideration, in its transformation of perceived values, falls unproblematically into that category. Likewise, I have not shied away from using the traditional term 'Golden Age' (often associated with the construction of the Spanish literary canon under Franco), precisely because of its propagandistic weighting.[11] Taking its origins from a mythological paradigm that connected the Spanish imperial regime with Augustan Rome, 'Golden Age' points to the conflictive ideological co-ordinates that connected an anxious *traslatio studii* to an increasingly fragile *traslatio imperii*. How lyric construction and linguistic policy in the period related to, and (re)negotiated, these revisionist ideals of empire is fundamental to this study.

The opening chapters concern the poetry of Garcilaso de la Vega and establish the intellectual parameters of the volume as a whole, identifying a dialectic of desire, amorous and artistic, that shapes lyric self-creation. Individual erotic desire (*eros*) of an unattainable beloved is compounded by a contradictory expression of *aemulatio* (*eris*), the desire to exceed the achievements of Classical and Renaissance vernacular models, which lies at the heart of the broader humanist project. The self that gains expression in this poetry of incessant movement, that is 'being' realised through the participatory agency of the reader, demonstrates a relationship between the individual and the world that can only ever be fleetingly harmonious. Enduring harmony would suggest a problematic stasis, stagnation even, that is antithetical to the lyric's autopoetic impulse to create, transform and recreate. History emerges in this process as an ever-shifting configuration, wherein time and space can be simultaneously entailed

---

[10]   The notion of deconstruction as I apply it here is much broader and more sociologically, even materially, grounded than its more conventional application, a concern with the disruption of elemental oppositions, rather than (or as well as) with the play of binaries contained within a text and operating at the level of language.

[11]   The term 'early modern' is not without its own problems. I address its more problematic overtones in Chapter 3 below.

and all periods can be made present. This desire to transcend the limitations of time and space accords the relationship between writing and Classical mythology a privileged status, while acknowledging the tensions that accompany access to, and appropriation of, otherness. Additional questions are raised here that shadow the subsequent chapters: how does the problematic self-fashioning of the lyric subject (anxieties surrounding the role of autonomous and imitative discourse; the interrogation of a fixed centre, the displacement of authorities, the tension between objective reporting and articulation of an excessively subjective gaze) reflect wider socio-cultural concerns about the instability of identity and status?; how does the poetry's performed dialectic of resemblance and deviance work as a catalyst for a transformative poetics that allows the reader to 'see' the real world differently through the fictional framing? And linked to all of this is an awareness of the paradoxes involved in the speaking subject's attempts to control both his own voice and the meanings inscribed within it. Rereading Garcilaso in these terms demonstrates that what we have come to accept as the defining features of Baroque lyric's reconfiguration of the Renaissance are already much in evidence in 'new poetry's' first incarnation: fluidity, transformation, eroticism, desire, and a less than stable epistemology.

Garcilaso's canonical status was confirmed in 1580 with the publication of Fernando de Herrera's edition plus *anotaciones*. Chapter 3 reviews the literary polemic surrounding Herrera's commentary (reaching our own time in the 'decentring' theory of Navarrete), to demonstrate how critical editions of the period participated in the invention and promotion of a national identity that was necessary for the legitimisation of the state. The canonisation of poetic texts, as evidenced by Herrera, constructed poetry as an ethnic heritage and communal treasure, and invariably employed the 'Spanishness' of the literary sign as a measure of aesthetic, and indeed ethical, merit. The cultural hybridity of 'new poetry' had been defended by Juan Boscán in two earlier poetic manifestos: the preface to his translation of Castiglione's *Il libro del Cortegiano* and the letter to the Duchess of Soma which appears as a preface to the posthumous 1543 edition *Las obras de Boscán y algunas de Garcilaso de la Vega*.[12] But the revisionary poetics which had caused so much controversy in the first half of the century are validated by Herrera as part of a belated *traslatio studii*. Their radicalism is so effectively 'purified' via sustained Neoplatonic allegory that they come to represent in the early decades of the following century, the enlightened, absolute, decorum against which Góngora's redirected eloquence is judged, and its perceived darkness deemed heretical. Moving away from the notion of a Garcilasian centre and a Herrerian margin, Herrera's own love poetry is redefined more positively in this chapter in terms of an audacious

---

[12]   See 'Three Literary Manifestos of Early Modern Spain: Juan Boscán and Garcilaso de la Vega'. Introduction and translations by Anne J. Cruz and Elias L. Rivers, *Publications of the Modern Language Association*, 126.1 (2011), 233–42.

poetics of interruption, in which the present is a critically determining and intrusive feature. Herrera's vision requires a new brand of collective, cultural heroism, allegorised both in his theoretical writing and in his poetry, as the individual creative will in action, and mobilised against the stasis of contemporary Spanish letters.

Góngora shares Herrera's intermediary self-consciousness, but rejects the symbolic activity of Herrera's conceptual schema; shattering the centric stability and iconic authority of Herrera's heliocentric formulations with alternative, metaphorical configurations. Clarity is rejected as an unrealisable attempt to impose order upon the world, to manage the crises of history and to temper the trauma of temporality. Extreme metaphorisation and a persistent erotic colouration of the principles of *aemulatio* are deployed within a radical rhetorical reshaping that subjects the linkage of imperial triumph and vernacular renewal to sceptical scrutiny. Whereas Herrera's poetry struggles to accommodate the material specificity of language, Góngora (even in his very earliest sonnets) gives a darker substance to the light and advocates a reimagined vernacular eloquence. Chapter 4 introduces analysis of Góngora's shorter poems with a reconsideration of the stylistic controversy generated by the major compositions, exposing the hermeneutical instability of his detractors' position as a conformist response to the extreme defamiliarisation of Castilian that characterises his deliberately opaque poetics. The *carpe diem* sonnets, and sonnets of invidious gazing, are analysed across both Chapters 4 and 5 as representative of a new 'new poetry' of becoming, of possibility, whose subjective remediation of poetic norms gestures towards a dynamic reciprocity of tradition and invention. Herrerian poetics are challenged, but also illuminated, in the dark materials of Góngora's erotic 're-membering', reminding us that the ellipse is the product of a circular emanation.

It is now generally accepted that locking Góngora and Quevedo into unstable silos of *conceptismo* and *culteranismo* has proven unsatisfactory. But this is not the only uncritical categorisation that has stifled appreciation of Quevedo's love poetry. The final chapter of this study reopens the debate around the perceived Neostoicism of the amorous verse, redefining lines of enquiry with reference to the transgression and dissolution of boundaries in Quevedo's persistent hyperboles, hypothesis and dream poems, and unrivalled 'mas allá de la muerte' [beyond death] sonnets. Despite Aristotelian confidence in the association of metaphor and mimesis, the operation of metaphor in Golden Age poetry is at its most effective when the 'new world' it creates trespasses across the boundaries of logical categories in order to challenge universal truths. This takes us beyond the issue of poetry as a creative imitation of reality and connects generic redefinition and renewal to broader politico-existential concerns. In Quevedo's love poetry the small space of the sonnet that is subjectively and irrationally reimagined in excess of language's referential functions is ultimately invaded by disturbing extra-textual realities, by the uncompromising fact of the human condition and by the abject failure of the poetic enterprise. But this failure is rhetorically constructed. Produced within an atmosphere of collective disillusionment, Quevedo's 'failed' poetic project attends to language as a material aspect of his world and its power structures. By positing the voice of the unrequited lover as an incomplete and anti-heroic self, Quevedo figures a fractured, central consciousness in uncompromising terms. Ultimately, the poetry's elaborate, condensed, metaphorical formulations challenge the limits of representation and reframe conventional allegories against the troubled backdrop of national history.

The book that has emerged from my thinking about love in the poetry of the Spanish Golden Age has been largely dictated by the poems themselves. My own preferences will no doubt emerge more clearly to the reader than to me, although some choices were deliberately made and may appear surprising. The absence of a chapter on Lope de Vega, for instance, and the omission of a formal conclusion were decisions not taken lightly. To some extent, limitations of space dictated the former, but other considerations were also pertinent. Ultimately, I felt that the internal coherence of the study, its intellectual shape and direction, were best served by balancing an extended analysis of Garcilaso's 'new poetry' with a more comprehensive discussion of Góngora's equally polemical poetics. The standard conclusion was also omitted because it could not be easily accommodated without undermining the book's commitment to open-endedness, to the premise that poetry thrives on the promise of a reading not yet realised. I have tried, therefore, to draw the strands of reiteration together as significant, recurring moments at the end of each chapter, while resisting the inevitable reductionism of a final 'concluding' word. My interpretation has benefitted from an eclectic use of critical theory, with the hope that this will facilitate new ways of looking, but not obscure with its own structures, or impose a rational order upon radical utterance. I have aspired, above all else, to let the poetry breathe.

'Pero tiempo es que el libro comience ya a dar razón de sí'.[13]

---

[13] The quotation is adapted from the penultimate sentence of Juan Boscán's preface to his own and Garcilaso's poetry, addressed to the Duchess of Soma (1543). The original line reads: 'Pero tiempo es que el segundo libro comience ya a dar razón de sí' [But it is time for the second book to account for itself]. See Juan Boscán, *Obras completas*, ed. Carlos Clavería (Madrid: Cátedra, 1999), p. 120.

Garcilaso de la Vega (*c*.1501–1536):
Transfiguration and Transvaluation

Introduction: *[not] out in the cold*

Roland Barthes' insistence on the death of the author (1968),[1] closely followed by Michel Foucault's equally provocative interrogation of the writing subject ('What is an Author?' 1969),[2] have been elaborated, qualified, denigrated and newly historicised in almost half a century's literary theorisings. Common sense alone suggests that in denying a critical need to relate the individual subject (whether author or reader) to a larger cultural, historically specific field of operations, Barthes' theory of textual construction went too far. But whatever its implicit contradictions (and current memory studies have identified several), there is no denying that the post-structuralist critique of authorship that became prominent in the late 1960s paved the way for several ground-breaking transformations in literature, art and in critical activity itself.

It was exactly at this time, coincidence or not, that the reception of Garcilaso de la Vega's lyric poetry experienced a sharp textual turn away from the dominant school of sentimental biography, an approach that had its roots in the Renaissance, but that acquired dimensions of almost iconographical stasis in the wake of Hayward Keniston's 1922 biography.[3] For some time belief in a central love story blocked complete analytical engagement with Garcilaso's poeticised story of love in all its diverse manifestations, until studies by Ter

---

[1]   Roland Barthes, 'The Death of the Author', in *Image, Music, Text*, trans. Stephen Heath (London: Fontana Press, 1977), pp. 142–48.

[2]   Michel Foucault, 'What is an Author?', in Michel Foucault, *Language, Counter-Memory, Practice: Selected Essays and Interviews*, ed. Donald F. Bouchard, trans. Donald F. Bouchard and Sherry Simon (Ithaca: Cornell University Press, 1977), pp. 133–38.

[3]   Hayward Keniston, *Garcilaso de la Vega: A Critical Study of His Life and Works* (New York: Hispanic Society of America, 1922). Later advocates include: Rafael Lapesa, *La trayectoria poética de Garcilaso de la Vega* (Madrid: Revista de Occidente, 1948); Elias Rivers, *Garcilaso de la Vega: Obras completas con comentario* (Madrid: Castalia, 1974); Bernard Gicovate, *Garcilaso de la Vega* (Boston: Twayne Publishers, 1975); Antonio Prieto, *Garcilaso de la Vega* (Madrid: S.G.E.L., 1975).

Horst (1968) and Woods (1969),[4] and subsequent articles by Goodwyn, Darst and Waley a decade later,[5] resulted in a recognition among critics that Garcilaso's poetry was finally a moving target for interpretation. Although this has not produced a definitive burial of the biographical bones of contention,[6] it has undoubtedly instigated more fluid lines of enquiry, including a growing number of theoretical studies.[7] The outcome is a much less sanctified view of Garcilaso's poetry on the whole, but more specifically, as the direct expression of interiority (the hallowed sense that the experience of the poem was present to the author at the moment of writing). And yet the vast majority of those readings that accept the self-conscious artistry of Garcilaso's verse also assume a trajectory of stylistic development that depends implicitly on biographical chronology (even where the latter has been explicitly denied to make the case). My own reading attempts to expose the paradox at the core of this approach and to address its most salient interpretive ramifications.

It is worth remembering that Garcilaso did not organise nor publish his poetry in his lifetime. So although there is sufficient documentary evidence to substantiate aspects of the poet's life, any attempt to construct a valid chronological sequence for the relatively small extant corpus (sixty-three poems in total; four in Latin, the rest in Castilian) would appear to involve excessive conjecture.[8] Nonetheless,

---

[4]   Robert ter Horst, 'Time and the Tactics of Suspense in Garcilaso's *Egloga Primera'*, *MLA*, 83.2 (1968), 145–63, and M.J. Woods, 'Rhetoric in Garcilaso's First Eclogue', *MLN*, 84 (1969), 143–56 initiated a school of thought that emphasised rhetoric and/or Garcilaso's engagement with the aesthetic conventions of his day. For instance: David Quinn, 'Garcilaso's Égloga Primera: Autobiography or Art?', *Symposium*, 37.2 (1983), 147–64; Anne J. Cruz, *Imitación y transformación: el petrarquismo en la poesía de Boscán y Garcilaso de la Vega* (Amsterdam: John Benjamins Publishing Co., 1988); Carroll B. Johnston , 'Personal Involvement and Poetic Tradition in the Spanish Renaissance: Some Thoughts on Reading Garcilaso', *Romanic Review*, 80 (1989), 288–304; Ignacio Navarrete, *Orphans of Petrarch, Poetry and Theory in the Spanish Renaissance* (Los Angeles: University of California Press, 1994); and Daniel Heiple, *Garcilaso de la Vega and the Italian Renaissance* (University Park: Pennsylvania State University Press, 1994).

[5]   See Frank Goodwyn, 'New Light on the Historical Setting of Garcilaso's Poetry', *Hispanic Review*, 46 (1978), 1–22; David H. Darst, 'Garcilaso's Love For Isabel Freire: The Creation of a Myth', *Journal of Hispanic Philology*, 3 (1979), 261–68; Pamela Waley, 'Garcilaso, Isabel and Elena: The growth of a legend', *Bulletin of Hispanic Studies*, LVI (1979), 11–15. See also Luís Iglesias Feijóo, 'Lectura de la Egloga 1', in *Academia Literaria Renacentista IV, Garcilaso de la Vega*, ed. Víctor García de la Concha (Salamanca: Ediciones Universidad de Salamanca, 1983), pp. 61–82.

[6]   Occasional attempts to revive the debate are evidence of its semi-enterred nature. See, for instance, recent articles by María del Carmen Vaquero Serrano: 'Doña Beatriz de Sá, La Elisa posible de Garcilaso. Su genealogía', *Lemir*, 7 (2003), 1–48; 'Dos sonetos para dos Sás: Garcilaso y Góngora', *Lemir*, 11 (2007), 37–44.

[7]   These are summarised by E.C. Graf in footnote 1 of his article, 'From Scipio to Nero to the Self: The Exemplary Politics of Stoicism in Garcilaso de la Vega's Elegies', *PMLA*, 116.5 (2001), 1316–33 (1328).

[8]   Antonio Prieto orders the poems in terms of an autobiographical *canzoniere*, an *imago vitae* which begins with Sonnet V and culminates in *Eclogue* III. See Garcilaso de la Vega, *Can-*

Rafael Lapesa's trajectory theory, which is based on mixed criteria of sharply observed (but inconclusive) stylistic and intertextual analysis, and persuasively argued (but ultimately speculative) biographical data, has dominated responses to Garcilaso's poetry since the commentary's publication in 1948.[9] Although recent readings take issue either with the dates attributed to individual poems, and/or with Lapesa's adherence to the Isabel Freire 'myth',[10] some fundamental principles of his aesthetic judgement, drawn directly from the flawed trajectory premise, have become subsumed into current thinking and have, therefore, remained largely unchallenged. A non-qualified acceptance that Garcilaso's poetry reflects an evolving aesthetic of indirectness is a clear case in point.

Lapesa's argument is underpinned by a binary opposition that pits authentic introspection, Petrarchism and subjectivity against the combined strength of self-elision, an emerging Classicism, and objective distance. Apprenticeship in the new art characterises the poems located in the former category (among them the four *canciones*, Sonnets I, IV, VI, XXVI, and *Eclogue* II), while progress towards technical perfection distinguishes the latter (including *Eclogue* I, poems in the three new genres of epistle, elegy and Ode, four 'classical' sonnets XXIII, XXIX, XI and XIII, and *Eclogue* III). In broad 'biographical' terms the death of Isabel Freire cleaves the categories asunder, as does the poet's period of exile in Naples. Somewhat perversely, current scholarship denies the biographical basis, but seems irrevocably committed to its concomitant system of mutually exclusive aesthetic principles. I have deliberately organised the poems under consideration in this chapter against the grain of Lapesa's categorisation, and independent of any alternative assumptions regarding dates of composition. This is a rather belated attempt to respond to Lázaro Carreter's appeal over two decades ago for a more 'flexible' reading of Garcilaso that would allow us to approach each individual poem on its own terms,[11] although always within a framework of discriminating difference. In other words, the broader aim is to delineate the parameters of

---

cionero, ed. Antonio Prieto (Barcelona: Bruguera, 1982), and his more recent *Imago Vitae: Garcilaso y otros acercamientos al siglo XVI* (Málaga: Universidad de Málaga, 2002).

9   I am not suggesting a universal, uncontested authority. Entwistle, for example, was one of the earliest to challenge the dating of a specific poem, also noting that 'the sonnets are gathered in inextricable confusion'. See William J. Entwistle, 'Garcilaso's Fourth Canzon and Other Matters', *The Modern Language Review*, 45.2 (1950), 225–28 (226). Margot Arce de Vázquez also cast doubt on Lapesa's dating of a 'canción', in her case, the third. See 'Cerca el Danubio una isla', *Studia Philologica*, 1 (1960), 91–100.

10   See, for instance, Bryant Creel, *The Voice of the Phoenix: Metaphors of Death and Rebirth in Classics of the Iberian Renaissance*, Medieval and Renaissance Texts and Studies, 272 (Tempe: Arizona Center for Medieval and Renaissance Studies, 2004), especially pp. 55–62.

11   See Fernando Lázaro Carreter, 'La *Ode ad Florem Gnidi* de Garcilaso de la Vega', in *Garcilaso: Actas de la IV Academia Literaria Renacentista, Universidad de Salamanca, 2–4 de marzo de 1983*, ed. Víctor García de la Concha (Salamanca: Universidad de Salamanca, 1986), pp. 109–26 (p. 126).

Garcilaso's lyric poetry in terms of its complex interaction and negotiation with its broader socio-cultural context.

More specifically my intention is to qualify our understanding of Garcilaso's aesthetic of indirectness, by exposing its problematic association with a distancing dynamic that separates emotion from the personal presence of the poet, but which also leaves the subjective reader out in the cold. The elocutionary disappearance of the subject voice in what is conventionally thought of as Garcilaso's later poetry (either through recourse to Graeco-Roman mythology, and/or conveyed within the contrived artifice of a timeless pastoral),[12] detaches emotion from a one dimensional point of origin, liberating it as 'an effect of language not of life',[13] in order to facilitate an infinite transfiguration and transferral that depends on the reader's active participation. The essence of Garcilaso's self-consciously crafted lyric is the creation of a reader who within a single poem is compelled to perform two roles at once: that of the critical observer whose rational response to the text's rhetorical strategies allows for an exploration of the nature of poetry, but also of human nature itself; and that of reader as compromised surrogate who, at manipulated moments, slips into the subjective space, and within it punctures the poem's pretensions of universality to experience instances of uniquely intimate encounter. From the perspective of appropriated subjectivity, the 'lack of intimacy' argument which, post Lapesa, has been a hallmark of responses to the mythological poems, emerges as an untenable position. Moreover, by adopting a less categorical approach we can reconcile the 'increasing aestheticisation'[14] of the Eclogues with a recognition that the pastoral poems also share the troubling dialectic of desire, amorous and artistic, that shapes lyric self-creation in the sonnets.

Mediating the distance

Central to a discussion of the new poetry of early Renaissance Spain was Garcilaso de la Vega's pivotal role in a national project of *traslatio studii*, which was closely, albeit tensely, related to a more overtly successful *traslatio imperii*. A new vernacular poetry was required to accompany Spain's imperial status and to provide the standard of cultural endorsement that had been accorded to Rome through

---

[12]   See, for instance, Gustavo Correa, 'Garcilaso y la mitología', *Hispanic Review*, 45.3 (1977), 269–81, for whom a process of objectivisation and distancing is the key function of mythology in the Eclogues, particularly relevant to the figuration of Elisa's death in *Eclogue* III (pp. 278–79).

[13]   See Paul Julian Smith, 'The Rhetoric of Presence in Lyric Poetry', in *Writing in the Margin: Spanish Literature of the Golden Age* (Oxford: Clarendon, 1988), pp. 43–77 (p. 53). Smith takes issue with Alonso's view that claims the production of emotion for modern writing, pointing out that this was a principal objective of both Classical and Renaissance rhetoric.

[14]   See Crystal Anne Chemris's recent study, *Góngora's 'Soledades' and the Problem of Modernity* (Woodbridge: Tamesis, 2008), in which she treats the issue of aestheticisation in the Eclogue cycle, though concentrates exclusively on *Eclogues* I and III (pp. 9–19).

the collaborative and contradictory writings of Virgil, Cicero and Ovid (among others). For early modern writers throughout Europe the imitative practices of Italian humanism provided the means to a linguistic enrichment that would match imperial expansion; within the bigger picture surpassing Petrarch as the most dominant vernacular model of *imitatio* became something of an end in itself. In early-sixteenth-century Spain, Garcilaso de la Vega's overtly allusive poetry responds most significantly to the problem posed by the Petrarchan model: how to accept, accommodate and indeed be nourished by the cultural/aesthetic other, without losing the self in the process. The purpose of the following brief analysis is to explore just some of the ways in which engagement with a codified Petrarchan poetics (and its intrinsic figuration of Classical myth and Neoplatonic philosophy) informs a project of lyric self-creation that was formulated in response to the contradictory pressures of imitative/emulative poetics.

Garcilaso's Sonnet XIII transfigures the Ovidian myth of Apollo and Daphne via Petrarch in an attitude of 'affection' and 'alienation'.[15] The 'yo lírico' (the poetic 'I') of Garcilaso's poem is doubled and duplicitous and exposes the identity crisis at the core of lyric self-creation. Moreover, by shifting the perspectives around the amorous poem's conventionally uncertain ontological centre, Garcilaso's reconfiguration of Ovid advocates a model of lyric subjectivity that is a revisionist correction of the Petrarchan. Sonnet XIII would become a dominant intertextual presence in subsequent reformulations of the Apollo and Daphne myth in sixteenth- and seventeenth-century Spain.[16] Within this mythical frame, later poets would dramatise anxieties of imitation that were inevitably more complex (Gabriel Bocángel's sonnet 'Miré un laurel' [I gazed at a laurel tree] is an obvious example), but they would do so on an erotic stage propped up by Petrarch, and reinforced by Garcilaso's rewriting of Ovid.[17]

---

[15]   I am indebted to the terminology of Sanders Regan, whose line of argument is clearly informed by the theories of Harold Bloom. See Sanders Regan, *Love Words*, p. 46.

[16]   Mary E. Barnard addresses the popularity of Garcilaso's poem in her excellent study *The Myth of Apollo and Daphne from Ovid to Quevedo: Love, Agon, and the Grotesque*, Duke Monographs in Medieval and Renaissance Studies, 8 (Durham: Duke University Press, 1987), and cites principal rewritings (p. 121). We might add Sebastián de Córdoba's version 'a lo divino' (see Glen Ross Gale, 'Garcilaso's Sonnet XIII Metamorphosed', *Romanische Forschungen*, 80 [1969], 504–09) and the various re-elaborations of Soto de Rojas. See, for instance, the *Fragmentos de Adonis* where Garcilaso XIII informs the metamorphosis of Myrrha, and also the *Fábula de la Naya* (from the lyric anthology *Desengaño de amor en rimas*) where Naya's transformation revolves around binary oppositions that acquire metapoetic depth in relation to Garcilasian and Ovidian intertexts. For an analysis of the former, see Isabel Torres, 'Transforming Desire: Metamorphosis and Metapoetry in Soto de Rojas's *Fragmentos de Adonis*', in *The Polyphemus Complex: Rewriting the Baroque Mythological Fable, Bulletin of Hispanic Studies*, monograph issue, 83.2 (2006), ch. 4, pp. 102–30 (Liverpool: Liverpool University Press, 2006).

[17]   The sonnet is included as no. 99 in Gabriel Bocángel y Unzueta, *Obras completas*, ed. Trevor J. Dadson, Biblioteca Áurea Hispánica, II, 2 vols (Madrid: Iberoamericana and Frankfurt am Main: Vervuert, 2000), I.

Thomas Greene has addressed the shock of confrontation experienced by early Renaissance writers in their fragmented rediscovery and recasting of the Classical world.[18] Mirroring Greene's ideas, Arthur Terry has urged the modern reader of Renaissance texts to resist a too easy assimilation, encouraging us to read the past with sympathy, but also with due deference to a sense of otherness.[19] The challenge for the modern reader of a Renaissance text that explicitly signals its own proximity to, and distance from, a Classical model is a considerable one, involving the ability 'to situate ourselves knowingly' in two distinct moments of cultural production.[20] Too often we weight our 'unknowing' in favour of the period less remote from us – prepared to acknowledge the limitations of our own historicity when dealing with the Renaissance text, and yet content to assume an unproblematic approximation in our reading of the Classics. There is a certain perversity in this. Located within an historical model that is 'intrinsically teleological and evolutionary' the modern reader's willingness to develop an imperfect 'working contemporaneity'[21] with the early modern (the cradle of our own time) may smack of a smug superiority; but at least it allows for readings that recognise the cognitive potential of analogical interpretation: points of identification with the past can become sites of interrogation for our own future. On the other hand, the imposition of modern and/or early modern epistemic assumptions on the cultural production of ancient times (what we might call in essentialist terms the 'pre-modern') produces acts of (mis)reading which encarcerate the ancient texts (and, inevitably, their Renaissance imitations) within anachronistic contextual co-ordinates. It follows then that any attempt to read Garcilaso's Classical and/or mythological texts, in the light of intertextual Classical and early modern antecedents, must acknowledge that the creative process under consideration is a fragile, indeterminate mix of synchronic and diachronic perspectives.

A first step in determining the degree to which we can approximate the dynamic relationship between Garcilaso's Sonnet XIII, for instance, and the early modern reader is through some reconstitution of the Ovidian–Petrarchan horizon of expectations which the poem itself provokes, plays with, and ultimately problematises. The story of Apollo's passion for Daphne holds the centre of Book I of Ovid's experimental epic, the *Metamorphoses*, preceded by two stories of transformation (Lycaon into wolf; Deucalion and Pyrrha's role in the metamorphosis of the stones) and followed by two stories of transformation (Io

[18]   See Thomas M. Greene, *The Light in Troy: Imitation and Discovery in Renaissance Poetry* (New Haven and London: Yale University Press, 1982), p. 293.

[19]   See Arthur Terry, *Seventeenth-Century Spanish Poetry: The Power of Artifice* (Cambridge: Cambridge University Press, 1993), pp. xii–xiii.

[20]   The ideas expressed here adapt and develop Greene, *The Light in Troy*, p. 293.

[21]   See Rosemond Tuve, *Elizabethan and Metaphysical Imagery: Renaissance Poetic and Twentieth-Century Critics* (Chicago: Chicago University Press, 1947), as cited by Terry, *Seventeenth-Century Spanish Poetry*, p. xii.

into heifer and Syrinx into reeds). Beyond the possible socio-political interpretations of the cosmological sections of the poem, we can also argue for a metatextual reading in which the process of literary creation is conveyed through deliberately non-conforming patterns of *concordia discors*. Thus the world/text comes into being when chaos yields to order through the agency of a higher authority. The initial metamorphosis, the story of Lycaon, gives graphic and violent representation to the dangers of imposing rigid boundaries, even on the basest human impulses. And so the divinely authorised chaos that ensues is fluid, 'iamque mare et tellus nullum discrimen habebunt: omnia pontus erat' [and now the sea and land have no distinction. All is sea]; embracing transgression in all its linguistic and conceptual forms, 'silvasque tenent delphines et altis / incursant ramis agitataque robora pulsant, nat lupus inter oves' [The dolphins invade the woods, brushing against the high branches, and shake the oak trees as they knock against them in their course, the wolf swims among the sheep].[22] Thus the ground is cleared for an alternative model of artistic creation in Pyrrha's story, one in which the language of the divine will yield meaning through a mediated process of performance and negotiated response. Pyrrha's misreading of the oracle's words is literally superficial and corrected by Deucalion's recognition of the representational and symbolic force of language. A new race comes into being and meaning takes shape, conveyed via an appropriately perverse metaphorical manoeuvre that compares the formation of human life to the transforming of marble into a work of art (*Met.* I, 403–06).

The Python episode (438ff) seems to inaugurate a more stabilised epic poetics with the archer god Apollo in conventional mode as bringer of order, symbolised in the initiation of the ritualistic Pythian games. But the text is ruptured by the intervention of Cupid who, in an act of calculated revenge, strikes Apollo with a golden arrow and casts the humiliated deity into the conventional role of elegiac lover.[23] The growth of desire that is plotted in Apollo's reaction to his first sight of Daphne admittedly owes much to this tradition and to the familiar posturing of the 'exclusus amator',[24] but within the context of the *Metamorphoses* the god Apollo is more significantly debased because he is humanly flawed. The uplifted

---

[22] See Ovid, *Met.* I, 291–92 and I, 302–04. All references to Ovid are taken from *Metamorphoses*, with an English translation by Frank Justus Miller, revised by G.P. Goold, 3rd edn, Loeb Classical Library (Cambridge, MA: Harvard University Press, 1977). Where Loeb editions of the Latin texts are cited I have used their accompanying translations. Where translations from Latin texts are my own, this is clarified in a note.

[23] The episode recalls and inverts the *recusatio* material of *Amores* I, where poetic self-fashioning is conveyed through a generic altercation between the poet and Cupid, and the poetic (elegiac) self is consequently defined in terms of a negation of epic objectivity. For a more detailed analysis, see W.S. M. Nicoll, 'Cupid, Apollo, and Daphne (Ovid, *Met.* I, 452ff)', *Classical Quarterly*, N.S., 30 (1980), 174–82 (175–77).

[24] See Barnard, *The Myth of Apollo and Daphne*, pp. 19–43 (the idea of Apollo as 'exclusus amator' is considered on pp. 42–43).

gaze that distinguishes the human subject from all other living creatures (*Met.*
84–86) is drawn downwards, away from contemplation of the heavens towards a
dangerously deforming objectivity. Daphne is fragmented, and dismembered,
beneath Apollo's searing glance, but it is the lover/god who seeks to reconstitute
a fractured sense of self in words. Apollo's *suasoria* to Daphne has been generally viewed in ludic terms,[25] but his assertion of self is not a Polyphemic delusion,
but a stream of consciousness grounded in objectively valid criteria (for instance,
Apollo is not a 'pastor' and is, as he points out, the son of Jove) that is entirely
invalidated by an illegitimate desire. Apollo's rhetoric fails. His narcissistic construction of self is word-based and words are shown here to be inadequate to the
task of bridging the gap between the god and his beloved. Language as a communicative tool is potentially powerful, but inevitably limited by the receiver's
perception of meaning. Daphne perceives Apollo's words in accordance with her
own resistance to them and flees, but immediately falls victim to the misinterpre-
tation of her own discourse.

When Daphne turns to her father — 'qua nimium placui, mutando perde
figuram' [transform and destroy this form, through which I pleased too well;
Met. I, 547] — her plea for help is potently ambiguous. There is a clear link to
the 'mutatas formas' [changed forms] of the epic's proem (I.1) which allowed
the narrator to speak of bodies and forms of poetry at the same time, alerting
the reader to the metapoetic potential of metamorphosis as a narrative device
that occupies an uneasy space between art and nature, and as a figure for the
processes of artistic creation. Daphne's words to her father demonstrate the
uncontrollability of language, the gulf that exists between experience and discourse, which separates articulation and interpretation.[26] Arboreal transformation
is a drastic dehumanising response to a plea to 'change form', or to lose beauty,
but it represents Peneus's literal interpretation of Daphne's words.[27] The metamorphosis of Daphne can be understood in this context as the tragic misreading
of signs. The indeterminacy of 'figura' in her plea also anticipates the purely

---

[25]   See, among others, Barbara E. Stirrup, who refers to Apollo's 'burlesque catalogue of
credentials': 'Techniques of Rape: Variety of Wit in Ovid's *Metamorphoses*', *Greece and Rome*,
2nd Series, 24 (1977), 170–84 (181); Peter E. Knox, who highlights the ludic element in the
metaphor of courtship as a chase made concrete ('In Pursuit of Daphne', *Transactions of the
American Philological Association,* 120 [1990], 183–202); and Barnard who views Apollo as
Ovid's fool, the comedy deriving from the contradiction between non-heroic behaviour and the
epic framework (*The Myth of Apollo and Daphne*, p. 34).

[26]   See Lynn Enterline, *The Rhetoric of the Body from Ovid to Shakespeare*, Cambridge Studies in Renaissance Literature and Culture, 35 (Cambridge: Cambridge University Press, 2000),
who considers this rupture across a range of myths in the epic, but with particular reference to the
rape of Philomela.

[27]   Peneus has already emerged as a partial, subjective interpreter of behaviour in the myth.
His reaction to Daphne's decision to preserve her virginity is rooted in his own desire for grand-
children (I. 481–82).

linguistic metamorphosis of the laurel into an eternal sign of artistic and imperial triumph; a transformation that has much more to do with Apollo as a projected act of self-assertion, than with Daphne.

The actual metamorphosis scene erupts so suddenly from the text that it is
difficult to know whose experience of change is being narrated; through whose
eyes are we indirect voyeurs:

> vix prece finita torpor gravis occupat artus,
> mollia cinguntur tenui praecordia libro,
> in frondem crines, in ramos bracchia crescunt,
> pes modo tam velox pigris radicibus haeret,
> ora cacumen habet: remanet nitor unus in illa.
> Hanc quoque Phoebus amat (*Met.* I, 548–53)

> [Scarce had she thus prayed when a down-dragging numbness seized her
> limbs, and her soft sides were covered with thin bark. Her hair was changed
> to leaves, her arms grew into branches. Her feet, but now so swift, stuck fast
> in sluggish roots, her head was now a tree top: only her gleaming beauty
> remained. But even now in this new form Apollo loved her.]

The fragmented vision and the fact that the persistence of beauty is connected
to Apollo's constant passion align the reader uncomfortably with the objecti-
fying gaze of the god. The coming into being of the laurel is the 'perfect'
Ovidian text, embracing transgression within an elegant, ordered, frame that
comes to a close while stubbornly resisting closure.[28] However, although
Daphne has become a 'multiply determined site of signification',[29] she continues to represent for Apollo the unfulfilment of desire, the *absentia in
praesentia*, that would become the very condition of Renaissance lyric poetry. When Apollo's active wooing of the tree (what Barnard has referred to
as 'on the surface a moment of triumphant self-assertion')[30] is rejected, he
articulates ownership in a speech designed to compensate for his earlier rhetorical and amorous failures (*Met.* I, 557–65). Apollo's is a subject voice
operating almost in excess, reconstituting itself in terms of appropriation of
and total identification with the object. The symbolic transformation offers
redemptive value for Daphne only from the perspective of Apollo.[31] Daphne's

---

28 Barnard offers an interesting alternative view of the transformation as 'grotesque', focusing on the fictional aspect of the metamorphosis, a lack of literal credibility, which highlights its
aberrant, dehumanising nature (*The Myth of Apollo and Daphne*, p. 37).

29 See *The Cambridge Companion to Ovid*, ed. Philip Hardie (Cambridge: Cambridge University Press, 2002), 'Introduction', p. 8.

30 *The Myth of Apollo and Daphne*, p. 41.

31 Ovid underscores the ambiguity of his finale – the rivers do not know whether to console
or to congratulate Daphne's father Peneus (l. 578).

privileged function as a sign of imperial and poetic apotheosis is really the transformation of Apollo's fragmented desiring self, conditioned by time and space, into an infinite, whole self, self-consciously engineered.

The authority of the voice, however, depends upon a response that will confirm its meaning. The text reads: 'finierat Paean: factis modo laurea ramis / adnuit utque caput visa est agitasse cacumen' [Apollo was done: the laurel waved her new-made branches, and seemed to move her head-like top in consent; *Met.* I, 566–67]. Motifs of hair and wind are brought together here in an elusive image that imposes the function of speech on a character whose voice has been taken away. Critics have been generally too ready to acknowledge Daphne's consent with, perhaps, only Apollo's flawed reading of the signs to go on.[32] The two stories of metamorphosis that follow, of Io and Syrinx, both associate loss of identity in metamorphosis with loss of articulation. In the case of Io the betrayal of experience in language is evidenced when her attempts to communicate her tragedy to her family bring sounds to her own ears so alien that she is terrified by them (*Met.* I, 635–38). In an anti-narcissistic splitting of self she flees in terror from her transformed image in the water. The expression of self in written form (letters in the dust; *Met.* I, 649–50) reveals how language can work sometimes in the speaker's favour, but its reliability is unsustainable. The interpolated story of Pan and Syrinx offers a succinct mirroring of the Apollo/Daphne myth, right down to the linguistic ambivalence of the ending.[33] Whose lament is heard as the soft air stirs in the weeds (*Met.* I, 689)? Whose experience is articulated? Pan's desire or Syrinx's fear? The patterns of repetition and reiteration of motifs throughout Book I of the *Metamorphoses* compel readers constantly to refigure our own relationship to Ovid's text. Our rereading of Daphne in the experiences of Io and Syrinx suggests that what has been traditionally viewed as her final act of paratextual speech is, in fact, Apollo's subjective inscription of meaning upon the other.

A non-dyadic subject/object relationship is at the core of a codified Petrarchan poetics which re-stages Ovid's linguistic play in an obsessive scene of unrequited love and unrealised/unrealisable demands. According to Sanders Regan, the uncontrolled and uncontrollable duplicity of language is the very condition for the writing of Petrarchan poetry: the vulnerable (male) speaking subject is a contradictory and fragile linguistic effect, lacking mastery in the face of the beloved's resistance to persuasion. The poems of the *Canzoniere* can be viewed, therefore, as the 'after-effect of language's failure'.[34] Such a reading

---

[32]   See, for instance, Alison Sharrock (referring to Daphne, Io and Pan): 'In each case, the changed woman is made to acknowledge her domination by an act of para-speech that accentuates her loss of voice. The laurel tree nods assent to becoming a symbol for triumphs' (*Cambridge Companion*, ch. 6, 'Gender and Sexuality', p. 100).

[33]   Enterline, *The Rhetoric of the Body*, pp. 77–79, draws our attention to this.

[34]   See Enterline, *The Rhetoric of the Body*, p. 15, where the Petrarchan speaker is portrayed as a 'second Apollo'.

is substantiated intertextually by the Ovidian aesthetic of *Metamorphoses* I which locates Petrarch's anagrammatic formulae in the self-texturing crisis of the Apollo and Daphne myth. Just as Laura is everywhere and nowhere in the *Rime sparse*, dismembered in the breeze (*l'aura*), transformed as the laurel (*lauro*), the poet/lover is equally unstable, sustained by the hope that love will cure the separated self and, like Apollo, seeking wholeness and the reconciliation of art and desire, by inscribing poetic glory in the name of the beloved.[35]

Garcilaso de la Vega is generally credited with the creation of lyric subjectivity in Spain, with Petrarch's own sense of literary belatedness transferred into a more complicated emulative context which, in addition to Classical writers such as Ovid, includes Petrarch himself as a dominant model.[36] Cascardi sums up the issue as follows: 'the post-Petrarchan tradition [...] presents a multilayered display of poetic self-consciousness in which the "original" desire for the lost or unattainable beloved is compounded by the desire to rival Petrarch's *canzoniere* book: the (impossible, unsuccessful) mimesis of desire is rivalled by the imitation (*imitatio*) of the model of a desire founded on lack'.[37] In Garcilaso's engagement with the Apollo and Daphne myth, this dialectic of desire, amorous and artistic, shapes lyric self-creation and exposes the paradoxes of the speaking subject's attempts to control not only his own voice, but the reader's responses to the meanings inscribed within it. Ultimately, Sonnet XIII depicts a poetic subject that moves involuntarily between control and capitulation, and whose voice emerges distinctly from the interdependency of imitative and autonomous discourse. The poem reads:

> A Dafne ya los brazos le crecían
> y en luengos ramos vueltos se mostraban;

35 On the 'split subject' of Petrarchan poetics see, for instance, John Freccero, 'The Fig Tree and the Laurel: Petrarch's Poetics,' *Diacritics*, 5 (1975), 34–40; Robert Durling, *Petrarch's Lyric Poems: The 'Rime sparse' and Other Lyrics* (Cambridge, MA: Harvard University Press, 1976), esp. pp. 1–33; Carla Freccero, 'Ovidian Subjectivities in Early Modern Lyric: Identification and Desire in Petrarch and Louise Labé', in *Ovid and the Body in the Renaissance*, ed. Goran V. Stanivukovic (Toronto: University of Toronto Press, 2001), pp. 21–37 (p. 23). Also of interest is Enterline's analysis of how Petrarch captures an 'Ovidian aesthetics of dismemberment' with specific reference to the construction of the subject and the myth of Actaeon (*The Rhetoric of the Body*, p. 93).

36 Garcilaso's indebtedness to Petrarch has been acknowledged by most commentators, but is central to the analyses of Cruz, *Imitación y transformación,* Heiple, *Garcilaso de la Vega,* and Navarrete, *Orphans of Petrarch.*

37 See Anthony J. Cascardi, *Ideologies of History in the Spanish Golden Age* (University Park PA: Pennsylvania State University Press, 1997), ch. 9: 'Instinct and Object: Subjectivity and Speech-Act in Garcilaso de la Vega', p. 251. Cascardi's argument emerges from engagement with the ideas of William Kerrigan and Gordon Braden, *The Idea of the Renaissance* (Baltimore: John Hopkins University Press, 1989) and Roland Greene, *Post-Petrarchism: Origins and Innovations of the Western Lyric Sequence* (Princeton: Princeton University Press, 1991).

en verdes hojas vi que se tornaban
los cabellos qu'el oro escurecían:
    de áspera corteza se cubrían
los tiernos miembros que aun bullendo 'staban;
los blancos pies en tierra se hincaban
y en torcidas raíces se volvían.
    Aquel que fue la causa de tal daño,
a fuerza de llorar, crecer hacía
este árbol, que con lágrimas regaba.
    ¡Oh miserable estado, o mal tamaño,
que con llorarla crezca cada día
la causa y la razón por que lloraba![38]

[Daphne's arms were already growing and turning into long branches; and
I saw hair that had once darkened gold become transformed into green
leaves; a harsh bark covering over tender limbs and organs, still throbbing;
and her white feet sank down into the earth, transforming into twisted
roots. He who was the cause of so much damage, made this tree grow
with the force of his weeping, watering it with his tears. What a miserable
state! What excessive suffering! Weeping over her every day he causes the
reason for his tears to grow.][39]

This is a clear case of textual corporeality that derives in great part from the
signifying universe of other texts. At first reading the imitative framework is
most evident in the quatrains, where the poem's negotiation with Ovid's metamorphosis scene determines composition, while the tercets demonstrate an innovative impulse grounded in a more autonomous voice, albeit one whose
subjectivity is linguistically ambivalent. In fact, the sonnet toys with a slippery
subject/object dynamic from the outset. Daphne is the emphatic object of the
metamorphosis itself (and, therefore, metaphorically, of the text in process), but
also of the voyeuristic scrutiny of the reader who is drawn into the text almost
in medias res, and encouraged to assume an Apollonian subjectivity, until the
sudden and disorientating intervention of a first person speaker ('vi')[40] reposi-
tions the reader outside the intertextual frame.[41] The speaker now enters the

[38]   All references to Garcilaso are taken from Garcilaso de la Vega, *Obra poética y textos en
prosa*, ed. Bienvenido Morros, estudio preliminar de Rafael Lapesa, Biblioteca Clásica, 27 (Barcelona: Crítica, 1995).
    [39]   Unless otherwise stated, prose translations of Spanish poems are my own. These are offered
as a guide for the non-Spanish-speaking reader without any claims to textual independence.
    [40]   Herrera (*Anotaciones*, p.366) found this so disconcerting that he felt it must have been
included only to rectify problems of metre.
    [41]   For Barnard, the intervention of a first-person speaker functions as a distancing device, spar-
ing the reader a direct confrontation with the monstrous ('grotesque') metamorphosis (*The Myth of
Apollo and Daphne*, p. 115). I would argue that the postponement of the verb works against this
reading. Compare the use of this device also in Garcilaso's Sonnet XXXVII, 1–4: 'A la entrada de

aesthetic and canonical space, either as Apollo or alongside Apollo, in an ambiguous relationship that anticipates the fluid identification of the tercets. Moreover, the fusion of poet/lover with Apollo results in a fusion of Daphne and the speaker's own idealised beloved, whose absence is undermined by the presence of a conventional Petrarchan iconography of beauty in the references to golden hair, tender limbs and white feet. Garcilaso's speaker steps in, and around him Ovidian and Petrarchan resonances emerge, are entangled and transformed, but continue to throb beneath the surface of the new text.

Petrarch's *Canzone* XXIII has been debated as a model for Garcilaso's poem. It is a poem concerned explicitly with the inscription of poetic subjectivity, and, while it moves through a series of Ovidian transformations, particular attention is paid to the Apollo and Daphne myth with which the cycle begins and ends.[42] The Petrarchan subject is also a direct witness *to* and narrator *of* metamorphosis, but, in a major deviation from Ovid, is also the object of the punitive and violent transformations that he relates.[43] These reiterated self-transformations express 'the incomprehensible changeability of the self in love',[44] but also foreground problems of communication and the inadequacy of language. As DellaNeva has suggested, the doubts expressed about the instability of language in the poem run counter to the permanence of the poet/lover's desire for Laura and obsession with the laurel as poetic symbol; and contribute to a deeper anxiety about the problems of innovative imitation.[45] Given Petrarch's recourse to the Apollo and Daphne myth in terms of an identification with his own writing, and the Ovidian myth's prominence in a poem which takes subjectivity to extremes, it seems valid to conclude that *Canzone* XXIII should inform any reading of Garcilaso's poem that prioritises these metatextual issues.[46]

---

un valle, en un desierto / do nadie atravesaba ni se vía, / *vi que* con estrañeza un can hacía / estremos de dolor con desconcierto' (emphasis added). See Cascardi, *Ideologies of History*, p. 276, who offers an insightful reading of Sonnet XXXVII around the question of poetic power.

[42] Consult, among others, Freccero, 'Ovidian Subjectivities', pp. 26–30, and JoAnn DellaNeva, 'Poetry, Metamorphosis, and the Laurel: Ovid, Petrarch and Scève', *French Forum*, 7 (1982), 197–209 (198–203).

[43] Contrast *Sestina* XXX, 1–2: 'Giovene donna sotto un verde lauro | vidi più bianca et più fredda che neve' in which the focus is on the woman's transformation.

[44] See Durling, *Petrarch's Lyric Poems*, p. 27, where he identifies this as the theme of the *canzone*.

[45] See DellaNeva, 'Poetry', pp. 198–200, where she also observes that Petrarch's transformation of Ovid points to the 'undeniable instability of even the most revered written texts' (p. 200).

[46] This is a view supported by María Jesús Cabañas Martínez, 'El mito de Apolo y Dafne: diferencias de tratamiento en Garcilaso y Quevedo a través de dos sonetos', in *La maravilla escrita. Antonio de Torquemada y el siglo de oro. Actas del Congreso Internacional Antonio de Torquemada y la literatura del Siglo de Oro, León-Astorga 7–9 de mayo de 2003*, eds Juan Matas Caballero, José Manuel Trabado Cabado and Juan José Alonso Perandones (León: Universidad de León, 2005), pp. 213–26 (p. 222). Moreover, Garcilaso's familiarity with Petrarch's poem is evidenced in Sonnet XXII, where verse 14 corresponds to 34 of *Canzone* XXIII.

It could be argued, therefore, that the intervention of the speaker in line 3 of Garcilaso's text is a narrative device exploited to distance Garcilaso's poetics from a Petrarchan model of lyric creation that is too explicitly forged in a crisis of language. The use of the past tense in the subject intervention of Garcilaso's poem is an important factor in the evocation of a controlling voice. This is a recollected revelation and the transfiguration occurring in the poem is the imagined transformation of a Petrarchan-inspired beloved into an Ovidian-metamorphosing Daphne – itself a figure for the poem as it unfolds before the reader. Garcilaso initiates in this poem a new type of ekphrasis, not the ur-ekphrasis that De Armas argues is the guiding principle of Cervantes, where art objects are created in the mind of the fictional character,[47] but an alternative form in which an image takes shape in the mind of the reader, *as if* it were an object of art. We know that Garcilaso was sensitive to the ekphrastic possibilities of Ovid's text (he casts the myth as the second tapestry of *Eclogue* III). Moreover, the plastic and pictorial qualities of Sonnet XIII have prompted several commentators to suggest that Garcilaso may have been viewing a painting as he wrote it.[48] Such a view, however attractive, undermines the complex play of perspectives at work in the poem, and the flexibility of the vantage point inhabited by a speaker whose speech is relayed via memory.

The 'yo' [I] of the quatrains is inside the inset text as participant, but not contained by it either in time or space. The reader, likewise, is drawn into the text as viewer, framed by it to some extent, but also left out as a non-participant in the scene on display. Persin argues that conventional ekphrasis can function as a 'special case of intertextuality'.[49] I would suggest that Garcilaso's freer ekphrastic model, flaunting its intertextual components, blurs the boundary between reader and poet in creative, receptive and interpretative terms. The fundamental transgression of formal ekphrastic texts resides in the indeterminate relationship between the 'I'/'eye' of the text and the subjects depicted; Garcilaso's aesthetic violations come much closer to Ovidian controlled chaos. In the quatrains, the creative subjectivity of the writer is displaced to the reader,

---

[47] See *Ekphrasis in the Age of Cervantes*, ed. Frederick A. de Armas (Lewisberg: Bucknell University Press, 2005), ch. 1: 'Simple Magic: Ekphrasis from Antiquity to the Age of Cervantes', pp. 13–31. De Armas takes the episode of the windmills as a prime illustration of art objects wrought in the mind of Don Quijote.

[48] Two recent editors who proffer this view are J.F. Alcina in his edition of Garcilaso de la Vega, *Poesía castellana completa* (Madrid: Espasa Calpe, 1998) and Bienvenido Morros, *Obra poética*.

[49] See Margaret H. Persin, *Getting the Picture: The Ekphrastic Principle in Twentieth-Century Spanish Poetry* (Lewisberg: Bucknell University Press, 1997), p. 23. I use 'conventional' ekphrasis to refer to a written text that makes explicit reference to a visual work of art, whether real or imagined. Heffernan offers a succinct, useful definition: 'the verbal representation of visual representation': see James A.W. Heffernan, *Museum of Words: The Poetics of Ekphrasis from Homer to Ashbery* (Chicago: University of Chicago Press, 1993), p. 3.

and in the tercets the shift from description to subjective interpretation (encapsulated in 'tal daño') mirrors the process of reading in the activity of the writer. Following Georges Poulet's argument, Sanders Regan observes that the reader of lyric poetry suspends disbelief in reading, that the reader is in fact 'on loan' to the text, in other words, the 'I' of the reader succumbs to the other.[50] In Sonnet XIII submission of authority is reciprocal as the 'I' of the text lends itself also to a very dynamically imagined receiver.

In the tercets subjective interpretation extends beyond Garcilaso's negative reading of Ovid's metamorphosis of Daphne to include a deflated vision of the god Apollo, who is denied identification on both a literal ('Aquel que' [He who]) and symbolic level ('este árbol' [this tree]). The diminution of Apollo in the one-dimensional role of lamenting lover suggests that this focus on the god is really another narcissistic contemplation of the 'stado' [state] of the speaker,[51] a condition of amorous stasis that is paradoxically circular, and expressed in ironically echoing language. The reiteration of 'causa' [cause; 14] is especially telling. Cut loose from any fixed referents, enclosed within a non-specific apostrophe, the ambiguity of the second 'causa' compels the reader to reconsider the first in a reconfiguring move similar to that provoked by the repetitive patterns of Ovid, *Metamorphoses*, I. The speaker now occupies the entire chain of referentiality of verse 9. He is the non-identified subject, the cause and the effect of his own 'loss'.[52] These final verses of the sonnet have generally been read as a metaphor for the self-perpetuating misery of the lover, and/or as representing the infinite self-renewal of poetry. The climactic alliteration, the symmetrical syntax, the rhyme and rhythm – in short, the almost oppressive order of these tercets – functions like the Apollonian voice in excess, protesting too much for us to accept unproblematically this illusion of closure and resolution. I would suggest that a second ekphrastic movement flows through the tercets. The tree grows and is *seen* to grow in the mind's eye of the reader (note the sudden switch to the present tense in verse 13: 'crezca'). The agent of this growth is left behind, entirely overwhelmed. Thus the controlling poetic voice expresses the inevitability of at least partial submission in the process of lyric self-creation. The effort of domination has the paradoxical effect of revealing the smallness of the self in the face of the other's unmanageability – whether that 'other' be overwhelming misery, the elusive 'dama', the unstable intertext, or the unpredictable, equally subjective, reader.

In Sonnet XIII Garcilaso's transvaluation of Ovid's Apollo and Daphne myth and of the Petrarchan model of lyric subjectivity recognises the values

---

50 See Sanders Regan, *Love Words*, p. 47.

51 Garcilaso, Sonnet I, 'Cuando me paro a contemplar mi "stado" ' [When I stop to contemplate my state] is an obvious illustration.

52 Barnard draws attention to the ambiguity and reciprocity of the epigrammatic ending, though reads the poem differently (*The Myth of Apollo and Daphne*, pp. 128–29).

and complexities of the antecedent texts, but is also aware of the destabilising consequences of interpretation. In accordance with Bono's theories of trans-valuation, the poem can be viewed as an 'artistic act of historical self-con-sciousness', in which these perceived values are re-created and transformed to serve the purposes of the poetic voice, and the uses of the present.[53] The ekphrastic dimension anchored in the fiction of eye-witness testimony is a provocative rhetorical strategy that exploits the visual to enhance aesthetic accessibility and immediacy, while simultaneously blocking direct access to the image through the intervention of a mediating 'eye/'I'. Thus the poem plays games with perception and with temporal distance, ultimately reassert-ing poetic power while bearing witness to the anxieties that underlie art that is constructed through borrowed authority.

Mischievous mediation: *Eclogue I*

As Anne J. Cruz has demonstrated, the language of Garcilaso's Eclogues owes much to his filtering of the Classical pastoral tradition through a deliberate misreading of Petrarchan poetics that involves an interrogation of the mimetic power of art.[54] This is a creative strategy that links the Eclogues to many of Garcilaso's amorous sonnets and belies the traditional linear readings of Gar-cilaso which would have us locate the Eclogues on the other, less neurotic, side of a fairly expansive Rubicon. In fact, this Petrarchan misreading acquires a more sophisticated interrogation in the context of re-iterated pastoral song. Within the emulative context of Spanish post-Petrarchan poetry, individual erotic desire of an unattainable beloved (*eros*), such as that expressed by Salicio for Galatea in *Eclogue* I, is compounded by a contradictory expression of eris-tic *aemulatio* (the desire to rival Classical and Renaissance vernacular models) which is central to the broader humanist project. Although the rhetorical nature of Garcilaso's pastoral poetry has gained widespread acceptance, and there has been sustained critical engagement with the symbiosis of *imitatio* and *inventio* that characterises the song of Salicio,[55] critics have been reluctant to tamper with the ecstatic vision of Nemoroso, and so have missed the paradoxes involved in the speaking subject's attempts to control both his own voice, and the meanings

[53] See Barbara J. Bono, *Literary Transvaluation: From Vergilian Epic to Shakespearean Tragicomedy* (Berkeley: University of California Press, 1984), p. 1.

[54] See Cruz, *Imitación y transformación*, pp. 97–99.

[55] There is relatively little engagement with Nemoroso in Woods or Lumsden Kouvel. The study of Virgil, *Eclogue* VIII as a foundation model for the creation of Salicio features in several studies, but is the single subject of an article by Sydney P. Cravens and Edward V. George: 'Gar-cilaso's Salicio and Vergil's Eighth Eclogue', *Hispania*, 64.2 (1981), 209–14. P.J. Smith also dedicates a study to Salicio: 'Homographesis in Salicio's Song' in *Busquemos otros montes y otros ríos. Estudios de literatura española del Siglo de Oro dedicados a E.L. Rivers*, eds Brian Dutton and Victoriano Roncero López (Madrid: Castalia, 1992), pp. 243–51.

(some of which are Salicio-inscribed) that are contained within it. Cruz sets her reading against that of Alexander Parker, whose analysis of the philosophical significance of the text's transfigured landscapes has had a substantial impact on subsequent scholarship.[56] For Parker, the landscapes are neither idealised, nor real, but rather poetic images conveying thoughts and clarifying feelings that move within the sphere of Renaissance Neoplatonism. Parker's compelling exploration of the relationship between form and content in *Eclogue* I forever silenced idiosyncratic theories about disparate genesis,[57] while his assertion that the identification of Galatea with Isabel Freire, 'though interesting in itself, adds nothing to our understanding of the poem as poetry', marked what was to be a premature dissention from the dominant school of sentimental biography.[58]

Many of Parker's early ideas about the poem were integrated into subsequent readings or accepted unquestioningly to support the analyses of others (for example Arce de Vázquez, Lumsden Kouvel and Fernández–Morera),[59] although his approach also acquired a certain predominance as a springboard from which diametrically opposed voices could launch their own alternative perspectives (ter Horst and Woods, for example).[60] The exposition of Renaissance Neoplatonism offered by Parker is certainly an exemplary exercise in clarity and precision. Essentially, it involves the idealisation of human love within a religious theistic view of life. Within this ethical system, the subjugation of sensuality through a rational recognition that love is perfected when dissociated from a mortal body removes conflict between human life and religion. In a paradoxically anti-Platonic move, love of a woman becomes a progressive stage in man's journey towards the divine. This idealised, 'philosophically sanctioned', concept of human love can then justifiably occupy the

---

56 Parker, in fact, only published twice on the poem. See Alexander A. Parker, *The Philosophy of Love in Spanish Literature: 1480–1680*, ed. Terence O'Reilly (Edinburgh: Edinburgh University Press, 1985), in which he offers a rather brief discussion of the poem, directing the reader to his earlier, lengthier article: 'Theme and Imagery in Garcilaso's First Eclogue', *Bulletin of Spanish Studies*, 25 (1948), 222–27; reprinted as 'Tema e imagen de la égloga 1 de Garcilaso', in *La poesía de Garcilaso: ensayos críticos*, ed. Elias L. Rivers (Barcelona: Ediciones Ariel, 1974), pp. 199–208. Parker's analysis is also heavily weighted in favour of Salicio.

57 See, for instance, Entwistle's suggestion that the Eclogues are poems of different dates assembled in a dramatic context. William J. Entwistle, 'The Loves of Garci-Laso', *Hispania*, 13.5 (1930), 377–88 (379).

58 In the intervening period, Parker opted ironically to row against the current he had helped set in motion – his attitude to the Freire question mellowed (See *Philosophy of Love*, pp. 44, 49 and 50). Interestingly, his advocacy of a Neoplatonic reading of Garcilaso emerged demonstrably more tenacious.

59 See Margot Arce de Vázquez, 'La Égloga Primera de Garcilaso', *La Torre*, L (1953), 31–68; Audrey Lumsden Kouvel, 'Nature and Time in Garcilaso de la Vega', *Kentucky Romance Quarterly*, 19 (1972), 199–209 (204); and Darío Fernández-Morera, *The Lyre and the Oaten Flute: Garcilaso and the Pastoral* (London: Tamesis, 1982).

60 See respectively 'Time and the Tactics' and 'Rhetoric'.

most eminent position in the scale of human values. According to Parker, its influence in Spanish literature via the writings of Ebreo and Castiglione is most clearly reflected in the poetry of Garcilaso de la Vega whose Eclogues are Italianate in their Neoplatonist content and form.

But Garcilaso's poetic practice does not quite fit the Neoplatonic paradigm, as Arthur Terry noted.[61] Unlike Parker's penetrating analyses of Quevedo's sonnets, which, to a large extent, bear out their Neostoic framing, his comments on Garcilaso's *Eclogue* I are directed by qualified argument and illustrative only in negative terms. Thus the resigned serenity which Parker sees as a hallmark of the Eclogue is attained *not* in the self-assurance of being in contact with the divine through the love of a woman, *but* in acceptance of the sadness inherent in life through the fact that love and beauty are perishable (*Philosophy of Love*, 49). The poem is informed by two kinds of suffering love: the pain of unrequited love as sung by Salicio, and the grief occasioned by the death of Elisa as lamented by Nemoroso. But this suffering, we are warned, is *not* a self-centred sorrow, because the personal is ultimately transcended into the universal, and transcendence is effected through the presentation of suffering love within the sympathetic and enduring peace of Nature, man's physical environment to which he *must* respond emotionally and spiritually (49). Philosophy, initially presented as a coherent system of thought and values, is thus transformed in the practical reading of Garcilaso's poetry into a methodological tool that is made to serve the purpose of the critic in his attempts to understand the text and to illuminate a meaning that matches a particular intellectual trajectory. In the context of a subsequent chapter (Chapter 4), Parker acknowledges that Neoplatonism is 'theoretically desirable', but has never formed part of human experience, and can 'scarcely inspire a literature that seeks to have a significant contact with reality' (*Philosophy of Love*, 109). Therein lies the problem with Parker's Neoplatonist reading of Garcilaso's Eclogues. By taking their pastoral artifice at face value, he denies the Eclogues the depth of thought and emotion that would encourage him to investigate the paradoxical sites of tension that connect word and world and which he perceives so clearly in the poets of the Baroque. Parker leaves his reader comforted, yet *Eclogue* I is an uncomfortable, if poignant, reading experience. This is precisely because the poem connects with the ambivalent reality of human experience at the level of language; and poetic iteration is a manipulative and mischievous mediator.

Elsewhere I have considered how Góngora regenerates pastoral poetry as a locus of poetic commentary.[62] Although the argument is valid in relative terms, it does underplay Garcilaso's generic experimentations in the Eclogues. The

---

[61]   See Terry's 'Review of *The Philosophy of Love*', *Bulletin of Hispanic Studies*, 65 (1988), 169–74 (171).

[62]   See Torres, *The Polyphemus Complex*, ch. 2.

pastoral idyll that these poems evoke is often out of step with the Neoplatonic rhythms of the Renaissance, but yet in harmony with the radical literary renewal of the Spanish 'new poetry'. *Eclogue* I, for instance, dismantles the competitive impulse of conventional pastoral in favour of a subtle coalescing of antagonistic impulses. Salicio's song is not echoed in Nemoroso's; it inhabits it in a tense interplay of individualistic and collective energies. The 'Petrarchist scene' of unrequited love and unrealised/unrealisable demands 'obsessively restaged' in Salicio's ontologically uncertain voice re-emerges in Nemoroso's lament, which then resonates with displaced anxieties. Within the carefully ordered and balanced structure of the Eclogue,[63] a fluid, tortured, lyric subject emerges in the voice of Nemoroso. But it is a voice that ultimately expresses a new model of individualistic thinking, one that brings near to healing the dissociative relationships of the poem: between the individual and the landscape/environment; past and present; objective reporting and excessive subjective articulation; experience and discourse; the demands of the body and the aspirations of the soul. In the final apostrophe to 'Divina Elisa' the poem teeters on the brink of a harmonious synthesis. The subjective imagination seems capable of effecting eternal preservation; but this heightened emphasis on imagination reminds the reader that its catalyst is the reality of the human condition, which proves to be its undermining.[64]

A defining feature of the early modern imperial condition is the substitution of a static concept of the universe with a dynamic one. Richard Helgerson has designated the new poetry of the sixteenth century a conspicuous 'movement' poetry, 'that sets out to impose a programme of literary renewal on the literature of its particular vernacular'.[65] Garcilaso's role in the re-making of the vernacular through imitation has been acknowledged; and we are beginning to debate the self-conscious politics of his poetry. But we cling to oversimplified views of harmony and stasis in the Eclogues, particularly the First and Third,[66] despite the fact that a re-elaboration of Virgilian and Italian Renais-

---

[63]   The poem imitates closely the formal structure of Virgil, *Eclogue* VIII (an introduction, a dedication, a transition, two songs, with a transition between them), even imitating the extra line in the second song. The enhanced symmetry and syntactical patterning in Garcilaso has been studied by, among others, Fernández-Morera, *The Lyre*, pp. 31–34, and Sharon Ghertman, *Petrarch and Garcilaso: A Linguistic Approach to Style* (London: Tamesis, 1975), pp. 93–128.

[64]   See Castiglione's exposition of Neoplatonic love, placed in the mouth of Bembo, which recognises the imagination's ambiguous relationship to materiality: Baldassare Castiglione, *Il libro del Cortegiano* (Venice: Aldo Manuzio and Andrea Asolo, 1528), IV, 67.

[65]   See Richard Helgerson, *A Sonnet from Carthage: Garcilaso de la Vega and the New Poetry of Sixteenth-Century Europe* (Philadelphia: University of Pennsylvania Press, 2007), p. 68.

[66]   Some readings of the sonnets have questioned tendencies to interpret Garcilaso's poetics in the context of Classical aesthetics. See, for instance, E.C. Graf, 'Forcing the Poetic Voice: Garcilaso de la Vega's Sonnet XXIX as a Deconstruction of the Idea of Harmony', *MLN*, 109 (1994), 163–85.

sance pastoral is the perfect site in which to answer Nebrija's call to fix the linguistic basis of the nation state and through which to convey revisionist ideals of empire.[67]

The key interdependent dynamics of poetry and power are established in the introductory stanzas of *Eclogue* I which include a dedication to Don Pedro de Toledo, Viceroy of Naples. Ter Horst has drawn our attention to the complexity of the art/state relationship and to the suggestion of a shared equality that emerges in Garcilaso's appropriation of epic energy to his lyric enterprise.[68] The reconfiguration of roles and a radical transvaluation is central to this project. The epic affirmation 'he de cantar' will be realised in the sweet lament ('dulce lamentar'), the single song of Salicio and Nemoroso. The shepherds' voices and their Orphic power will be recreated in the voice of the narrator/poet. The tranquility of the Arcadian setting is disrupted by the frenetic activities of upper nobility – diplomacy, state business, imperial warfare, hunting. This is a poetry in motion that draws art away from its origins and towards a contemporary scene of power and recognition. But the transformative counter-current is just as potent. The metamorphosis of laurel into ivy heralds the substitution of *negotium* by *otium* and a collapsing of generic and art/life boundaries as the Viceroy is integrated into the Arcadian audience. Art is the supreme seducer and political power is drawn towards its authority.

The public figure sustains the private poet (there are debts to settle), but the poet's promised promotion of Don Pedro plays against the Viceroy's horizon of expectations – patronage is repaid not in a speculative epic in the future, but in a pastoral text in the present. But this is not a suspended present. Don Pedro may be required to stop and listen, but the reader is never intellectually immobilised. Time, a vital protagonist of *Eclogue* I, never stands still in these opening stanzas, it is never experientially stable. The reader is shuttled back and forth through diverse intertextual and socio-historical spaces, amid blatant metafictional markers,[69] and adversely engaged with reality. The experience of art promises infinite renewal, just as Salicio and Nemoroso sense eternity in love. But the poem reminds us in the (con)flated image of fleeing deer and artist working against the clock

[67]   See the often-cited 'siempre la lengua fue compañera del Imperio, y de tal manera lo siguió, que juntamente comenzaron, crecieron, y florecieron, y después junta fue la caída de entrambos'. Antonio de Nebrija, *Gramática de la lengua española,* eds Pascual Galindo Romeo and Luís Ortiz Muñoz, 2 vols (Madrid: CSIC, 1946), Preface.

[68]   See Robert Ter Horst, 'Poetry and Power in Garcilaso's Égloga Primera', *Revista de Estudios Hispánicos,* 21 (1987), 1–10 (1–2). On the protean potential of the Eclogue, see Aurora Egido, 'Sin poética hay poetas: sobre la teoría de la égloga en el siglo de oro', *Criticón,* 30 (1985), 43–77.

[69]   See Howard B. Westcott, 'Garcilaso's Eclogues: Artifice, Metafiction, Self-Representation', *Calíope,* 3.1 (1997), 71–85. Westcott reads the three Eclogues in relation to each other; locating the coherency of narrative discourse in the development of the character of Nemoroso. The argument makes little allowance for sensuality in a trajectory of grief-recovery-transcendence.

(stanzas 2–3) that a rational perspective sets parameters that can be overcome only through the materialisation of memory in our imaginings.

A poetics of memory that requires the co-operation of the reader as co-creator systematically undermines the idea of a frozen past in the lament of Nemoroso (stanzas 18–29). But before Nemoroso sings the narrator intervenes in a transitionary stanza which rewrites and expands upon Virgil's invocation to the Muses in *Eclogue* VIII (62–63). The additional verses are integrated at 231–34: 'la blanda Filomena, / casi como dolida / y a compasión movida, / dulcemente responde al son lloroso.' [The nightingale, softhearted, as though sharing the pain, is moved to pity, and responds sweetly to the sorrowful song.] 'Filomena' is a provocative plural sign that draws from its mythological origins the powerful articulation of tragedy: Ovidian rape victim metamorphosed into aesthetic symbol; Virgilian lover, suspended in the nightingale analogy between culpability and overwhelming loss, caught somewhere between self and other.[70] Within Garcilaso's text it signals a mediating moment when the authority of the narrator ('ejercitar *mi pluma*') is transferred to the culminating voice of the text, anticipating Nemoroso's sustained engagement with the Georgic model at stanzas 24 and 25. It represents also a determined subsuming of the idolatrous, self-estranging resonances of Salicio's song, the 'son lloroso', into the responsive, melancholic, 'new poetry', of Nemoroso. Salicio had made insubstantial Orphic claims for his own music at stanza 15 ('Con mi llorar las piedras enternecen' [The rocks are softened when I weep]),[71] but his failed relationship with the sustaining muse, Galatea, results in the failure of communication to effect order out of chaos. In stanza 16 he exits the bucolic space he has failed to recreate.

Salicio's relationship with his environment is hindered by exaggerated self-absorption. Disorder exists in the natural world only from the subjective perspective of a voice which inhabits the margins ('siempre está en llanto esta ánima mezquina' [but this miserable soul of mine is always bathed in tears; 81]), and which embodies confusion of the natural cycles. When Salicio looks back to the past (landscape), it is indeed a foreign country(side):

> Por ti el silencio de la selva umbrosa,
> por ti la esquividad y apartamiento
> del solitario monte m'agradaba;
> por ti la verde hierba, el fresco viento,
> el blanco lirio y colorada rosa
> y dulce primavera deseaba[72]

* pleading for love

---

70   The story of Tereus, Procne and Philomela closes Ovid, *Metamorphoses* VI; Orpheus is compared to the nightingale in the Virgilian epyllion of *Georgic* IV, 511–15.

71   See Cruz, *Imitación y transformación*, pp. 102–06, who explores the Petrarchan subtext of Salicio's verses.

72   Cruz refers to a 'paisaje subjetivizado' which, described in terms of the absent beloved, unites the two songs of the poem (*Imitación y transformación*, p. 98).

[For you alone did I take pleasure in the silence of the shady forest, for you did I withdraw to the deserted wood; for your sake alone I longed for the green grass, the cool breeze, the white lily, the red rose and sweetness of springtime.]

Harnessing allusion to make present the absent elusive beloved, Salicio makes metaphors out of the traces of memory, and credits Galatea not with his capacity to participate positively in the world, but with the construction of an idyll in language that has no reality in past or present, and which even he knows cannot be sustained: 'Ay, ¡cuánto m'engañaba!' [How deceived I was!; 105][73] His attempt to reconcile the irreconcilable results in the anti-Orphic poetry termed by Horace 'a sick man's dreams' (stanza 9).[74]

The elegiac opening of Nemoroso's song reconstitutes Salicio's *cancionero*-inflected refrain, 'Salir, sin duelo, lágrimas corriendo' [Flow, flow freely, streams of tears; stanzas 5–15],[75] within a new progressive poetics that respects continuity while advocating renovation: 'Corrientes aguas puras, cristalinas, / árboles que os estáis mirando en ellas' [Pure streams of crystalline waters, trees that see yourselves reflected in them; 239–40.] The *locus amoenus* depicted in stanza 18 represents art, nature and human suffering in empathetic co-existence. The mirror figure negates the narcissistic self-fashioning of the previous song (stanza 13; 175–81),[76] positing a counter-ideology in which *eros* is entirely transfigured. Desire, which is debased in Salicio's self-determined Polyphemic identification to the lowest level of materiality,[77] recuperates its Platonic potential as a force that compels the human being to overcome his human condition and to look upwards.[78] Within the context of Salicio's ontological and aesthetic

73   In an idiosyncratic reading, David Quinn interprets the 'por ti' passage as reflecting a decision taken by Salicio to move from city to country. See 'Autobiography or Art?', 153.
74   The analogy is used by Horace to emphasise the importance of unified form in artistic creation. See *Ars Poetica*, 1–9.
75   Patrick Gallagher explores Garcilaso's debt to Garci Sánchez de Badajoz's adaptation of Jeremiah for Salicio's refrain. See 'Garcilaso's First Eclogue and the Lamentations of Love', *Forum for Modern Language Studies*, IX (1973), 192–99. See also Brian Dutton, 'Garcilaso's *sin duelo*', *MLN*, 80.2 (1965), 251–58, who investigates precedents and meaning.
76   Several pretexts have been identified for these verses: Virgil's adaptation of Theocritus (Corydon, *Eclogue* II, 22–27); Ovid's buffoonish Polyphemus (*Metamorphoses* XIII, 789–865), and Sannazaro's *Arcadia* IX, 41; but with a tendency to miss the Polyphemus/Narcissus association. This is all the more surprising given Garcilaso's sustained engagement with the Narcissus myth (fused with Orpheus) for his depiction of the deranged Albanio in *Eclogue* II.
77   The parodic potential of this scene is realised in Lope de Vega's burlesque epic *La Gatomaquia*. See Isabel Torres, 'Lope de Vega's *La Gatomaquia* and positive parody', *Calíope*, 14.1 (2008), 5–22.
78   Jeanne Nightingale connects the use of the mirror metaphor as a governing metaphor of the courtly lyric tradition to the Neoplatonic concept of creation as a descent from the ideal realm of intelligible and static forms into an illusory material world of mirror images. See 'From Mirror to Metamorphosis: Echoes of Ovid's Narcissus in Chrétien's *Eric et Enide*', in *The Mythographic*

crisis, the mirror functions as a locus of deception that invites transgression. In Nemoroso's transformation of matter into articulated 'memorias llenas d'alegría' [joy-filled memories; 252], the mirror bridges a higher level of reality and initiates a process towards transcendence.

Nemoroso as poet is conscious of his role in the relentless movement of time. In stanza 20 he converts the deceptively realist surfaces of memory into an actualisation of reality in its most concrete form. Desire is encoded within the conventional rhetorical strategy of the 'ubi sunt' theme, aligned with a positive act of artistic creation that recalls the iconographical stasis of *carpe diem* (and Sonnet XXIII), but in reaching the reader 'mas allá' mobilises an image of Elisa that is poignantly soulful and utterly (and paradoxically) present.[79] The interrogative mode allows silence a role in the subtle articulation of the ineffable, but words confront the reality of death in starker, more uncompromising terms: 'Aquesto todo agora ya s'encierra, [...] en la escura, desierta y dura tierra' [But all that is buried now [...] in the dark, desolate, unyielding earth; 279–81]. Nemoroso's reality is determined by the fact of this confrontation. Stanzas 21–23 encapsulate the darkness, isolation and entrapment of a life that is lived in death's shadow and in the persistent grip of fear:

> El cielo en mis dolores
> cargó la mano tanto,
> que a sempiterno llanto
> y a triste soledad me ha condenado;
> y lo que siento más es verme atado
> a la pesada vida y enojosa,
>   solo, desamparado,
> ciego, sin lumbre en cárcel tenebrosa. (288–95)

[Heaven, heavy-handed in my sorrow, has condemned me to ever-lasting lament and wretched loneliness; but I am dragged down most by the frustrating weight of life's chains, alone, helpless, blind, without light in a gloomy prison.]

Art, ed. Jane Chance (Gainesville: University of Florida Press, 1990), pp. 47–82. Within the European tradition of Neoplatonic philosophy the most significant innovation was the fusion of this theory of Platonic forms with Aristotle's concept of an ordered universe. According to the logic of the Great Chain of Being, perceived by Macrobius as a chain of mirrors, the lowest level was the material world of the senses which, being the farthest from God, was also the least real. Within this Neoplatonic schema, *eros* was an essentially contradictory force, a sign of the human being's weakness and attraction to superficial and inferior beauty, and yet the force that compelled souls to overcome their imperfection and ascend the scale of Being.

79 Contrast stanza 13, where Galatea, absent from Salicio's self-inflationary discourse, is replaced by a mocking rival (see Smith, 'Homographesis') and attacked in interrogative mode in the following stanza as a perpetrator of crimes against Salicio and nature.

This is the catalyst for the implicit death wish of verses 321–23 ('hasta que muerte'l tiempo determine / que a ver el deseado / sol de tu clara vista m'encamine') [until death determines that it is time for me to see the longed-for brillance of your sun-like gaze] and the context of *desengaño* [disillusion] against which we must read its explicit articulation in the final apostrophe to 'Divina Elisa'.

As Paul Ilie has pointed out, the concept of reality 'takes its ontological status from the phenomenology of language' and arises through language's ordering process.[80] In stanza 26, Nemoroso's systematic ordering of a lock of Elisa's hair into a keepsake on a string transforms it from its passive role, as recipient of almost unbearable experience, into an active participant in the formulation of a palliative mnemonic art. As in many of Garcilaso's sonnets, especially Sonnet X, memory is a subjective perspective that negotiates the boundaries between two worlds, not past and present, but the reality of a painful present and the recollection of past pleasure within that agonising context.[81] Also at play is the reminiscing voice of the emulative poem, with its own ordering of previous articulations that depends on the reader's recollection and recognition to complete meanings.[82] But memory functions on the basis of an irreversible chronometry and an unpredictability that can defy ordering. When Nemoroso opens the door on the past he is besieged by the darkest memory of all, the night of Elisa's death (stanzas 27 and 28),[83] which invades perception in the present with a deceptive vitality: 'verte presente agora me parece […] me parece que oigo' [I seem to see you before me […] I seem to hear]. Memory becomes the mirror in which Nemoroso is pulled back towards Salicio ('siempre aflige esta ánima mezquina', 368 echoing 81), in which he sees the self deceived. This is part of what drives the angry outburst against the god Lucina, but it is also what produces the expressive triumph of stanza 29:

> Divina Elisa, pues agora el cielo
> con inmortales pies pisas y mides,
> y su mudanza ves, estando queda,
> ¿Por qué de mí te olvidas y no pides
> que se apresure el tiempo en que este velo

[80]   See 'Purifying Poetry: The Ineffable and the Dehumanized', in *Studies in Honour of Bruce W. Wardropper*, eds Dian Fox, Harry Sieber and Robert Ter Horst (Delaware: Juan de la Cuesta, 1989), pp. 163–79 (p. 169).

[81]   Critics have long made autobiographical associations between *Eclogue* 1, stanza 26 and the 'dulces prendas' of Sonnet X (e.g. Entwistle, 'The Loves', 382). For alternative readings of the sonnet, see Johnson, 'Personal Involvement', 290–92, and Navarrete, *Orphans of Petrarch*, pp. 23-27.

[82]   See Cruz, *Imitación y transformación*, pp. 99–102, who reads the poetics of ordering in Garcilaso as an anti-Petrarchan strategy, noting a tragic Dido subtext via a link with Sonnet X.

[83]   For an alternative reading, see Stephen Lipmann, 'On the Significance of the "Trance de Lucina" in Garcilaso's First Eclogue', *Neophilologus*, 67 (1983), 65–70, in which he argues that Nemoroso has been separated from Elisa before her death and that these stanzas represent an act of imagination rather than memory.

rompa del cuerpo y verme libre pueda,
y en la tercera rueda,
contigo mano a mano,
busquemos otro llano,
busquemos otros montes y otros ríos,
otros valles floridos y sombríos
donde descanse y siempre pueda verte
ante los ojos míos,
sin miedo y sobresalto de perderte? (394–407)

[Divine Elisa, now with immortal feet you measure and tread the heavens, and motionless, you see their changes. Why do you forget me and not ask for time to pass quickly, for the veil of this body to be broken, for me to be free, so that hand in hand with you, in the third sphere, we might search out another plain, other woods and other rivers, other valleys with flowers, and with shade, where I can rest and hold you ever before my eyes, without this fear and dread of losing you?]

The past does not perish in Nemoroso's vision, but its ground has shifted. Memory brings the past into the present, but a timeless imagination can reconstruct the past in order to push the present towards the future, and generate a new reality. In the poem this takes the form of a recreated bucolic space that recognises the anxieties and autonomy of the self ('¿Por qué de mí te olvidas …'), while even syntactically emphasising its dependence on the other.[84] Thus Nemoroso's imagined reunion with Elisa represents an attempted reconciliation of the material and spiritual in the poem, but it also celebrates the interdependency of its competing strands of literary discourse – the Christianised imagery of Renaissance Neoplatonism, the pagan echoes of Classical and Italian intertexts and the aesthetic experimentations of a new poetic consciousness. *Elements*

Cruz has identified an Orphic tension in the antagonistic endings of the shepherds' songs.[85] Within the surface space of the poem and the renegotiation of Salicio's flawed Orphic stance into Nemoroso's nightingale, this is incontrovertible. But stanza 29 opens up a more problematic intertextual interrogation. Those commentators who have noted the pagan tone of Nemoroso's Neoplatonic vision have either failed to account for it,[86] or stressed the concretising potential of pagan reminiscences as a negation of the text's Neoplatonic impulses.[87] But the strategy

---

84   The ecstatic vision of the stanza is constructed in terms of a question that originates in an expression of selfhood and moves outwards to embrace the other.

85   See *Imitación y transformación*, p. 104.

86   See Fernández Morera, *The Lyre*, p. 31.

87   See, for example, Arce de Vázquez, 'La Égloga Primera', 55. For a different perspective, see Otis H. Green, 'The Abode of the Blest in Garcilaso's Égloga Primera', *Romance Philology*, VI (1953), 272–78. Green takes issue with those who interpret the pagan elements of the ending

at work is consistent with the shifting intertextual dynamics that have informed the entire eclogue. What has been identified as disconcertingly pagan is one strand in a slippery system of evolving temporal, aesthetic and ideological synergies. As Nemoroso searches for a location in which to reinterpret past experiences in relation to present pain and projected pleasure, the figure of Elisa moves accordingly. Regardless of the emphasis on her immobility in the Empyrean (396),[88] Elisa defies fixation and is not really there, or anywhere, in a complete sense. But it is not a question of where she is, or is perceived to be, rather that the creative collaboration inherent in the reading process allows her to move through several spaces at once. When Elisa descends into the sphere of Venus (400),[89] textual traces coalesce to convey amorous and artistic apotheosis in emulative terms. The Orphic tragedy of Virgil's *Georgics* (and the 'sempiterno llanto' [eternal lament; 290]) is subsumed in an Ovidian reunion scene (Ovid, *Met.* XI, 64–66) that also echoes Garcilaso's own Sonnet 25: 'hasta que aquella eterna noche escura / me cierre aquestos ojos que te vieron, / dejándome con otros que te vean' [until that dark and eternal night closes those eyes that saw you, leaving me with others that will see you again; 12–14]. The 'otherness' of Nemoroso's vision effects estrangement by fusing Sannazaro's Christian apotheosis (*Arcadia* V, 1–16),[90] with Claudian's Elysium in the *De Raptu Proserpinae*: 'amissum ne crede diem; sunt *altera* (nobis) / sidera, sunt orbes *alii*, lumenque videbis purius' [don't consider the day lost; we have other stars, other orbits and you will see a purer light; II, 282–85]. In accordance with the imperatives of secular humanism, Garcilaso manipulates a range of models to restore sensuality to its rightful place in human experience (although never at the expense of our more sublime metaphysical moments),[91] while Nemoroso transcends the conditions of his own death wish, retaining 'sentido' as he attempts to overcome 'dolor'.

as indicative of a conscious abandonment by the poet of Christian (Catholic) dogma.

   88   The static/motive dialectic of verse 3 functions through the figure of hypallage. The heavenly spheres below the Empyrean move, while it alone of all the heavens remains immobile. See Green, 'The Abode', 272–74.

   89   The 'tercera rueda' is designated the circle of Venus within a Ptolomaic conception of the universe. It is the temporary dwelling place of the *spiriti amanti* in Dante (Green, 'The Abode', 274) and exploited as the traditional destination of poet lovers by Petrarch (Cruz, *Imitación y transformación*, p. 105). Both Green and Cruz comment on the ambiguity of the location.

   90   The soul of Androgeo is imagined in a solitary apotheosis by the lamenting shepherd Ergasto, whereas Nemoroso transcends lament in a self-apotheosizing vision that emphasises the amorous reunion.

   91   Edward Dudley takes this further, arguing that Garcilaso turns traditional Neoplatonic metaphor into an image of sexual fulfilment. See 'The Lady is Out of this World: Erotic Conceits and Carnal Displacements in Three Protocols of Desire', in *Negotiating Past and Present: Studies in Spanish Literature for Javier Herrero*, ed. David Gies (Charlottesville, VA: Rookwood, 1997), pp. 176–93 (p. 185); a line of enquiry pursued more recently by Álvaro Llosa Sanz in 'El tacto invisible. Relectura erótica del soneto VIII de Garcilaso: del eros fantástico a la fantasía erótica', *Hispanic Review*, 77.4 (2009), 413–25 (422–23).

The voice of Garcilaso's 'new poetry' is borne on artifice, its compelling rhetoric residing in the range of its correspondences, and in the power of its words to communicate limitations – linguistic and human. The emotional anguish at the core of Nemoroso's apostrophe to Elisa is identifiable because reason is not overturned 'más allá de la muerte' [beyond death]. Quevedo would confidently assert the survival of a unified love experience in a series of untenable future tenses. Garcilaso's poem exposes its existential and aesthetic crisis in a crescendo of subjunctives which, rather than defying death, depends entirely upon it. Parker alerted us to the presence of Neoplatonic imperatives in the poem, and countered structuralism's objectivity with an insistence on poetry's relation to its contextual external reality. But Neoplatonism is only one aspect of the Eclogue's prevailing counter-harmonising principles that encompass the material, the spiritual and the aesthetic. In *Eclogue* I representation comes into being through a counterposing of the opposites that are the permanent structures of the world, the early modern, but also our own: unity and loss; rest and motion; origin and originality; memory and imagination. The dialectic is closer to the value-recognising philosophy of aesthetic realism than to structuralism. In Garcilaso's eclogue freedom and order are beautifully and musically made one: the strands of a lost beloved's hair are counted 'uno a uno' [one by one]; the souls of lovers rematerialise to walk together 'mano a mano' [hand in hand]; and in the shadow of death the rhythms of life are persistently renewed in the twilight song of shepherds who withdraw with their flocks, 'paso a paso' [step by step].

Indirectly to the point(s): ekphrasis and echoes

In Sonnet XI a motion through opposites combines with a pseudo-ekphrastic poetics (similar to that of Sonnet XIII) to unfold a plurality of temporal perspectives that interact within a complex spatial conceit:

> Hermosas ninfas, que en el río metidas,
> contentas habitáis en las moradas
> de relucientes piedras fabricadas
> y en columnas de vidrio sostenidas,
>   agora estéis labrando embebescidas
> o tejendo las telas delicadas,
> agora unas con otras apartadas
> contándoos los amores y las vidas:
>   dejad un rato la labor, alzando
> vuestras rubias cabezas a mirarme,
> y no os detendréis mucho según ando,
>   que o no podréis de lástima escucharme,
> o convertido en agua aquí llorando,
> podréis allá despacio consolarme.

[Beautiful nymphs, submerged in the water, you dwell in contentment in mansions made of shining stone, supported by columns of glass; now, absorbed, you embroider or weave delicate fabrics, now, separated out in groups you share stories of life and love. Put aside your work for just a moment, raising your golden heads to gaze on me, and I will not detain you long as I pass by, either you'll be too moved to listen to me, or I, through weeping, transformed to water here, will be consoled by you forever there.]

The mythological scene that is recreated in the quatrains of this sonnet, the underwater world of the beautiful nymphs, thematises an ekphrasis (image/text of vv. 5–6) that is never explicitly forthcoming, yet involves the reader in a voyeuristic image construction that overcomes formal ekphrastic rupture with a smooth suturing of space and time. Paradoxically, the passage towards integration is energised by assertive figures of difference and alterity, which, as well as encompassing gender and emotional states, implicitly cites (and sights) the sterile rhetoric of the petitioning courtly lover against the eloquence and collective creativity of the subaquatic sphere of the nymphs. The speaker objectifies and makes 'real' a utopian image of visual pleasure whose sustained radiance is in stark contrast to the dark well of unfulfilled desire from which it arises. The sonnet is a magnificent gesture of aesthetic over-compensation in which the nymphs, captured in the frame of the poem, substitute for the absent, unresponsive beloved and emblematise the potential for alternative integrated relationships: communion with nature, the reciprocality of the reader and the mutually sustaining interarticulations of artistic emulation.[92]

Unlike formal ekphrastic mode the static and spatial qualities of the image are temporalised so that, despite its heightened artificiality, the scene appears to co-exist with speaker and reader in an open-ended, gravity-defying present ('habitáis' [2], 'agora estéis labrando' [5], 'tejendo' [6], 'contando' [8]). The reader is drawn in as viewer and seems, as in Sonnet XIII, to share the frame with the speaker, but here the reader's interpretive space is more tightly controlled, determined by the point of view and attitude of a deliberately understated poetic 'I'/'eye'. The fantasy feigns a liquid fluidity but its constituent parts are corporeal and solid, already completed as they come into being ('ninfas ... metidas'; 'moradas de piedras fabricadas'; 'columnas de vidrio sostenidas'). The self-other encounter of speaker and mythical nymphs operates as a figure for the lover's imaginative manipulation of memory and desire, and although it might appear to be triply inscribed, opening out to include the reader,

[92] Multiple models have been cited for this sonnet. Heiple adds two poems by Bernardo Tasso to the long list of sources (*Garcilaso de la Vega*, p. 211); among them the dwelling place of nymphs as described by Virgil in *Georgic* IV, 333–85 and by Sannazaro in *Arcadia* VIII and XII, 15–16. Navarrete, following Herrera's identification of the Petrarchan origins of line 1, considers the erotic ambiguity of the poem in the light of Petrarch's recourse to water-related erotic myths in *Canzone* XXIII (*Orphans of Petrarch*, pp. 99–101).

it carries an allegorical weight of value and power that negates third-party neutrality. On the surface the poem presents itself as an objective site of aesthetic contemplation, but access to its alien underworld involves immersion in a subjective imagination that is rendered in deceptively material terms.

The oblique apostrophising gesture of the quatrains acquires an explicit intensity in the tercets, as if the speaker recognised that the fragile scaffolding of fantasy might collapse (anticipated in the eloquent border crossing of verse 8), or that the desired compassionate reciprocality was prohibited by courtly convention. As Ter Horst has noted, the crucial word here is 'labor', which unites the activity and eloquence of the nymphs with the double condition of the speaker as poet and as courtly lover.[93] The qualified tone of the lover's petition belies its inherent audacity. By asking the nymphs to turn their gaze towards him, the speaker requests an act of communication that would reverse the attitude of the beloved and reset the conventional perspective of the amorous sonnet. Moreover, the move from seeing subject to seen object negates the Medusa metaphor of artistic creation, allowing the speaker to turn the power of the nymph's artistry and eloquence back upon the self. Caught in the luminous gaze of his own eroticised fantasy, the speaker seeks to overcome the threat of emotional and artistic stasis through an emblematic metamorphosis of tears into water that recalls Petrarch's evocation of the myth of Byblis (*Canzone* XXIII).[94]

Within the sonnet's dialectical structure the 'either'/'or' dilemma of the final tercet is necessarily inadequate, designed to recognise and reconcile both propositions (the ebb and flow of effective communication and affective response) through the intermediary link of transcendent art. Narrative logic locates the speaker at the water's edge, his situation pathetically inflected by a sense of imminent self-destruction ('y no os detendréis mucho según ando'; 11). But the potential transformation of tears into spring is a transgressive strategy which resists the regulation of borders (spatial/temporal, literal/metaphorical) in order to promote an infinite system of cultural free exchange that gives positive universal significance to self-perpetuation. A world of individual suffering and redemption is encapsulated in the antithetically positioned deictics 'aquí' and 'allá'. Once again, as in *Eclogue* I, 'allá' is a locus of consolation, an imagined space beyond pain, which derives its power from its distance and difference from 'aquí'. Ultimately, however, the poem attempts to transcend narcissistic

---

93 See Robert Ter Horst, 'In an Echoing Grove: Quijote II and a Sonnet of Garcilaso', in *Studies in Honour of Bruce W. Wardropper*, pp. 335–46 (p. 339).

94 See Navarrete's discussion, *Orphans of Petrarch*, pp. 99-100. Navarrete returns to this sonnet to substantiate his erotic reading in terms of connections between Garcilaso's poetry and erotic burlesque poems of the period. See 'La poesía erótica y la imaginación visual', in *Venus venerada: tradiciones eróticas de la literatura española*, eds J. Ignacio Díez and Adrienne L. Martín (Madrid: Editorial Complutense, 2006), pp. 73–87 (esp. pp. 83–84).

contemplation by prioritising time ('despacio') over space, but there is an unsettling circularity in the intermingling of the speaker's tears and the sonnet's
imagined site of artistic creation; a regressive turn to self which communicates
a residual burden of cultural geography and personal history.

In *Eclogue* III, traditionally considered to be Garcilaso's final poem, the
golden-haired nymphs emerge from the water, now specifically the River Tagus,
and transfer the artifice of their 'labor' to a conventional *locus amoenus* that has
been displaced to the Castilian banks. The poem is conceived in a strongly arch-
itechtonic way, reflected in the choice of the more formal *octava real* over the
alternation of heptasyllables and hendecasyllables of *Eclogue* I. Two outer parts,
thirteen dedicatory/prologue stanzas and thirteen final stanzas with an amoebean
coda, act as dual points of reference, framing and intersecting a central pastoral
scene of formal ekphrasis.[95] The structure is balanced, even sculptural, but the
poem's pure plasticity and striking visuality reflect a carefully crafted illusion.
For Bergmann, Garcilaso's attention to the materials of the tapestries, their subtle-
ties of colour and perspective – in short, the way in which the poem offers up its
artifice at every opportunity – serves to expose the tension between the illusion
itself and recognition of its inherent deception.[96] And yet, the effect of the artifice
works against artificiality. The 'cultivation of the aesthetic' in *Eclogue* III does
not involve the complete containment of lyric emotion, which threatens to out
itself at any time.[97] On the contrary, the poem (*ut pictura*) portrays with exquisite
sensuality what the mind's eye can clearly see, but also what the human heart
perceives with uncertainty. The connotative contours of the Eclogue are multilayered, confused but intimately connected, suggested by contrasts of water and earth,
nymphs and shepherds, harmony and discord, origin and originality, past and
present. A conflicted sense of the transient and the eternal in art, in love and in life
flows through the poem in the form of a ubiquitous water motif that issues from
an appropriated Orphic underworld, streams across the surface of the tapestries,
merges with a contemporary Tagus, and finally discharges into the sea of Lusita-
nia. The motif figures a fluid, reshaping poetics in progress; potentially unifying,
but constructed in tense relation to its politico-aesthetic surroundings (the sym-

95   This follows Darío Fernández-Morera's adaptation of the scheme offered by Elías L. Rivers. See *The Lyre*, p. 74.

96   See Emilie L. Bergmann, *Art Inscribed: Essays on Ekphrasis in Spanish Golden Age
Poetry* (Cambridge, MA: Harvard University Press, 1979), pp. 102–05. See also Alan K.G. Paterson, 'Ekphrasis in Garcilaso's "Egloga Tercera"', *Modern Language Review*, 72 (1977), 73–92.

97   The idea that the self-conscious cultivation of the aesthetic in *Eclogue* III is incompatible
with the expression of lyric emotion has been an implicit, though dominant, approach to the poem
since Lapesa. More recently it has been defended by Chemris (*Góngora's 'Soledades'*, pp. 12–14),
although this seems contrary to her very pertinent observations regarding the undermining of
pastoral conventions and the exhaustion of the Neoplatonic ideal, as demonstrated in the violent
description of Elisa's death: 'the Platonic artifice encasing the death of Elissa does not, in the end,
totally absorb the discord of reality' (p. 15).

biosis of literary prestige and empire), and conscious that its expansionist impulses endanger its identifying nature. At the end of the poem the water recuperates its essence, re-emerging as the liquid mantle of the departing nymphs.

At the heart of conventional ekphrasis lies a negatively charged borrowing which in *Eclogue* III becomes transformed into a compelling interrogation of the power of transfiguration itself. Garcilaso offers a second version of Ovid's Apollo and Daphne myth, now formally ekphrastic as the second of the four tapestries woven by the water nymphs. The nymph Dinámene represents the three stages of the story in three stanzas that convey a distillation of the Ovidian narrative sequence: the vengeance of Cupid, Apollo's pursuit and Daphne's metamorphosis. The third stanza of the tapestry reads as follows:

> Mas a la fin los brazos le crecían
> y en sendos ramos vueltos se mostraban;
> y los cabellos, que vencer solían
> al oro fino, en hojas se tornaban;
> en torcidas raíces s'estendían
> los blancos pies y en tierra se hincaban;
> llora el amante y busca el ser primero,
> besando y abrazando aquel madero. (161–78)

[But in the end her arms began to grow and change into long branches; and hair, which had once outshone fine gold, turned into leaves; her white feet, transforming into twisted roots, sank down into the earth; the lover weeps and seeking out the former being, kisses and embraces the wooden trunk.]

The witnessing role of the speaker-narrator is more subtle than in Sonnet XIII, and is twice removed (at least) from this scene. As an interloper in the mythical world of the nymphs, and voyeur of the weaving scenes, the task of the narrating subject is to weave in words the visual images of the tapestries. The speaker perceives, interprets and transforms (the tapestries) what has already been perceived, interpreted and transformed (the myth), and the end product (the poem) is opened up to the potentially transforming interpretation of the reader. The artistic process that is uncovered here suggests that there can be no authoritative centre in art, just the swings and roundabouts of unpredictable transmission.

Against this, the Eclogue seems structured to convey supreme confidence in the potency of Garcilaso's poetic word. The Ovidian tapestries, as subtextually significant as *Eclogue* I for the poem's contemporary story of love and loss, are unravelled and rewoven in a dynamic reading. The violent death of Elisa, the 'ninfa degollada',[98] filtered through the textual fragments of interpenetrating

---

98   The authenticity of the term 'degollada' (of the first edition) over 'igualada' (preferred by Morros), has been a subject of much critical debate. The major studies are cited by Navarrete, *Orphans of Petrarch*, p. 252, note 34. The significance of 'degollada' has been equally polemi-

sources, emerges as a unified and culminating image/text that reaches the reader as simultaneously 'real' and represented. The sense of a collective poetic contin-uuum is violated by a subjective personal memory (impelled by the devastation of Nemoroso) that penetrates into past histories and impacts upon the future. But unlike *Eclogue* I the emotional responses evoked within and beyond the text by the story of an individual's sorrow are counter-balanced, if not quite controlled, by invasive conceptual attitudes about myth and history, reality and art and, most pervasively, about the fragile condition of universal humanity. The *vanitas* that stills the images of the Ovidian tapestries is mobilised in the more immediate matter of the Elisa tragedy, only to be reformulated by the poetic voice as the shared sweet song of the shepherds Alcino and Tirreno.[99]

The first three Ovidian tapestries do not just end badly, they are ended badly, the evolution of their mythical narratives arrested at moments of divine failure. Orpheus, now alienated from the natural environment he once held enthralled, is deprived of an effective voice and pours forth a futile lament. Venus, the supreme deity of love, is brought to her knees before the lifeless body of Adonis, her sensuous mouth unable to breathe life into the beloved. And Apol-lo, potent god of poetry (one of his many titles), is reduced to the level of the frustrated 'amante', futilely seeking out the essence of the human beloved beneath the dehumanising bark. Only Garcilaso's own story of Nemoroso and Elisa, three times as long as the others, is presented to the reader as a completed image, tragically and iconically unalterable, yet opened out at the end to the possibil-ity of artistic apotheosis.[100] Ovidian strategies of redemption are transformed somewhat paradoxically by the wilful subject voice of Nise in a new Spanish context that rejects events located in an irrelevant past: 'La blanca Nise [...] no quiso entretejer antigua historia' [The fair Nise [...] did not wish to weave an

cal. Cobarrubias's 1611 dictionary gives two primary meanings: 'to bleed to death' and 'to behead'. The first has been easier to reconcile with a biographical reading (the idea that Isabel Freire bled out in childbirth); the second has been variously interpreted within the Orphic frame of the poem and in relation to Virgilian and Ovidian precedents (see studies by Enrique Martín-ez-López, 'Sobre aquella bestialidad de Garcilaso [égl. III, 230]', *Publications of the Modern Language Association*, 87 [1972], 12–25; Cruz, *Imitación y transformación*, p. 117; Terence O'Reilly, 'The Figure of Elisa in the Eclogues of Garcilaso', in *Spanish Poetry of the Golden Age*, eds Stephen Boyd and Jo Richardson [Manchester: Manchester Spanish and Portuguese Studies, 2002], pp. 85–96).

99   Although the singers reflect contrasting attitudes to love (Tirreno more positive than Alcino), the emphasis is on a single song and a singular effect (vv. 289–90; 295–96; 301–04; 369–71). The element of competition, foregrounded in the Virgilian model (*Eclogue* VII), is only subtextually present.

100   If the manner of Elisa's death heralds the re-emergence of a poetic voice forged with Orphic assumptions, then the swan analogy is perfect in this context, evoking the immortalising power of poetry via the ironic assertions of Horace who depicts his own metamorphosis into a swan in *Odes* II, 20, 1–8. The poet/swan association was famously exploited in Ben Johnson's 'Sweet Swan of Avon' with reference to Shakespeare.

ancient story; 193–96]. The unresponsive laurel bark of the Apollo and Daphne myth becomes the speaking surface of the 'álamo' upon which is inscribed an epitaph that articulates timeless love and loss within an Orphic frame:[101]

> en la corteza
> de un álamo unas letras *escribía*
> como epitafio de la ninfa bella,
> que hablaban ansí *por parte della*:
> *'Elisa soy*, en cuyo nombre suena
> y se lamenta el monte cavernoso,
> testigo del dolor y grave pena
> en que *por mí* se aflige Nemoroso
> y llama: "Elisa", "Elisa"; a boca llena
> responde el Tajo, y lleva presurosa
> al mar de Lusitania *el nombre mío,*
> donde será escuchado, *yo lo fío'*. (237–48; emphasis added)

[(one of the goddesses) [...] wrote a few words on the bark of a poplar as epitaph to the beautiful nymph, which spoke as though the words were Elisa's own: 'I am Elisa, with my (lit. whose) name mountains, honeycombed with caves, resound and lament as witness to the sorrow and pain that Nemoroso suffers for me, calling out "Elisa", and "Elisa" responds the Tagus, full-mouthed, and its swift current carries my name to the Lusitanian sea, where it will be heard, of this I'm sure.]

The dynamic interplay of past, present and future, as well as a provocative insistence on shifting agency and an ambiguous final subject, expose the limits of poetic autonomy at the very moment of lyric self-assertion. Although Garcilaso demonstrates in *Eclogue* III 'his ability to do all the things required of a poet',[102] intervening at every stage in the process of poetic creation and transmission, there is a certain insecurity in 'yo lo fío' which recalls the linguistic excesses of Ovid's Apollo.[103] The authority of the poetic voice is dependent upon knowledge (erudition), but also upon the signifying work of the writer as

---

[101] See Virgil, *Georgic* IV, 523–27. Among the many critics who have commented on this passage, Barnard is particularly relevant to this discussion: Mary E. Barnard, 'Garcilaso's Poetics of Subversion and the Orpheus Tapestry', *PMLA*, 102 (1987), 316–25. She draws attention to the 'extraordinary complexity of interdependent voices' (323).

[102] See Carroll B. Johnson, 'Personal Involvement', 303. The full text continues: 'to imitate a Latin poet in Spanish; to replace that Latin poet as the model to be imitated; to do something that Latin poet did not do, which is to create an entirely new text [...] which in turn may be turned into a new myth and depicted in future art works.' Navarrete reads the self-figuration at work here as an act of metalepsis in which Garcilaso 'reduces his sources to the status of predecessors' (*Orphans of Petrarch*, p. 124).

[103] Cascardi sees this too 'obvious' affirmation as the least convincing of Garcilaso's assertions of poetic authority. See *Ideologies of History*, p. 285.

reader. The poem opens up a space for slippage (between Nise creator 'tan informada' [so well informed], and Nise receiver) in the potentially subjective inscription of meaning that is provoked by emotional and/or manipulated response: 'que llorando el pastor, mil veces ella / se enterneció escuchando su querella' [for a thousand times over she had listened with compassion to the lament of the weeping shepherd; 255–56].

In the final tapestry of *Eclogue* III the poem moves beyond 'the question of the power of poetic verse',[104] to offer a three-dimensional analysis of the process of lyric self-creation, encompassing 'other' that is source (past), and 'other' that is reader (future). This palimpsest-like finale is marked by a deliberately qualified self-referentiality. 'Elisa' is an autonomous sign, but transmitted via familiar Ovidian referents: Eurydice, Daphne, Adonis. In this poem the narcissistic voice of Renaissance lyric is explicitly redefined via its antitype, the echo. The subject seeks authority, and stability, through a reconciliation of autonomous and imitative discourse. The anxieties expressed in the text about the vulnerability of the voice, and of the written artefact itself, as it takes shape and is shaped in time, are integral to Garcilaso's self-conscious poetics. But in *Eclogue* III such concerns are balanced by a sophisticated self-elaboration that is enabled and sustained through appropriation, and by the sheer rhetorical force of a sensed infinity that promises infinite renewal.

---

[104] Cascardi, *Ideologies of History*, p. 281.

2

Garcilaso de la Vega:
Luz de Nuestra Nación?[1]

Introduction

In the prologue to *Eclogue* III, Garcilaso addresses the tension between the demands of his professional life as a soldier and his poetic vocation:

> Entre las armas del sangriento Marte,
> do apenas hay quien su furor contraste,
> hurté de tiempo aquesta breve suma,
> tomando ora la espada, ora la pluma. (37–40)

[In the midst of bloody battle, where scarcely anyone can withstand the fury of Mars, I stole this brief measure of time, now taking up the sword, now the pen].

These verses suggest a close relationship between two potentially conflictive realms of experience, arms and letters; one in which parity of value is the implicit ideal. There is, as Navarrete has indicated, a strategy of self-fashioning at work here which allows Garcilaso to write himself into literary history as 'the courtier poet who healed the theoretical split' between the two.[2] However, as Anne J. Cruz has pointed out, Garcilaso never actually attained in his life, nor expressed through his poetry, the equilibrium between these two categories which has been attributed to him by early modern and modern critics alike.[3]

---

[1]   The reference is to Ambrosio de Morales's well-known designation of Garcilaso as: 'Luz muy esclarecida de nuestra nación' [The most splendid light of our nation]. See *Discurso sobre la lengua castellana*, ed. Valeria Scorpioni, *Studi ispanici*, 3, 177 –94 (187).

[2]   See Navarrette, *Orphans of Petrarch*, p. 117.

[3]   See 'Arms versus Letters: The Poetics of War and the Career of the Poet in Early Modern Spain', in *European Literary Careers. The Author from Antiquity to the Renaissance*, eds Patrick Cheney and Frederick A. de Armas (Toronto: University of Toronto Press, 2002), pp. 186–205 (esp. pp. 193–94).

Moreover, it is misleading to see reconciliation of an arms versus letters opposition as a major preoccupation of Garcilaso's poetry. Rather, it is a distinctive strand in a more broadly conceptualised dialectic, where tension derives from the fraught interaction of the macrocosm with the smaller world of the resisting, sentient individual. This is true, in differing ways, of Sonnets X, XXIII, XXIX and XXXIII. In poems such as *Eclogue* II, however, coincidence and correspondence is effected when art (or letters), through a complex merging of intimate, mythological and historical discourses, simulates a transition from disorder to order. Even here, however, any sense of complementarity of categories in the abstract is ultimately compromised by an insistence on the real price that must be paid for this in human terms.

Critics have long struggled to find the military theme in the poetry of the soldier poet,[4] let alone any trace of justification for war.[5] This has led to ahistorical conclusions such as Dámaso Alonso's argument for Garcilaso's pacifism.[6] Indeed, a more recent and somewhat reactionary stance seizes upon incidences of discord in the imperial soldier's poetry in order to identify an unequivocal rejection of imperial ideology. E.C. Graf, for example, identifies political dissent in Garcilaso's elegies (I and II) and argues persuasively that even the Italianate love poetry should not be read in isolation from the political realities of Hapsburg Spain. But his emphasis on a repudiation of imperial ideology, rather than an ambiguous questioning of it, is difficult to substantiate across a wider range of poems.[7] The textual evidence available to us urges greater caution; conveying an ambivalence that is self-consciously constructed through a reformulation of lyric and epic literary models. There is no doubt that the sword that Garcilaso wields is textually scarce and more double-edged than Hernando de Acuña's synthesising symbol of Spanish hegemony ('un monarca, un imperio y una espada' [one monarch, one empire, one sword]);[8] and it is this dualism, which engages provocatively with the Renais-

---

[4]   See, for instance, Lapesa who notes that war as a literary topic is treated only exceptionally in the poetry (*La trayectoria*, p. 118), and more recently Morros, who observes that the theme of war is scarcely considered by critics (p. LXXIX).

[5]   María Soledad Arredondo addresses not only the lack of military fervour in Garcilaso's poetry, but also the absence of justification for war that was common to imperial propaganda in the early part of the sixteenth century. See 'El exceso de guerras, de peligros y destierro: de Garcilaso a Quevedo', in *Garcilaso y su época: del amor y la guerra*, eds José María Díez Borque and Luís Ribot García Morros (Madrid: Sociedad Estatal de Conmemoraciones Culturales, 2003), pp. 265–73.

[6]   Dámaso Alonso designates Garcilaso a 'pacifista' in *Cuatro poetas españoles*, 'El destino de Garcilaso' (Madrid: Gredos, 1962), pp. 19–46 (p. 43).

[7]   Certainly *Eclogue* II, as will be argued below, offers a more conflicted engagement with political realities. See 'From Scipio to Nero'. For a lively discussion of Graf's views see the 'Forum' section of *Publications of the Modern Language Association of America*, 117.2 (2002), 324–28.

[8]   For a new and thoughtful reading of Hernando de Acuña's sonnet in terms of its ambiguous poetics, see J. Ignacio Díez Fernández, 'La inspirada poética del soneto "Al rey, nuestro señor", de Hernando de Acuña', *Hispanic Review*, 79. 4 (2011), 527–46.

sance belief in the intimate relationship between microcosm and macrocosm, that marks the poetry as very much a product of its own time. Where counter-heroic impulses are discernible, for instance in the dedication of *Canción* V, they are not easily disentangled from this mutually intrusive context; nor, as in Sonnet XXX-III, from a subjectively experienced dialectic of private and public selfhood.

Garcilaso's 'double-edged sword'

In the fifth *canción*, also entitled *Ode ad florem Gnidi*, a deliberately reiterative metalinguistic strategy operates throughout the poem to separate and associate military activity and erotic persuasion; a complex elaboration of the conventional love as war metaphor (which informs Sonnets II and XVII, and is explicitly thematised in Sonnet XXX) that is instigated under the ambiguous sign of 'el fiero Marte'. The god of war who is also the cuckolded jealous lover of Venus is simultaneously evoked and rejected in the poem's opening sequence (13).[9] The mutual intrusions of *Elegy* I are more explicitly unsettling. Addressed by Garcilaso to his friend Fernando, the Duke of Alba, on the occasion of his brother's death in Sicily after the Tunis Campaign (1535), the poet conflates and rewrites a range of Classical and Italian models to offer an unconventional poem of consolation.[10] All the standard ingredients are included: a eulogy of the deceased, an exposition of stoic exemplarity, a culminating vision of the afterlife which transcends the temporal ruptures of mortality in a touching reunion of grandfather, father and son. But the last word fails to mitigate entirely against the 'furia', both individual (II, 56) and collective (82–90), that drives the poem. Fernando's rage, which motivates the elegy, is a subsequential picture in miniature of the war fury that brought about Bernaldino's death (the 'furor del sangriento Marte' of *Eclogue* III), and which infuses a poetic voice angered at, and by, the interconnections. The individual, undone in tears ('deshechas tus entrañas en lágrimas'; 22–23), who reaches out and calls out in vain for the lost other who would make his soul complete (25–45), is merely a symptom of the deeper human tragedy, which the

9   For a detailed reading of this poem which takes into account the question of genre, principal models and the implications of the title, see Peter N. Dunn, 'La Oda de Garcilaso "A La Flor de Gnido"', in *La poesía de Garcilaso: ensayos críticos*, ed. Elías L. Rivers (Barcelona: Ediciones Ariel, 1974), pp. 129–62. See also Lázaro Carreter's discussion 'La *Ode ad Florem Gnidi* de Garcilaso de la Vega'. Mary E. Barnard offers an interesting reading of the poem's rhetorical strategies and its exploitation of ekphrasis. See 'Myth, Rhetoric and the Failure of Language in Garcilaso's "Ode ad Florem Gnidi"', in *Brave New Words: Studies in Spanish Golden Age Literature*, eds Edward H. Friedman and Catherine Larson (New Orleans: University Press of the South, 1996), pp. 51–65.

10   Garcilaso's poem is schematically close to the elegy by Girolamo Fracastoro, *In obitum M. Antonii Turriani Veronensis, ad Joannem Baptistam Turrianum Frater*, and to Fracastoro's source, the *Consolatio ad Liviam*. But it is overlaid with echoes of Bernardo Tasso, Bembo, Virgil and Horace, among others. Morros identifies all the principal models.

conditions of the age have aggravated and made contagious, and which must provoke a more generalised and, through a future interpretation of letters, an immortalised 'undoing' (76–96). The latter stages of the poem hold out a hope of redemption, but the aesthetic distance contrived through the highly stylised exposition of Neostoicism[11] is at variance with the anguished questioning of a subject voice which confronts the complicity of a nation whose story has universal ramifications (93) – the tragedy thus transcending generic expectations.

Garcilaso's awareness of generic convention is made explicit with a certain irony in *Elegy* II when the poet berates himself for slipping into satire (22–24). This is one of three poems addressed to his closest friend Boscán (the others are the Epistle to Boscán[12] and Sonnet XXXIII), and, like the first elegy, is also geographically and historically anchored by its connection to Trapani in Sicily and to the imperial army's victory at Tunis. The contextual similarities appear to end there. The second elegy is a much more overtly self-centred poem. Once set back on track, the central premise is an amorous lament which exploits the geographical distance between subject and addressee to expose the circumstantial and emotional gulf which divides them. Depicted as happy and secure in love (145–57) Boscán functions both as recipient of, and target for, the speaker's jealous outpourings. The lyric subject that emerges, and is dominant in the poem, is marked by difference (from the community of courtiers, from the world of lovers, from the soldier/lovers fortunate enough to die in battle) and by an ambivalence which he seems to perform uncertainly, but to which he ultimately resigns (192–93). Mar Martínez Góngora and E.C. Graf both identify a repudiation of the expansionist policies of Charles V in the opening tercets of the poem,[13] which would connect the emergence of this ambivalent self to a very concrete ideological scepticism. The authority of Charles's *traslatio imperii* is certainly undercut by the subsequent satirical pen pictures of a less than cohesive, hypocritical and self-seeking 'conquering people':

> Aquí, Boscán, donde del buen troyano
> Anchises con eterno nombre y vida
> conserva la ceniza el mantuano,
> debajo de la sena esclarecida

---

[11]   For an alternative reading of the poem, see Steven F. Rendall and Miriam D. Sugarmon, 'Imitation, Theme and Structure in Garcilaso's First Elegy', *Modern Language Notes*, 82 (1967), 230–37.

[12]   Despite the very fluid style and content of this poem, characteristic of the epistolary genre, it is grounded in the shared significance of its temporal and geographical context. Written in Avignon, the birthplace and burial site of Petrarch's Laura, on 12 October, the anniversary of her death, Garcilaso's letter to Boscán in Spain re-enacts the trajectory of cultural transfer which their 'new poetry' proposes.

[13]   See respectively 'Relaciones homosociales, discurso antibelicista y ansiedades masculinas en Garcilaso de la Vega', *Calíope*, 10.1 (2004), 123–40, and 'From Scipio to Nero', esp. 1322–24.

de César Africano nos hallamos
la vencedora gente recogida:
diversos en estudio, que unos vamos
muriendo por coger de la fatiga
el fruto que con el sudor sembramos;
   otros, que hacen la virtud amiga
y premio de sus obras y así quieren
que la gente lo piense y que lo diga,
   destotros, en lo público difieren,
y en lo secreto sabe Dios en cuánto
se contradicen en lo que profieren.
Yo voy por medio, (1–16)

[Here, Boscán, where the Mantuan (Virgil) preserves the ashes of the great Trojan Anchises, whose name and life are everlasting; (here) beneath the glorious standard of Caesar Africanus, we the conquering people are gathered; all of us different, some of us go to our deaths to reap the fruit of our suffering which by our sweat we sowed; others make a virtue and prize of our effort and wish it to be recognised and spread abroad; these differ from the first group in public, but in private God knows the extent to which they contradict what they say. I take the middle ground ...]

By assuming the role of the outsider within (or 'betwixt and between') Garcilaso's poetic subject is perfectly placed to interrogate the nature of the *traslatio imperii* (and, indeed, the nature of human love, which is conceived in strikingly similar terminology), but he does not deny, as Graf seems to suggest, the authority of a *traslatio studii*. Rather, in a clever play of geopolitical and ideological dynamics, he positions himself as the most appropriate heir to Virgil, the conflicted singer of Roman greatness. Heiple recognised the possibilities of these verses: 'the poem seems to conflate the stature of Charles V with the glories of the Roman past. The comparison is, however, curiously incomplete. [...] Surely, Charles V would not find his Virgil in Garcilaso'.[14] But the poet who defines his epic tone, however tongue in cheek in *Elegy* II, in the ashes of Troy and in the dark night of Anchises's final departure from his beloved son Aeneas, would presumably beg to differ.

The analogical ambiguities could hardly have been lost on Boscán, to whom Garcilaso addresses his most provocatively Virgilian sonnet, no. XXXIII, entitled 'A Boscán desde la Goleta' [To Boscán from La Goulette]. The poem reads:

Boscán, las armas y el furor de Marte,
que, con su propia fuerza el africano
suelo regando, hacen que el romano
imperio reverdezca en esta parte,

---

14 See Heiple, *Garcilaso de la Vega*, pp. 320–21.

han reducido a la memoria el arte
y el antiguo valor italiano,
por cuya fuerza y valerosa mano
África se aterró de parte a parte.
    Aquí donde el romano encendimiento,
donde el fuego y la llama licenciosa
solo el nombre dejaron a Cartago,
    vuelve y revuelve amor mi pensamiento,
hiere y enciende el alma temerosa,
y en llanto y en ceniza me deshago.

[Boscán, the arms and the fury of Mars, which, watering the African soil with
its own strength, make the Roman Empire flourish again in this region, have
brought back to memory the art and the ancient courage of Italy, by whose
strength and courageous hand Africa was razed from end to end. Here, where
the Roman inferno, where fire and licentious flame left a Carthage in name
only, love returns and turns my mind, wounds and sears my fearful soul, and
in tears and ash I am undone.]

On 14 July 1535, Charles V captured the fort of La Goulette, near the site of ancient
Carthage. Garcilaso was wounded twice in the campaign and this poem was ostensibly written while he was still in Africa (vv. 4 'this region' and 9 'here').[15] The
poem has been expertly analysed in a recent book by Richard Helgerson as defining a new literary programme in terms of a recasting of Classical models, especially of Virgilian epic, which involves a break from the Petrarchist manner.[16]
Helgerson follows Rodríguez García in identifying the tragedy of Carthage, Aeneas's
abandonment of Dido and her subsequent suicide, as the major intrusive and
conflicting subtext of the sonnet.[17] Both critics detect an evolving poetic voice,
which moves from the position of the conquerors in the quatrains to identify, in
extreme terms, with the defeated Dido in the tercets. The sonnet thereby opens up
a space in which the new poetry can interrogate both its 'aestheticised politics'
and its 'political aesthetics' from a suitably ambiguous site of estrangement.[18]

[15] Garcilaso's injuries are mentioned in a letter by the Duke of Alba's son Enrique (see Keniston, *Garcilaso de la Vega*, 1922–25, I, 481, n. 134). Garcilaso also composed an ode in Latin in
praise of the emperor's victory, addressed to the chronicler Juan Ginés de Sepúlveda (*Ode ad
Genesium Sepulvedam*).

[16] See *A Sonnet from Carthage*.

[17] See José María Rodríguez García, 'Epos delendum est: The Subject of Carthage in Garcilaso's "A Boscán desde La Goleta"', *Hispanic Review*, 66. 2 (1998), 151–70. He also identifies
a second major subtext in Augustine's *Confessions*; see pp. 160–62.

[18] My reading of an unsettling ambiguity in the speaker's identification with Dido differs in
emphasis, if not in overall design, from Rodríguez García and from Anne Cruz, who also sees in
this poem, as elsewhere in Garcilaso's poetry, an identification with the vulnerability of the con-
quered, rather than with military conquest. See 'Arms versus Letters', pp. 193–98.

Dido, the building sacrifice of the empire builder, captures a dynamic of artistic self-creation that involves both destructive and restorative impulses; wherein the 'undoing' and 'remaking' have both private and collective ramifications.[19]

Rodríguez García reads the shift in perspective from quatrains to tercets as the destruction of an epic impulse in favour of the lyric.[20] However, as Helgerson[21] points out, epic inevitably embodies the lyric, none more so than the *Aeneid*, whose monolithic structure is persistently punctured by elegiac interludes. The intentional and controlled ambivalence of Virgil's epic is announced in the first line of the proemium: 'Arma virumque cano' (I sing of arms and of a man). The thematic and structural relationship between two wars – the Trojan, which precedes the time frame of the epic but is reconstructed through the mnemonic experience of the hero as narrator (*Aeneid* II), and the future conflict in Latium, which will reverse the fall of Troy – is balanced by an attention to the human relationships which will ultimately be subordinated to the historical mission. The first verse of Garcilaso's sonnet encourages Boscán, and the wider reader, to read the poem as a reconceived and radically abridged *Aeneid*. Ironically, epic expectations are frustrated by the lyric poet's strict adherence to epic abstractions. The human and humanising aspects of Virgilian epic are erased in favour of a reinforcement of the warfare through which imperial objectives are accomplished.[22] In fact, the quatrains prioritise 'fuerza' (2 and 7), a quality (in Latin 'vis') without which empire cannot be won, but which is manipulated by Virgil to engender ambivalence in the reader regarding the virtue of its practitioners. The figures against whom Aeneas and the Trojans direct their force (and Dido can be counted among these) are often depicted with uncompromising sensitivity.

The central correspondence of the quatrains, Charles V's victory as a re-enactment of Scipio's destruction of Carthage, is not, of course, neatly Virgilian, despite the fact that the broader analogical frame, which relies heavily on the notion of continuity with, or restoration of, the (more distant) past,[23] is most

---

19   Limitations of space prevent a comparison of this sonnet with the dynamics of memory which inform Sonnet X and in which the poetic subject's identification with Dido is signalled in the opening verse (a very clear echo of *Aeneid* IV, 651).

20   See especially his discussion of verse 11, supplemented by the note: 'To name Carthage is to name the lyric impulse, since the non-referentiality of the word opens up a space of signification for subjective expression' ('Epos delendum est', 163, n. 16).

21   See *A Sonnet from Carthage*.

22   Garcilaso may have conflated the authentic opening of Virgil's epic with an echo from the apocryphal. The latter constitutes four additional verses which were popular in the Renaissance (used both by Milton and Spenser) despite a lack of manuscript authority: 'Ille ego qui quondam gracili modulatus avena / carmen, et egressus silvis vicina coegi / ut quamvis avido parerent arva colono, / gratum opus agricolis, at nunc *horrentia Martis* / *arma* virum*que cano*' (my italics). See R.G. Austen, 'Ille qui quondam …', *The Classical Quarterly*, 18.1 (1968), 107–15, who summarises the arguments for and against, but concludes against Virgilian authorship.

23   Just as Augustus would wish to forget the antagonisms and rivalries of the civil wars, Charles was eager to move beyond events such as the *comunero* rebellion.

certainly in keeping with the imperial propaganda that informs both texts. The 'imperium' towards which the hero Aeneas is striving is a prototype of the one being realised by Augustus in the real world of the writer Virgil. Thus the actions and attitudes of Aeneas might be viewed (though not without some qualification) as emblematic of those of Augustus, and any ambivalence surrounding Aeneas might raise questions about the manner and methods of contemporary Roman politics. If Garcilaso's purpose in the quatrains is to legitimise the cultural experience of which he is a direct witness and active participant, there can be no place for such Virgilian ambiguity. To engage explicitly with Virgil's *Aeneid,* however, only to deny its characteristic ambivalence works as a clever double bluff on Garcilaso's part that makes all the more compelling the ideological reversal of the tercets. History can repeat itself for good or bad on its own terms but, as Garcilaso's poem demonstrates, the historical past which is inscribed in literature gives particular resonance to the constructed nature of collective memory,[24] and also to the subjective impulses which manage the twin towers of remembering and forgetting.

The operation of memory which occupies the centre of the quatrains (5) is motivated by a process of visualisation that captures, retains, decodes and reconstructs an image of post-conflict devastation. The interplay of sight, memory, interpretation and articulation is similar to that which informs Sonnet V 'Escrito está en mi alma vuestro gesto' [Your face is written upon my soul]; is activated by a similar subjective agency; and is informed by a circular, conflicted reasoning which, in this poem to Boscán, conveys concepts that are political, as well as psychological and literary. There are clear indications that the end has to be written into the beginning: the epistolary function, for instance, makes sense only in retrospect; and this is supported by the sonnet's shifting tense patterns that connect the degenerate, jealous lover, who comes undone in the final tercet, with the soldier who reflects on imperial regeneration in the opening quatrain. From this perspective, the 'furor de Marte' (we recall the fifth *canción*) is a product of the wounded and fearful soul (13), and infects the imperial project with dangerous, uncontrollable desire from the outset. Likewise, the suicidal subtext which (to adapt García Rodríguez) 'dwells in Dido' becomes threatened when the speaker, overwhelmed in the present by the past, seems 'to dwell' simultaneously in Aeneas.

The force that dominates the speaker is, of course, *eros*, whose essential nature is Phoenix-like (the ash of v. 14 may be subversively redemptive) in its circular conflagrations: 'vuelve y revuelve amor mi pensamiento, / hiere y enciende el alma temerosa' (11). These verses recall Ovid's characterisation of Cupid as warrior (*Amores* I, 21–25 and I, ii, 43–46) and capture the violence,

---

[24]   For allusion as a form of poetic memory, see Gian Biagio Conte, *The Rhetoric of Imitation: Genre and Poetic Memory in Virgil and Other Latin Poets*, ed. Charles Segal, Cornell Studies in Classical Philology 44 (Ithaca and London: Cornell University Press, 1986), pp. 23–95.

pain and humiliation of submission to erotic love. The rhyme advises that we associate the speaker's moment of self-effacement ('me deshago'; 14) with 'Cartago' (11), an historical site surviving as a mnemonic force. Clearly to be wounded by love in Carthage is to identify with Dido and to value the private over the public, to prioritise emotion over state and to focus on the specific at the expense of the abstract (or even prophetic).[25] But the flipside of 'Amor' is 'Roma'. To carry 'Cartago' beyond its limits (historical, geo-political, literary and psychological); to renounce it, however unwillingly, for duty, is to identify with Aeneas.[26] The rhyme also advises that we associate 'mi pensamiento' (12) with 'el romano encendimiento', the subject-partner-in-crime of 'fuego' and 'llama licenciosa' (10). Fire is the force that lingers in Aeneas's mind and makes memory causative in the epic,[27] whether the flames symbolise Troy, the fiery passion of Carthage or Dido's burning pyre. In Book VI of the *Aeneid* the hero is made to confront the ghosts (and victims) of his past (Palinurus, Dido, fellow Trojans, Anchises) in order to embrace the future. But Dido complicates catharsis by reversing abandonment. When she turns silently from Aeneas, it is he who is left weeping and 'undone'.

The speaker of Sonnet XXXIII experiences abandonment in the ambivalent terms of victim and perpetrator – as both its subject and its object. The poem condenses the memorialising responsibilities of epic (to challenge the present and future with the past) by articulating a nation's politico-cultural navel-gazing in the intimate experience of a poet/soldier-lover who is wrestling with the combined weight of private and collective histories. Garcilaso's reformulation of Virgil is never one-dimensional; and the new literary and political orders he proclaims are marked very deliberately with the anxieties of the old.

Sites of speculation: metaphor and memory in Eclogue II

Just as meaning in the lyric sonnet is determined through a system of dialogical relations, the pastoral eclogue keeps its significance active and fluid in the relativity of its various voices. All three Eclogues share a sense of pastoral as a complex site of encounter, which encourages the reader to think through relationships with the past, with desire and with aesthetic pleasure. But Garcilaso's pastoral has more shapes than one. The presentation of different speakers who

---

[25] In *Aeneid* II, Cupid plays a major role in the destruction of Dido by impersonating Aeneas's son Iulus at the command of Venus (Aeneas's mother).

[26] In *Aeneid* VI, Aeneas tells Dido: 'invitus, regina, tuo de litore cessi' [My Queen, I departed from your shore unwillingly]. Unfortunately, this is a clear echo of his tactless speech in IV, in which he claims that he does not go to Italy of his own free will ('Italiam non sponte sequor'), and that if he did have a choice his heartfelt wish would be to return to Troy (IV, 340–44).

[27] A clear example of this occurs in *Aeneid* XII, where motivation to attack the Latin capital is connected to the memory of Troy (e.g. 560 and 572–73).

move through and among the words of others serves to meld time, but it also plays with pastoral's thematising of the personal or general. The Second *Eclogue*, more than the first or third, harnesses the persistent ambiguity of water/mirror imagery, to convey this private/public dialectic, this troubling interdependence of microcosmic and macrocosmic meaning. It is not that the subjective yields to the collective in Garcilaso's Eclogue, nor that (against the movement of XXXIII) lyric impulse becomes epic, or an unstable idealised Arcadia collapses under the real weight of the House of Alba, but rather that the problematic amalgam of these and other irreconcilables ultimately exposes the tensions that underlie a rational, but deeply flawed, imperial actuality.

Ever since Lumsden Kouvel connected *Eclogue* II with a series of aesthetic 'problems', much has been made of the generic, thematic and tonal schisms that separate the unrequited love of the shepherd Albanio from Nemoroso's account of eulogistic ekphrasis.[28] I would suggest that these 'problems' (the polymetric system, dialogic form, re-elaboration of incompatible pastoral/epic models, among others),[29] are deliberately jarring strategies designed to support the central opposition of the poem: that is, the juxtaposition of the imagined and real that forms interconnecting patterns of perception within individual episodes, but which is also integral to the cohesion of parts and heterogeneous whole. Attempts to reconcile textual conflicts through identification of elements common to both spheres of action (conventionally designated as the first half play or pastoral episode and the second half ekphrasis or epic section) have floundered

[28]   See Audrey Lumsden Kouvel, 'Problems Connected with the Second Eclogue of Garcilaso de la Vega', *Hispanic Review*, 15.2 (1947), 251–71. Generic classification in particular has been a dominant issue for critics. Both Pamela Waley ('Garcilaso's Second Eclogue is a Play', *Modern Language Review*, 72 [1977] 585–96) and Darío Fernández-Morera ('Garcilaso's Second Eclogue and the Literary Tradition', *Hispanic Review*, 47.1 [1979], 37–53 [38–40]) posit the view that *Eclogue* II was conceived as a masque to be performed. Peter M. Komanecky ('Epic and Pastoral in Garcilaso's Eclogues', *Modern Language Notes*, 86.2 [1971] 154–66) explores Garcilaso's concept of the 'égloga' as a genre with two sub-genres in the Medieval tradition that had categorised the Virgilian Eclogues according to the generic schema of Plato's *Republic*. *Eclogue* II thus belongs to the same 'mixed' genre as two Virgilian Eclogues (I and IX), and the *Aeneid*. Rather than developing this association of pastoral and epic in the context of Garcilaso's fluid pastoral, Komanecky takes a more reductive approach, proposing Virgil, Eclogue IX, as a source of Garcilaso's poem.

[29]   Critics have tended to approach the poem's eclectic range of models at the level of identification rather than analysis of function. See, for instance, Lapesa (*La trayectoria*, pp. 113–14), who identifies a range of precedents, with Sannazaro's *Arcadia* dominating in the Albanio story, Virgil's *Aeneid* in the panegyric. Lumsden Kouvel likewise, focuses on Sannazaro and Virgil and is concerned with compatibility issues ('Problems', 254–57). Inés Azar presents an insightful analysis of the Eclogue's dialectical framework along antithetical axes (including literary conventions, poetic and philosophical ideologies, irreconcilable models) which are synthesised through the rhetorical strategies of *inventio, dispositio* and *elecutio (Discurso retórico y mundo pastoral en la "Égloga segunda" de Garcilaso* [Amsterdam: Benjamins, 1981]).

because commentators have failed to see the bigger picture.[30] The gaps the reader cannot easily close are a symbolic representation of the distance between the reality of individual human suffering, and the broader 'ideal text' of empire. In this ambitious 1185 line poem, water imagery is the major structural principle and the key that unlocks a challenging critical commentary. The following brief analysis will demonstrate how the figurative possibilities of water are mobilised throughout the eclogue at the level of 'histoire', but demand to be deciphered at the level of 'discours'.[31]

From Albanio's opening apostrophe to the 'claras ondas' of the 'clara fuente', water is established as a dynamic intratextual interlocutor; a polyvalent figure which stimulates a universe of reader responses that feed off one another and play off one against the other. Traditionally associated with life, birth, rebirth, creation and creativity (associations that are exploited in Sonnet XI and *Eclogue* III), water is also a threatening agent of oblivion and annihilation. Transcendence in metapoetical terms (permanent form bestowed on the inherently fleeting) is potentially transgressive in the context of liminality, whether the borders broached are real (land and sea) or figurative (art and nature). The co-presence of motion and stillness as essential components of water and human time can symbolise the human being's complex interaction with temporality (the interplay of past and present), but also signal infinite progression. Water can pour cool rationality over fire's passion, yet also encapsulates the fundamental ambivalence of erotic experience, embracing the polarities of pleasure and pain within the antithetical metaphor of life and death. Sonnet XXIX, for instance, which focuses on Leander's fatal swim across the Hellespont, derives much of its symbolic energy from these antitheses. Most significantly for a reading of *Eclogue* II, water's poetic transfiguration into mirror correlates perfectly with the fundamental illusion/reality contradictions that lie at the heart of self-identity, self-creation and self-knowledge.[32] Looked at the other way round, mirror's transfiguration into water distances the mirror motif from the demands of *mimesis* and encourages a more fluid exploration of perspective.

---

30 Lumsden Kouvel forces the issue of unifying the poem in the figure of Severo 'whose character blends in almost equal proportions traditional, symbolical and literary qualities with factual details' ('Problems', 264–66, [264]).

31 See Tzvetan Todorov, 'Les Catégories du récit littéraire', *Communications* 8 (1966), 125–51 (126).

32 The 'mirror stage' is central to Lacan's theory of child development: the idea that the child's awareness of selfhood as a whole and separate entity begins when he/she sees him/herself reflected in a mirror. See Jane Gallop, *Reading Lacan* (Ithaca: Cornell University Press, 1985), p. 38. The psychological effect of mirrors is that they both confirm and question the individual, the mirrored viewer becoming both observer and observed identity (see Michael Schlig, *The Mirror Metaphor in Modern Spanish Literary Aesthetics* [Lewiston: The Edwin Mellen Press, 2004] p. 20). It follows that if the observer exists simultaneously as subject and object, then the distinction between subjective and objective perspective becomes ambiguous.

At the opening of the poem the shimmering surface of the water acquires a curious autonomy when reflection becomes recollection:

Albanio:
> En medio del invierno está templada
> el agua dulce desta clara fuente,
> y en el verano más que nieve helada.
> ¡Oh claras ondas, cómo veo presente,
> en viéndoos, la memoria d'aquel día
> de que el alma temblar y arder se siente!
> En vuestra claridad vi mi alegría
> escurecerse toda y enturbiarse;
> cuando os cobré, perdí mi companía. (1–9)

[In mid winter this clear spring has sweet, warm water and in summer it freezes more than snow. Oh, clear waters, in you, I see before me, the memory of that day which still fills my soul with fire and fear! In your clarity I saw my own joy darken and cloud over; when I recovered you, I lost my companion.]

The figure of Narcissus is clearly behind this moment of destructive self-knowledge, anticipating the explicit identification that will come later in the poem.[33] But the interwoven temporalities of self-reflection that undermine an empirical act of seeing[34] strip the mythical paradigm of any didactic dimension and provoke a crisis in the text's visual, verbal and temporal orders. From the outset representation is the informing reality. The artifice of the pastoral landscape is a frame that draws the reader towards its image and implicates us in the circular gaze of Albanio. The subject's visual field in the here and now of the text is corrupted by the painful memory of another's reflection on another day. Albanio, subjective poet and subject of his own poetry, loses linguistic grip on the present ('*vi* mi alegría ...'; emphasis added) and the tears that trouble the surface of the water (22–23) are represented as memories that mist the mirror of the mind.[35] In this indeterminate

---

[33] See Cruz, *Imitación y transformación*, p. 93. More recently, Mary E. Barnard has examined how Garcilaso enlarges the role of the mirror (mirroring pool) as mediator of self-definition by having Albanio/Narcissus share it with Camilla as an anti-Narcissus figure. This twin mapping of the self is considered against the background of the trope of self-portraiture in contemporary painting ('The Mirror of Narcissus: Imaging the Self in Garcilaso's Second Eclogue' in *Ovid in the Age of Cervantes*, ed. Frederick A. De Armas [Toronto: University of Toronto Press, 2010], pp. 137–57).

[34] See Lynn Enterline, *The Tears of Narcissus: Melancholy and Masculinity in Early Modern Writing* (Stanford: Stanford University Press, 1995), p. 169.

[35] Sabine Melchoir-Bonnet has drawn our attention to the role of the mirror image in the construction of subjective truth: 'The mirror opens up a space of play between the visible and the invisible, between dream and reality, with which the subject takes account of himself by projecting himself into images and fictions' (*The Mirror: A History*, trans. Katherine H. Jewett [New York: Routledge, 2001] p. 184).

environment Camila's rejection of herself as object of Albanio's desire is memorialised as the catalyst that brings the equivocal and alienated subject into being: 'yo solo en tanto bien morir me siento' [I, alone, amidst such beauty, feel like dying; 18].

Albanio might be considered a post-Lapsarian subject, constituted as the after-effects of *eros*'s intervention. His predicament has paradoxical metapoetic implications, for while he can articulate a sensuous version of the landscape from which he feels excluded (13–15), drawing on erotic experience to reconfigure reality, external reality is but a shadow when confronted with the substance of his tragic sense of loss.[36] But Albanio's attempt to recuperate a sense of self through a dissolution of the boundaries between self and lost beloved actually involves a subtle self-elision. The absent beloved rematerialises in a precarious iconographical image that is a concrete indication of Albanio's 'vain imaginings' (28) and displaces him from within the frame of his own figural and psychic mirror. A metaphysical gesture of perverse messianic proportions allows him to effect an exit of sorts from an alienating Arcadia. Disillusioned, he commits his weary body to sleep, fully aware that the regenerative capabilities of temporary absence are not definitive (35–37). But the presence of the disillusioned and sleeping Albanio gives a problematic temporal weight to the timeless and illusory *locus amoenus* subsequently celebrated by his fellow shepherd Salicio (38–76). In direct opposition to Albanio's introspective engagement with the pastoral environment, Salicio conceptualises a landscape that is imitated more from art than life,[37] and which is recognisably rhetorical as the pagan counterpart of the Garden of Eden. As such it is a potentially mutable space, open both to moral ambiguity and to reconstitution through subjective perception. Salicio's harmonious idyll in which a gentle, murmuring stream invites a 'dulce sueño' [sweet dream 64–66) has undergone an ironic process of collapse even before Salicio's linguistic re-creation.[38]

36 Lapesa (*La trayectoria*, pp. 114–17) considers Albanio in Petrarchist terms, a context substantially developed by Cruz who sees in the conflicted Albanio a personification of 'el acto poético del petrarquismo' (*Imitación y transformación*, p. 94). Navarrete (*Orphans of Petrarch*, pp. 20–23) also focuses on Garcilaso's critique of Petrarchism and suggests that the predominance of over-flowing still waters in the latter half of the poem symbolises a shift from adolescent fantasy (associated with the Petrarchan love code) to a more mature, active male sexuality.

37 The 'locus amoenus classicus' is Theocritus's *Idyll* VII, 134–42. However, the primary model for Salicio's 'Cuán bienaventurado' speech is Horace's 'Beatus ille' poem (*Epodes* II) combined with other re-elaborations of the topos, such as Virgil (*Georgics* II, 458–542) and Seneca (*Hippolytus* 483–564).

38 Azar (*Discurso retórico*, p. 193, n. 21) notes how the final stanza of Salicio's monologue reiterates the dominant motifs of Albanio's previous description, but the former's objectively distanced stance is exemplified in the switch from 'this' to 'that': 'el dulce murmurar *deste* ruido' (13) to '*aquel* manso ruido' (65).

Sleep for Albanio is an underworld of insubstantial forms that spills over to undermine his waking presence and to invalidate his future.[39] The memory of Camila's 'blanca mano' [white hand] touched in dreams will be replicated in an actual reaching out that will precipitate a complete rupture from reality and a narcissistic regression.[40] But while the poem depicts the tenacity of a past that returns and re-enacts itself with negative consequences, it also speaks powerfully against the idea that a traumatic past should be forgotten. At Salicio's insistence Albanio interrogates the possibility of articulating painful memory as a process of liberation and renewal (150–60). As a lover whose wounds have healed (356–64), Salicio functions for the reader as Albanio's empathetic mirror *in potentia*. But he also represents Albanio's first point of contact with a mutually sustaining homosocial network which, via Nemoroso as mediator, will convert the underlying (erotic) chaos of 'narcissistic … subject and reflections' into the contained ekphrastic space of an 'ordered masculine geneology'.[41]

Although Albanio's extensive account of the cause and development of his lovesickness is a clear adaptation of Carino's story in Sannazaro, *Arcadia, Prosa 8*, the differences between the Italian model and the Spanish imitation are deliberately conspicuous.[42] The addition of a character such as Salicio, recently returned to the pastoral bower, is a case in point. Whereas Carino's linear and retrospective story emerges from the perspective of a recuperated, whole self, Salicio's intervention provokes an unresolved version of Albanio's past that continues to destabilise the speaking subject in the present. Albanio's split narration (Salicio forces the climax of the story when Albanio offers an abrupt ending at v. 337) anticipates the fracturing of identity that lies at the core of his madness, but it also exposes the early modern subject as an unstable cultural and linguistic product whose potential for re-affirmation lies in an interweaving of the self in the wider social framework. Albanio loses authority over discourse, and this disintegration of language as emblematic of

---

[39]   The 'ebúrnea puerta' [ivory gate; 117] recalls the reference to the empty figments of form at the entrance to Hades in *Aeneid* VI, and Aeneas's exit through the ivory gates of false dreams after his father Anchises's prophecy in the same book. Thus Virgil subtly calls into question the dream vision of Aeneas's and Rome's glorious future.

[40]   Azar discusses verses 802–49 as a symmetrical inversion of Albanio's dream scene (*Discurso retórico*, p. 205).

[41]   For quotation see Smith, 'Homographesis', p. 140. Interesting also in this context are Helgerson's observations regarding the new poetry's engagement with homosociality: 'As much as the new poetry is committed to empire, to art, to place and to erotic undoing, so it is committed to the homosocial bonds of male friendship and male collaboration' (*A Sonnet from Carthage*, p. 15). Martínez Góngora reads Albanio's exchange with Salicio differently, seeing in his reluctance to articulate the past a fear of emotional exposure that reveals acute masculine anxiety. See 'Relaciones homosociales'.

[42]   Azar (*Discurso retórico*, pp. 180–91) explores the structural relationship between *Eclogue* II and Sannazaro's text, taking into account the fact that Carino of Prosa 8 can be considered a pastoral transfiguration of the courtly Sincero of Prosa 7.

the dissolution of the symbolic order prefigures his madness. It is explicitly associated in the text with the contamination of pure love by carnal desire, and with a deviant anti-sociability.[43]

Eros makes chaotic the text's own symbolic system by infecting the distance between memory and metaphor with a deceptively sequenced subjectivity. The depiction of a postrate, suicidal Albanio (491–95) recalls the violent image of the trapped crow (269–74),[44] but it also reveals Albanio as the author of a text that is ostensibly outside the erotic frame, in which his complex feelings of guilt and rejection re-emerge in brutal and bloody images of hunting. Thus the crow, 'crucified' in a symbolic well of Narcissus,[45] prefigures the self-sacrificing, victim-perpetrator dementia that Albanio has already begun to experience. Moreover, beyond the conflicted intimately conceived image of the trapped bird, the collective cost of the crows' solidarity suggests a misconception of imposed values at the level of community which will lend a muted resonance to the heroic endeavours trumpeted in the poem's latter half. In addition, when Albanio recounts the details of Camila's first rejection, the poem's fluid *locus amoenus* resurfaces as a projection of his insecure self-fashioning on two relatively reversed levels of significance (431–42). Thus the landscape that is nostalgically recalled has a much greater ontological status than the natural environment which is being observed. And once again the 'fuente' occupies the literal and figurative centre:

> y en medio aquesta fuente clara y pura,
> que como de cristal resplandecía,
> mostrando abiertamente su hondura, (443–45)

[and there, at the centre, that pure, clear spring, which shone like glass, openly revealing its depth]

Two distinct forms of self-negation (symbolic and literal) inform Albanio's focus on the water as surface and depth. When Camila gazes into the pool's

---

43   The complex relationship between *eros* and articulation is expressed at verses 314–19; 331–36; 367–70; 380–81 and 390–91. When Albanio agrees to resume his story he does so under the condition that Salicio will promise to leave him to lament alone (407–12).

44   Roger Boase's reading of the crow-hunting episode in the context of its relationship with the source in Sannazaro, as well as with related passages in Ariosto's *Orlando furioso*, concludes that Garcilaso's rewriting was determined by moral as well as aesthetic considerations. See 'The Meaning of the Crow-Hunting Episode in Garcilaso's *Égloga Segunda* (ll. 260–95)', *Journal of Hispanic Philology*, 13 (1988), 41–48. Boase's interpretation follows a line of didactic enquiry initiated by Royston O. Jones which stresses the text's conformity with Neoplatonic teaching and sees in Albanio's madness the consequences of the dethronement of reason. See 'The Idea of Love in Garcilaso's Second Eclogue', *Modern Language Review*, 46.3/4 (1951), 388–95.

45   In the *Roman de la Rose*, verses 1588–94, the well of Narcissus is depicted as a perilous mirror that constitutes a kind of bird snare in which illicit desire for pleasure catches its victims.

natural mirror to ascertain the object of Albanio's desire, she finds herself (not entirely unlike the Ovidian Io) inscribed into an alienating visual field. Forced into a negative appropriation of the male gaze as both its subject and object, she confronts herself as 'other' and refuses to identify with the idealised image against which the male subject has constructed itself:

> le dije que en *aquella fuente clara*
> vería *d'aquella* que yo tanto amaba
> *abiertamente la hermosa cara.*
>   Ella, que ver *aquésta* deseaba
> con menos diligencia discurriendo
> *d'aquélla* con que'l paso apresuraba,
> a la *pura fontana* fue corriendo,
> y *en viendo el agua, toda fue alterada,*
> en ella su figura sola viendo.
>   Y no de otra manera, arrebatada,
> *del agua rehuyó* que si estuviera
> de la rabiosa enfermedad tocada,
>   y sin mirarme, desdeñosa y fiera,
> no sé qué allá entre dientes murmurando,
> me dejó aquí, y aquí quiere que muera. (470-84; emphasis added)

[I told her that *in that clear spring* she would see *revealed the beautiful face of the one* I loved so much. And she, desperate to see *her* and faster on *her* feet than in *her* thinking, ran to the *pure fountain* and, *seeing only her own face in the water, was totally distraught.* In a rabid-like frenzy *she fled,* wild and scornful, *from the water,* muttering incoherently to herself. Without a single glance she abandoned me here, and here she would have me die.]

In Albanio's case the watery depths offer an authentic form of self-negation through drowning (984–85), an impulse which is conveyed in the poem as an anti-Orphic/Aristaean response to a complex and unresolvable narcissistic dilemma.[46] Abandoned by Camila, Albanio wallows in self-pity and in isolation. He bemoans his 'loco error' [mad mistake; 489] in a 'largo llanto' [long lament; 495] that makes a river of his tears (490). But his lament is heard as an agonised 'gemido' [moaning, 527] which frightens and alienates the inhabitants of his bucolic world (516–17). On the point of suicide Albanio seeks a self-inflationary identification with the song of the dying swan (554–62) and grasps at the possibility of eternal celebration of his death for love (528–32). But the correlation of Albanio's voice with that of Echo (598), who functions as both a 'sym-

---

[46]   The motif can be traced to the origins of pastoral. In Theocritus, *Idyll* III, the speaker's self-destructive impulse is expressed as a desire to leap into the waves from a cliff (25–27).

bolically translated Narcissus'[47] and the aural equivalent of the text's deceptive mirror symbolism, strips the speaking voice of the materiality that would give it meaning. The subsequent state of madness, prompted by a complete capitulation to desire and by Camila's second rejection, will involve a similar shedding of the body that results in a denial of authentic selfhood. Albanio, a lover in name only, can only identify himself as a signifier emptied of a signified.[48] Addressing his own reflection, which he believes to be his stolen body, he says: '[…] sal ya fuera / a darme verdadera forma d'hombre, / que agora solo el nombre m'ha quedado' [come out of there and give me a man's true form, for now I am man in name only 935–36]. Most commentators, following Rivers, have identified a Neoplatonic re-elaboration at the core of the poem's Ovidian Narcissus episode (*Met.* III, 413–503).[49] Translation of specific verses from the Latin text certainly enhances the impression of a relatively controlled textual surface, but immersion in the murkier allusive depths reveals a more disjunctive reading that is in keeping with the poem's generic and thematic play of doubling and distortion.

Camila, for instance, symbolises the uncontrollable composite allusion that underpins the ambiguity of the eclogue. Like her counterpart in Sannazaro, she is a chaste virgin, huntress and devotee of Diana, understandably outraged by the violation of her person.[50] In an associated pre-figural context she is the goddess's stand-in, in hot pursuit of the invasive Actaeon/Albanio whose bestial

[47]　See Enterline, *The Tears of Narcissus*, p. 154.

[48]　Umberto Eco dedicates a chapter to the workings of mirror reflection in order to explain and define the 'sign', commenting that 'the mirror image […] is present in the presence of a referent which cannot be absent' (*Semiotics and the Philosophy of Language* [Bloomington: Indiana University Press, 1984], p. 216). Albanio's madness or dislocation from reality might be understood, therefore, in semiotic terms as the impossible perception of self as an absent referent.

[49]　See Elías L. Rivers, 'Albanio as Narcissus in Garcilaso's Second Eclogue', *Hispanic Review*, 41.1 (1973), 297–304. Before Rivers' analysis of the literary influences that mediated the Ovidian model in order to shape Garcilaso's moralistic use of the myth, Lumsden Kouvel had read the episode in terms of an 'invading schizophrenia' ('Problems', 269), with Albanio agonising to reconcile the two sides of his personality (flesh–lust/spirit–aspiration). Waley's anti-moralistic reading is a notable exception, denying Albanio any indication of excessive sensuality. Unfortunately she chooses not to explore what she refers to as 'the ingenious use of the narcissus myth' ('Garcilaso's Second Eclogue', 593).

[50]　See Boase, 'The Meaning of the Crow-Hunting Episode', 4. Correa argues that Camila does love Albanio but her devotion to Diana prevents the union ('Garcilaso y la mitología', 274). He focuses on the mythical subtext as a strategy exploited to reflect both the personal circumstances of the poet and the contradictions inherent in a society subject to a rigid code of honour. The quest to 'identify' Albanio has resulted in several theories: for example, Lumsden Kouvel ('Problems', 262) had also identified Albanio as Garcilaso; Lapesa opted for the Duke of Alba's younger brother Bernardino (*La trayectoria*, pp. 107–10); while Jones insisted that although not strictly speaking autobiographical, the character of Albanio allowed the poet to pass moral judgement on an attitude to love through which he himself had passed ('The Idea of Love', 394–95).

metamorphosis heralds moral degradation.[51] But the stag wounded on its left side confounds the moral connotations, reinstating Albanio as the ultimate icon of Christian self-sacrifice, but within an unsettling epic/erotic frame that merges Christ with Dido and with the stag which unwittingly starts Virgil's war in Latium.[52] These are contradictions which coalesce in Camila's name, resonant with that of the warrior princess Camilla of Virgil's *Aeneid* (VII, 808–11). The epic Camilla epitomises 'furor' in feminine form, and her complex ambivalence crystallises the tension that exists between heroism and sacrifice throughout the epic. She too is a follower of Diana, but also a tragic female counterpart to Marcellus, Pallas and Euryalus. Indeed, as I have remarked elsewhere, she functions in the *Aeneid* as a potent site of multiple correspondences. She is unique to Virgil and her role is exploited by him to question the glories celebrated in epic battle.[53] In *Eclogue* II, Camila's absence from the second part of the poem is offset by epic reminiscences that lend a subdued personal cadence to the traditionally impersonal form.

Camila's symbolic transmutation in the eclogue realises on the figural plane a desire for self re-creation that is articulated in the poem as an illusory conviction that sleeping can transform the traumatic memory she associates with the 'fuente', into an act of forgetting (753–63). But upon awakening she must confront a more violent re-enactment of herself as other that compels her to call on the natural mirror as a mnemonic verifying site that embeds the pool in a deliberately flawed enunciative context. The water, implicated fully in Albanio's indirect declarations, now incarnates an ironic witnessing role (828–29), not only testifying to Camila's accusations, but also substantiating her own deliberate violation of the bond between speech and action. Her misfired oath (844–46) is an attempt to control her world by creating a future that is in direct opposition to the 'reality' she expresses. She has no intention of remaining still if Albanio releases her, and the story of the lost 'prendedero d'oro' [gold brooch] is a ruse to distract him while she makes good her escape. From Albanio's perspective Camila is indeed a treacherous oath-breaker (865–66), but given that Albanio's authority is not maintained by any degree of reciprocation, the rules governing verbal interaction no longer apply and there is no obligation to truthfulness.

The whole episode, from the moment Albanio spots Camila asleep by the pool until his demented dialogue with his own reflection, is marked by escalating loss – of self-control, of agency in language, of Camila (now definitive), and of any

---

[51]   The Actaeon/Diana myth also has water/mirror poetics at its core. The metamorphosis is effected when Diana sprinkles Actaeon with water from the spring in which she was bathing. It is only when Actaeon sees his own reflection that he realises what has happened to him.

[52]   In *Aeneid* VII, 479–502, Iulus/Ascanius finds himself an unwitting pawn of divine powers when the fury Allecto enflames his dogs to attack the prized stag of Latium and thus provoke the first strike of the war.

[53]   See Torres 'Lope de Vega's *La Gatomaquia*', 16.

authentic sense of self. Moreover, the fractured subject is replicated in a mythical paradigm that splits in two, arguably three, antagonistic directions. Although Albanio compares himself to Orpheus in a threat to invoke the powers of darkness (938–45), the analogy is sustainable only at the basest level of Eurydice's inter-pretation of Orpheus's actions as madness (*Georgic* IV, 494–95). Albanio's violent treatment of Camila is consistent with the intertextual 'furor' that informs these lines, so reminscent of *Aeneid* VII (310–12) and brings into stark relief his jarring misappropriation and misreading of the Orphic role (942).[54] In fact, Albanio's irrational behaviour is more in keeping with the action of Aristaeus, the Virgilian anti-hero whose illicit passion for Eurydice manifested itself in a violent assault. Eurydice's subsequent flight results not only in her own death, but also has casti-gatory consequences for Aristaeus himself, whose bees fall victim to a fatal disease (*Georgic* IV, 315–558).[55] Garcilaso's fusion of both Virgilian figures in the char-acter of Albanio/Narcissus would suggest an awareness of Virgil's depiction of Orpheus as a flawed egotistical lover with Aristaean tendencies.[56] But it is impor-tant for the structure and meaning of *Eclogue* II that the sequence of events as presented in *Georgic* IV are inverted. In this way, the thin line separating 'amor puro' [pure love] from 'amor insano' [mad love] (and Albanio from his own reflec-tion) operates as a shifting and subjective interface. The uncertainty created by the narcissistic subject contemplating a double, a misleading surrogate form, in-stigates a rupture into representation that works to corrode identity at the level of the individual subject in the first half of the poem, but which in the latter half will salvage a collective identity through the inter-related continuum of selves de-picted on the urn ekphrasis.

A subtle transition to the second half of the poem is also provided by the *Georgic* subtext. As Albanio stands on the brink of suicide at verse 983, intending to hurl himself into the water, Salicio and Nemoroso appear in time to restrain him. They

---

54   The Virgilian verses read: 'quod si mea numina non sunt / magna satis, dubitem haud equidem implorare quod usquam/flectere si nequeo superos, Acheronta movebo' [If my own divine power is not enough, I shall not hesitate to ask for aid from any power, anywhere. If I cannot change the will of the Heavens, I will release Hell]. Juno decides to oppose fate by calling on Allecto, one of the Furies. Allecto's instructions are to disrupt peace and to sow the seeds of war. She sets about doing this by filling Queen Amata with such Bacchic furor that she becomes inca-pable of rational thought or action (*Aeneid* VII, 341–405).

55   Orphic analogy is tempered by Aristaean overtones throughout *Eclogue* II: Albanio's la-ment recalls Aristaeus's plea for his goddess-mother Cyrene to come to his aid (*Georgic* IV, 321–32); in Virgil's epyllion the nymph Arethusa raises her golden head out of the water in response to Aristaeus's distress (*Georgic* IV, 351–52), a scene recalled when Albanio seeks the aid of the water nymphs in *Eclogue* II, 611–13.

56   Correa identifies the Orpheus/Narcissus ambivalence in the presentation of Albanio, but limits his analysis to a commentary of verses 938–45 ('Garcilaso y la mitología', 274). Boase also identifies the Orphic analogy but fails to understand its significance: 'the Classical allusion could hardly be more inappropriate' ('The Meaning of the Crow-Hunting Episode', 52).

introduce us to the character of Severo, an omniscient magician whose eloquence will hold the key to Albanio's cure. The reader is reminded of Aristaeus's descent to his mother Cyrene at the source of all rivers and of her description of the all-knowing seer Proteus. The Severo/Proteus correspondence is anticipated in *Eclogue* II by Salicio and Nemoroso's attempts to restrain Albanio – a darkly comic episode which offers a deflationary response to Aristaeus's encounter with the god who can be overcome only by force (*Georgic* IV, 443–44).

In Virgil's epyllion, Proteus is an essential figure in whom the oppositional forces of Aristaeus and Orpheus symbolically confront each other.[57] Likewise, despite differences in emphasis, critics have been unanimous in highlighting the crucial unifying function of Severo in Garcilaso's poem, stressing either the shared literary origins of Albanio and Severo in Sannazaro (Lumsden Kouvel and Waley),[58] or positing a relationship of dialectical opposition (Komanecky). More recently, Martínez Góngora (2004), following a Lacanian approach adopted by Mitchell, credits Severo with the restoration of a specifically male heterosexual order that has been thrown into chaos by Albanio's madness.[59] In other words, Severo represents an ideological world in which the split masculine subject can be made whole and reintegrated. Severo has also been read in more conventional reconciliatory terms from a Neoplatonic/Orphic perspective. Azar interprets the seer's power over natural and physical phenomena (vv. 1161–68) as a demonstration of *coincidentia oppositorum*, the operating principle of Pico's Natural Philosophy,[60] while others interpret the prophet as metapoetic symbol, an epic poet with Orphic powers of ordering, divine sight, and rhetoric (for instance, Komanecky).[61] In this context the artistic potential of the inspired poet emerges as an effective solution

---

[57]   See Charles Segal, *Orpheus: The Myth of the Poet* (Baltimore: John Hopkins University Press, 1989), pp. 42–50.

[58]   See Lumsden Kouvel, 'Problems', 265, and Waley, 'Garcilaso's Second Eclogue', 594. As Morros points out in his note to *Eclogue* II, 1074, Severo's catalogue of magical powers has several Classical antecedents (most notably Ovid, *Amores* I, viii, 3–15), but given the extent of dependence on Sannazaro's *Arcadia* throughout the Spanish poem, a primary prototype for Severo must be Enareto in Prosa IX. Not surprisingly Garcilaso rejects the certainty of Clónico's cure, preferring to exploit Severo's role to confront concerns that are metatextually and ideologically ambiguous. See also Komanecky, 'Epic and Pastoral'.

[59]   See 'Relaciones homosociales', 34, where Martínez Góngora cites Juliette Mitchell (*Feminine Sexuality; Jacques Lacan and the Ecole Freudienne*, eds Juliette Mitchell and Jacqueline Rose [New York: Norton, 1982]), p. 26.

[60]   See *Discurso retórico*, pp. 194–95.

[61]   Correa and Cruz have also noted Severo's association with Orpheus. Correa speaks of his 'visión apolínea y hechizo orfeico' ('Garcilaso y la mitología', 275), while Cruz comments that Severo 'reúne en su persona y en sus acciones … ciertas cualidades que pueden asociarse con el poeta, en particular su comparación con los poderes órficos' (*Imitación y transformación*, p. 94). By designating Proteus 'vates' (*Georgic* IV, 387), Virgil had indicated an affinity between the sea-god and Orpheus which Garcilaso may be exploiting in *Eclogue* II. See also Komanecky, 'Epic and Pastoral'.

to the narcissistic neurosis of courtly love. It is this poetic potential, in fact, which Garcilaso realises in *Eclogues* I and III when, as narrator, he appropriates the Orphic art for himself.

While all of these readings are persuasive, they are also to some extent limited by a misguided desire to solve the perceived problem of the text's disunity. It is this drive to close the gap between the imaginative reality of Arcadia and the material reality of the House of Alba that has led us to miss how these seemingly distinct planes interact in the poem in a fractious mediation between experience and abstraction. The site of encounter is the prime identificatory medium of idealised pastoral, the 'fuente clara y pura' (1152), which now actively encourages a discourse (the 'dulce trato' [sweet conversation]; 1153) that will elide the intimate, ephemeral contemplation of the solipsistic subject in favour of an ekphrastic illusion of prophecy that is itself a distinct form of disciplined reverie. The *locus amoenus* is simultaneously natural setting and visual artwork as the pastoral pool becomes subject to an expansive, linguistic transformation. Mirror imagery is recuperated in this process as the enabling condition of a properly referential (collective) identity that is both nationally specific and imperially ambitious. Within Nemoroso's experience-authorised monologue the 'fuente' emerges figurally as the River Tormes, its regenerative energy explicitly associated in the poem with the lands and House of Alba (1041–73), only to rematerialise as the river-god's '*cristalina* urna' [*crystalline* urn; 1172; emphasis added], in which Severo sees and conveys the history of the Dukes of Alba (1154–1828), including his own role in their fortunes, 'como si *en espejo* se mirara' [as if reflected *in a mirror*; 1317; emphasis added].[62]

The River Tormes is a non-negotiable symbol of national identity in *Eclogue* II, just as the Tagus is in Sonnet XXIV and *Eclogue* III. As a transvalued River Tiber, it allows Garcilaso to bridge the gaps between the grandeur of Rome's past, the socio-political presumption of Spain's present and the deluge of ambiguities that shadow the future.[63] Book VIII of Virgil's *Aeneid* opens with the personified deity of the Tiber rising out of the water in a dream to Aeneas. In a reassuring prophecy Aeneas is informed that Ascanius, his son, will found a city of illustrious name, Alba Longa, whose kings will provide a direct line of descent to Romulus, founder of Rome. The book ends with an ekphrastic description of the shield forged for Aeneas by Vulcan (VIII, 617–731) and a rec-

---

62   The character Severo shares the name of Frey Severo who would have been familiar to early modern readers as the former tutor to the young Duke of Alba. As Lumsden Kouvel notes: 'while Severo's reported account of Alban history and exploits is heightened in prestige by his supernatural and symbolic character, it is also strengthened by his obvious authenticity' ('Problems', 265).

63   In Sannazaro's *Arcadia*, Prosa XI, the River Sebeto is introduced in similar vein as a Neapolitan Tiber, which is consistent with its role in the eulogy of Naples and which anticipates its participation as river deity in Prosa XII.

ognition that behind the glory of empire lies the very sadness of it all. Aeneas gazes upon the personified forms of rivers, the Rhine, the Euphrates, the Araxes, whose participation in Augustus's triumph symbolises the bloody conquest of defeated nations and peoples (VIII, 724–28). In fact, water functions as a cohesive element throughout the Virgilian epic, a repeated motif especially in the fabric of the book's first half, from the seascape that is the backdrop of the Trojans' journey towards their destination and destiny, to the rivers of the underworld that take Aeneas back through time and space, to confront the presence of his past before being challenged with a vision of Rome's future.[64] In the second half of the epic the rolling Tiber, as we have seen, marks out the site of future Rome and water is the force that bonds and integrates scenes of past, present and future on Aeneas's shield, containing the expansiveness of empire within a dynamic image of silver, circling dolphins (VIII, 671–74).

In the latter half of *Eclogue* II the illusion of ekphrasis tends to a unification of space (co-extensive with that of the pastoral narrator Nemoroso, and the reality of the contemporary reader) in which everything seems to form part of a continuous and unbroken totality that flows out from the crystalline urn of the River Tormes. The River Rhine facilitates Don Fernando's journey (1470), the River Danube which was 'frontera en otro tiempo del imperio romano'[65] now witnesses, approves and foretells the imperial project (1575; 1588–89; 1590), and a magnificent sea battle is the setting for the ekphrastic centrepiece, the relief of Vienna, which is more impressive (we are told) than Vulcan's Actium (1619–22) both in political significance and aesthetic representation. This prioritisation of water poetics in Nemoroso's narration of the visual description conveys the hierarchies and complexities of focalisation.[66] Narratologically the visual scenes described function as a story, told by Severo, but interpreted, ordered and framed by Nemoroso from Severo's written transcription. Ultimately the values and point of view inscribed are those of the speaker whose authority is as precarious or as powerful as that of any reader (1818–27). Nemoroso's epic ekphrasis ends with an alternative vision of the pastoral idyll (1720–37), which restores nature's function as a symbol of the moral and cosmic order. In this new macro-pastoral scheme of things with the River Tormes at its centre, desire is not renounced, but deftly revalued within a reciprocated conjugal context. Nemoroso's verbal third-party description may appear to hold up a more translucent mirror, but its broad ideological refiguring is no less subjective than Albanio's intimate quest for self-authenticity.

[64]   See Harry C. Rutledge, 'The Opening of *Aeneid* 6', *The Classical Journal*, 67.2 (1971), 110–15.

[65]   [The border, in another time, of the Roman Empire.] See Margot Arce de Vázquez, 'Cerca el Danubio una isla', *Studia Philologica*, 1 (1960), p. 96.

[66]   See D.P. Fowler, 'Narrate and Describe: The Problem of Ekphrasis', *The Journal of Roman Studies*, 81 (1991), 25–35.

At the micro level of transformative aesthetics there are key water-structuring connections (Tormes/Tiber, Alba de Tormes/Alba Longa, urn/shield, etc.) that encourage a reconstructed reading of the pastorally motivated ekphrasis in Virgilian/epic terms.[67] Such a generic reframing has ramifications for the depiction of Don Fernando whose transformed heroism must be determined comparatively by the reader in the context of the ethical and political values of the intertextual Aenean model, but measured in emulative terms in adherence to contemporary ideologies. The result is an analogic empowering according to which Fernando, beneficiary of a perfect humanist education (1302–53), transcends the flaws of the Virgilian hero and emerges as a new guardian of cultural inheritance, embodiment of Christian morality and model of Spanish aristocracy. Whereas Aeneas struggles to conform to the ideals of Stoicism, and ultimately must stoop to impious 'furor' in order to conquer,[68] Fernando's Neoplatonic credentials remain intact. Even involvement in 'la inhumana furia infernal, por otro nombre guerra' [infernal, inhuman, fury; in other words, war 1066][69] can be legitimised when military prowess is exercised against the Turkish infidel in the service of the state, authorised by the Holy Roman Emperor himself (1502–04), and tempered by a capacity for legitimate married love (1354–68 and 1714–26).[70] While this designation of Fernando as a desiring subject ('en amoroso fuego todo ardiendo' [burning with love's fire; 1702][71] contributes to a counter-heroic spirit that works to deconstruct the dominant discourse, the most poignant intrusion occurs much earlier. Before Garcilaso introduces Fernando, he harnesses Virgil's own self-transgressive strategy, the allusive multi-correspondence simile, to explore the price of Empire in human terms. Fernando's father García falls at the age of twenty-three in a disastrous campaign to conquer Djerba:

---

[67] The conventional machinery of epic is also in place, for instance the complement of divinities or quasi-divinities that are invoked to take an interest in or move along the action (the presence of divinities at the birth of Fernando which recalls Ariosto, *Orlando*, XLVI, lxxxv, 5–8; the depiction of envy [1558ff]), the extended simile (1253–66), and the brutal battle scenes.

[68] By ending the *Aeneid* with an act of rage (the death of Turnus provoked by the sight of Pallas's belt worn by Turnus as triumphant spoils), Virgil leaves the reader contemplating the darker side of humanity rather than celebrating Trojan/Roman victory.

[69] Morros suggests that the representation of war as 'Furia infernal' has its source in Erasmus's representation of war, which is in turn inspired by passages from Virgil, *Aeneid* VI and VII. This strengthens the case for considering the individual 'furor' of Albanio (also related to scenes in Virgil), which dominates the early part of the Eclogue, as being inextricably bound up with the collective 'furor' of war as depicted in the latter stages. See 'El tema de la guerra y de la caza en Garcilaso', in *Garcilaso y su época*, pp. 227–40.

[70] Westcott suggests that if the three Eclogues are read in relation to one another and in the order in which they were written, they recast the ideas that appear in the Neoplatonic dialogues of Ficino, Bembo and Castiglione. Fernando's love story, grounded within the norms of matrimony, thus confirms the presentation of a self-conscious ideological statement ('Garcilaso's Eclogues').

[71] This verse is also used by Garcilaso of Leander in Sonnet XXIX, 2, and imitates Ariosto, *Orlando*, XIX, xxvi, 8.

> puso en el duro suelo la hermosa
> cara, como la rosa matutina,
> cuando ya el sol declina al mediodía,
> que pierde su alegría y marchitando
> va la color mudando; o en el campo
> cual queda el lirio blanco que'l arado
> crudamente cortado al pasar deja,
> [...]
> tal está el rostro tuyo en el arena,
> fresca rosa, azucena blanca y pura. (1253–66)

[and he laid his lovely face upon the hard earth, like the morning rose when the sun declines at noon, its vigour lost, withers and gives up its bloom; or like the white lily left lying in the field, cruelly cut down by a passing plough [...] such is your face upon the sand, fresh rose, pure, white lily.]

The already 'troubled integration of ekphrasis'[72] is intensified by such a radical mode-switching. Whereas Virgil constructs a network of similes which coalesce to create a psychological continuity that is pivotal to the working out of the epic, Garcilaso distils interwoven strands of intertextuality into a single concentrated image that goes nowhere in the narrative, but is impossible to shake off.[73] The power of apostrophe ('el rostro *tuyo*') creates an intimate space between an implied-speaker-reader 'yo' [I] that breathes renewed life into imitated words and form.[74]

Putnam has demonstrated how ekphrasis in the *Aeneid* serves as a *mise en abîme*, its circularity of form and content positing a cyclical view of history that counter-balances the epic's linear, historical trajectory.[75] I would suggest that the analysis of the contemporary world in *Eclogue* II, via the reformulation of literary monuments, is much more consciously Virgilian than has been recognised,[76] but that the belated nature of the Spanish text's transvaluation of ekphrasis constitutes a more complex interrogation of the relationship between art and time. Within the Renaissance context of an emerging vernacular human-

---

72   See Fowler,'Narrate and Describe', 35.

73   A catalogue of 'victims' in the *Aeneid* are connected by elements common to the double simile that describes the young Euryalus at the moment of death (VIII, 433–37). See, for instance, Dido (IV), Pallas and Camilla (XI), Lavinia and Turnus (XII). For Virgil's models in Homer and Catullus, and the subsequent re-elaboration of the same sources in Claudian, see Torres, *The Polyphemus Complex*, 89–90.

74   Garcilaso would use aspects of this image again in the elegy on the Duke of Alba's brother (118-26) and in *Eclogue* III, 133–36.

75   See Michael C.J. Putnam, *Virgil's Epic Designs: Ekphrasis in the Aeneid* (New Haven and London: Yale University Press, 1998).

76   Lapesa, for instance, notes that 'la influencia del latino, menor que la de Sannazaro en la égloga II, es superior en la I, y las dos se combinan en la III' (*La trayectoria*, p. 182).

ism and a developing struggle for national and political self-definition, the forward thrust of the poetic continuum is at once advanced and challenged by an emulative contribution that leaves deliberately unresolved the aesthetic and political questions which it reiterates and recasts. The value of Virgil in *Eclogue* II does not lie in specific scenes or events, but in the broader situation of the individual protagonists and their world – a relationship that carries a weight of struggle and power. The determining dichotomy of *Eclogue* II is the poem's desire for integration and its simultaneous resistance to it. The tensions that characterise the shift out of Arcadia to Alba and back again are paradoxically uncovered by a very fluid, but persistent, water/mirror poetics, poised significantly between reality and illusion, and emblematic of a larger struggle between present and past.

It is highly appropriate that the culminating image of the *locus amoenus* should celebrate the fecundating principle of water as a potent image of recreativity.[77] *Eclogue* II may close down conventionally at sunset, but the static, reflective, Arcadian pool has been definitively replaced by the culturally specific and transforming River Tormes, a force that sustains the essence of what is already there, but subjects it to a wholly original, open-ended, formulation ('mas con diversos modos lo decían' [but each expressed it differently; 1723].[78] Ultimately, Garcilaso's 'new poetry' exposes the 'literariness' of ideologies such as nationalism or imperialism, as well as the anxious authority of the poet who claims transmission. Moreover, *Eclogue* II also addresses the informing contradiction of identity formation, demonstrating how the totemic system is fashioned out of and haunted by a fundamentally indeterminate human condition. Individual and community are interdependent rather than oppositional, yet the success of one is often realised through the sacrifice of the other. It is this conundrum that Garcilaso provocatively confronts when he adamantly refuses to square the imperial circle in poems such as Sonnet XXXIII and *Eclogue* II.

[77]   The topos of water as an agent of oblivion is explicitly rejected at verses 1738–41.
[78]   In a clear departure from Sannazaro's *Arcadia*, Garcilaso leaves the question of Albanio's cure unresolved.

3

Fernando de Herrera (1534–1597): *'Righting' the Middle – Centres, Circles and Algunas Obras (1582)*

Introduction: *in medias res ...*

In our post-modern or *post* post-modern present, we pay little more than lip service to a flawed sense of a continuously unfolding linear temporality. Within an apparently dynamic frame of moving horizons which, on the surface, recognises that meaning does not settle easily within segregated presentism, we have locked the *early* modern into a temporal pocket on the lower end of a value-added sequential scale. Our contemporary understanding of linear history, as an accumulation of personal and communal experience, is, of course, more complex and, indeed, less 'linear' than the Aristotelian concept of the numerical estimation of movement. But while we may not have sacrificed the phenomenology of how individual human beings participate in three-dimensional time (past/present/future), and have expended considerable energy on unlocking the secrets of the hermeneutic circle,[1] our insistence on the 'early' modern betrays an unwillingness to recognise that human nature, at any point or place in time, could be said to exist 'in medias res'[2] – that is, that our communal beginning comes only after beginning; and that the corporeal individual exists somewhere between life and death, an intermediate state destabilised by the incommensurable complicity of accessible 'temporal' time as we experience it and an awareness of 'cosmic' time, absolute, somehow 'purer' and experientially absent.

Intermediary self-consciousness was a defining feature of a Renaissance humanism that is understood in broad terms as an intellectual, cultural activity

---

[1] The bibliography related to critical thinking around hermeneutics is vast. For analysis of the beginnings of modern hermeneutics see, among others, Gayle L. Ormiston and Alan D. Schrift, eds, *The Hermeneutic Tradition: From Ast to Ricoer* (New York: State University of New York Press, 1990), and Gerald Bruns, *Hermeneutics: Ancient and Modern* (New Haven: Yale University Press, 1992).

[2] The term originates in Horace's *Ars Poetica*, 147–48, where it refers to the narrative technique of the ideal epic poet, Homer.

centred upon the rediscovery, interrogation, assimilation and transference of ancient Greek and Latin texts. Humanism's operational literary field encompassed critical and creative endeavour which articulated the belated anxieties of its dialogical interplay between past and present, while also writing itself into the middle of a bigger diachronic picture.[3] The present, in this context, can be conceptualised in terms of interruption or intrusion; predicated upon an intermediary function which opens out into an indeterminate future, thereby transcending the limitations of its situatedness within history. I would argue that it is this sense of provocative intrusion that is a co-determining condition of both the critical and creative voices of the Sevillan writer Fernando de Herrera (1534–1597);[4] a self-affirming strategy in individual and nationalistic terms, which undermines the monolithic formulations of the past with an insistence on language's capacity to yield meaning over (and above) time.[5] Indeed, stasis emerges as the principal antagonist both of Herrera's literary theory as expounded in the *Las Obras de Garcilaso con anotaciones de Fernando de Herrera* (1580) and of his poetic practice, as exemplified in *Algunas obras*, the collection of poetry he published only two years later, in 1582. Whether or not the love poems were inspired by Doña Leonor de Milán, the wife of Herrera's patron, the Count of Gelves, is a matter of some debate. If positions have been drawn less vehemently than in the case of Garcilaso's alleged muse Isabel Freire, this may be down to an erroneous belief that less is at stake when it comes to Herrera.

Arguments in favour of considering the *Anotaciones* and *Algunas obras* as co-dependent have been made by a range of critics, with differing and inevitably fragmentary emphases, for instance: Woods, Cuevas García, Navarrete, Montero, Ruíz Pérez, Schwartz, and most recently by Middlebrook.[6] It is my

---

3   In a recent analysis of passages from Rabelais and Montaigne, Wes Williams has effectively demonstrated how Renaissance texts imagined their readers 'to be not at the start (early), nor at the end (post), but somewhere in the middle (always, already, modern)'. See Williams, '"Being in the Middle": Translation, Transition and the "Early Modern"', in *Theory and the Early Modern*, eds Michael Moriarty and John O'Brien, special issue, *Paragraph*, 29.1 (2006), 27–39.

4   Paul Julian Smith approaches Herrera in terms of this blurred distinction between the creative and the critical in his *Writing in the Margin*.

5   A recent study of Herrera's poetry by Scott Sigel emphasises its 'eternalising' aspects. See *The Baroque Poetry of Fernando de Herrera, 1534–1597: Decoro in the Spanish Poetry of the Sixteenth and Seventeenth Centuries* (Lewiston: Edwin Mellen Press, 2007).

6   See M.J. Woods, 'Herrera's Voices', in *Medieval and Renaissance Studies on Spain and Portugal in Honour of P.E. Russell*, eds F.W. Hodcroft, D.G. Pattison, R.D.F. Pring-Mill, R. Truman (Oxford: The Society for the Study of Medieval Languages and Literatures, 1981), pp. 121–32 (p. 129); Fernando de Herrera, *Poesía castellana original completa*, ed. Cristóbal Cuevas García (Madrid: Cátedra, 1985); Ignacio Navarette, *Orphans of Petrarch*, p. 150; Juan Montero, 'Las anotaciones, del texto al lector', in *Las anotaciones de Fernando de Herrera: doce estudios*, ed. Begoña López Bueno (Sevilla: Universidad de Sevilla, 1997), pp. 91–105 (p. 104); and in the same volume, Pedro Ruíz Pérez, 'De la teoría a la práctica: modelos y modelización en "Algunas

intention in this chapter to synthesise and develop key strands of their arguments around the notion of an overarching allegorical system in which shared 'metaphors of purpose',[7] particularly those prioritising *claridad* [clarity] and *osadía* [daring], and conventional motifs (such as the *homo viator*), undergo an interdependent process of transvaluation as a means of negotiating a very slippery aesthetic, epistemic and ontological middle ground – a 'middle ground' whose inherent transitory and provisional nature is itself reconceived through a melding of *imitatio* and *inventio*, which, both in theory and in practice, fuses the horizons of there and here, then and now.

The canon ... and other controversial 'caminos'

Ambivalent and mixed responses to Herrera's creative work stand in stark contrast to the undisputed historical significance of the textual criticism. And yet, on almost every level of engagement, the *Anotaciones* continue to generate their fair share of critical controversy. Persistently open questions include: the identification and significance of Herrera's sources (Morros versus Pepe Sarno on this);[8] whether the *Anotaciones* can or should stand as a legitimate and coherent substitute for a hypothetical *Ars Poética* (Gallego Morell versus Cuevas García and others);[9] whether or not this treatise formed part of the Herrerian corpus that was 'swept away' in the symbolic wreckage of what Duarte, one of Pacheco's 1619 *prologuistas*, referred to as a *naufragio* [shipwreck];[10] and the relative

obras"', pp. 239–61; Lía Schwartz, 'Herrera, poeta bucólico, y sus predecesores italianos', in *Spagna e Italia attraverso la letteratura del secondo cinquecento*, eds E. Sánchez García, A. Cerbo and C. Borrelli (Napoli: Instituto Universitario Orientale, 2001), pp. 475–500 (p. 481); Leah Middlebrook, *Imperial Lyric: New Poetry and New Subjects in Early Modern Spain* (University Park, PA: Pennsylvania University Press, 2009), pp. 138–74.

    7   See Edwin Honig, *Dark Conceit: The Making of Allegory* (London: Faber and Faber, 1959), p. 12.

    8   See Inoria Pepe Sarno's article on the relationship between Herrera's work and Bembo's edition of Petrarch (1501), 'Fernando de Herrera creador del Petrarca español: *Las anotaciones a la obra de Garcilaso*', *Calíope*, 10 (2004), 69–86, an argument previously articulated in Fernando de Herrera, *Anotaciones a la poesía de Garcilaso*, eds Inoria Pepe Sarno and Jose María Reyes (Madrid: Cátedra, 2001). For Bienvenido Morros' aggressive response to her argument see 'Idea de la lírica en las anotaciones a Garcilaso de Fernando de Herrera', in *Idea de la lírica en el Renacimiento (entre Italia y España)*, eds María José Vega and Cesc Esteve (Barcelona: Mirabel Editorial, 2004), pp. 211–29 (p. 211, n. 1).

    9   Although both Herrera and Medina refer to this as a future work in the preliminaries to the *Anotaciones*, the jury is still out. See, for instance, Antonio Gallego Morell, *Garcilaso de la Vega y sus comentaristas* (Madrid: Editorial Gredos, 1972), pp. 39 and 43–44; Cristóbal Cuevas García, 'Teoría del lenguaje poético en las anotaciones de Herrera', in *Las anotaciones de Fernando de Herrera: doce estudios*, pp. 157–71 (pp. 158 and 171).

    10   The relevant section of Duarte's prologue reads: 'I es cierto que su memoria uviera quedado sepultada en perpetuo olvido, si Francisco Pacheco, célebre pintor de nuestra ciudad i afectuoso imitador de sus escritos, no uviera recogido […] algunos cuadernos i borradores que escap-

validity of seventeenth-century and contemporary speculation around the circumstances of this posthumous silencing. Indeed, the loss of much of Herrera's work and the gap between his death and the publication of *Versos* (1619) constitute an unresolved intrigue which has turned out to be just one act in a more elaborate 'drama textual';[11] a 'drama' that has divided and dominated responses to the authenticity, and authority, of Pacheco's text over the earlier *Algunas obras*.[12] Clearly, then, all contentious *caminos* around Herrera's critical work lead us eventually, albeit inconclusively, back to the problem space between theory and practice.

Yet we have not broached the polemic sparked by early detractors of the *Anotaciones*, a dispute that has reached our own time in the 'decentring' theory of Ignacio Navarrete.[13] As Navarrete reminds us, Herrera's contemporary readers reacted strongly to what was perceived to be a subversive exploitation of the genre of commentary for overtly biased purposes.[14] The first shot was fired by Don Juan Fernández de Velasco (Condestable de Castilla), writing under the pseudonym Prete Jacopín. The very title of the work signals the Castile/Andalucía 'in-fighting' that characterised individual contributions to the controversy.[15] It reads in full, *Observaciones del licenciado Prete Jacopín,*

aron del naufragio en que, pocos días después de su muerte, perecieron todas sus obras poéticas, que él tenía corregidas de última mano, i encuadernadas para darlas a la emprenta. Dexo en silencio la culpa d'esta pérdida' [And his memory would certainly have been consigned to oblivion if Francisco Pacheco, a famous artist of this city, and affectionate imitator of Herrera's writing, had not gathered together some of the notebooks and rough drafts which survived the shipwreck in which, a few days after his death, his complete poetic corpus had perished; texts which he had put the finishing touches to and bound for printing. I will draw a veil of silence over responsibility for this loss.] Andreina Bianchini analyses the interconnected social, political and literary factors underpinning a system of power abuse that would result in the sacrifice of Herrera's work; see 'Herrera and Prete Jacopín: The Consequences of the Controversy', *Hispanic Review*, 2 (1978), 221–34.

11   See Oreste Macrí, 'Autenticidad y estructura de la edición póstuma de *Versos de Fernando de Herrera*', *FR*, VI (1959), 1–26 and 151–84.

12   For a detailed summary of the major players and positions of the 'drama textual' see Cuevas García, *Fernando de Herrera*, pp. 87–99. See also Begoña López Bueno, *La poética cultista de Herrera a Góngora* (Sevilla: Alfar, 1987), pp. 38–42 and p. 50; Francisco Javier Martínez Ruíz, 'Fernando de Herrera ante la crítica', in *Las anotaciones de Fernando de Herrera: doce estudios*, pp. 280–81 and p. 285.

13   Navarrete, *Orphans of Petrarch*, pp. 137–68.

14   Macrí ('Autenticidad') extracts an intellectual anti-*culto* position from Prete Jacopín's attack. This is echoed by López Bueno who beneath the vitriol perceives aesthetic 'cuestiones de fondo de mayor interés' (*La poética cultista*, p. 58). Against this view, see Antonio Alatorre, 'Garcilaso, Herrera, Prete Jacopín y Don Tomás Tamayo de Vargas', *MLN*, 78 (1963), 126–51 and Andreina Bianchini, 'Herrera: Questions and Contradictions in the Critical Tradition', *Caliope*, 1 (1995), 58–71.

15   The *Observaciones* and a *Respuesta* which may have been written by Herrera in the guise of a friend ('por ser andaluz como él') were first published in 1870: José María Asensio, *Controversia sobre sus Anotaciones a las obras de Garcilaso de la Vega* (Seville: [n.p.], 1870). The

vecino de Burgos, En defensa del Príncipe de los Poetas Castellanos Garci Lasso de la Vega, vecino de Toledo, contra las anotaciones que hizo a sus obras Fernando de Herrera, Poeta Sevillano' [Observations by the university graduate Prete Jacopín, *resident of Burgos*, in defence of the *Prince of Castilian poets*, Garcilaso de la Vega, *resident of Toledo*, against the annotations written by the *Sevillan poet*, Fernando de Herrera]. But what really is at stake, then as now, is the *intentionality* of Herrera's enterprise, which, even if deemed intrinsic on the basis of derivative textual evidence, is ultimately ascribed by an external agent, but is perhaps no less legitimate for residing in the eye of a subjective beholder/reader. The offensive-defensive strategies underlining Herrera's own interpretations of Garcilaso would certainly support the hermeneutic validity of reader response.

   Navarrete's reading of the *Anotaciones* as an attack on a Castilian-controlled canon boils down evidentially to the distinct methodologies employed by Herrera and his predecessor Francisco Sánchez de las Brozas (1574 and reprinted 1578); whose absence from Herrera's roll-call of references did not pass unnoticed.[16] Whereas *El Brocense's* more conventional editing project was limited to the purification of Garcilaso's text and a solid identification of sources, Herrera swamps Garcilaso's poetry with an overwhelming (and sometimes bewilderingly tangential) array of learned source citations and translations (including some of his own and of contemporary Andalusian writers).[17] Garcilaso is thus subjected to a non-neutral humanist hermeneutic which, following Navarrete's argument, has two primary goals: firstly the reconceptualisation of the ideal poet in Herrera's own image (whereby Garcilaso soldier-courtier becomes Garcilaso scholar-artisan, and poetry itself emerges as the sophisticated product of an *arte-ingenio* alliance distanced

---

'respuesta' also makes reference to a now lost censure written by a certain Damasio (de Frías y Bilbao, from Valladolid). Alatorre extends the limits of the dispute to, at least, 1622, providing evidence that Tamayo Vargas's anti-Herrerian edition of Garcilaso relied heavily on the comments made by 'Prete Jacopín' ('Garcilaso, Herrera, Prete Jacopín y Don Tomás Tamayo de Vargas'). For a detailed exposition of the controversy, see Bienvenido Morros, *Las polémicas literarias en la España del siglo XVI: a propósito de Fernando de Herrera y Garcilaso de la Vega* (Barcelona: QC, 1998), ch. 3.

   16   On the relationship between these two commentaries see, among others, Gallego Morell, *Garcilaso de la Vega y sus comentaristas*, pp. 39 and 43.

   17   So prevalent are these references that the commentary has been read by several scholars as the aesthetic manifesto or *florilegio* of a so-called *escuela sevillana*. Critics who tend towards this view include María del Pilar Palomo, 'La herencia de Herrera', in *La Poesía de la edad barroca* (Barcelona: SGEL, 1975); Eugenio Asensio, 'El Brocense contra Fernando de Herrera y sus Anotaciones a Garcilaso', *El Crótalon. Anuario de Filología Española*, I (1984), 13–24; Montero, 'Las anotaciones, del texto al lector'; and, most recently, Ignacio García Aquilar, *Poesía y edición en el siglo de oro* (Madrid: Calambur Editorial, 2009). However, Bianchini finds no evidence that Prete Jacopín identified the existence of a homogenous group sharing an aesthetic ideal and also disputes Herrera's leadership role in such a grouping ('Herrera: Questions and Contradictions'), pp. 66–67.

from any sense of spontaneous *sprezzatura*); and, secondly, a displacement of Garcilaso from the centre of a vernacular canon that is reconfigured within broader European and Classical contours.

The paradoxes that permeate Navarrete's Bloomian-inspired theory are too easily dismissed as ironies – most obviously, the fact that Herrera's attempt to subvert the notion of authority by undermining canonicity would so effectively confirm the canonical status of 'the overwhelming predecessor' whose central position he sought (and failed) to challenge. Perhaps if we stop thinking of the commentary as *disrupting* the reading of the primary text and, therefore, emblematic of the discontinuities in the literary tradition, and think instead in terms of normative *interruption*, then it is not Herrera as alternative poet nor the *Anotaciones* as alternative text which decentre Garcilaso, but rather a model of objectivity that is deliberately (and yes, ironically) centred on a highly subjective reader. Herrera's intrusions upon the source text can then be viewed positively as the creative will in action – a daring attempt to stake out his own path to potential meanings within his own and Garcilaso's intellectual horizons ('osando abrir el camino' [daring to open the way], he states from the outset).[18] By talking into, and back at, Garcilaso's text, Herrera engages with authorities that precede his own, and while these are not, nor are meant to be, uniformly dismantled, there is little sense of submission in the dialogue. Against the Gadamerian view that we do not confront canonical texts but, rather, that having travelled authoritatively through time, they come to challenge us and our way of life, the heightened autonomy accorded to explication and interpretation by Herrera significantly softens and reverses the temporal collision. The empowerment of the present in this encounter is entirely in keeping with the concern for the condition of the Spanish language which is a dominant theme of the *Anotaciones*; and the self-conscious Andalusianism of the text, insofar as it articulates a persistent site of linguistic renovation within a vernacular continuum, can therefore be re-evaluated as a symbolically recurring reactualisation of the past in the present. With privileged hindsight we can trace this from the Sevillan Nebrija through to Lorca via Góngora.[19]

Undoubtedly there is a certain tension between the dimension of individuality claimed by Herrera as present-day reader and the sense of uncontrollability generated by the sprawling intertexts and extended generic discourses. But anxieties surrounding the individual's ability to 'master' the text of the past are balanced by a confidence in the undertaking, if not the outcome, of a collective nationalistic project – a drive to secure a temporally unfettered imperial self-determination through passionate engagement with 'la gran belleza

---

18   See Fernando de Herrera, *Anotaciones a la poesia de Garcilaso*, p. 264. All references to the *Anotaciones* are taken from this edition.

19   Interestingly in the 'Respuesta' [Response] to Prete Jacopín, Herrera anticipates the emergence of 'otro andaluz' [another Andalusian] who will continue along the path which he has carved out.

y esplendor de [nuestra] lengua' [the great beauty and splendour of our language].[20] Suffused throughout the *Anotaciones* with the solar energy and radiance of an informing Neoplatonic allegory, the Spanish language mirrors the aspirational movement of humanity; which means shedding its body-politic and material specificity to inhabit a celestial sphere where it may move continuously forward and last for all time.

However, the realities informing the analogical frame contradict the aspiration. The antagonism is explicit in Medina's prologue to the *Anotaciones*:[21]

> Siempre fue natural pretensión de *las gentes virtuosas procurar estender no menos el uso de sus lenguas que los términos de sus imperios,* de donde antiguamente sucedía que cada cual nación tanto más adornava su lenguage cuanto con más valerosos hechos acrecentava la reputación de sus armas. [...]

> [It was always the natural objective of *virtuous peoples to try to extend the use of their language in accordance with the limits of their empires.* Consequently, in the ancient world, each individual nation adorned their language all the more as their heroic deeds enhanced the reputation of their arms.]

> Crecieron, por cierto, las lenguas griega i latina al abrigo de las vitorias i *subieron a la cumbre de su esaltacion con la pujança del Imperio.* I fueron tan *prudentes ambas naciones* que, pretendiendo con ardor increíble *la felicidad de sus repúblicas para la vida presente i la inmortalidad de su fama para los siglos venideros,* entendieron que con ningún medio podían conseguir mejor lo uno i lo otro que con el *esfuerço de sus braços i con el artificio de sus lenguas.* [pp. 187–88]

> [Of course the Greek and Latin languages grew under the protection of their victories and *reached the height of perfection with the power of the Empire.* Both nations, with unbelievable fervour, sought *the happiness of their republics in the present and the immortality of their reputation in the future.* They were *wise enough* to understand that there was no better way to realise both these objectives than *with a strong arm and an elegant tongue.*]

At the core of Medina's communication to the reader is an unsettling integration of the national mission (the 'pujança del imperio'), into a broad ethical system whose moral principles are consequently revalued. The summit of all virtue and

---

20 *Anotaciones*, p. 202.
21 For discussion of the prologue, see, among others, Gaetano Chiappini, ed.,'Estudio preliminar', in *Fernando de Herrera y la escuela sevillana* (Madrid: Taurus, 1985), pp. 7–26 (pp. 22–25); Pepe Sarno, 'Fernando de Herrera creador del Petrarca español', 72–73.

wisdom is attained through dedication to a common linguistic goal – success will redefine the present and determine the future. What the Spanish nation has the potential to become depends, therefore, upon a sophisticated, emulative, speech-act. But this cross-fertilisation of language and empire, envisioned for national cohesion by Nebrija almost a century before,[22] and modelled now, as then, on a policy of linguistic imperialism which, centuries earlier, had consolidated the dominion of Rome across three continents, is contradictory in itself. The Roman empire is dead, whatever positive spin Medina might put on the memorialising function of its ruins; and its linguistic companion, Latin, by Herrera's own admission in the *Anotaciones*, is dying and, therefore, less 'relevant' then the evolving vernaculars.

No less contradictory is the ever-widening gap between the advancing glory of Spanish arms and the belated, static, condition of its letters:

> Por lo cual me suelo maravillar de nuestra floxedad i negligencia, porque haviendo domado *con singular fortaleza i prudencia casi divina* el orgullo de tan poderosas naciones *i levantado la majestad del reino de España a la mayor alteza* que jamás alcançaron fuerças humanas [...] ¿somos – diré – tan descuidados (o tan inorantes) que dexamos perderse *aqueste raro tesoro* que poseemos? [...] i no ai quien se condolesca de ver *la hermosura de nuestra plática tan descompuesta i mal parada. [Anotaciones* p. 189]

> [And so I tend to marvel at our weakness and negligence, because having vanquished such powerful and proud nations *with extraordinary bravery and divine-like wisdom*, and *having elevated the majesty of the Kingdom of Spain to heights* never before reached by human power [...] are we, I ask, so careless (or so ignorant) that we allow *that rare treasure* to be lost? [...] And I doubt that anyone is content to see *the beauty of our speech in such an unfortunate state of disarray.*]

The present moment is its own split subject; but Medina postulates the possibility of healing a dichotomised national selfhood by negating the distance between its two competing, and distinct, semantic fields. In other words, language functions as both corollary subject and object of the dilemma. Thus the daring deeds of empire are 'translated' into the *osadía* required by Spanish writers and poets to confer on the vernacular the Olympian dignity it deserves. Garcilaso, 'príncipe de los poetas castellanos', emerges as the protagonist of a less immediate struggle, of an ideological project of *traslatio studii* which involves the transmission of cultural authority and value between past and present; but also the translation of the other into the terms of an idealised self. From Medina's perspective, this has been effectively realised (though in precariously unique terms)

---

[22] See Chapter 1 above.

through a process of eclectic imitation and *con dichosa osadía*. Thus the implicit mythological paradigm is appropriately reconfigured and the impiety of the Giants' revolt is positively recast. Emulative art, through Garcilaso, has established itself in the void of temporal and cultural difference as the mechanism for bridging their respective ruptures and rivalries:

> [...] Garci Lasso de la Vega, príncipe de los poetas castellanos, en quien claro se descubrió cuánto puede la fuerça de un ecelente ingenio de España i que *no es impossible a nuestra lengua arribar cerca de la cumbre donde ya se vieron la griega i latina si nosotros <u>con impiedad</u> no la desamparássemos.*
> [...]
> *En las imitaciones sigue los passos de los más celebrados autores latinos i toscanos*, i trabajando alcançallos, se esfuerça <u>*con tan dichosa osadía*</u> que no pocas vezes *se les adelanta.* [p. 197].

> [Garcilaso de la Vega, Prince of Castilian poets, who revealed just what could be achieved by an exceptional Spanish talent; that it *is not beyond our language to scale heights previously reached by Greek and Latin, if we had not so impiously abandoned it.* [...] *As an imitator, he follows the footsteps of the most celebrated Latin and Italian writers,* and in his *daring* efforts to catch them up, often *overtakes them.*]

Medina grants Garcilaso a central position at a distinct point in time; without invalidating the poetic continuum, nor denying the connectedness of the *traslatio* to his own day (enfolding Garcilaso 'en nuestra edad' [in our age]). But he does thrust Herrera into the middle of this project, identifying him as a new, exemplary, protagonist of a more urgent, internalised *traslatio* – an innovative *poeta artifex* through whose erudition and heroism the terms of an idealised (imperial) self in 'armas' can be translated into an equally idealised self in 'letras'.

Herrera's declaration of purpose at the opening of the *Anotaciones*, in a preface to his commentary on Garcilaso's first sonnet,[23] conveys a certain confidence in this innovatory role:

> I aunque sé que es difícil mi intento i que está desnuda nuestra lengua del conocimiento d'esta disciplina, *no por esso temo romper por todas estas dificultades, osando abrir el camino a los que sucedieron, para que no se pierda la poesía española en la oscuridad de la inorancia.* [...] Pero desseo que sea esta mi intención bien acogida de los que saben, i que se persuadan a creer que *la onra de la nación* i ecelencia del escriptor presente me obligaron a publicar estas rudezas de mi ingenio [p. 264]

23 Herrera's comments on the sonnet are analysed by, among others, Montero, 'Las anotaciones, del texto al lector'.

[And although I know that my enterprise is difficult and that our language is stripped of knowledge of this discipline; *for all that, I am not afraid to break through these obstacles and to dare to open up a path for those who follow me, so that Spanish poetry is not lost in the darkness of ignorance.* [...] But I would like my intention to be well received by those who know and for them to believe that *the honour of the nation* and the excellence of this writer (i.e. Garcilaso de la Vega) compelled me to publish these simple offerings of my own.]

The 'heroic vision' identified by Gaylord Randel as the common denominator of Herrera's writing is tempered here by a recognition of the difficulties which have had to be, and which will have to be, surmounted.[24] The literary past, for Herrera, is not a foreign, but a dark country that lies within. In accordance with the ambivalent, non- antagonistic, conditions of *claro-oscuridad* in which the poetic project is emblematised throughout the text, the Spanish language must rise above obscurity (without *claridad* 'no puede la poesía mostrar su grandeza' [poetry cannot demonstrate its grandeur]), but yet depends upon it for authentic revelation of its radiance.[25] The positive ambivalence of the allegorical frame, however, is challenged by *osadía*, a problematic reconciliatory sign whose mutually exclusive significations in arms and letters defy easy co-existence. This shift into ambiguity, and perhaps even towards a more problematic de Manian 'undecidability', conveys a somewhat negative dialectic which, like the violence occasioned by Herrera's intrusive citations, denies the reader the comfort of a homogenising, totalising narrative of literary history which constant reiteration seems to offer. For instance, Santillana's imitation of the sonnet (*singular osadía* [exceptional daring]) is connected to Garcilaso's invigoration of the language through neologisms (also *osadía*), which, as we have seen, is in turn linked to the very circumstances of Herrera's writing and implicitly informs his clarion call to poets of his own time – who must dare to *alzar mayor vuelo* [fly higher]. The Icarian pretext underlying this is predicated upon the individual reaching beyond the self, stretching towards the sublime, extending beyond time – in fact, moving right out of the epistemic and ontological middle ground.[26]

The entry on *claridad* makes explicit Herrera's transcendent aspirations for Spanish poetry and implies a corresponding, albeit destabilising, Icarian profile for the ideal poet:

---

24   See Mary M. Gaylord Randel, *The Historical Prose of Fernando de Herrera* (London: Tamesis, 1971), p. 4.

25   The emphasis on *claridad* throughout the *Anotaciones* is so pronounced that Herrera was subsequently associated with the anti-*cultista* movement. See, for instance, López Bueno, *Las anotaciones de Fernando de Herrera: doce estudios*, pp. 20–22. Navarrete draws attention to the fact that Herrera's comments on metaphor prioritise clarity (sight), and how figurative images of light/sight are even employed in the discussion of sound (*Orphans of Petrarch*, pp. 151–54).

26   Middlebrook makes a good case for identifying self-restraint in Herrera's entry on 'valiente' in the *Anotaciones* and in relation to the second *canción* (see *Imperial Lyric*, pp. 149–52), but the textual evidence works against this as a reading of the entire collection.

> Es importantíssima la claridad en el verso; y si falta en él, se pierde toda la gracia y la hermosura de la Poesía. [...] Cáusase la clareza de la puridad y elegancia. La elegancia es modo que trae claridad a todos los modos de la oración. La puridad de sí mesma es clara y abierta; mas la elegancia está en la grandeza y magnificencia del decir; *y es como el Sol, que deshace la oscuridad*. [p. 351]

> [Clarity in verse is of the utmost importance; without it, all the grace and beauty of poetry is lost. [...] Clarity derives from purity and elegance. Elegance is a way of giving clarity to all types of speech. Purity is inherently clear and open; but elegance resides in the grandeur and magnificence of speech; and *is like the sun which dispels the darkness.*]

Within a Neoplatonic system of cosmic coherence, poetry which meets the highest standards of linguistic purity, is envisaged in the celestial sphere; its incorruptible nature confirmed in its association with the circular motion of the sun. The poet, however, is a material, sublunary being whose rectilinear movement through time, according to Ptolemy, is 'a symbol of the contrast between the eternal and the transient, hence also between the psychical and the physical, even the divine and the mortal'.[27] The vulnerability of Herrera's allegorical elevation of poetry is exposed in its dependency upon the poet's Icarian ambition, which ultimately breaks the logic of the cosmic arrangement. Moreover, and still keeping within Herrera's Neoplatonic/mythically conflated scheme of things, this heliocentric representation of linguistic elegance turns language into an idealised feminine object of desire. The highest pretensions of poetry are thus expressly written in ambiguity and, potentially, in resistance to rationality.

Throughout the *Anotaciones*, then, the connotative contours of *claridad* and *osadía* [clarity and daring] operate as a master image upon which Herrera maps various conflicting and contradictory ideas. Compelling and coherent readings have emerged when critics have prioritised one over the other. For instance, Rachel Schmidt has very effectively demonstrated how the concept of the battlefield 'as the proving ground of personal virtue' (14) is applied throughout the work to the field of literature, particularly in Herrera's development of a metaphor for literary imitation as the 'taking of Italian spoils'.[28] And most recently, Middlebrook, following Patricia Parker, has read Herrera's poetics of the lyric in the context of sixteenth-century anxieties regarding the possible effeminacy of the pursuit of letters, concluding that Herrera advocates a new 'poetics of masculinity' against the effeminate affectation of *sprezzatura*. But more difficult to sustain is Mid-

---

[27]   See Ptolemy, *Almagest*, trans. and ed. G.J. Toomer (London: Duckworth, 1984), p. 36.

[28]   See Rachel Schmidt, 'Herrera's Concept of Imitation as the Taking of Italian Spoils', *Caliope*, 1 (1995), 12–26. Interestingly the metaphor itself is a 'spoil' in Herrera's own struggles to assimilate the Italian theorists. Much has been written on the sources of Herrera's *Anotaciones*, although Bienvenido Morros's scholarship is unsurpassed in this area. See, especially, *Las polémicas literarias*.

dlebrook's argument for the 'remasculinization of the Spanish language'[29] itself; against it: the archetypal feminine object status of the solar trope, but also its anticipation in Medina's culminating image of the Spanish language, in all its beauty and splendour, as a radiant Helen of Troy, snatched from barbarian darkness. Helen, of course, had a central role to play in Neoplatonic interpretations of the Trojan war, representing that worldly beauty, the imperfect copy of the form of the beautiful, which inhabits the material world and entices souls (that is, the Greeks) to abandon their true abode and to enter a conflictive existence for which war is the most appropriate metaphor.[30] Whether seen, therefore, as the passive, idealised female of amorous lyric or the powerful instigator of ambiguous heroic endeavour, language is central to the imperial order, but cannot be active in its own destiny: *i veremos estenderse la magestad del lenguage español* [...] *hasta las últimas provincias* [and we will see the majesty of the Spanish language extend as far as the farthest provinces]. The extension of linguistic sovereignty beyond the borders of the nation state hangs on passionate 'buenos ingenios', like Herrera, brave enough to intervene.

Rising above mediocrity ...

[Herrera] *'understood everything about poetry except how to do it.'*[31]

Notwithstanding a more positive, recent surge of interest,[32] Bianchini's provocative evaluation has been an unsettling shadow narrative of contemporary criticism's emphasis on the *Anotaciones* over the poetry. I would like to qualify, if not counter, Bianchini's view with a brief consideration of Herrera's 1582 anthology, entitled *Algunas obras*, perhaps an intentional echo of the first edition of Boscán and Garcilaso. The motifs of the *Anotaciones* persist in the poems of *Algunas obras*, but within a radical embracing and abandonment of the macrostructure of Petrarchan *canzoniere*, these achieve an even greater symbolic scope and an enhanced range of interpretation.

29   See Middlebrook, *Imperial Lyric*, pp. 155–56, and Parker, 'Virile Style', in *Premodern Sexualities*, eds Louise Fradenburg and Carla Freccero (New York: Routledge, 1996), pp. 199–222.
30   This Neoplatonic allegorical meaning is implied in Plotinus (*Enneads* 1.6.8. 16–21), generally considered to be the founder of Neoplatonism (204/5–270). Proclus, the last major Greek Platonic philosopher (410/12–485), and author of many Platonic commentaries, offers a similar interpretation of the Trojan war in the second part of his essay on *The Republic*. See Anne D.R. Sheppard *Studies on the 5th and 6th Essays of Proclus' Commentary on the Republic* (Goettingen: Vandenhoeck and Ruprecht, 1980), pp. 92–95.
31   See Bianchini, 'Herrera: Questions and Contradictions', 65. The specific charge against Herrera's poetry is its lack of 'afectos', glossed as an inability to move the reader.
32   The 500th anniversary of Herrera's death in 1997 produced two key publications (*Las anotaciones de Fernando de Herrera: doce estudios* and a special issue of *Insula*, 610) which was the catalyst for a resurgence of interest in Herrera and his work.

The patterns of repetition and contradiction that pervade the *Anotaciones* are played out across the collection in the tighter space of sonnet fragments, thereby undermining, in theory, the pre-eminence assigned to textual wholeness and order. However, the sonnet form is lauded by Herrera in the *Anotaciones* in particular because, in its reading (or enactment), centripetal constraints can be counteracted by less secure, centrifugal significances. In fact, as the opening poem of the anthology demonstrates, the inward-looking subject matter of metapoetic reflection is opened up precisely because the sonnet collapses under Neoplatonic ascent and fails to live up to the established set of specifications of the Petrarchan proemium. Unlike the *imitatio vitae* of Petrarch and Boscán, the poem is not a palinode, nor does it announce a narratological trajectory that will end in repentance, or transcendent resolution.[33]

The sonnet reads:

> Osé y temí, mas pudo la osadía
> tanto que desprecié el temor cobarde;
> subí a do el fuego más m'enciende i arde
> cuanto más la esperança se desvía.
>
> Gasté en error la edad florida mía;
> aora veo el daño, pero tarde:
> que ya mal puede ser qu'el seso guarde
> a quien s'entrega ciego a su porfía.
>
> Tal vez pruevo (mas, ¿qué me vale?) alcarme
> del grave peso que mi cuello oprime,
> aunque falta a la poca fuerça el hecho.
>
> Sigo al fin mi furor, porque mudarme
> no es onra ya, ni justo que s'estime
> tan mal de quien tan bien rindió su pecho.[34]

[I dared and I feared; my daring so strong that I disdained cowardly fear; the more I climbed to where the fire enflames and burns me, the more I lost track of hope. I wasted the flower of my youth in error; I see the damage now, but too late: for the mind is powerless to safeguard the man who delivers himself blindly to daring. Perhaps I could try (but what good would it do me?) to

---

[33] Much has been written on the vexed issue of Herrera's Petrarchism. See, for instance, the differing emphases of Santiago Fernández Mosquera, 'De nuevo sobre la consideración de "Algunas obras de Herrera" como cancionero petrarquista', *Insula-Revista de Letras y Ciencias Humanas*, 610 (1997), 14–17; and Navarrete, *Orphans of Petrarch*, p. 170.

[34] This opening sonnet was included by Lope de Vega in his *Laurel de Apolo*. All poems from Herrera's *Algunas obras* are cited according to Cuevas García's edition, *Poesía castellana original completa*.

break free from the great weight that bears down on my neck, although I lack even the slight force needed to see that through. I follow my own madness along to the end, because there would be no honour now in changing, nor would it be right to hold in such low esteem the one who surrendered his heart to one so exalted.]

The attitude of 'melancholic heroism' which is central to the construction of the Petrarchan male subject, and usually associated with frustrated desire and loss, is prominently overturned in the opening lines of this sonnet in a dynamics of resistance and contradiction that owes much to the antithetical narcissism of courtly lyric. The structural, binary tensions relate to the dilemma of the affective being in a context of dynamic, belated, self-creation and subjugation. The packaging of the past in preterites is revealed to be misleading in verse 3. The intrusive present tense interpolates a subject who *appears* to speak from stasis; but even this present condition is itself temporally and spatially uncertain. The immediate experience which is being recounted is the direct result of having acted on *osadía* [daring] over *temor* [fear] and of the subsequent, but now simultaneous, slipping away of hope (*más – cuanto más*; 3–4) into a future that is destined to repeat the failed aspirations of the past. Memory, operating a retrospective, perverse *carpe diem* through visualisation (not conventionally of a beloved seen in absence, but of the speaker's own youthful day 'not seized'), activates a temporal circularity that is contingent upon compelling verbal self-expression. The creative continuum traced around the quatrains reinforces Carruther's connecting of memory and strategies of invention,[35] and so extends its operation beyond the private.

As Navarrete has pointed out,[36] the allusive context of Herrera's sonnets forces a circular reading that opens up multiple sites of ambiguity, challenging and drawing the reader into the meaning-making process. In this context the first word 'osé' [I dared] is a potent intertextual trigger. Ruíz Pérez identifies a motif of 'vuelo osado' [daring flight] here which pervades both poetic anthologies, the *Algunas obras* and the 1619 *Versos*, where it is more explicitly connected to the 'mitos asencionales' [ascending myths] of Icarus and Phaeton – irrefutable evidence, he argues convincingly, of the thematisation of poetic consciousness. The female object of desire plays a strong emblematic role in this analysis 'como [materialización de] la suprema belleza perseguida por el poeta y emparentada con el sol, es astro de Apolo, dios de la poesía y padre de Faetón, el audaz aspirante a regir el carro de la luz, elevándose por encima de sus émulos, aun con la conciencia de lo arriesgado de su empresa'.[37] Middlebrook

35   See Mary Carruthers, *The Craft of Thought: Meditation, Rhetoric and the Making of Images. 400–1200* (Cambridge: Cambridge University Press, 1998), p. 7.

36   *Orphans of Petrarch*, p. 170.

37   [as (a concretization of) the supreme beauty pursued by the poet and equated with the sun; (she) is the star of Apollo, god of poetry and father of Phaethon, who dared to guide the chariot of

applies this Phaethon analogy directly to the poet's ascent in Sonnet 1 wherein 'the function of light and its energy for the sequence is established'.[38] But *Luz* is not yet figured in the sequence (we have to wait until Sonnet IV), and her or 'its' substitution by 'fuego' [fire] defies harmonic expectations. To adapt Walker's 'verbal dissonance' theory, it is not so much the 'wrong word at the right time', but the right word in the wrong place.[39] The spatial deictic 'do' [where] underlines the illusion of decipherable Neoplatonic ascent only to set up irreconcilable tensions along an axis of similarity and difference.[40]

Heroic 'daring' in Sonnet I forces a confrontation with the dark side of the sun; sexuality making of the speaking subject an incandescent material object, on fire with passion, morally blind, and irrationally finding comfort in a *servitium amoris* that signals surrender (final tercet). To rise upwards is to overcome resistance, to transcend materiality; but to descend, to be weighted down, as Arnheim reminds us, 'is to surrender to the pull from below, and, therefore, is experienced as passive compliance'.[41] As we shall see, willing submission in Herrera's sonnets becomes, throughout the collection, the path of least resistance. Icarus and Phaethon are persistently negated in the dead weight of Sisyphus (here and in Sonnet XXVI where the persistent renewal of futile ascent is couched as a credo to suffering), elsewhere in the castigations of the rebellious Giants, or trapped between Scylla and Charybdis at the mercy of the Sirens – the first node ends, in Sonnet VI with the verse: *ni osar me vale en el temor perdido* [nor is there any point in daring when I am so lost in fear]. The conflicted subject emerges as the non-transforming centre of gravity in Sonnet I; anti-Platonic certainly, but also fundamentally anti-Aristotelian. Attempts to transcend the imitation (limitation) of human nature are ontologically doomed.

Throughout the love poetry of *Algunas obras* the dichotomous domains of fear (*temor*) and daring (*osadía*) interact through a set of mutually implicated elements which externalise a process of dialogical self-creation. The key components emerge from antithetical categories of the pure and the corrupt: fear that the pure is fragile and always at risk, that the corrupt dares to threaten basic

the Sun, setting himself above all who would emulate him, fully aware of the risks involved in the enterprise]. See Pedro Ruíz Pérez, 'Mitología del ascenso en los sonetos herrerianos', *Insula*, 610 (1997), 6–9 (8).

38   See Middlebrook, *Imperial Lyric*, pp. 168–70 who has interesting things to say about daring as display and the image of noble subjection in this sonnet.

39   See Steven F. Walker, 'The Wrong Word at the Right Time: Verbal Dissonance and the Social Function of Mannerist Hermeticism', in *Proceedings of the Xth Congress of the International Comparative Literature Association*, eds Anna Balakian, James J. Wilhelm *et al.* (New York: Garland, 1985), pp. 582–86.

40   Herrera's commentary on Garcilaso's Sonnet XXXIII glosses the poet's use of the verb 'subir' [to ascend] in terms of a 'camino estrecho de la virtud' [a narrow path of virtue].

41   See Rudolph Arnheim, *Art and Visual Perception: A Psychology of the Creative Eye* (Berkeley: University of California Press, 1954), p. 188.

principles of order, and, most challenging, that their relational character (the fact that each derives its meaning from co-existence with the other) denies authority and autonomy to both. These issues, ethically and epistemologically fraught, inform the speaker's explicit engagement with the myth of Daedalus and Icarus in Sonnet XLIII:

> ¡O, cómo buela en alto mi desseo,
> sin que de su osadía el mal fin tema!;
> que ya las puntas de sus alas quema
> donde ningún remedio al triste veo.
>
> Que mal podrá alabarse del trofeo
> si, estando ufano en la región suprema
> del fuego ardiente, en esta vanda extrema
> cae por su siniestro devaneo.
>
> Devía en mi fortuna ser exemplo
> Dédalo, no aquel joven atrevido,
> que dio al cerúleo piélago su nombre.
>
> Mas ya tarde mis lástimas contemplo.
> Pero si muero, porque osé, perdido,
> jamás a igual empresa osó algún ombre.

[Daring desire ascends on high, fearless of the tragic end! wing tips already on fire where I see no solution to sorrow. Tragic that desire should boast of victory when being proud in the upper realm of burning fire comes before a fall to this lower land – pulled down by its fateful affair. I should have drawn my destiny in Daedalus, not followed the example of that reckless youth who gave his name to the cerulean sea. But too late I contemplate my pain. And if I die, because I dared, already lost; (I know) there was never a man, nor daring, like me, like mine.]

There is no illusion of experiential unity in this sonnet. Rather, several relatively interconnected 'I' positions speak from, or are seen in, fluctuating temporal and spatial spheres. In the opening quatrain, for instance, the subject's cognitive and perceptual powers are split across two oppositional manifestations of selfhood: one dominant, active, desiring ('deseo', 1); the other dependent, passive, observing ('veo', 4). This perverse dyadic interaction, in which the self is positioned against its own erotic aspirations, articulates the radical nature of *eros*'s protagonism, while rendering its revolution-in-progress (already) impossible. Despite the ecstatic tonal implications with which the flight motif is introduced, strategies of self-deferral and self-distancing appear to deny any possibility of humanity transcended, exalted or rarefied. The myth of Daedalus and Icarus, which will make its intertextual presence felt more forcibly as the

poem unfolds, charges the speaker's sustained act of contemplation with a dynamism whose value is citational and, therefore, uncomfortably relative. The
first quatrain initiates a circular process (from 'ya [...] donde ningún remedio
[...] veo', 4, to 'ya tarde mis lástimas contemplo', 12, echoing 6 of the opening
sonnet) through which self-knowledge and retrospective revelation can produce
only a problematic paradigm for stasis.

From the outset Herrera's transgressive Icarian flight, with all its contingent
codifications of poetic daring, creativity and immortality, offers no secure base
from which the speaker can negotiate frustration, shattered hopes, lost time
and a future that is foreclosing. Mythical interplay forces a reframing of the
relationship between subjectivity and temporality. Desire is spoken from
within an immediate present, but this self-forming speech-act, which depends
on memory constituted upon literary reminiscences, functions outside the immediate temporal context. Timing, that is both literal and symbolically analogous is, therefore, everything and nothing to the speaker. But it is also here
and, yet, really nowhere at all. For it is in the spatial terms of an image-based
narrative of desire's collapse from ethereal heights to a world of concrete reality that the (Edenic-like) tragedy of human finitude is most effectively conveyed
(5–8). '*Esta* vanda extrema' [*This* lower land] is not an impartial transcript of
a realm of essence,[42] but a contingent reality in which dreams are connected to
disappointments, ambitions struggle against material limitations, and human,
historicised options are limited. Against this, the 'beyondness' of intertextuality, and the inherent 'doubleness' of the Icarus myth, allow extreme polarities
to sustain an enabling ambiguity. As a relational model of selfhood, identification with Icarus makes of the subject an all too solid 'vanitas' object, but the
drama of Icarus falling has a transformational, liminal dimension which embraces the temporal and the spatial, the textual and the extra-textual, the material and the metaphysical. It is in this more fluid space that the speaker invites
us to read the present 'historically'; and to call into question monolithic assumptions about the past.

The essence of intertextuality, as Vanhoozer reminds us, is that 'it allows free
association with voices across time and beyond canonical boundaries'.[43] Just
some of the voices 'already read' in Herrera's poem include previous engage-
ments with the Minoan flight myth, such as references in Horace, *Odes* 1.3,
2.20, and 4.20; the more sustained narrative treatments of Ovid (*Ars Amatoria*
2.17–98 and the *Metamorphoses* 8.183–235); Italian sonnets by Tansillo and
Spanish allusions, both explicit and implicit, in poems by Garcilaso de la Vega

42   Costner, disputed by Cuevas García, reads this as a specific reference to Spain (*Poesía
castellana completa*, p. 410, n. 7).
43   See Kevin J. Vanhoozer, *Is There a Meaning in This Text? The Bible, the Reader, and the
Morality of Literary Knowledge* (Grand Rapids: Zondervan, 1998), pp. 134–35.

and Gutierre de Cetina.[44] Like the labyrinth itself, the symbolic associations mediated via these interlocking allusions constitute a multicursal maze of contradictory values. The Horatian text (I.3), which informs Ovid and is generally considered to have inspired the psychological context of Tansillo's poems, is framed as an elegant *prompentikon* (farewell poem) conventionally addressed to Virgil and the ship which will convey him on his journey. This is but a springboard to a more sweeping denunciation of progress which climaxes in an ethical meditation on human presumption, stupidity and sinfulness. Reader expectations of the *prompentikon* genre are defeated in a sequence of three individual mythological *exempla* employed by Horace to illustrate the collective audacity of the human race:

> Audax omnia perpeti
> gens humana ruit per vetitum nefas,
>   Audax Iapeti genus
> ignem fraude mala gentibus intulit [...]
> expertus vaccum Daedalus aera
>   pennis non homini datis,
> Perrupit Acheronta Herculeus labor.
>   Nil mortalibus ardui est;
> caelum ipsum petimus stultitia neque
>   per nostrum patimur scelus
> iracunda Iovem ponere fulmina. (I. 3, 25–28; 34–40)

[Daring all, humankind rushes on through sin and the forbidden; daring and disobedient, Prometheus provided humanity with fire [...] Daedalus tried the empty air on wings denied to man, Herculean labour broke through Acheron. Nothing is beyond the human being; our stupidity scales the very heavens and our sin keeps active the angry thunderbolts of Jove.]

In this Ode, Horace exploits the figure of Daedalus, along with that of Prometheus, Hercules and, implicitly, the Titans, in order to implicate a particular 'self' in a universal scheme of fallen humanity. Daring is the catalyst which commits human beings to persistent renewal of transgressive action, to symbolic, self-determined and, ultimately, frustrated, acts of defiance of death. In opposition to this, Horace's poetic self, transformed in ironic vein into a swan in Odes 2.20, can transcend earthly limitations and, in a fatidic flight more celebrated than Icarus's, is permitted a positive turn towards eternity. Metamorphosis is, for Horace as for many artists, a potent symbol of subjective creation, a relinquishing of boundaries, that locates poetic self-becoming beyond material being.

---

[44]   Joseph Fucilla offers a succinct survey of these models in 'Etapas en el desarrollo del mito de Icaro en el renacimiento y en el siglo de oro', *Hispanófila*, 3 (1960), 1–34.

If metamorphosis is the reframing that shifts the evaluative consequences of daring from negative to positive in the Horatian Odes, then it is precisely non-metamorphosis in Ovid – its substitution by the incomplete invention of Daedalus (whose wax-feather wing contraption turns out to be a flawed imitation of nature) – that renders the audacity of the *homo faber* ambiguous.[45] Ovid's rewriting in the *Metamorphoses* of his own earlier version of the myth (*Ars Amatoria*), especially the development of the character of Daedalus-artisan,[46] seems to codify poetic achievement as the transgression of boundaries, while simultaneously suspending the Aristotelian law of non-contradiction. Combining knowledge and imitation with invention, Daedalus emblematises the challenge and conflicts at the heart of artistic creation. He is a symbol of the human imagination at its most heroic, but also a paternalistic model of moderation. In Daedalus the transcendent aspirations of the sublime style co-exist in context with an authorised decorum.

These complex intertextual tensions inform the reader's engagement with the tercets of Herrera's poem. Daedalus's entry into the frame at verse 10 is deliberately postponed and temporally duplicitous. The speaker's calculated attempt to bring order to present chaos via a conjectured transformation of analogical models (a swapping of Icarus for Daedalus) initiates a disjunctive strategy in which general poetic memory seems to be at variance with the speaker's asynchronous re-mythologising of his own past. In this fluid and highly subjective space, the temporal closure of 'should have' ('devía') is momentarily meaningless. 'Remembering' Daedalus on two distinct planes, speaker and reader collaborate in the illusion of a parallel reality (a 'what if') that might have been. But Daedalus is the speaker's path not taken (9–10), and identification with him would only have led, like the labyrinth itself, to frustrated attempts to locate an identifiable centre. Icarus, quite literally for all his tragic flaws, emerges the more stable model of poetic self-creation (10–11); and analogy with the defiant youth is secured by 'mis lástimas' [my pain], bringing the poem full circle.

Reflecting on the fate of a substituted self in the past allows the speaker to anticipate and contemplate his own death in the future. The analogical strategy, as in Horace, is a powerful affirmation of the individual's relationship to col-

---

[45] For a survey and analysis of the varying interpretations of the nature of metamorphosis in the myth of Daedalus and Icarus in Ovid's *Metamorphoses*, see Marjorie Hoefmans, 'Myth into Reality: The Metamorphosis of Daedalus and Icarus (Ovid, *Met.* 8, 183–235)', *L'Antiquité Classique*, LXIII (1994), 137–60.

[46] As well as several additions in the extended narrative of the *Metamorphoses*, there are two striking differences between the two versions: the Daedalus of the *Metamorphoses* does not ask Jupiter for forgiveness before embarking upon two activities which violate the natural order – changing the condition/form of the human being and transgressing the forbidden celestial sphere; Icarus of the *Metamorphoses* is silenced (in the *Ars Amatoria* Icarus is more vividly drawn and calls out to his father before Daedalus calls to him).

lective human experience; underlining the participation of a particular self in a universal scheme. The flip side is the fact that death subordinates individual agency to universal laws; thereby reinforcing the anonymity of common mortality. The Icarian model is crucial in this context, facilitating an emerging self through and in language that is structured by the eternalising potential of art. There is no final integration of death in the poem, nor reconciliation; rather a 'tense' assertion that this daring desire which determines the speaker's humanity also sets him apart from all other men. 'Contemplo' [I contemplate; 12], which could have been the ultimate figure of stasis in the poem, telescopes the plurality of the trans-temporal narrative into an intrusive present textual moment, giving some power back to the poetic 'I'/('eye'), and conveying the re-actualising capacity of language when it is effectively deployed in heroic and emulative action.

Mobilising metaphor …

'Herrera may have traveled the Platonic staircase in reverse'[47]

Bianchini suspects that the Neoplatonic substance of Herrera's poetry has been exaggerated: 'in support of a definition of Herrera's love poetry as Neoplatonic in character there are only seven sonnets and one *canción* in which there occur a kind of metahuman transfiguration of the beloved'.[48] The issue has certainly split commentators. Coster, Parker and Cuevas García are representative of those who have identified a Platonising direction;[49] while others, such as López Bueno and Maglione, recognise Herrera's familiarity with the most striking ideas of Neoplatonism,[50] but deny that this informs his poetry at any significant

---

47 Bianchini, 'Herrera: Questions and Contradictions', 61.

48 Bianchini, 'Herrera: Questions and Contradictions', 60. Bianchini (like Maglione) develops the arguments of Gabriel Celaya, *Exploración de la poesía* (Barcelona: Seix Barral, 1964), p. 33: 'ha buscado la contemplación pura pero lo que encuentra es la pasión turbia' [(Herrera) sought pure contemplation, but found murky passion]. See Sabatino Maglione, 'Fernando de Herrera and Neoplatonism', *Hispanófila*, 69 (1980), 4–71.

49 See Adolphe Coster, *Algunas obras de Fernando de Herrera* (Paris: Champion, 1908), p. 55; A.A. Parker, 'Ideal Love and Neoplatonism', in *The Philosophy of Love in Spanish Literature*, esp. pp. 41–61; and Cuevas García, *Poesía castellana*, esp. pp. 20–22.

50 Central Platonic arguments as expounded by Marcilio Ficino in his translation and commentary of Plato's *Symposium* of 1469, and by Pietro Bembo in his treatise on love, *Gli Asolani* (1505), were popularised by Castiglione in *Il Cortegiano* [the Courtier], written *c*.1516 and first printed in 1528, and by León Hebreo in his *Dialoghi d'amore* [Dialogues of Love], 1535. Maglione argues against Coster's assumption that Herrera's comments on Neoplatonic love in the *Anotaciones* are based solely on the *Cortegiano* (the famous exposition of Neoplatonic theory placed in the mouth of Bembo at the end of the last book, IV, 51–73, contains the conceit of 'spiritual eyes' which informs Garcilaso's Sonnet VIII). Maglione argues that the three kinds of love described in the *Anotaciones* conform with Hebreo's division of love ('Fernando de Herrera and Neoplatonism').

philosophical level.[51] Terry seems to have a foot in each camp. He identifies a strong sense of ennoblement through suffering which recalls *cancionero* insistence upon the visceral effects of the speaker's passion, and which undermines the notion of an easy Platonic ascent (Sonnet XLVI, in which desire devours the speaker's heart in a re-enactment of the punishment of Prometheus, might have been called forth in evidence); but he also argues that beauty is often given its full weight of Platonic meaning. Ultimately, for Terry (and others), Herrera's poetry remains firmly attached to Neoplatonic values.[52]

What all of these conflicting views have in common is a shared recognition that Herrera's speaker has at least a foothold on the Neoplatonic ladder. The highest aspiration of Renaissance Neoplatonism (which coalesces in its development with the conventions of courtly love) is the coupling of the soul with the heavenly beauty, which is attained on the final rung of the ladder (the seventh grade, or 'sabbath of divine love' as Pico called it). This is articulated via the symbolic transformation of an inherently circular and static schema into a systemic mobile and mystical ascent. These 'ascending steps' might be summed up as follows: from contemplation of particular beauty; to generalisation of universal beauty; followed by introversion; then intellectualisation (the senses and imagination are placed in abeyance under the command of reason); and finally, the contemplation of the summit of all beauty which leads to the merging of the individual intellect with the universal. In short, Neoplatonic love represents a perfect example of value transfer, a seemingly closed circuit which can be opened up across the poetic collection as a form of extended metaphor. Herrera plays with Neoplatonism's linguistic system as a poet, not as a philosopher, and designates its signs accordingly. Metaphorical extension becomes, therefore, in *Algunas obras* a mechanism for empowering language; a process that enables an even more anxious exploration of the larger project of linguistic renovation that was announced in the *Anotaciones*. In this context, attempts to read the Neoplatonic ladder into Herrera's profane love poetry are misleading.[53] Herrera's poetry shows no promulgating interest in Platonism as a system of thought. In his emphasis on the human rather than on the metaphysical aspect of love, Herrera is not seeking to identify or explain the nature of reality, but rather to interrogate how our individual and collective connections with reality, embedded in language,

---

[51] López Bueno denies that there is any Neoplatonic ascent (*La poética cultista*, pp. 49–51); while Maglione argues that the point of departure for Herrera's allusions to Neoplatonic concepts, including truncated ascent towards the perception of the highest beauty, is prevailingly aesthetic ('Fernando de Herrera and Neoplatonism', esp. the conclusions drawn on 70–71).

[52] See Terry, *Seventeenth-Century Spanish Poetry*, ch. 1, pp. 22–28 and ch. 2, pp. 49–52.

[53] Even those critics who deny Neoplatonism in Herrera and concede that the speaker desires beauty incarnate, rather than Beauty's self, allow the speaker to ascend to the second grade before he is inevitably flummoxed by an inability to displace the image of the particular beauty of the beloved with a universal conceit.

at a specific historical moment (but also in any time or place), are more complex, multilayered and, consequently, even more vital.

As we have seen, Herrera's transcendent aspirations for the Spanish language are emblematised in the *Anotaciones*, not without a degree of uneasy ambivalence, within an overarching allegorical frame which prioritises hyperbolic heliocentric metaphors. However, within the 'theatre of desire' that is the Petrarchan love poem,[54] emphasis shifts away from the more abstract, theoretical considerations of linguistic sovereignty, towards the self-defining struggle of the individual (male) poet, who has to speak himself (and language) into being, in the very act of articulating desire for the unattainable. 'Contemplation' in this context of infinite deferral works against the conventional Neoplatonic paradigm, subverting the terms of its synchronic unity. Rather than signalling the apprehension of beauty severed from the body – the catalyst for a relational reciprocity of matter and spirit that is sublimely envisaged –'contemplation' is made to connect with the negative dichotomies of conventional Petrarchism (absence/presence; silence/eloquence; passivity/activity; and, of course, fear/daring) and so thrives on the ambiguous relationship of spirit (soul, consciousness) to matter (the body).[55] Just as praising Beatrice beatifies Dante (Beatrice/beatitude) and idealising Laura legitimises Petrarch (Laura/laurel), *contemplating* 'Luz' is, at its most superficial level in Herrera's poetry, a straightforward act of artistic self-creation, wherein the question of ontology is reduced to its most fundamental terms (I and you). The transformation of the poetic object of amorous adoration into a composite symbol which conflates metaphysical principles, human desire and a broadly iconic anthropomorphic characterisation is not, therefore, in itself, a strategy that might shatter the expectations of Herrera's readers. What differentiates Herrera's love poetry, then, is not that erotic loss might result in aesthetic gain (it is, after all, the absence of Laura in Petrarch's *canzoniere* that creates the space of desire that engenders the poetic process), but the way in which the temporal (and sometimes spatial) anxieties articulated by the speaker betray broader concerns: for the belated condition of the vernacular in the writer's present; and for the fragile and intermediary nature of individual human existence at any point or place in time.

The introduction of Petrarchan lyric in Golden Age Spain accompanied both the promotion of Castilian and the political expansion of the crown in the Americas. A self-defining male desire that focused on female beauty was symbolically coupled with the aspirations of empire; and the ultimate goal, posses-

---

54   See Gary F. Waller, 'Struggling into Discourse: The Emergence of Renaissance Women's Writing', in *Silent But for the Word: Tudor Women as Patrons, Translators and Writers of Religious Works*, ed. Margaret Patterson Hannay (Kent: Kent State University Press, 1985), pp. 238–56 (p. 242).

55   As Robert Durling has pointed out, 'critical tension between contemplative form and sexual content is a major theme of the *Rime sparse*'. See *Petrarch's Lyric Poems*, p. 20.

sion of the beloved, translated often into colonial ownership. The consummation of passion in Herrera's third *Elegy*, for instance, is made to coincide, allusively speaking, with the Battle of Lepanto, thereby underlining the Petrarchan pursuit of beauty as a strategic site of heroic endeavour. Cervantes, who lost the power of a hand in that battle, would parody such pretensions in the form of a protagonist whose adventures are framed with praise for a beloved who is far removed from the Petrarchan ideal. The co-dependence of the *Anotaciones* and *Algunas obras,* however, suggests that challenging the imperial project *per se* was not on Herrera's combined theoretical/practical agenda. What he does interrogate is whether the Spanish language itself, and those scholars who would wield it creatively, are up to the task. Working within the thematic and structural parameters of the Petrarchan *canzoniere*, Herrera can convey the writer's struggle to transform the inadequacies of this language into a compelling performative text, while also integrating confrontation with certain failure into a positive concept of self. Cultural pretensions are thus unsettled, rather than denied, in a process of unregulated reinterpretation which plays a pivotal role in the formation of aesthetic identity that is also referential in political terms. The writer, as interpretive reader, generates broader anxieties about the future out of the subjective reconfiguration of an individual amorous 'history'.

A key element in this strategy is the dislocation of any sense of an authorising centre, in the speaker's present, which could validate the project. The speaker's role is portrayed as unique and prominent, but it is forged in shifting, multiple, mostly mythical, profiles which undermine the power of privileged perspective. Forward, upward, movement in the poetry allegorises the potential for progress across several interdependent contexts. But the perpetual redefinition of agency, the rearticulations of memory, the circular motion of intertextual allusion, all point to a poetic universe of unstable orbit in which even *Luz* has no fixed abode.

In his lyric anthology, then, Herrera writes within and against established patterns of love poetry, including the conventional confluence of Neoplatonic ascent and the 'flight' of the aspiring poet, or even poesy itself, by seizing the subject positions usually constructed in mythical archetypes, such as Icarus and Phaethon, and complicating their potential idealism with material matter(s). This is very clearly the case in Sonnet XLIII, discussed above, but it is also evident in Sonnet XLV. 'Clara suave luz, alegre i bella' [Clear, gentle light, joyful and beautiful] unproblematically designated 'a breakthrough into Neoplatonism' by Parker.[56] As in many of Herrera's sonnets, the speaker of this poem interrogates the problem of erotic passion in terms of its basic metaphor, fire, and by extension via the Petrarchan antithetical motif of 'icy fire':

---

[56]   See Parker, *Philosophy of Love*, p. 58.

Clara, suäve luz, alegre i bella,
que los safiros i color del cielo
teñís de la esmeralda con el velo
que resplandece en una i otra estrella;

divino resplandor, pura centella,
por quien, libre mi alma, en alto buelo
las alas roxas bate i huye el suelo,
ardiendo vuestro dulce fuego en ella:

Si yo, no sólo abraso el pecho mío,
mas la tierra i el cielo, i en mi llama
doi principio immortal de fuego eterno,

¿por qu'el rigor de vuestro antiguo frío
no podré ya encender? ¿por qué no inflama
mi estío ardiente a vuestro elado ivierno?   [Sonnet XLV]

[Clear, gentle light, joyful and beautiful, who dyes the sapphire-coloured sky
with the emerald veil that shines in both your stars; divine splendour, pure
spark, for you my soul, freed, flies high, fleeing the earth, with red wings
beating and your sweet fire burning within it; (But) if I burn beyond my
breast, igniting the earth and sky, and can feel the beginning of immortal fire
in my flames, why can I not yet set fire to your constant and callous coldness?
Why does my searing summer not burn your frozen winter?]

Characteristic Platonic conceits establish an organising frame in the quatrains
centred upon an implied optics of desire. Divine beauty is experienced upon
sight of the beloved and stirs within the speaker a subconscious memory of his
divine origins, impelling his soul to transcend the material limitations of an
imprisoning body and to soar towards the freedom of the celestial realm. But
when the apostrophising turns inward in the tercets and the speaker reflects
critically on the utter futility of the enterprise (the fact that the present perfect
moment is an unsustainable illusion), the frame collapses under the weight of
persistent negation. The metaphorical formulation of the lady as the source of
cosmic light in a microcosmic world of love veers uncontrollably off-course
when the speaker's 'Platonic' identity shifts into the territory of Phaethon with
all its devastating macrocosmic consequences.

There are more dynamic boundaries breached in this poem than the conventional dividing line between physical and spiritual love. The symbolic mapping
of Phaeton's reckless ascent (uncontrollable, limitless desire), his fall to earth
(failure), and untimely demise (finite power of human beings), against the rational thrust of the quatrains, constitutes a new 'blended' conceptual space out
of which emerges meaning that is antagonistic to the dominant Neoplatonic
'message' of the quatrains. Phaethon was, after all, considered the very em-

bodiment of unreason by Renaissance Christian moralists; often equated with
Lucifer's attempts to get too close to God (Isaiah 14.12). Of course, there is
always the possibility of redemption in aesthetic terms. The 'eternal fire' can be
usefully recuperated in the context of compensatory art. But, ultimately, the
presence of such a discordant mythical intertext underpins the irreconcilability
of the amorous relationship, and contaminates timeless union with a strong,
subjective sense of a goal that is always out of reach.

This paradoxical interdependency of oppositional forces (conveyed via a
sustained ice/fire conceit) is explored in many poems of the collection. It provides
the framework for an ascent towards 'la luz pura' [pure light] in *Elegy* V which
collapses explicitly in the face of language inadequacy:

> La fría nieve m'abrasó en tu fuego
> la llama que busqué me hizo ielo;
> el desdén me valió, no el tierno ruego.
>
> Subí, sin procurallo, hasta el cielo,
> – que se perdió en tal hecho mi osadía –;
> cuando m'aventuré, me vi en el suelo (*Elegy* V, 22–30)

[Cold snow burned me in your fire, the flame I sought turned me to ice; your
disdain was of more use to me than tender pleading. I soared towards heaven
without reaching it, losing my nerve in the deed, and grounded when I dared]

In the sonnets a sense of significance beyond the amorous struggle often belies
a circular, claustrophobic rhyme and reasoning. Sonnet LXXII, for instance,
sets the lovers outside the norm of the transforming power of desire (and, indeed,
disdain) in order to keep destructive polarities in splendid isolation:

> Amor en mi se muestra todo fuego,
> i en las entrañas de mi Luz es nieve,
> fuego no hay, que ella no torne nieve,
> ni nieve, que no mude yo en mi fuego.
>
> La fría zona abraso con mi fuego,
> la ardiente mi Luz vuelve helada nieve,
> pero no puedo yo encender su nieve,
> ni elle entibiar la fuerza de mi fuego.
>
> Contrastan igualmente hielo y llama,
> que de otra suerte fuera el mundo hielo,
> o su máquina toda viva llama.
>
> Más fuera; porque ya resuelto en hielo
> o el corazón desvanecido en llama,
> ni temiera mi llama, ni su hielo.

[In me love is all fire; within my Luz it is all snow; there is no fire that she turns not to ice, nor snow which I turn not to fire. I burn cold zones with fire, my Luz turns zones of heat to frozen snow. But I cannot set her snow on fire, nor can she cool my fire's glow. Ice and fire are equally opposed, if not the world would be all ice; or all its structure living flame. But more than that; were my heart reduced to ice or hers dissolved in flame, she would not fear my flame, nor I her ice.]

Parker argues that the technical mastery of this sonnet is let down by an insubstantial conceptual argumentation which fails to follow through on the implications of a dualistic philosophy of body and soul.[57] But it is this very gap between the linguistic signs of the sonnet and any corresponding philosophical 'scene' which exposes its emotional complexity. The poem is self-consciously construed as a linguistic house in order, its reiterated metaphors measured, their effects coldly calculated. Resignation rather than rebellion seems to be the order of the day. Yet the sonnet's patterns of simultaneity, which promote a status quo grounded in the harmonious irreconcilability of opposites, challenge the credibility of traditional Renaissance value systems. A site of shameless self-deception, the poem's tight interlocking textual order reveals a restricted language that is not stripped down, but built up in metre, rhetorical artifice, and chiastic connections. In a novel subjective take on the familiar *adynata* topos, the speaker must seek infinite separation so as not to turn all creation upside down (the 'coldness' of Luz is, after all, the poem's perverse point of departure). Sonnet LXXII draws the reader into its own enactment and what has been considered an abstract response to a codified system is, in fact, a subjective construction of alterity – a zone 'controlled' by frustrated aspirations (a transfigured stasis is still static after all) and by underlying erotic (and chaotic) impulses.

In Sonnet XXXVIII *eros* is required to play against type, and the lyric persona is cast as a bit player, secondary (once again) to rhetorical design. Nonetheless, the speaker's one prominent line, an aside, manages to steal the whole Neoplatonic show:

> Serena Luz, en quien presente espira
> divino amor, qu'enciende i junto enfrena
> el noble pecho, qu'en mortal cadena
> al alto Olimpo levantar s'aspira;
>
> Ricos cercos dorados, do se mira
> tesoro celestial d'eterna vena;

---

57 Parker, *Philosophy of Love*, pp. 56–57. Sigel seeks the same in the sonnet but, unlike Parker, actually finds it: 'Sonnet LXXII exemplifies Herrera's use of reference to the idealized, neo-Platonic concept of love in combination with the technical craftsmanship of poetic *decoro* as he builds a poem that literally enacts itself, in style and content' (*The Baroque Poetry of Fernando de Herrera*, p. 46).

armonia d'angelica Sirena,
qu'entre las perlas i el coral respira:

Cual nueva maravilla, cual exemplo
de la immortal grandeza nos descubre
aquessa sombra del hermoso velo?

Que yo enessa belleza, que contemplo,
(aunqu'a mi flaca vista ofende i cubre)
la immensa busco, i voi siguiendo al cielo.

[Serene Luz, in whom divine love, present and breathing, ignites and yet
restrains the noble heart which, in mortal chains, aspires to scale Olympian
heights. Rich, golden curls display a celestial treasure mined in the eternal;
and the harmony of an angelic Siren, issues forth between coral and pearls.
What new marvel, what example of immortal grandeur is revealed to us by
that shadow of the beautiful veil? For in that beauty which I contemplate
(although it assaults and obscures my weak sight) I seek infinite beauty and
pursue it to heaven).]

Elegant dispassionate images flaunt their Platonic pedigree centre stage in the
quatrains,[58] calling too much attention to the sheen of a reflecting surface
whose substance is challenged in the first tercet. But, as McNair has so persuasively argued, it is the parenthesis of verse 13, with its extrovert marginal-
ity and flagrantly incongruent word choices, that most effectively destabi-
lises the poem's contrived intellectualised aura.[59] McNair reads the effacement
of the lyric persona as a symbolic Attis-like castration; the cost of a wilful
suppression of the sensual appetite in a noble attempt to transcend the corporeal self:

---

[58]   This poem is most often cited as a clear example of pure Neoplatonism. See, for instance,
the comments of Vicente García de Diego, *Poesías* (Madrid: Espasa-Calpe, 1962), p. xvi; M.
Romera Navarro, *Historia de la literatura española*, 2nd edn (Boston: D.C. Heath, 1966), p. 159;
Antonio Vilanova, 'Fernando de Herrera', in *Historia general de las literaturas hispánicas*, ed.
Guillermo Díaz-Plaja (Barcelona: Vergara, 1968), pp. 687–751 (p. 727); and Parker, *Philosophy
of Love*, p. 59.

[59]   See Alexander J. McNair, 'Re-evaluating Herrera's Sonnet XXXVIII: Notes on Sense and
Intellect in the Lyric Persona of *Algunas Obras*', *Hispanic Review*, 71 (2003), 565–84. McNair
reads the poem as Herrera's rewriting of Garcilaso's Sonnet XXIII and as an extension of his
commentary on that poem in the *Anotaciones*. He argues also for a recontextualisation of the sonnet within its original editorial context, demonstrating how the Neoplatonic aspirations of the poem
are undermined by the antagonistic content of other sonnets in the collection, focusing particularly on how elements of verse 13 are most often conveyed within the context of the 'guerra de
amor' [war of love] motif and resonate with allusions elsewhere to the myth of Attis (Sonnet
XXXIX).

Lest we forget it is a sensual 'yo' rather than an entirely intellectual one contemplating the beauty, looking for a more immense beauty and hopefully flying 'al cielo', Herrera inserts verse 13 [...] It is as if Herrera were trying to close in the sensual appetite to which the verse points; as if he were trying to keep it from influencing the otherwise exemplary contemplation carried out in the other thirteen lines of the sonnet.[60]

The problem is that the 'enclosure' of verse 13 is so deliberately different that it must influence the rest of the poem. The parenthesis draws the reader right to a fixed point of interruption, a point of discontinuity that breaks the flow of the paradigmatic images (golden hair, pearl-like teeth, corral-red lips etcetera) and thus frees the speaking subject from subordination to them. Textual wholeness and order is disturbed by the intervention of the speaking subject in an act of creative interruption, which makes sense in 'real' terms and gives sense to 'real' time. Inherited, preordained images are, in this moment, released and open to re-evaluation. The poems ends, but it is not over. The speaker is suspended on the knife edge of possibility – of contemplating, reaching, or creating '*new marvels*' that might uncover 'immense' meaning beyond mortality.

The metaphoric repertoire of Sonnet XXXVIII is mobilised very differently in a more explicit metapoetic poem (Sonnet VI), which harnesses ominous epic resonance against Herrera's lofty lyric objectives:

> Al mar desierto, en el profundo estrecho,
> entre las duras rocas, con mi nave
> desnuda, tras el canto voi suave
> que forçado me lleva a mi despecho.
>
> Temerario desseo, incauto pecho,
> a quien rendí de mi poder la llave,
> al peligro m'entregan fiero i grave,
> sin que pueda apartarme del mal hecho.
>
> Veo los uessos blanquear, i siento
> el triste son de la enganada gente,
> i crecer de las ondas el bramido.
>
> Huir no puedo ya mi perdimiento,
> que no me da lugar el mal presente,
> ni osar me vale en el temor perdido.

[Out towards empty sea in my open boat, through deep straits and between harsh rocks, I pursue the gentle song that forces me forward, despite myself.

---

60   See McNair, 'Re-evaluating Herrera's Sonnet XXXVIII', 578.

I handed power over to that fearless desire and unsuspecting heart which
surrender me to fierce and grave danger; I cannot now steer clear of the
damage done. I see the bones whiten, I hear the wretched sound of the
seduced (deceived people) and the rising roar of the waves. It's too late to
flee my own loss, present suffering offers no space, and there's no point in
daring when I am already lost in fear]

The symbolic use of the sea and of sea-faring as images for epic poetry, and
in some cases for original poetic enterprise, was extensively exploited by
Latin poets of the first century BC and may well have reached back beyond
an Homeric allusion (to the Argonaut saga, *Odyssey*, 12.69–72), to a lost pre-
Hellenistic epic.[61] The metaphor dominates the opening of Catullus 64, is a
subtle presence at the start of Virgil's First *Georgic* (I, 40–42), is inescapable
in the *Aeneid* (where the literal voyage of the plot converges with the symbolic voyage of the progressing epic), and determines Propertius's generic
choices in the Elegies (especially Book 3, wherein the scale of epic is a vast
sea [3.9.3], too dangerous for the poet's fragile 'craft'). Since then the 'voyage out' as poetic metaphor has persisted in a multitude of contexts, but the
departure point for striking out in new directions has continued to be Homeric (the opening of Ezra Pound's modernist epic *Cantos*, for instance, is a
case in point). Likewise epic/mythic heroism, as an embodiment of the principles of boundary violation and maintenance, is a powerful metapoetic figure
in itself which allows the writer to comment on the process of poetic composition. The mythic hero, as shaped by Homer in writer-function mode, may
boast a divine parentage which enables transgressive acts beyond the ordinary
limits of humanity (even access to 'other' realities beyond the profane), but
he is always subject to death, and defined by mortality. Both Achilles and
Odysseus must travel to establish themselves as heroes, often ignoring, along
the way, the limits set by death's sphere of influence. The impression of motion communicated by their sea-faring narrative configures language temporally within the poem's episodic succession, thereby offering a model of
constructing dynamic, blended conceptual spaces. In the case of the *Odyssey*,
for instance, the ordeals of the human condition are symbolised in the perils
the hero Odysseus confronts on his voyage away from conflict, and in all the
struggles (both external and internal) with which he must engage. But the
textual movement also facilitates an on-going exploration of the possibilities
and limitations of the materiality of language. If metaphor means the possibility of creating new meanings when signifiers are merged, replace each other,
or collide, then navigation is a useful mechanism for thematising this move-

[61] For voyaging and poetic analogy in general, see J.V. Cody, *Horace and Callimachean
Aesthetics*, Collection Latomus, 147 (Brussels: Latomus Revue D'Etudes Latines, 1976) and P.
Fedeli, *Sesto Properzio: il terzo libro delle elegie* (Bari, 1985).

ment of the signifying chain; and heroic navigation becomes a powerfully ambiguous symbol of the writer's complex role in this transformative and transforming process.

When Herrera's speaker 'voyages out' through the dire emotional straits of Sonnet XXXVIII, he charts a voyage of lyric rediscovery around some very familiar epic narrative and symbolic coastlines.[62] Episodes from Homer's *Odyssey*, Book 12, are particularly resonant. The book opens with Circe's forewarning to Odysseus of the dangers that will beset him on the next stage of his voyage. His first encounter will be with the Sirens – fierce winged women who live among desolate rocks amid a wild and stormy sea, and whose enchanting song lures sailors to certain death. Their seductive music is belied by the pile of human bones, flesh still rotting, scattered about them. Odysseus, tied to his own mast, his sailors' ears plugged with wax, passes unharmed. But from there he must navigate his ship through a dangerous, narrow strait. On the one side lives the many-headed hydra Scylla; on the other, the omnivorous whirlpool Charybdis. The choice is not a false dichotomy, for it is made clear to Odysseus that there are no others. Victory over these liminal creatures requires a new form of heroism, far removed from the uncompromising physical and emotional aggression of the *Illiad*'s Achilles. Strategy and foresight overcome the temptation of the Sirens, while cautious decision-making and careful navigation minimise losses against Scylla and Charybdis. These monsters cannot be defeated by sword-wielding soldiers. Their call to oblivion can only be resisted if the hero is forewarned, and has the inner strength to drown out the voices of self-destruction which the music of the Sirens can awaken from within.

As in all intertexual dialogues, Herrera's rewriting of the Odyssean model allows authority and transgression to co-exist in the same ambiguous synchronic time and space, thereby contravening any sense of ideological unity or stable centre. What emerges are two competing sets of human heroic and anti-heroic attributes: on the one hand, the strength, action, power, strategies of self-preservation and timeless voice of the Homeric hero; on the other, the weakness, passivity, compliance, impulse to self-destruction and the certain voiceless oblivion of Herrera's poetic persona. In this antagonistic encounter there seems to be little attempt to personify through myth the transcendent impulses of the poet or lover. The heroic response to human mortality, which is conveyed via 'osadía' in other poems, is here explicitly negated in the self-determined portrayal of the speaker as an Odyssean anti-type. It is also denied in the reconfiguration of the conventional topos of the shipwrecked lover who, rather than celebrating survival with a votive offering on the nearest temple wall, submits his free will to the control

---

[62] Ruíz Pérez cites this sonnet as an example of Herrera's approach to imitative poetic practice; that is, a refusal to be straitjacketed by his reading and filtering of the Classics and a determination to carve out his own path. See 'De la teoría a la práctica', p. 248.

of *eros*.[63] Consequently, erotic passion appropriates and redesignates sight and hearing (the two senses permitted within the Platonic love system)[64] as ministers of macabre images of *memento mori*. Thus Herrera's voyage of vernacular poetic consciousness not only carries a sense of the failure of his own deluded role in the cultural *traslatio*,[65] but also locates broader existential concerns in the subjective experience of the individual unrequited lover. These anxieties are elaborated more expansively, and with a heightened sense of urgency, in the fourth elegy addressed to Medina, where the speaker slips through a series of associated subject positions: *caminante, amante, navegante, combatiente*. Life is a laborious path or journey ('senda tabajosa'; 22), a brief space and narrow prison ('espacio breve', 'estrecha prisión'; 42–43), a dangerous strait from which the shipwrecked lover emerges only to be cast back into the stormy depths (140–47). The satisfaction of human desire, at the expense of authentic freedom, is conveyed as a cycle of Sisyphean struggle[66] relieved only by the siren-like deceptions of the beloved (163–71), and culminates in a realisation that death on the battlefield of love is a *fait accompli* (259–61).

Inserted within this broader field of reference, Sonnet VI suggests a lack of resolve to slay the 'monsters' (intertextual and/or existential) which beset the text. However, in Herrera's lyric recreation of heroism (a reading against the grain of the epic intertext), there is a resistance to authority which allows for a dynamic transference of agency. As Barolini reminds us, it is this type of subjective interpretation by the writer that compels the reader to put 'hermeneutic pressure' on the poem.[67] This heightened autonomy accorded to interpretation is yet another instance of Herrerian theory in practice.

[63] The equation of the lover as a shipwrecked sailor was a standard topos of Roman elegy (for instance, Horace, *Odes*, 1.5) variously reimagined by lyric poets of the Renaissance. See, for instance, Lía Schwartz's comments on Quevedo's re-elaboration of the topos in 'Prisión y desengaño de amor: dos topoi de la retórica amorosa en Quevedo y en Soto de Rojas', *Criticón*, 56 (1992), 21–39 (31–32).

[64] In the *Anotaciones*, Herrera outlines three kinds of love: divine, human and bestial. In this categorisation, as demonstrated by Maglione, he seems to follow more closely the *Diálogos de amor* of León Hebreo, rather than Castiglione (See 'Herrera and Neoplatonism'). Hebreo includes a discussion of the kind of love perceived by sight and hearing: 'La de la vista es imagen de la belleza intelectual [...] la que se capta por medio del oído es la imagen del alma del mundo' [The beauty perceived by sight reflects intellectual beauty (...) that perceived by hearing is the image of the world's soul]. *Diálogos de amor*, trans. David Romano (Barcelona: José Jones, 1953), p. 240.

[65] Navarrete identifies references to generic choice (lyric over epic) as part of a broader, self-conscious assertion of Herrera's relationship with literary predecessors (particularly Petrarch) and his role in the *traslatio*. He draws particular attention to a node of three sonnets (XLVIII, XLIX and L), the first of which uses the shipwreck metaphor to recall and rewrite the epic diction of Homer and Virgil. See *Orphans of Petrarch*, pp. 176–78.

[66] Throughout *Algunas obras* the ceaseless renewal of suffering speaks eloquently in symptoms of sighs and lament (e.g. Sonnets III, XI, XIV, XXI, XXVII, XXXIV, LXXVI, LXXVII), often despite protestations to the contrary.

[67] See Simon Gilson, 'Historicism, Philology and the Text. An Interview with Teodolinda Barolini', *Italian Studies*, 63.1 (2008), 141–52 (141).

Conclusion: *Forward and back to the middle*

However debatable the etymological connection between hermeneutics and the god Hermes, the idea of the writer as an interpreter, accessing knowledge from elsewhere and mediating this otherness, has often placed him under the sign of the messenger deity whose very essence is mobile and marginal.[68] As Otto notes, 'It is Hermes' nature not to belong to any locality and not to possess any permanent abode; always he is on the road between here and there'.[69] This sense of transitional and provisional being, which is as significantly temporal as spatial, finds expression in Herrera's poetry through a contamination of the conventional motif of the *homo viator* with a reconfiguration of the normative trajectories of courtly love and the *peregrinatio amoris*.[70] The experience of the human being as a traveller who sets out, as soon as he leaves the womb, on a journey through the time and space of his existence, is intensified and acquires a more negative valuation in the figure of the wayfarer as unrequited lover. In this latter context, faith, self-denial and sacrifice result not in the attainment of self-knowledge (nor ultimately, as in the case of the believer, eternal life), but in a deceptive sense of open-ness and mobility that seem to signal surrender to pre-determined aesthetic and ontological outcomes. As we have seen, several poems of *Algunas obras* exploit the flight or journey motif to convey a condition of stasis which foils a cyclically set and continuously evolving process (for example, Sonnet XXX, *Canso la vida*). However, the concentration of the topos in the node of sonnets which immediately precedes the last (Sonnets LXXIIII–LXXVI), suggests a path towards individuation that is not finite.[71] The final sonnet, in particular, frustrates all expectation of closure:

68   See especially Martin Heidegger's discussion of Hermes and Hermeneutics in 'A Dialogue on Language: Between a Japanese and an Inquirer', in *On the Way to Language*, trans. Peter D. Hertz (New York: Harper and Row, 1971), pp. 1–54.

69   Walter F. Otto, *The Homeric Gods: The Spiritual Significance of Greek Religion*, trans. Moses Hadas (New York: Thames and Hudson, 1979), p. 117.

70   The pilgrim of love as a literary figure goes back to Boccaccio's *Il Filocolo* and the *dolcistilnovisti* poets. Early modern Spanish representations culminate in the *peregrino* subject of Góngora's *Soledades*, though we find the 'pilgrim of love' in the pastoral novel and in Cervantes's *Los trabajos de Persiles y Sigismunda*. In Dante's *Divina Commedia* the pilgrimage of love becomes a religious pilgrimage to Paradise; a transit from human to divine love. For general discussion of the pilgrimage metaphor, see F.C. Gardner, *The Pilgrimage of Desire: A Study of Theme and Genre in Medieval Literature* (Leiden: Brill, 1971), pp. 11–15, and Gerhart B. Lacher, '*Homo viator*: Medieval Ideas on Alienation and Order', *Speculum*, 42 (1967), 233–59.

71   Navarrete reads these sonnets in the light of specific connections to the theme of love as a journey in Garcilaso's Sonnets IV, VI and especially XXXVIII; arguing that the motif has poetic as much as erotic connotations: 'the repeated allusions to Garcilaso's journey poems convey Herrera's portrayal of himself as both surpassing but also limited to the path his predecessors trod' (*Orphans of Petrarch*, p. 174).

AMOR: En un incendio no acabado
ardí del fuego tuyo, en la florida
sazón, i alegre, de mi dulce vida,
todo en tu viva imagen trasformado.

I aora, ¡o vano error!, en este estado,
no con llama en cenizas ascondida,
mas descubierta, clara i encendida,
pierdo en ti lo mejor de mi cuidado.

No más; baste, cruel, ya en tantos años
rendido aver al yugo el cuello ierto
i aver visto en el fin tu desvarío.

Abra la luz la niebla a tus engaños,
antes qu'el lazo rompa el tiempo, i muerto
sea el fuego del tardo ielo mío.

[LOVE: I burned from your flames in an unfinished fire; (it was) the flower
of my youth, the joyful season of my sweet life, (and) I became the living
image of you. And now, oh vain error! in this state, my flame not concealed
in ash, but (still) ablaze, uncovered and clear, I lose in you the greatest of my
cares. No more. Let it be enough cruelty to have submitted my stiff neck to
your yoke for so many years, and to have seen your madness at the end. Let
light break open the fog of your deceits, before time breaks the bond, and the
fire dies out in my belated ice.]

In his apostrophising of Love, Herrera's speaker stands both outside and within himself in a highly self-conscious questioning of his amorous and poetic
trajectory. The sonnet stages the poetic persona's process of perception in the
present by working together disparate temporalities into a 'balanced' configuration that reflects the writer, speaker and reader's experience of being, always,
in medias res, in the world.[72] The controlled patterning of associative imagery
(fire and ice in particular) is carefully engineered to play up these temporal tensions, and still carries the traces of the efforts made throughout the anthology
to bring materiality and metaphysics into some sense of equilibrium.

Padrón tells us that the opening poem, Sonnet I, encodes undifferentiated
heroism, but in its abstract poetics 'does not tell the whole story' of *Algunas*

[72] We might contrast Boscán's tense usage when he draws his poetic sequence to a close.
Middlebrook points out the difference between the tense drifting which takes place in earlier poems
and the insistence on the then and now of these final poems. Thus Boscán conveys 'his triumph
over old ways of loving and singing' and declares his 'emergence as the new self-contained, and
self-contented author of a new type of courtly song' (*Imperial Lyric*, p. 194).

Obras.[73] Maybe not. But the semantic links between the final group of sonnets and the first are incontrovertible.[74] The speaker of this final, non-finite, sonnet, speaking from an intensely inward, exacerbated sensuality, seeks to build a new structure of meaning out of and beyond its intertextual fabric,[75] but opened up in a subjective, subjunctive space. Perhaps the circular insolvability of the whole, its sustained paradoxes, its deliberate defiance of trajectory, its resistance to tidy parcels of meaning, and the ultimate racing of light against time does say *something* of the little stories inside the bigger picture – once, and always, linguistically 'upon a time'.

The sense of time that emerges both from Herrera's *Anotaciones* and *Algunas obras* is an expansive one, encompassing a past that is historical, mythic, as well as intensely personal. It is this broad perspective that allows for an awareness and manipulation of the patterns, repetitions and pitfalls of human experience. And it is a vested interest in the application of these inherited patterns of significance to subjective experience that makes the present such a critically determining and intrusive feature of Herrera's vision. For the solutions to the problems identified by Herrera, in either guise (as theorist or practitioner), lie always in the present, but the issues of responsibility for action that they raise make of the present a problem in itself. The strategic response proposed by the poet requires a new brand of collective, cultural heroism, allegorised as the individual creative will in action and mobilised against the stasis of contemporary Spanish letters. Supreme virtue is, therefore, the constancy of heroic aspirations for perfectability within the perpetual dynamics of a mutable world. But heroism demands daring and daring exists in relation to fear. Out of this dichotomy emerge the following: Herrera's emphasis on the Sisyphean nature of his artistic endeavour; temporal tensions which underline the relation and disparity between mythic and historical time; erotic chaos that is barely contained within the small space of the sonnet or the structured specifications of Petrarchan narrative; descent in free fall from Neoplatonic summits; and lyric misreadings of mythic and epic intertexts. The result is an idealisation of process over product; a sense of the lasting value of the poet as a figure of transformation. Whether exerting 'hermeneutic pressure' on the words of Garcilaso or rewriting Classical and Renaissance intertexts in his own poetry, Herrera thematises lan-

---

73   See Ricardo Padrón, 'Exile and Empire: The Spaces of the Subject in Fernando de Herrera', *Hispanic Review*, 70 (2002), 497–520 (512).

74   See Santiago Fernández Mosquera's analysis of the structure and organisation of the collection in which he emphasises its circularity and, in particular, the relationship between the final group of sonnets and the first: 'De nuevo sobre la consideración de "Algunas obras de Herrera" como cancionero petrarquista', *Insula-Revista de Letras y Ciencias Humanas*, 610 (1997), 14–17.

75   Navarrete draws attention to the way in which Herrera constructs a complex set of opposites out of the Petrarchan 'icy fire' antithesis, so that what is oxymoronically united in Petrarch is fragmented and ultimately internalised into 'a self-centred love song to his own poetic creation'. See *Orphans of Petrarch*, p. 172.

guage's power to order and to violate the world. Moreover, in prioritising a defiance of patterned ways of thinking, he demonstrates both the potential for vernacular renewal and the importance of the poet's role in this broader project.

> *Some men are born mediocre, some men achieve mediocrity, and some men, like Herrera, have mediocrity thrust upon them.* (Joseph Heller, *Catch 22*, adapted)

Hindsight, especially in the context of critical reception, has twenty/twenty vision. The great irony of Herrera's legacy is that, despite this very self-conscious reclaiming and reconceptualisation of the 'middle' ground as a distinctly dynamic site in the present, and despite a confident carving out of new steps on the path of self-individuation, 'el divino' [the divine one] is generally located (temporally and spatially) in a negative transitionary position: somewhere on the road between Garcilaso and Luis de Góngora; no longer the former, but not yet the latter.[76] It is time perhaps to rethink Herrera's role in the development of early modern Spanish poetics, to shine a light on Herrera via Góngora rather than the other way round.

---

[76] Dámaso Alonso situates Herrera half way along a line that runs from the Platonism of Garcilaso to the enflamed sensuality of Góngora (*Poesía española. Ensayo de métodos y límites estilísticos* [Madrid: Gredos, 1956]), p. 387; Palomo discusses the 'paso' from Herrera to Góngora in the natural evolution of *cultista* poetry (*La poesía de la edad barroca* [Barcelona: SGEL, 1975], p. 50); Terry emphasises Herrera's 'transitional' role (*Seventeenth-century Spanish Poetry*, pp. 51–52). Even Navarette, who recognises Herrera's self-consciousness about literary history and his own role in it, concludes that his 'achievements would shine brighter if not for Góngora' (*Orphans of Petrarch*, p. 189). Sigel tries to resist the transitionary tag for Herrera, but there is some slippage between the caution which he urges and his own critical apparatus; his language often suggesting what it simultaneously denies (e.g. Herrera 'follows' the innovations of Garcilaso while 'pointing towards' the poetry of Góngora). See *The Baroque Poetry of Fernando de Herrera*, p. 9.

4

Luis de Góngora y Argote (1561–1627):
Into the Dark

Introduction

Herrera's heliocentric formulations fixed the linguistic aspirations of the late sixteenth century upon the iconic authority of natural and perfect form, the circle. In a post-Copernican allegorical system, the vernacular 'sol' was figured as the ideal centre around which not only the fates of individual poets, but the destiny of the Spanish empire itself could, and should, revolve in conterminous motion. Notwithstanding the anxieties and ambivalences which, as we have seen, complicated this correlative arrangement, other paradoxes would ultimately destroy the illusion of centric stability. Firstly, the allegorical frame itself was intrinsically flawed. Herrera's new brand of collective cultural heroism, conveyed as the audacious transformation of tradition by an individual poet on his own terms, was designed to promote progress (that is, linguistic renewal) over stasis, but the symbolic activity of its conceptual schema furnished allegiance to a fixed point of conventional transcendental reference. To engage creatively with the problem in poetry would inevitably involve some shattering of the representative system in which the upwardly mobile aspirations of the language were forged. This was a strategy adopted by Luis de Góngora, whose response to the exhausted generic, modal and metaphorical possibilities of Spanish post-Petrarchan lyric was to refocus it in the direction of a new kind of beauty. Góngora opted not to resist the limitations placed on self-expression by language, or the ironies of timeless assertions that are caught up in the stream of time, but rather to embrace the deceptions embedded in language and to encourage a carefully crafted violence. In other words, Góngora's poetry shatters allegorical logic and order through linguistic processes which reaffirm and renew, while also boldly resisting traditional generic, thematic and tonal frames of reference.

The discussion that follows, in this chapter and the next, of representative sonnets with reference to Góngora's longer, mythological fable, the *Fábula de Polifemo y Galatea*, will draw attention to a number of these processes: in particular, to Góngora's radical deployment of periphrasis, hyperbaton and mythological allusion. The result is a self-conscious evocation and elision of meaning, a dislocation of time and space and a celebration of freedom from referents. Readers are compelled to see words as material things in themselves, but are also made to grasp at meanings which multiply and can seem to recede, like Virgil's Eurydice, into the vanishing air. But from this thin air significance is rendered and *admiratio* provoked by innovative and extravagant figural combinations. Extreme metaphorisation or, as Sarduy puts it, metaphor that is raised to its power squared,[1] transforms relations of remoteness into areas of contiguity, always seeking the points where light and dark meet in their greatest disproportion. Within this system of converging symbolic boundaries, *eros* emerges as a dominant agent,[2] energising transferences that reconceive even the basic properties of speech and silence, a catalyst for the 'silencio creador'[creative silence] identified by Aurora Egido.[3] Love is turned into the direction of the dark, and positioned at the centre of a new poetry that seeks alternative figuration: a poetics of heightened *aemulatio* whose unconventional decorum requires new compliantly creative readers; a reimagined vernacular eloquence that corrupts the circle and obscures the sun.

The idea of a negative trajectory from light to dark in Góngora's poetic development (which Menéndez Pelayo attributed to Francisco Cascales) has long been rendered invalid.[4] Equally spurious is the charge that essentially radiant meaning is suppressed beneath the dark materials of a technically overwrought *cultismo* – a subject we will return to when considering the controversy generated by the *Polifemo* and Góngora's other major work, the *Soledades*. Although it is now generally recognised that luminosity and shadows coincide throughout the image system of Góngora's poetry, both early and late,[5] Alonso's notion of

---

[1] See Severo Sarduy, *Barroco* (Buenos Aires: Editorial Sudamericana, 1974), ch. 3.

[2] The exaltation of *eros* in Góngora's poetry has been most recently treated by Jesús Ponce Cárdenas, whose study of the *Polifemo* embraces Salcedo Coronel's notion of 'honesta oscuridad' in order to interrogate the relationship between eroticism and ellipsis in the *Polifemo* and, ultimately, to expose the creation of a new 'decorum'. See *El tapiz narrativo del Polifemo: eros y elipsis* (Barcelona: Universitat Pompeu Fabra, 2010).

[3] For Egido's insightful analysis of the power of the 'palabra eludida' [the elided word] in Góngora, see 'La poética del silencio en el siglo de oro: su pervivencia', in *Fronteras de la poesía en el Barroco* (Barcelona: Crítica, 1990), pp. 56–84 (p. 82).

[4] Dámaso Alonso challenges the concept of the so-called 'dos épocas' (two periods differentiated in terms of a stark transition from natural clarity to artificial dark enigma) in *Góngora y El Polifemo*, I (Madrid: Gredos, 1961), 4th edn, pp. 87–101.

[5] The fact that we can date Góngora's individual poems with reasonable accuracy distinguishes him from his major contemporaries and from the other poets treated in this study. It is generally accepted, based on the evidence of the poet's letters among other substantial indicators, that the so-called *Chacón* manuscript represents the last revision of the poems by the poet himself – assembled and organised in collaboration with Antonio de Chacón – during Góngora's final years in Madrid. This was first published in three volumes in 1921, edited by R. Foulché-Delbosc. See *Poesías completas*, 3 vols (New York: Hispanic Society of North America, 1921). For a useful overview of editorial history, see R.P. Calcraft, *The Sonnets of Luis de Góngora* (Durham: University of Durham, 1980), pp. 10–12. As Arthur Terry warns us, the value of read-

dualism in the *Polifemo* (darkness and monstrosity aligned with Polifemo, light and beauty with Galatea) seems to have extended beyond engagement with this single work and continues to hold sway.[6] Regardless of whether the critical perspective ultimately celebrates unity (Parker), or the triumph of positive or negative values (Jones, Jammes on the one hand; Lehrer, McCaw, Wagschal on the other), this dualistic stance tends to prioritise antagonism over interchange and, thereby, to some extent, denies to Góngora's most intricate pattern its play of paradox and illusion.[7] I would suggest that we rethink Góngora's elaborate matrix of light and dark, recognising that the world it apprehends often inhabits both realms, together, often at once, yet also separately. As demonstrated in the depiction of Galatea, the shifting tensions of this matrix cannot be reduced to binary contexts that give the illusion of balance, permanence, even wholeness: where light is to dark as the spiritual is to the physical; the mind to matter, good to evil or principles of life to those of death.[8] Seldom is Góngora's world of changing colours so certain, seldom are its revelations and resolutions so 'relatively' straightforward. It is not just that Góngora's poetry rebels against the transparency of the word, shaking the stability of the sign and of signification itself, but that the acceleration of vernacular expansion inherent in this process decentralises the broader project of linguistic homogenisation, which, as we have seen in Herrera's *Anotaciones*, had connected the pursuit of elegant majesty (based on principles of dark-dispelling elegance) with 'la onra de la nación'[9]

---

ing the poems in chronological order must be balanced against the temptation 'to construct a partly fictitious "life" into which the poems themselves can be conveniently slotted' (*Seventeenth-Century Spanish Poetry*, p. 65).

   6   See Alonso, *Góngora y El Polifemo*, pp. 196–218 (esp. pp. 213–18).

   7   See A.A. Parker, *Polyphemus and Galatea: A Study in the Interpretation of a Baroque Poem* (Edinburgh: Edinburgh University Press, 1977); *Poems of Góngora,* ed. R.O. Jones (Cambridge: Cambridge University Press, 1966), esp. pp. 36–37; Robert Jammes, *Études sur l'oeuvre poétique de Don Luis de Góngora* (Bordeaux: Institut d'études ibériques et ibéro-américaines de l'Université de Bordeaux, 1967), pp. 533–54; Melinda Eve Lehrer, *Classical Myth and the 'Polifemo' of Góngora* (Potomac, Maryland.: Scripta Humanistica, 1989), p. 57; R. John McCaw, 'Turning a Blind Eye: Sexual Competition, Self-Contradiction and the Impotence of Pastoral in Góngora's *Fábula de Polifemo y Galatea*', *Hispanófila*, 127 (1999), 27–35 (esp. 32); Steven Wagschal, 'Góngora on the Beautiful and the Sublime', in *The Literature of Jealousy in the Age of Cervantes* (Columbia and London: University of Missouri Press, 2006), pp. 157–87.

   8   Parker, whose 'conceptista' reading of the fable is offered to a large extent as an extension of Alonso's 'cultista' study (*Polyphemus and Galatea*, pp. 51–53), recognises that this dualism is not based on a straightforward 'conflict of opposing principles' (p. 76), yet his insistence on two dominant image complexes often suggests the opposite. See, for instance, his reading of Galatea as the 'principle of concord in human life' (p. 65).

   9   Even when Gongorist poetics had infiltrated the opposition (Juan de Jaúregui's *Orfeo* being a prime example of this), some, like Quevedo and Lope de Vega, would continue to endorse authentic Castilian poetry in terms of purity, clarity and elegance, and connect this to national honour. As Aurora Egido has shown, whereas Quevedo turned back to Fray Luis as his exemplar, Lope championed the contemporary poetry of the Aragonese Argensola brothers as saviours of a Castilian

[the honour of the nation]. Certainly, as we will see, Góngora's detractors perceived the splendour of Castilian to be under threat from a 'new' poetry which revelled, somewhat perversely, in its own obscurity.

There were, of course, other factors that destabilised the Herrerian alignment of linguistic renewal, imperial expansion and heliocentric symbolism. In fact, Herrera's own pressing for the development of letters as a professional activity (realised in the court-based careers of prominent poets of the early seventeenth century) contributed to a cleaving of the relational categories of his own analogical transfer system. But perhaps, most significantly, the always fragile relationship between arms and letters which, as Anne Cruz has demonstrated, 'assumed various and varying perspectives' from the Middle Ages onwards,[10] had acquired weakened ideological impact by the early Baroque. The oppositional stance of the Middle Ages, predicated on class standing and, notably, the superiority of arms for the attainment of social recognition, passed through a forced, politicised, conciliation in the late fifteenth and sixteenth centuries which, as we saw in Chapter 4 had allowed for Herrera's allegorised transfer of heroicisation from warrior to poet. A generation later, however, the affiliation seemed to have lost all positive emblematic potency (certainly from the perspective of letters).[11] No single reason can account for this shift at a very complex historical moment,[12] but key contributing factors (none of them straightforward) include: the realignment of subject positions, which saw in the dismantling of historical structures; the emergence of a new aristocracy of letters in opposition to essentialist concepts of subjectivity that were based on purity of blood line and status; a disproportionate accumulation of cultural capital linked to enhanced literary autonomy that existed, nonetheless, in tension with monarcho-seigniorial interests and the demands of patronage.[13] And all of this set against a back-

---

language that was drowning in its own confusion. Interestingly, Cervantes (in his *Galatea* of 1585) had celebrated the brothers in 'Herrerian' terms, as 'dos luceros, dos soles de poesía' [two shining stars, two suns of poetry]. See '"Dos soles de poesía": Lupercio y Bartolomé Leonardo de Argensola', in *Dos soles de poesía. 450 años. Lupercio y Bartolomé Leonardo de Argensola*, eds Aurora Egido and José Enrique Laplana, *Argensola*, special monograph issue, 119 (2009), 15–39 (20).

10 See 'Arms versus Letters,' p. 186.

11 Thus the exaltation of arms over letters in *Don Quijote* (I, 38) ironically underscores the deranged protagonist's deluded quest for fame and social advancement through out-moded social discourses and practices. This discourse has been read at face value, most recently by John T. Cull who explores a possible model in Francisco de Guzmán's *Digresión de las armas y letras* (1565). See '"Mas no lo saben todo los letrados/ni todos son ydiotas los soldados". Francisco de Guzmán's *Digresión de las armas y letras* (1565)', *Cervantes*, 29.2 (2009), 5–31.

12 Cruz suggests that advances in the development of artillery played their part by making obsolete the ideals of individual courage in battle ('Arms versus Letters', pp. 186–87).

13 For a detailed discussion of these issues, see Carlos M.G. Gutiérrez, 'The Challenges of Freedom: Social Reflexivity in the Seventeenth-Century Spanish Literary Field', in *Hispanic Baroques.Reading Cultures in Context*, eds Nicholas Spadaccini and Luis Martín-Estudillo (Nashville: Vanderbilt University Press, 2005), pp. 137–62.

drop of diminishing returns on the nation's investment in military conquest. Much had changed, therefore, since Nebrija had published his Rome-based model of seamless union for language and empire, with its sinister outworking that portended inevitable and simultaneous collapse. As the linguistic project of self-determination continued to gain momentum (aided by the dissemination via printing of culturally divergent viewpoints), the empire sustained its global position in a context of growing national crises and reactionary counter-reformational conservatism. It is not surprising, in this context, that the linkage of imperial success and vernacular renewal should come under sceptical scrutiny, and that inventive poets such as Góngora would seek to reconfigure the metaphorical scaffolding that held it together. Confronting the sun with other regenerative figures was one such manoeuvre.[14]

The writings of Severo Sarduy have clearly informed attempts in recent years to find a correlation between the 'disfigured language' of Góngora's major works and contemporary debates concerning other fields of activity, notably painting and cosmology.[15] Within a broader argument which foregrounds the ellipse as a figure of the Baroque as a whole, Sarduy identifies in the shifting perspectives and generative possibilities of Góngora's poetics the literary equivalent of anamorphosis; the process that transformed the fixed-centred Ptolomaic circle, with its closed set of absolute principles, into the double-centred Keplerian ellipse. Moreover, the former's analogy to the Pythagorean scale secured a symbolic universe of symmetrical and harmonious motion;[16] a vision of the world as a manifestation of divine harmony that was challenged by Copernicus, whose revolutionary solar system not only altered the centuries-old scientific foundation upon which rested the entire knowledge of an age,

[14] It is worth remembering that the sun analogy was frequently exploited to promote the image of Phillip IV, the 'rey planeta' [planet king], especially by his 'privado' [favourite], Olivares. See Jonathan Brown and John H. Elliot, *A Palace for a King: The Buen Retiro and the Court of Phillip IV* (New Haven: Yale University Press, 1980), p. 33. Whether or not such overt political 'hijacking' contributed to the diminishing metapoetic power of the image is difficult to say, but it is a tempting theory, nonetheless. Góngora, of course, was not averse to exploiting solar imagery for political purposes, as evidenced in his *Panegírico al duque de Lerma*. This aspect of the text is analysed in a recent study by Jesús Ponce Cárdenas. See 'Taceat superata vetustas: poesía y oratoria clásicas en el *Panegírico al duque de Lerma*', in *El Duque de Lerma. Poder y literatura en el siglo de oro*, eds Juan Matas Caballero, José María Micó y Jesús Ponce Cárdenas (Madrid: Centro de Estudios Europa Hispánica, 2011), pp. 57–103 (esp. pp. 63–70)

[15] See Severo Sarduy, *Barroco*, ch. 3; reproduced recently in English in *Baroque New Worlds: Representation, Transculturation, Counterconquest*, eds Lois Parkinson Zamora and Monika Kaup (Durham and London: Duke University Press, 2010), ch. 15; and Matthew Ancell's recent article, 'Este....Cíclope: Góngora's *Polifemo* and the Poetics of Disfiguration', *Hispanic Review*, 79.4 (2011), 547–72.

[16] The analogy can be summarised as follows: the moon, Mercury, Venus, the sun, Jupiter, Mars and Saturn corresponded to the seven notes on the scale; the sun stood between two fourths in the middle; the eighth note was the heaven of fixed stars, which stood for the octave.

but also directly opposed Church doctrine. The heliocentric model was inherited, and accepted, by Kepler, who struggled, within it, to find the physical causes underlying the movements of the planets (*Mysterium Cosmographicum*, 1596) and to construct a rational theory that would restore to the world the harmony that Copernicus had taken from it. It was during the preparation of the *Harmonice mundi* (not published until 1619, though planned for 1599) that Kepler discovered the orbit of Mars to be elliptical rather than circular, thereby, according to Sarduy, transferring the reference point of all symbolic activity and giving rise to an alternative, revolutionary, figuration that prioritised what was absent (from the Greek 'elleipsis', a deficit or 'falling short'), while also cutting loose from the static strictures of the perfect circle. It has been a small step for critics from here (the ellipse) to the predominance of rhetorical ellipsis in Góngora, a mechanism of linguistic repression which operates beneath the surface to liberate alternative, hidden, meanings, thus bringing into focus deeper, darker, structures. The result is a new oppositional, pluri-centred, coherence.

Whereas Sarduy's emphasis tends to downplay the interconnectedness of the circle/ellipse relationship (the fact that they are to all intents and purposes figural cohorts), critics such as Arnaldo Cruz and Jesús Ponce Cárdenas have recognised in Góngora's inventiveness a simultaneous affirmation and exclusion of traditional meanings.[17] A recent analysis by Ancell of the elliptical, anamorphic poetics of the *Polifemo*, with an emphasis on the disfiguration of established poetic forms, offers a more sustained engagement with Sarduy's Keplerian premise.[18] The Cyclops, Polyphemus, emerges as a figure for contemporary astronomical debates: 'The grotesque, disproportionate image of Polyphemus, with his large, circular and solar eye, recalls this transitional moment in the history of cosmology and its coincidence in the movement from Renaissance to Baroque aesthetics'. Within Ancell's schema, Polyphemus is at once a poetic embodiment of a 'tangled Ptolomeic system' and 'the circular fiction of Copernicus'; yet with the proper perspective a 'symmetry of Keplerian geometry' comes into view to belie Polyphemic monstrosity.

Alonso's dualistic system is clearly an informing dimension of Ancell's reading. Beauty and monstrosity are the primary oppositions held in tension throughout the fable and, out of which, an alternative, Heraclitean-type 'dark harmony'

---

[17]   See Arnaldo Cruz, 'Exclusión y afirmación en Góngora', *Dispositio*, IX, 24–26 (1984), 167–82; Ponce Cárdenas, *El tapiz narrativo*, esp. pp. 27–28, where Sarduy is cited to inform the argument.

[18]   See Ancell, 'Este....Cíclope'. Enrica Cancelliere also defines the *Polifemo* in terms of an elliptical dynamism in which the relationship between the individual subject and the cosmos is articulated via a schism of centrality, a principle which also governs anamorphic perspective. See *Góngora. Itinerarios de la visión*, trans. Rafael Bonilla and Linda Garosi (Córdoba: Diputación de Córdoba, 2006), esp. pp. 25–26, 158–65.

emerges.[19] However, Ancell's attempt to 'fit' Keplerian geometry neatly into the practice of the reading serves only to reveal that such neat analogies, even of the disfigured variety, are difficult to sustain in a poem that prioritises imperfect communication,[20] as are conclusions based on these sets of closed-off binaries. Let us take, for instance, the assertion that 'Petrarchism meets its end, in Góngora at least, with the *Polifemo* and *Soledades*'.[21] This is not easily reconciled with Polyphemus's performance of Petrarchan song, into which the Cyclops's telluric tones seem to slip all too comfortably, reaching us both as a neurotic monument to Petrarchan authority and as an indictment of its inherent treacheries. Góngora's 'new art', as I have argued elsewhere, gives the reader enhanced responsibility for the production of meaning, but it also operates paradoxically upon the reader's senses.[22] Polyphemus's 'dark harmony' does shed a new sceptical light on the Petrarchan tradition, illuminating its cultivated obsessions, its calculating claims for compensatory immortality, and its submission to idealisation. But it also makes us complicit in its fundamental proposition – the value of prolonged desire over its end in satisfaction. For we are seduced by it and it stands as a substitute for the culmination of Acis's seduction of Galatea, which is silenced and elided. The Edenic paradise of mutual love, problematically built upon Acis's contrived ritualistic courtship and charged with the idolatry of courtly love, is already absent to readers before it is timed out of the narrative. Indeed, its subverted gender norms of venery fantasy and linguistically embedded sense of impending collapse dismantle the *locus amoenus* even as it is being created. When, in the final stanzas, the expansive ego of the counterfeit suitor-poet erupts in violence, the primary problem of Petrarchism – that

[19] Equally pertinent is Ancell's engagement with more recent criticism (such as Barnard, Wagschal, McVay, Hunt Dolan and Chemris) which reads Góngora's poetry as a response to the epistemological crisis of the seventeenth century that dominated artistic production in Spain. A strength of the study is the way in which he moves beyond these to contextualise the *Polifemo* within the broader currents of European scepticism, following Robbins in drawing our attention to Spain's intellectual dialogue with the rest of Europe during this period, but adding Góngora into the mix. See 'Este....Cíclope', esp. 548–52. See also Jeremy Robbins, *Arts of Perception: The Epistemological Mentality of the Spanish Baroque 1580–1720* (Abington, UK: Routledge, 2007).

[20] Ancell is careful to preface his reading with the caveat that it is difficult to substantiate the influence of these astronomical writings on Góngora ('Este....Cíclope', 557). It is worth noting that Kepler's 'world harmony' may even have had little influence on his scientific contemporaries. Modern editors note that a sympathetic friend like the Chancellor of Bavaria, Herwart von Howenberg, complained that the whole theory was grounded in conjecture. With the rise of experimental science, the general trend of the seventeenth century was towards a mechanical natural philosophy where metaphysical speculation played little part. See *The Harmony of the World by Johannes Kepler*, Translated into English with an Introduction and Notes by E.J. Aiton, A.M. Duncan and J.V. Field (Philadelphia: American Philosophical Society, 1997), 'Preface', pp. vii–x.

[21] See Ancell, 'Este....Cíclope:', 564.

[22] See, Torres, '"Sudando néctar": (Re)Constructing *aemulatio* in Góngora's *Fabula de Polifemo y Galatea*', in *The Polyphmeus Complex*, pp. 23–78.

is, the poetical illusion and political impasse of language and reality – is re-interpreted and made significantly anti-heroic. Ultimately, the 'ending' writes itself into a new beginning. The metamorphosis of Acis allows a compromised, threshold poetics to flow forward in lament and acclamation. Within its para-doxically 'purified' current, Petrarchism is not lost, but regained *in potentia*. In other words, readings that are tempted by cause–effect critical solutions run the risk of simplifying the complexity of the poetry, and what could, and should, be an exciting, innovative form of criticism falls into the trap of excluding tradition from its deconstruction of traditional paradigms. By suppressing aware-ness of the literary dynamics in operation (including the range of alternatives from which Góngora made his stylistic and thematic choices), the potential to open up broader lines of enquiry is limited and, somewhat perversely, the socio-historical scope is narrowed.[23] As Jerome McGann argued some twenty years ago, an historical and ideological dimension needs to be restored to discussions of literature, but reductionism is a perennial danger.[24]

The relationship of literary patterns to the larger culture is complicated and, as both sociologists and literary historians point out, even now still not entirely understood. It is, however, generally accepted that the poetry or art of a period can reveal a distinctive configuration. Góngora's very fluid poetics should be read in terms of a reciprocal interaction between it and a *broader* realm of evolv-ing ideas and contemporary socio-cultural practices, if only to appreciate, as distinctive, its textual mobility, within a heightened play of temporal contingen-cies. Góngora's poetic texts move syntactically and emotionally. But as social events they are also embedded in a dynamic, multilayered historical and ideo-logical context. The valorisation of language as a transitive and transforming force, expressed in unceasing movement from one state, place, and perspective to another (and most forcefully represented in the roaming *peregrino* subject of the *Soledades* and the meandering metatextuality of its *torcido discurso*), chal-lenges univocal designation and operates against an embryonic national iden-tity that was being developed and defended upon principles of purity, orthodoxy

---

[23]   It is doubtful that future generations will look back upon early-twentieth-century artistic production and map its anxieties unproblematically on to a new post-Hubble awareness of cosmic acceleration and 'dark energy', setting aside engagement with literary history, along with the broader socio-political co-ordinates of global warming, economic collapse, religious extremism, ethnic cleansing, and international conflict. That is not to deny the validity of astronomy as a subject matter for contemporary poetry, as a recent edition of poems testifies: *Dark Matter: Poems of Space*, eds Maurice Riordan and Jocelyn Bell Burnell (London: Calouste Gulbenkian Founda-tion, 2008). This volume was a collaborative venture between scientists and commissioned poets; and, therefore, wears its cosmological credentials, quite literally, on its sleeve. Reading cosmol-ogy into Góngora is a much more speculative exercise.

[24]   These ideas inform McGann's thinking as reflected particularly in two short books published in 1983: *The Romantic Ideology: A Critical Investigation* (Chicago: University of Chicago Press, 1983) and *A Critique of Modern Textual Criticism* (Chicago: University of Chicago Press, 1983).

and homogeneity. The sense of self which is shaped in and by the language of Góngora's poetry interrogates these tenets inasmuch as they impact upon the representation of individual identity, and upon the status and evolution of the Spanish language itself. But Góngora's 'heretical' sense of radical motion is equally important for the interrogation of an evolving national selfhood out of which the poetry emerges. Barbara Fuchs reminds us that the notion of a stable 'natio' was central to a master discourse which reacted to the threat of racial and cultural otherness by embracing exclusionist ideals of pure blood and honour.[25] The polemic around Góngora's poetry, and the poetry itself, is only partially understood if we disconnect it from this centralising imperative. A stable vernacular (equally illusory) was integral to its success. The defence of this, as expressed by Góngora's detractors, was, as we shall see, similarly regulative.

A major achievement of Gongorist poetics was, therefore, the liberation of the Spanish vernacular, as vehicle, from the static strictures of meaningless symbolic tenors. A far cry from 'pure poetry',[26] Góngora's reformulations do not exist apart from the affairs of the nation or, as Fuchs puts it, the 'nation in the making';[27] nor is the subjective space a closed off safe haven, but invaded by a consciousness (social, historical, aesthetic) that is ideologically charged. This is as true of Góngora's 'carpe diem' and love sonnets, tempered with awareness of human failings and hypocrisies, as it is of the longer *Soledades* where disenchantment with colonial expansion is a more overtly disintoxicating presence. The union of imagination and actuality as conveyed by Góngora heralded a linguistic rebellion which, to adapt Walter Benjamin, wrested tradition away from the conformism that was threatening to overpower it.[28] In fact, as Bultman, Kluge and Vitulli have all argued recently (with varying emphases),[29] the sty-

[25] See Barbara Fuchs, *Passing For Spain. Cervantes and the Fictions of Identity* (Chicago: University of Illinois Press, 2003), esp. pp. 3–4, where she cites and engages with the ideas of Josiah Blackmore and Gregory Hutcheson around 'limpieza de sangre' [blood purity] and 'honra' as manifestations of the same dominant discourse.

[26] Beverley's reading of the *Soledades* in terms of their connectedness to the socio-historical realities of their moment of origin, offered the first sustained challenge to the 'pure poetry' arguments that had characterised twentieth-century responses and which had been central to the 27 generation's re-evaluation of the poet. See Luis de Góngora, *Soledades*, ed. John Beverley (Madrid: Cátedra, 1980), *Introducción*, pp. 17–61. Beverley's work on the *Soledades* has been recently reprinted as Part One of his *Essays on the Literary Baroque in Spain and Spanish America* (Woodbridge: Tamesis, 2008), pp. 23–85.

[27] See Fuchs, *Passing For Spain*, p. 2.

[28] In thesis VI of *On the Concept of History*, Walter Benjamin wrote that 'every age must strive anew to wrest tradition away from the conformism that is working to overpower it', where 'tradition' is understood as a tool of the ruling classes if it is abandoned to conformism. *Walter Benjamin: Selected Writings*, vol. 4, eds Howard Eiland and Michael W. Jennings, trans. Edmund Jephcott *et al.* (Cambridge: Harvard University Press, 2003).

[29] The studies in question are: Dana Bultman, 'Góngora's Invocation of *Prudente consul*: Censorship and Humanist Doubts about his Lyric Language', *Hispanófila*, 142 (2004), 1–19;

listic controversy generated by Góngora's poetry should also be considered within these conflictive ideological co-ordinates. From a Sarduy-inspired Keplerian perspective, we might dare to envisage the tension between Góngora's poetry and his detractors in the symbolic terms of an elliptical orbit unsuccessfully restrained by a heliocentric moral order.

Is there 'res' in this 'verba'?

The literary polemic surrounding the publication of Góngora's *Polifemo* and *Soledades* was a dominant focus of twentieth-century scholarship.[30] Thanks to the fervour of the debate, instigated in 1614 by Juan de Jáuregui's *Antídoto contra la pestilente poesía de las Soledades* [*Antidote to the Pestilent Poetry, 'Soledades'*], scholars have been able to document in some detail the reactions of the poet's first readers to his most aggressively experimental texts, the *Soledades*, as well as the *Polifemo*. Both poems, in accordance with the elitist pretensions of their author, circulated in numerous manuscript copies during Góngora's lifetime.[31] There was some concern that absorption in the minutiae of the theoretical positions informing the *culteranismo* controversy might mean that broader imperatives would be overlooked or, indeed, result in the erasure of the poet.[32] However, the figure of the poet has never really been lost in the conventional biographical studies that are standard features of every edition, and in fact, in recent years, has been recuperated from a more collectively resonant socio-economic perspective. Beverley's ground-breaking work on the *Soledades* merits particular mention.[33] The portrayal of Góngora as a marginal-

---

Sofie Kluge, 'Góngora's Heresy: Literary Theory and Criticism in the Golden Age', *Modern Language Notes*, 122.2 (2007), 251–71; Juan M. Vitulli, 'Polifemo reformado: imitación, comentario y diferencia en la poética de Góngora', *Revista de estudios hispánicos*, 41.1 (2007), 3–26.

[30] See the following representative sample of literature on the topic: *Documentos gongorinos*, ed. Eunice Joiner Gates (Mexico: Colegio de México, 1960); Emilio Orozco Díaz, *Lope y Góngora frente a frente* (Madrid: Gredos, 1973); Ana Martínez Arancón, *La batalla en torno a Góngora (selección de textos)* (Barcelona: Antoni Bosch, 1978); David H. Darst, *Imitatio: polémicas sobre la imitación en el siglo de oro* (Madrid: Orígenes, 1985), pp. 51–82; Antonio Carreira, 'La controversia en torno a las *Soledades*. Un parecer desconocido, y edición crítica de las primeras cartas', in *Hommage à Robert Jammes (Anejos de Criticón)*, ed. Francis Cerdan, 3 vols (Toulouse: Presses Universitaires du Mirail, 1994), I, pp. 151–71.

[31] Góngora died in 1627 without having published his poetry. The first printed edition, by López de Vicuña, appeared the following year, but was withdrawn by the Inquisition in June 1628. Salcedo Coronel published his *Polifemo comentado* in 1629, and then in 1630 Pellicer de Salas y Tovar's edition was published with the title *Lecciones solemnes a las obras de don Luis de Góngora y Argote, Píndaro andaluz, príncipe de los poetas líricos de España*.

[32] See W. Pabst, *La creación gongorina en los poemas Polifemo y Soledades*, trans. Nicolás Marín (Madrid: C.S.I.C, 1966), pp. 6–8.

[33] See John R. Beverley, *Aspects of Góngora's 'Soledades'*, Purdue University Monographs in Romance Languages, 1 (Amsterdam: John Benjamins, 1980).

ised aristocrat who used his poetry as a means of attaining cultural and social distinction has had a considerable impact on subsequent scholarship; restoring some legitimacy to the notion of authorial intentionality, without tying the poetry down to a circular model of meaning that absorbs poetic voice into author and vice versa. A significant reconciliation was effected as a result: the generic and rhetorical construction of lyric subjectivity in Góngora's poetry is now generally recognised, but without discounting a connection with history. Thus words that eschew the comfort of order are not made to point back to an identifiable, 'authorial', sense of self, but rather embody the experiences of particular selfhood as traces within a chaotic confrontation with past time and present language. In fact, an added advantage of this approach is the way that it draws us back to the poetry at the heart of the Gongorist debate.[34] For, as I have argued elsewhere,[35] among the 'losses' sustained by scholarship in its too narrow engagement with the Gongorist polemic were the poetic texts themselves and the agency of their co-creating readers.[36] Even the identifiable readers/protagonists of the controversy have emerged in one-dimensional fashion (as literary critics whose black and white reception of the new-style poetics has rarely been scrutinised outside the boundaries of the aesthetic), with little regard for their firm rooting in what Fish termed distinct 'interpretive communities'.[37] When the acts of reading which gave rise to the polemic are located within their historical dimensions they emerge as more provocatively interferential. The meanings read into the texts were certainly determined by earlier reading experiences and by the intellectual tools of the receivers,[38] but it is worth remembering that Góngora's poems were not abstract entities easily detached from the material

[34] A view convincingly demonstrated by Beverley and defended by Edward Friedman and Carlos M.G. Gutiérrez. See (respectively): 'Creative Space: Ideologies of Discourse in Góngora's *Polifemo*', in *Cultural Authority in Golden Age Spain*, pp. 51–78; and Gutiérrez, 'Las *Soledades* y El *Polifemo* de Góngora: Distinción, capitalización simbólica y tomas de posición en el campo literario español de la primera mitad del siglo XVII', *Romance Languages Annual*, 10.2 (1998), 621–25 (622).

[35] In a study of the *Polifemo* published in 2006, I sought to establish the context which would allow us to accept the centrality of the *fábula* in the defence of *gongorismo*, and explored the contradictory parameters of a reconceived *aemulatio* which is inextricably connected to that defence. It was my contention then that by interrogating the metaliterary markers and the function of literary allusion in the fable, and by implicating the reader in this process of signification, we can recreate potential meanings which extend beyond the surface-searching investigations that have traditionally characterised source studies. See Torres, *The Polyphemus Complex*, 'Introduction', pp. 3–22.

[36] Carlos Gutiérrez has suggested that the emergence of modernity in Gongorist poetics is directly linked to the way in which the reader is involved in decoding the linguistic and conceptual difficulties of the text. See 'Las *Soledades* y El *Polifemo* de Góngora'.

[37] See Stanley Fish, *Is there a Text in this Class? The Authority of Interpretive Communities* (Cambridge, MA: Harvard University Press, 1980).

[38] See Roland Barthes, *S/Z*, trans. Richard Miller (Oxford: Basil Blackwell, 1974), p. 10.

forms and spaces through which they were received, nor from the differing ideologies which were invested in their reading.

In the Gongorist climate of literature written 'no para los muchos' [not for the many], but for the select few 'ideal' readers[39] whose erudition and 'ingenio' [ingenuity] rendered them worthy recipients of such elevated poetics,[40] the intellectual contours of a reader's horizon of expectations are not difficult to delineate. Moreover, as Beverley pointed out, Góngora's poetry is exemplary of a certain form of Baroque literature that was designed to resist even the already-existing possibilities of commercial publication and distribution. Its instrumentality was not to 'reach a mass audience, but rather to intervene in discrete circuits of aristocratic power and patronage'.[41] We need only look to the prologue of Pellicer's edition of 1630, addressed to 'los ingenios doctíssimos de España, bienméritos de la erudición latina' [the most learned intellectuals in Spain, most worthy of Latin erudition], for an explicit statement about the poetry's intended readership.[42] In fact, Gutiérrez goes so far as to suggest that Góngora wrote for other writers, for a small group of proto-intellectuals who could confer on him the literary distinction he craved.[43] Prominent among this group was Pedro de Valencia, an influential humanist and friend of the poet, who was singled out by him to receive a copy of the first *Soledad* and *Polifemo* in May 1613.[44] Valencia's objections to some of Góngora's more extravagant images, stylistic features and, indeed, 'todo lo oscuro' [everything dark] were accepted by the writer, who was prepared to amend or expunge the offending passages from his

---

[39] Beverley, working from a premise established by Godzich, points out that 'even a text as evidently "dialogical" as *Don Quijote* presumed in its own time an ideal reader ...'. See *Against Literature* (Minneapolis and London: University of Minnesota Press, 1993), p. 45.

[40] See Pablo Jauralde Pou on the topic of the Baroque as the first 'cultura de masas': '... de qué modo los poetas de la época intentan no ser devorados por la plebe, por el vulgo fiero de esos prólogos insultantes, aquilatando su forma, escribiendo un arte exquisito y minoritario, para los pocos, que no se entregará a las prensas, sino en copia manuscrita al amigo erudito, al sabio, al poeta de la corte, al humanista, etc., que lo dará a conocer, a su vez, a los restantes colegas'. 'El público y la realidad histórica de la literatura española de los siglos XVI y XVII', *Edad de Oro*, I (1982), 55–64 (63).

[41] See Beverley, *Against Literature*, p. 50. Rivers notes the significance of the first collection of the poet's work, brought together by Chacón Ponce de Léon, Lord of Polvoranca, under the supervision of the poet himself, and presented as a gift to the Count-Duke of Olivares a year after Góngora's death: 'This aristocratic gesture, deliberately avoiding the mass-producing mechanics of the printing press, with its commercial buyers, featured a skilfully crafted and uniquely authoritative copy of the famous poet's works to be presented in a lordly manner to a single reader, who was the King's prime minister, the *de facto* ruler of Spain'. See 'Góngora and his Readers', in *The Image of the Baroque*, ed. Aldo Scaglione, with Gianni Eugenio Viola (New York: Peter Lang, 1995), pp. 109–21 (p. 114).

[42] As discussed in Rivers, 'Góngora and his Readers'.

[43] Gutiérrez, 'Las *Soledades* y El *Polifemo* de Góngora', 621.

[44] See Alonso, *Góngora y El Polifemo*, pp. 62–63; Manuel M. Pérez López, *Pedro de Valencia: primer crítico gongorino* (Salamanca: Ediciones Universidad de Salamanca, 1988).

final version. Góngora's readiness to revise his work was undoubtedly due to the respect he had for Valencia's judgement, but the censure was made more palatable by Valencia himself, who framed it within a rhetoric of eulogy informed by an intuitive responsiveness to Góngora's linguistic ambitions. For although Valencia may have struggled with aspects of Góngora's experimental lyric, and his comments certainly convey ambivalence regarding the extent to which the limits of standard Castilian usage should be breached,[45] ultimately he endorsed the validity of Góngora's project to raise Castilian to the level of Latin as a poetic language.[46] It is especially in this regard that the moderation asked of the writer is conspicuous by its absence from the critic/reader's response. For Valencia judges Góngora's work to be better, by far, than the best Greek and Latin poets: '[…] juzgando de sus poesías que se aventajan con grande exceso a todo lo mejor que he leído de griegos y latinos en aquel género […]'[47] [considering his poetry to be far superior to the best Greek and Latin work that I've read in that genre]. There is also, in this first, requested reading, an implicit recognition of what Alonso would designate centuries later an 'anhelo de superación' – an exemplary eristic energy impelling extraordinary artistic creation.[48]

The intensity of *cultismo* in Góngora can certainly, therefore, be understood and valorised within the parameters of a calculated strategy of *aemulatio*,[49] a perspective that permits appreciation of the broader diachronic imperatives of his self-consciously progressive poetics, while still acknowledging the dialectic of continuity and rupture that is articulated within the allusive frame. But we must be careful not to privilege the 'reality' of diachrony over other temporal relationships, as María Rosa Menocal has reminded us.[50] Otherwise we

45   See Bultman, 'Góngora's Invocation', 7–10, where she argues that analysis of the differences between two existing drafts of Valencia's letter to Góngora reveals that he was (a) 'initially hesitant' to praise Góngora's works and that (b) this hesitancy was due in great part to his sense of frustration with a linguistic obscurity which challenged even the most learned.

46   This argument is central to Rose Lozano's analysis of Gongorist poetics and their reception. See Joaquín Roses Lozano, *Una Poética de la Oscuridad: la recepción crítica de las 'Soledades' en el siglo XVII* (London: Tamesis, 1994).

47   See Luis de Góngora y Argote, *Obras Completas*, eds Juan Millé y Giménez and Isabel Millé y Giménez, 5th edn (Madrid: Aguilar, 1961), p. 1084.

48   Alonso, *Góngora y El Polifemo*, pp. 255–57.

49   Curtius reminds us that 'cultismo' is actually a Latinism, used for instance by Quintilian (VIII, 3. 6) and Ovid (*Ars Amatoria* III, 341 where his poems are called 'culta carmina'). See Ernst Robert Curtius, *European Literature and the Latin Middle Ages*, trans. Willard R. Trask (New York: Pantheon Books, 1953), p. 294, footnote 56. Affinity between Spanish and Latin is, therefore, at the core of the 'cultista' movement in Spain. Initiated in the fifteenth century, it is not surprising that it would gather momentum in the imperial context of the sixteenth century, galvanised by Herrera. As most commentators have noted, the elements of Góngora's 'culto' style were not new, nor indeed was his promotion of obscurity as a hallmark of distinctive and distinguishing language. Carrillo y Sotomayor writes in a similar vein in his *El libro de la erudición poética* in 1611.

50   See *Writing in Dante's Cult of Truth: From Borges to Boccaccio* (Durham: Duke University Press, 1991), p. 3: 'For literary history is itself not diachronic but rather synchronistic: time

run the risk, in this case, of inferring from Góngora's efforts to create a transcendent imperial language, a sense of order which the writing process itself
undermines. The diachronic background gains sense only when it is perceived
in tension with the synchronic space of instability and contingency that was
invaded by imperial failures. As such, the language of Góngora's poetry is
bound up with the ideologies that legitimised colonisation (and cannot be
disconnected from a master discourse of emerging nationalism); but rather than
imagining, and re-presenting, with the ultimate aim of 'vaulting the nation',[51]
its difficult readings resist the orthodoxies of single significance and, in their
plurality, challenge the idea of history as smooth narrative. In fact, the cleaving
of differences (most notably between poetry and the vulgar tongue), the collapsing of time periods into the present and the dissolution of conventional
connections are all characteristic of an 'altered consciousness of language' in
Góngora which finds its most pervasive expression through reinvigoration of
hyperbaton,[52] a figure from Classical rhetoric (*Rhetorica ad Herennium*, 4. 44)
which the Romans translated as 'transgressio' in recognition of its disruptive
as well as ornamental effects.

   Hyperbaton, understood by rhetoricians as the linguistic phenomenon whereby logical syntactical relations are disturbed, is deployed by Góngora as part of
a strategy of intentional obscurity in communication.[53] His heightened use of
the device, which corresponds with the poetic practice of canonical Latin writers such as Virgil, Ovid and Horace (especially in the *Odes*), also demonstrates
that Góngora knew exactly how to deal with the problem of literary tradition;
how to be enabled, authorised and renewed by it; without being repressed and
subsumed in its 'vast passing away'.[54] For the inherently antithetical premise of
Góngora's writing demanded a dialectical response; one that would encompass
a respect for continuity (and reinforce the elevation of Castilian to the rank of
its predecessor Latin), while also recognising distinction through gestures of
rebellion (thereby ensuring that while keeping within the Roman imperial

is all jumbled up everywhere, authors from different centuries and different mindsets sit one next
to another and shape each other's work, both proleptically and retrospectively'.

   [51]   Patricia Palmer's analysis of how language and power move into alignment in the context
of conquest in early modern England is a useful point of reference and contrast here. See *Language
and Conquest in Early Modern England* (Cambridge: Cambridge University Press, 2001), ch. 1.

   [52]   Richard Waswo's study, *Language and Meaning in the Renaissance* (Princeton: Princeton
University Press, 1987), demonstrates how a 'generally altered consciousness of language' (p. 113)
was the outworking of a process set in motion by humanist philologists such as Lorenzo Valle,
whose analysis of the flux of Latin in/through time revealed language to be a socio-historical
construct.

   [53]   A very obvious example occurs at the opening of the first *Soledad* (vv. 42–51) where the
main verb 'escala' is postponed.

   [54]   Curtius encapsulates the dichotomy. His observations on the complexity of the literary
tradition conclude that: 'Like all life, tradition is a vast passing away and renewal' (*European
Literature*, p. 393).

model, Castilian would ultimately escape Latin's inevitable extinction). Thus creative emulation in Góngora tends towards achieving defamiliarisation in language – a non-conformist enactment that was rejected by those who would champion a continuous literary decorum. Moreover, hyperbaton, operating at the level of combination, rather than selection, accords a privileged status to the word, thereby freeing it from the shackles of referential commitment. In this respect, hyperbaton is not unlike Góngora's extravagant mechanisms for meta-phorisation which also compel the reader to interrogate complexity and, in so doing, to rethink the question of how language relates to physical reality.

According to Foucault's classification of the sixteenth-century episteme, Renaissance Europe's understanding of the connection between language and reality was one which bound language to the world through a system of analogical correspondences. A corollary argument is that language usage in the seventeenth century is marked by a heightened awareness of its constitutive power; in other words, language operating under the conditions of a new epistemic system is discovered as a maker, not just 'namer', of meaning.[55] As Palmer points out, such dichotomous thinking is problematic in that it fails to acknowledge the dynamic operations of language that are apparent in both creative and theoretical writing prior to the 1600 epistemic threshold.[56] Garcilaso's and Herrera's poetry, as we have seen, are just two cases in point and are illustrative of Renaissance writers' instinctive appreciation of language's inherently creative potential. Moreover, by focusing our attention on the seventeenth century as the decisive locus of discontinuity, we lose sight of an earlier, equally fundamental fracture in the Western history of thought – what has been recently termed the 'transvaluation of values' by means of which Renaissance secular culture is said to have overthrown the asceto-monastic traditionalism of the Middle Ages.[57] Notwithstanding the unresolved issues that persisted at the heart of this transition, a highly significant development of the Western intellectual tradition was realised; the rise of empirical science, which laid the foundations for the Scientific Revolution of the eighteenth

---

55   See Michel Foucault's *L'Archéologie du savoir* (Paris: Gallimard, 1969), where he defines the episteme as follows: 'Par épistémè on entend, en fait, l'ensemble des relations pouvant unir, à une époque donnée, les pratiques discursives qui donnent lieu à des figures épistémologiques, à des sciences, éventuellement à des systèmes formalisés ... l'épistémè, ce n'est pas une forme de connaissance ou un type de rationalité qui traversant les sciences les plus diverses, manifesterait l'unité souveraine d'un sujet, d'un esprit, ou d'une époque, c'est l'ensemble des relations qu'on peut découvrir, pour une époque donnée, entre les sciences quand on les analyse au niveau des régularités discursives' (p. 250). As Ian Maclean has noted, many Renaissance specialists have given Foucault's Renaissance episteme 'short shrift' (see 'Foucault's Renaissance Episteme Reassessed: An Aristotelian Counterblast', *The Journal of the History of Ideas*, 59.1 [1998], 149–66 [p. 149]). Also, see, among others, Murray Cohen, *Sensible Words: Linguistic Practice in England 1640–1785* (Baltimore and London: John Hopkins University Press, 1977), p. 25.

56   See Palmer, *Language and Conquest*, p. 25.

57   Creel, *The Voice of the Phoenix*, pp. 277–9, where this argument is synthesised.

century. Scientific discoveries of the period, such as the achievements of Copernicus discussed above, challenged authorities which had held sway for centuries (most notably the 'sacred' triad of Aristotle, Ptolemy and Galen). But another 'intellectual revolution' was less fully realised. The shift from the referential semantics of the Medieval period to the relational and constitutive semantics of the Renaissance was a major insight which Renaissance culture struggled to articulate. The fact that Renaissance writers and theorists lacked the theoretical vocabulary to effect a full-scale semantic rebellion certainly impeded the project, but, as Waswo's study points out, a more deliberate strategy of containment can also be identified.[58] A counter-movement, impelled by politico-ideological conservatism and/or a concern for religious orthodoxy (under threat from science's negation of *a priori* judgement), worked to adjust semantic insights to a traditional view of language as nomenclature. A 'considerable discrepancy between theory and practice'[59] resulted from the tensions between those who sought to see through words to essence (often with some moral purpose)[60] and those who reflected upon the employment of language in terms of contexts and effects, revelling in the operation of words as spatio-temporal phenomena. This state of disjuncture extended beyond the sixteenth and into the seventeenth century and finds expression in Spain in the *cultista* polemic, when ideologically suppressive tendencies, dressed up as aesthetic theory, were set against an exuberant poetic practice.

This view is not at variance with received wisdom which sees the Gongorist 'battle', and its central *res/verba* conflict, as a reflection of a crisis of confidence in the assumptions that underpinned the Renaissance model of *imitatio*.[61] On the contrary, the unconventional functioning of emulative allusion, which gives precedence to opposition over analogy in Góngora's lyric, is better understood when viewed as the poet's re-evaluation of an inherited framework that he found insufficient, both for the communication of new knowledge and as a means of decipher-

---

58   See Waswo, *Language and Meaning*.

59   Waswo discusses this split between theoretical observations (referential) and language practice (constitutive) in *Language and Meaning*, p. 80.

60   See Darst, *Imitatio*, p. 72, where he sums up the main thrust of the argument of Góngora's detractors (from Cascales through Lope de Vega to Juan de Jáuregui) as: 'una crítica contra la presencia exclusiva de palabras sin fin doctrinal'.

61   Aurora Egido comments: '[...] la batalla gongorina no es sino un reflejo de la crisis que en los inicios del siglo xvii enfrenta a los defensores de la imitación renacentista y a los que tratan de desvincularse de ella. Pero unos y otros, áticos y llanos, buscan en el pasado modelos que justifiquen su postura'. See 'La *Hidra bocal*: sobre la palabra poética en el Barroco', in *Fronteras de la poesía en el barroco* (Barcelona: Crítica, 1990), pp. 9–55 (p. 41). See also Darst, *Imitatio*, pp. 51–52, who notes a radical change of emphasis in Spanish poetic theory post 1610, the date of publication of Carrillo y Sotomayor's treatise *Libro de la erudición poética* and the date of composition of Góngora's first *cultista* poems. Prior to that date, Spanish poetic theorists were 'comentadores' [commentators] who aimed to construct a poetic system based on imitation of the ancients. Post 1610, all theorists were 'defensores' [defenders] of specific poetic styles, using ancient texts as justification for their arguments.

ing 'the temporal, cosmic and metaphorical representation of man' in his particular socio-historical environment.[62] Likewise, the hermeneutical instability of the detractors' position is fully exposed when the negative values they ascribe to aesthetic concepts are considered beyond the framework of continued allegiance to a fading analogical world view. In fact, it is feasible that accusations that point to semantic hollowness, and/or violations of similitude, participate in a less than benign discourse of power – one that mediates the concerns of the Old World (in which humanist commentaries operate as a controlling tool in tension with individual, unorthodox, engagement with tradition, religion, identity and race), while also filtering anxieties about the New. If words spinning free from extra-linguistic correlatives could 'make' meaning, then language, at its most anarchic, could call heterodoxy into being.

The stabilisation of Castilian as the dominant mother tongue had gained ground in the peninsula through the establishment of a relatively strong administrative apparatus and through print culture, both playing a role in embodying for citizens the ideal of a linguistically shared public sphere.[63] It was, as Elliott has noted, a collective identity 'laboriously achieved' and challenged by the continual pursuit of new territorial acquisition.[64] Sustaining Castilian's centralising and 'civilising' function in expansion became key to subsuming and sanitising alien components within a system of communication that rationalised inequitability. For instance, intellectual speculation on the nature and status of Amerindians included an evaluation of their native languages, which, by giving expression to unintelligible heresy, confirmed the barbarity of the speakers.[65] Castilian was conveniently vaulted as a luminous mirror projecting universal Christian truth, a position made ever more precarious by a poet like Góngora whose language usage thrives, productively, on the dark side. Bultman points, in particular, to how Góngora's engagement with 'linguistic drift in meaning' demonstrates that 'texts are bound to time, are not eternally the same, and by extension nor are the cultures they represent'[66] – an ideological position that clearly cut across any sense of a unitary 'reality' (stabilised in religion and ethnicity), as well as the universalising tenden-

---

[62]   See Antonio Carreño's discussion of the cultural identity of texts and of those, like Góngora, who give them voice: 'Of "Orders" and "Disorders": Analogy in the Spanish Baroque Poetry', in *The Image of the Baroque*, pp. 139-56 (p. 152).

[63]   An insightful, succinct account of the issues involved in this is provided by Bultman, 'Góngora's Invocation', 1–3, with reference to Ralph Penny, *A History of the Spanish Language* (Cambridge: Cambridge University Press, 1971).

[64]   See J.H. Elliott, *Spain, Europe and the Wider World 1500–1800* (New Haven and London: Yale University Press, 2009), p. 6.

[65]   See Anthony Pagden, *The Fall of Natural Man: The American Indian and the Origins of Comparative Ethnography* (Cambridge: Cambridge University Press, 1987), who writes: 'Not only was the concept of "barbarism" in origin a linguistic one, but [...] the evaluation of Indian languages played a crucial role in assessing the status of their users' (p. 70).

[66]   See Bultman, 'Góngora's Invocation', 3.

cies of imperialism. Moreover, if a community is 'imagined' on the basis of a 'coherent nation of speakers', functioning as 'simultaneous participants',[67] then the extreme defamiliarisation of Castilian in Góngora's opaque poetics (which rendered it 'meaning-less' to many of his contemporaries) may have been received as a disturbing onslaught from within, a deconstruction of Baroque political fictions through an admission of 'otherness' which extended far beyond a perceived allegiance to heretical Judaism.[68]

The turnabout of the expected in Góngora is effected through a cultivation of perceptual doubt (exemplified, for instance, in the *Polifemo*, in his pervasive use of the 'A if not B' structure), but also through the enhanced temporality of the sign. This is marked especially in the movement of words across linguistic borders (especially from Latin or Italian), or in the imaginative extension of historical linguistic practices, through which familiar words are appropriated and differently conditioned. Even a sympathetic reader like Pedro de Valencia had a consensual limit and urged moderation in the use and frequency of what he termed 'vocablos peregrinos' [unusual words],[69] perhaps anticipating the aggression that would follow from recasting Castilian in such novel and 'obscure' terms.[70] Francisco Cascales would not disappoint, attacking Góngora's 'modo de hablar peregrino' as wolverine aesthetics purposefully constructed to destroy legitimate poetry.[71] Jáuregui, too, had sensed a wilful irrationality in the depiction of the poem's 'principal figura':

[67]   Benedict Anderson's seminal study, *Imagined Communities: Reflections on the Origin and Spread of Nationalism* (London and New York: Verso, 1983), locates the 'thinking' of nationalism post the early modern, but its arguments are suggestive for nation-making in the earlier period. The quoted text is taken from p. 13.

[68]   Criticism of obscurantism and deviation from poetic norms, from Jáuregui through to Quevedo, was often expressed in terms that suggested Góngora's allegiance to Judaism and exposes the intricate dialectic between language and ethnicity that was pervasive in the period. See Andrée Collard, 'La "herejía" de Góngora', *Hispanic Review*, 36.4 (1968), 328–37.

[69]   The full reference reads: 'También siguiendo esta novedad, usa de vocablos peregrinos italianos, y otros del todo latinos, que los antiguos llaman glosas, lenguas, y ahora llamamos así a las interpretaciones de los tales y de todo lo oscuro. Estos conviene moderar y usar pocas veces; y no muchas tampoco [...]'. See Millé and Millé, *Obras Completas*, pp. 1085–86. Bultman draws our attention to the 'semantic impreción' of the word 'peregrino/a' itself, its difference from the more concrete 'cultismo', and the request for transparent poetic language which underpins Valencia's use of it ('Góngora's Invocation', 8–9).

[70]   In fact, Valencia is explicit on these two points: he warns that even the most erudite readers (in an earlier version of the letter he refers to himself as the frustrated reading subject) will find Góngora's obscurity frustrating; and he observes that the extreme defamiliarisation of the poet's style does not sit easily with the natural structures of Castilian (Millé and Millé, *Obras Completas*, p. 1085).

[71]   See Francisco Cascales, *Cartas filológicas*, ed. Justo García Soriano (Madrid: Espasa Calpe, 1959), I, 188. See also Mary Gaylord Randel 'Metaphor and Fable in Góngora's *Soledad Primera*', *Revista Hispánica Moderna*, 40 (1978–9), 97–112, who situates metaphor at the heart of the controversy and as central to Cascales's defence of more conventional humanistic poetics.

Sale un mancebito, la principal figura que Vm introduce, y *no le da nombre*. Éste fue al mar y vino de el mar, sin que sepáis cómo ni para qué; *él no sirve sino de mirón, y no dice cosa buena ni mala*, [...] *Tampoco dice Vm* jamás en que País o Provincia pasaba el caso: *todo lo cual es contra razón*. [emphasis added][72]

[A youth appears, the protagonist you present, and *you give him no name*. He went to sea and came back from the sea, regardless of how or why; *he serves no purpose except to observe, and says nothing, neither good nor bad*, [...] *Nor do you ever tell us* in what country or province this takes place: *there's no reason to any of it*.]

As Lorna Close suggested some years ago, there is a diacritical dimension to the *peregrino*'s deliberate indeterminacy.[73] By denying his protagonist a name, Góngora denies the traditional view of language as nomenclature, figuring his new progressive poetics in the intangible 'value' of a sign that contains traditional traces within it, but wanders 'lejos de la patria'[74] [far from the homeland]. Defenders of Góngora do, inevitably, assign a more positive value to the 'peregrino' concept. Pedro Díaz de Rivas, in his textual commentary on the *Polifemo*, transforms transgression into a celebration of autonomy, identifying in Góngora's 'wandering wit' a capacity for distinction rather than dissonance.[75] Góngora speaks for his own poetry in these terms in the single letter that constitutes his contribution to the *cultista* polemic. His comments reveal a self-conscious awareness of the distinct status that will accrue to him as the instigator of a new elitist poetics: '[...] honra me ha causado hacerme escuro a los ignorantes, que esa es la distinción de los hombres doctos, hablar de

---

72   See *Antídoto contra la pestilente poesía de las Soledades por Juan de Jáuregui*, ed. José Manuel Rico García (Sevilla: Universidad de Sevilla, 2002), p. 7. I have discussed elsewhere the question of the *peregrino*'s passivity and various acts of seeing. See Torres, '*Broaching the Void*', 107–29.

73   See 'The play of difference: a reading of Góngora's Soledades', in *Conflicts of Discourse: Spanish Literature in the Golden Age*, ed. Peter W. Evans (Manchester and New York: Manchester University Press, 1990), pp. 184–98 (pp. 191–92). Close read the *Soledades* in Derridean terms, as a process of endless deferral in which 'peregrinación' is privileged as an act of postponement.

74   The *Diccionario de Autoridades* offers the following as its primary definition of 'peregrino': 'que se aplica al que anda por tierras extrañas o lejos de su patria' [applied to whoever travels through foreign lands or far from his native land]. Its currency in the controversy derives, however, from the following: 'por extensión se toma algunas veces por entraño, raro, especial en su linea, o pocas veces visto'[by extension it is sometimes understood as strange, unusual, special of its kind, or rarely seen].

75   See Melchora Romanos's useful study of the *Anotaciones*, 'Los "tan nuevos y peregrinos modos" del *Polifemo*. Ponderación de la poética gongorina en los comentaristas del siglo XVII', in *Góngora Hoy VII: El Polifemo. Actas del Foro del Debate Góngora Hoy celebrado en la Diputación de Córdoba del 22 al 23 de abril de 2004*, ed. Joaquín Roses (Córdoba: Diputación de Córdoba, 2005), pp. 215–31. For Díaz de Rivas's text, see Joiner Gates, *Documentos gongorinos*; see also Marsha S. Collins, *Góngora's Masque of the Imagination* (Columbia: University of Missouri Press, 2002), pp. 27–39, for an interesting reading of Díaz's defence.

manera que a ellos les parezca griego' [Honour accrues to me from being obscure to the ignorant, that's what distinguishes learned men, speaking in such a way that it is all Greek to them].[76] The letter itself has been the subject of much discussion, mostly because its conventionality, lack of satirical edge and/or vision are at odds with the sharp intellect that informs the author's poetry.[77] I have made the case elsewhere that we have, perhaps, accorded the document an enhanced position in the front line of Góngora's defence, one that was never intended; and that we should look to the poetry itself for a 'manifesto' of *gongorismo*, where the role of the reader as co-artificer in the construction of meaning is most apparent.[78] I stand by the substance of that earlier assertion, but now believe that if we attend to the allusive texture of the letter itself, specifically to the biblical reference to Babel, and recognise in this return to the inaugural scene of linguistic diversity a confrontation with the critical provisionality of language itself, then the letter comes to represent a more provocative intervention in the politico-linguistic debates of the period than has been acknowledged to date.

Góngora's letter answers specific charges brought against his major compositions, and he uses it to outline how the poetry does in fact demonstrate the conventional norms demanded of it: 'lo útil, lo honroso, lo deleitable' [utility, honour, pleasure]. According to the letter, Góngora's lyric is 'útil' [useful] as a cerebral exercise, designed to stimulate and enliven the wit; it is 'honroso' [honourable] because the writer's artistic labour has elevated the vernacular to the 'perfection' of Latin; and it is 'deleitable' [pleasurable] as an intellectual journey of exploration and discovery to the mysteries concealed within the poetic text.[79] It is this latter point, more precisely, the metaphor used to express it ('quitar la corteza' [remove the bark]), that has attracted (and, in the process, distracted) the attention of critics. Góngora's recourse to Neoplatonic Christian allegory has been seen as a defence of didacticism,

---

[76]   For the text of Góngora's letter, *Carta de don Luis de Góngora en respuesta de la que le escribieron*, see Millé and Millé, *Obras completas*, pp. 894–98. Carreira ('La controversia', pp. 168–71) argues for the authenticity of Góngora's reply against Jammes's view that at least part of the text was written by someone else.

[77]   Carreira suggests that the letter is ineffective because it was written in response to an anonymous detractor and Góngora found it impossible to harness his satirical wit against an invisible enemy and should have resisted the temptation to do so ('La controversia', p. 170). Most commentators, however, accept that this first letter was written by Lope de Vega.

[78]   See Torres, *The Polyphemus Complex*, 'Introduction', esp. pp. 7–10. Friedman ('Creative Space', p. 54) also places Góngora's poetry at the centre of the Gongorist debate with the *carta en respuesta* as complementary to it.

[79]   More specifically, the metaphor is exploited to indicate the meticulous exegesis required on the part of the reader to penetrate beyond the linguistic complexity of the poetry in order to open up the layers of interpretation that lie beneath. The 'fruta' of Góngora's heretical new poetry might be forbidden to those too ignorant to appreciate it, but would satisfy the intellect of the learned.

problematic in that it is not sustained anywhere in his poetic practice.[80] Moreover, the poet's recourse to Augustine sententiousness in order to stress the meticulous exegesis required of readers appears to substantiate this anachronistic commitment to hidden truths and to undermine an earlier confident claim to a restorative originality that we have tended to overlook. Having been accused of inflicting violations upon the natural tongue in his *Soledades*, and warned that this might set a precedent for future poets, Góngora takes unambiguous pleasure in the creation of an elevated Castilian that has its origins in the artificiality of Classical Latin (citing Ovid, in his letter, as his own 'obscure' predecessor): 'me holgara de haber dado principio a algo; pues es mayor gloria en empezar una acción que consumarla' [I am delighted to have initiated something; there is greater glory in beginning an act than ending it]. Against those who would invoke tradition in terms of conventional limitations and claim ownership of clarity as a key virtue of 'traditional' discourse, Góngora articulates a belief in obscurantism both as a locus of communion with literary history and as a creative medium of linguistic renewal. In the light of this opening offensive, the poet's 'Platonic' discourse might be viewed as ironic signposting, directing his detractors to a placating conformity, from which there is no escape from absolute truths ('como el fin de el entendimiento es hacer presa en verdades' [given that the aim of understanding is imprisonment in truth]), while at the same time making 'clear' to those with the 'agudeza' [wit] to see in and through the dark that the realm of conceptual reality is more subjectively speculative, built on approximations that embrace experience, sensation and, as the poetry reveals, the assaults of involuntary memory. Read either as linguistically ambiguous (where the objective of 'entendimiento' is reflexive and its exercise, therefore, an end in itself),[81] or as a 'play' on Platonism, rather than adherence to it, Góngora's metaphor emerges as a more significant gesture of resistance. The reflection upon the Tower of Babel that follows, and that 'resolves' Góngora's response, appears less enigmatic in this context. It is the poet's parting shot against an ignorant type of reading (coherently derided and manipulated throughout), but it also contributes to a broader linguistic debate which troubled contemporary culture – the issue of multiple European vernacular languages and their inherent exilic conditioning.

---

[80]   See, for instance, Darst, *Imitatio*, p. 81; Beverley, *Aspects*, p. 15. Note, however, a more recent study by Sophie Kluge who argues via a reading of the navigation passage of the *Primera Soledad* (vv. 366–506) that Gongorine allegory does remain within the boundaries of Christian allegory, as suggested in his letter, but stretches that worldview to its breaking point: 'Góngora's Heresy'. For an alternative reading of Gongorist poetics in relation to the *Primera Soledad* see my 'Broaching the Void'.

[81]   See Beverley, *Aspects of Góngora's 'Soledades'*, p. 16, who takes this view against Jones's Platonic interpretation.

The biblical narrative of the Tower of Babel (*Genesis* II, 1–9) purports to explain the origin of the world's diversity of languages as a curse laid down by God upon human presumption. The myth offered aristocratic humanism a symbolic schema that drew much of its power from its reiteration of the tensions between the infinite and the finite which emanated from the Edenic garden and the Adamic fall. The building of a tower from mud bricks that would reach 'unto heaven' was a project shrouded in post-Lapsarian darkness, a projection of the human community's contamination by iniquitous self-discovery and a monument to wilfulness and delusion. The task was impossible and the collapse inevitable. Divine knowledge could not be attained through misguided means and the way of reparation could not be built upon a collective illusion of limitless ascent. A consensus that denied the reality of embodiment floundered in fragmentation and the language that subsumed individuality in order to articulate this flawed univocality was confused and, subsequently, confusing. The original Fall from the lightness of the spirit into the heaviness of the body was seen to be rehearsed again at Babel in a descent from linguistic clarity into darkness. An organic syntax of image, metaphor and symbol emerged, however, from this tragic collision and dialectically informed the main currents and counter-currents of humanist thinking on the subject of Romance languages. For some, Babel offered a means of condemning the multitude of vernaculars as a linguistic fall from grace, a state of exile from the perfect sublimity of Latin;[82] for others, Babel was exploited to hold in check the emerging emancipation of aesthetics from theology and to recall language to its lost Edenic origins when, in the supreme act of clear signification, God's naming created substance.[83] It is not surprising, therefore, that when Góngora's detractors took issue with the lexical polyphony and multivalency of his major poems, they would denounce them in terms of Babelic heresy, with all that this imputation implied. Góngora's response is a condescending and determined declaration of intent:

> Al ramalazo de la desdicha de Babel […] quiero descubrir un secreto no entendido de v.m. al escribirme. No los confundió Dios a ellos con darles

---

[82]   See, for instance, Aldrete's grammar of 1606 in which Spanish is considered a corrupt Latin which has to be cleansed from all trace of decadence. Nitsch sets Góngora's Babel reference in this context. See Wolfram Nitsch, 'Prisiones textuales. Artificio y violencia en la poesía española del barroco', *Olivar*, 5 (2004), 31–47 available at: http://wwwfuentesmemoria.fahce.unlp. edu.ar/art_revistas/pr.3259/pr.3259.pdf

[83]   This theological celebration of clear significance, which reduced the ambivalence of poetic discourse through insistence on a deep structure in which true univocal meaning is revealed, is evidenced in El Brocense's attempts to account for ellipsis and other related phenomena. See Malcolm K. Read's discussion in *Visions in Exile: The Body in Spanish Literature and Linguistics 1500–1800*, Purdue University Monographs in Romance Linguistics, 30 (Amsterdam and Philadelphia: John Benjamins, 1990), pp. 17–18.

lenguaje confuso, sino en el mismo suyo ellos se confundieron, tomando piedra por agua y agua por piedra; que ésa fue la grandeza de la sabiduría del que confundió aquel soberbio intento. Yo no envío confusas las *Soledades*, sino las malicias de las voluntades en su mismo lenguaje hallan confusión por parte del sujeto inficionado con ellas. A la gracia de Pentecostés querría obviar el responder, que no quiero a v.m tan aficionado a las cosas del Testamento Nuevo; y a mí me corren muchas obligaciones de saber poco de él por naturaleza y por oficio; y ansí sólo digo que [...] no van en más que una lengua las *Soledades*, aunque pudiera, quedando el brazo sano, hacer una miscelánea de griego, latín y toscano con mi lengua natural, y creo no fuera condenable.

[With regard to being touched by some branch of the misfortune of Babel [...] I would like to reveal a secret misunderstood by you when you wrote to me. God didn't confuse them by giving them confused language, but rather they were confused themselves, taking stone for water and water for stone; that was the great wisdom of the one who confounded that presumptuous project. I don't send the *Soledades* out into the world confused, rather the wilful malice of those who would infect them, find confusion in the language. With regard to my non-participation in the grace of Pentecost, I prefer not to respond, as you seem not too fond of New Testament affairs; while I, on the other hand, am obliged to know something of them both by inclination and by occupation; so I will only say that [...] the *Soledades* are written in a single language, although without too much effort I could have mixed up my natural tongue with a miscellany of Greek, Latin and Italian, and I don't think that would have called for condemnation.]

The poet is explicit on three key issues: his adversary has misunderstood the Babel myth; this misreading has allowed for a wilfully negative, interpretive judgement of the *Soledades*; confusion, therefore, is imposed upon the poetry by those who would infect it with their ignorance and malice, and is not integral to the poetic discourse itself. The subtle shock tactic of the letter, however, is Góngora's insistence on a single language in the *Soledades*, but one that celebrates an anti-Babelic unity and to which he implicitly accords the redemptive potential of Pentecost. Within the New Testament's reconfiguration of the Fall, Christ's sacrifice restores humanity's ruptured relationship with God, and the Spirit's descent in tongues of fire at Pentecost symbolises the re-emergence of language purified and redeemed from its post-Babelic state (St Augustine, *Tractate* 6.10). Góngora's allegiance to New Testament orthodoxy not only re-directs accusations of covert Judaism back on to his accusers (reminded that he is a priest after all), but offers a paradoxical authorisation of linguistic non-conformity in transcendent terms. Extended to language, the concept of the 'felix culpa' [fortunate Fall] enables the existence of multiplicity and yet sanctions each language's own complexities and ambiguities – the characteristics of language that are most at play in poetry. Robert L. Entzminger has demonstrated just how appealing the paradigm was for Milton.[84] I would suggest that it was more subversively attractive to Góngora. Where Pentecost restores communication and consensus in the context of a single Church into which all nations are integrated, Góngora proclaims the inauguration of a single, sublime, language, 'perfected' rather than perfect, in which unity and plurality aspire to reconciliation.[85]

A sonnet written by Góngora in 1600 testifies to the anxieties that haunt such a project. The traditional syntax of the sonnet form, its stanzaic sequences of rhymed and metrically equivalent verses, forces order and logical proposition out of a multilingual mosaic. The result is a site of struggle involving potent questions of genealogy and identity:

> Las tablas del bajel despedazadas
> (signum naufragii pium et crudele),
> del tempio sacro con le rotte vele,
> ficaraon nas paredes penduradas.
>
> Del tiempo las injurias perdonadas,
> et Orionis vi nimbosae stellae
> racoglio le smarritte pecorelle
> nas ribeiras do Betis espalhadas.
>
> Volveré a ser pastor, pues marinero
> quel dio non vuo, che col suo strale sprona
> do austro os assopros è do oceám as agoas,
>
> haciendo al triste son, aunque grosero,
> di questa canna, già selvaggia donna,
> saudade à as feras, e aos penedos, magoas.[86]

[The shattered planks of the boat (a sign of shipwreck that is both merciful and cruel), along with the torn sail, will hang upon the walls of the sacred temple. Once the insults of time have been forgiven, as well as those inflicted

---

[84]   See Robert L. Entzminger, *Divine Word: Milton and the Redemption of Language* (Pittsburgh: Duquesne, 1985). Collard reads Góngora's reference to Pentecost less provocatively, on the basis that he is reacting to insinuations made by his anonymous detractor: 'se acusa a Góngora de confuso y obscuro, insinuando que "no ha participado en la gracia del Pentecostés"' [Góngora is accused of being confused and obscure, insinuating that 'he has not participated in the grace of Pentecost']. See 'La "herejía" de Góngora', 331.

[85]   Mercedes Blanco's meticulous analyses of Góngora's unique poetic language are well known. Unfortunately, her most recent study (which includes discussion of the sublime) became available after the present book had gone to press and too late to inform this reading. See *Góngora o la invención de una lengua* (León: Universidad de León, 2012).

[86]   All references to Góngora's poems are taken from the following edition: Luis de Góngora y Argote, *Obras Completas*, ed. Antonio Carreira, I (*Poemas de autoría segura. Poemas de autenticidad probable*) (Madrid: Biblioteca Castro, 2000). For this sonnet, see pp. 180–81.

by Orion, constellation of storms, I will gather the lost sheep, scattered across the banks of the Betis. I will be a shepherd again, since the god who whips up the South wind and ocean seas with his arrows, will not have me sailor. With the sorrowful, though crude, sound of this reed pipe, I will reach a now rustic lady, move wild beasts to sadness and make rocks feel pain.]

The poem sets up an assemblage of linguistic discourses (Latin and three Romance languages: Castilian, Portuguese and Italian) that point to a fragmented subjectivity and to particular historical conditions which language struggles to accommodate. As in the *Soledades*, the motif of survival in the wake of shipwreck implicates language in the intimacy of a personal trauma. The speaker's identity crisis (lover, shepherd, sailor, survivor, shepherd again, pastoral poet) constitutes more than a parable of the Romance languages' fraught love affair with Latin or a Darwinian reflection on linguistic 'fitness'. The quatrains evoke the ambivalence of signification; the role of subjective experience in interpretation; self-renewal through immersion in ritualistic, symbolic action, the promotion of cultural continuance; and, in the recovery of the abandoned and dispersed sheep, the possibility of redemption through a unified attitude to the world. The elision of Latin in the tercets coincides with a return to origin, to authentic selfhood, but the decision is prompted by an external (and, in the narrative, erotic) force. It is, therefore, if read against the grain of Walter Benjamin's account of ideal language, a regression to progress, a mobility that is productive, but marked by passion and by signs of the past.[87] The final verses open out into an Orphic promise of lyric transmission in which epic appears to cede to pastoral in the celebration of a new type of heroism. The subject voice has fallen into modernity, but communicates its personal catastrophe through an instrument of cultural resonance. The tragedy of Syrinx triggers the mnemonic power that lies at the most archaic core of poetry. And so we are returned to Latin, to the scene of origin for the vernaculars, and specifically to Ovid (*Met.* I, 689–713), and, therein, to transformation and dynamic re-membering. Throughout the sonnet the different languages exclude immediate and complete comprehension. The reader is seduced by their sound patterns, by their musicality. The weight of linguistic excess is lightened in this seduction, and the poem's potentially repressive materiality is mitigated. In the final verses, we are attuned to a music of

---

[87]   In his essay 'On Language as Such and on the Language of Man' (1916), in *One-Way Street*, trans. Edmund Jephcott and Kingsley Shorter (London: Verso, 1997), pp. 107–23, Walter Benjamin posits the genesis of an ideal language as an Adamic, pre-Lapsarian, divine gift, not complicated by passion: 'Man is the namer, by this we recognise that through him pure language speaks. All nature, insofar as it communicates itself, communicates itself in language, and so finally in man. Hence he is the lord of nature and can give names to things. Only through the linguistic being of things can he gain knowledge of them from within himself – in name. God's creation is completed when things receive their names from Man' (p. 111). The loss of linguistic mimesis, according to Benjamin, is an allegory of a fall into history.

loss, to the creation of a poetic voice that sings of desire destroyed, substituted and deferred, but a song communicated on an instrument fashioned by Pan from the union of reed canes of differing lengths that once were Syrinx.

In this sonnet, as in the 'carta en respuesta' [letter in response], there is no investment in the representation of a single reality. Rather we find a quest to create a distinct language that might generate the complex depths of human experience via the reader's intellectual movement through shifting signifiers which multiply upon the surface. Góngora announces in the letter a poetry of becoming, of possibility ('dar principio a algo'), and it unfolds throughout his work in tension with the contradictory reality of being. For there is no acceptance by Góngora in the letter, or in the poetry itself, of prevailing notions of Edenic language, no sense of a search for pre-Lapsarian clarity. Instead, there is a sustained commitment to linguistic obscurity which bears witness to the absence that it fills, which speaks what is absent and for what is absent. The dense metaphoric eloquence, generic marbling and transgressive attitude to tradition which characterise his lyric demonstrate that, unlike Nebrija, Góngora did not find language threatening in its materiality. The grammarian's promotion of Latin as a model language that was not subject to change imposed potential paralysis on linguistic development, a 'flight from death into stasis' which both Garcilaso and Herrera had identified and challenged.[88] Góngora, like his poetic predecessors, had no desire to create a language lifted out of time. If Góngora's poetic purpose was to embrace the experiential world in all its plenitude, as Molho observes,[89] then clarity, as understood by his opponents, had to be rejected as a myth, as an unrealisable attempt to impose order and structure upon the world and to manage the crises of history and the trauma of temporality. When the 'político serrano' [the politic mountain dweller] of the *Soledad Primera* critiques the cost of empire and condemns the 'codicia' which impels imperial overreaching, a collective crisis is given a subjective articulation which self-consciously oversteps conventional linguistic limits. What Beverley has designated a 'language of discovery' is too riddled with paradox and contradiction to suggest a neat substitution of 'the economics of art' for the 'economics of an imperial project that had become problematic'.[90] In the *serrano*'s

---

[88]   See Malcolm K. Read's discussion of Nebrija's project in *Visions in Exile*, pp. 8–9, where he notes: 'It should not be forgotten that grammarians lived in the same precarious world as lyric poets, such as Garcilaso de la Vega, who found favourite themes in those of *tempus fugit* and *carpe diem*. The grammarian realised that language was sufficiently terrestrial to possess one of the fundamental defects of sublunary things: it was subject to change and the process of generation, growth and decay' (p. 8).

[89]   See Maurice Molho, *Semántica y poética (Góngora, Quevedo)* (Barcelona: Crítica, 1997).

[90]   See Beverley, *Aspects*, p. 23. Johnson accepts Beverley's premise but with the caveat that it 'depends inordinately' on readers who can convert the poet's 'hyperbolic currency'. See Christopher D. Johnson, *Hyperboles. The Rhetoric of Excess in Baroque Literature and Thought* (Cambridge, MA, and London: Harvard University Press, 2010), ch. 5, p. 162.

digression, as elsewhere in Góngora's lyric, language is darkly eroticised via myth and metaphor (Vasco da Gama, for instance, is figured as Phaethon and Actaeon) and the desire that drives poetic ambition is interconnected with the perversions, but also the wonders of navigation and conquest. Ethics (whether aesthetic, political or moral) are frustratingly indeterminate in Góngora's poetry, but they are not absent. This is not a free-for-all of empty floating signifiers. As his detractors perceived, when 'nothing' appears to be at stake, a great deal often hangs in the balance.

Art in 'nada' ...[91]

Appreciation of Góngora's art has been largely defined by the controversy over his major compositions, the *Soledades* and *Polifemo*, and by critical engagement with the poems themselves. His shorter works, in particular the sonnets published prior to 1613, have suffered from relatively negative value judgements, and have been presented as evidence of a period of apprenticeship in the poet's trajectory.[92] The love poetry, especially, has emerged as the highly stylised communicative utterances of a voice, weighted down by tradition, that was struggling to find its own way. A common complaint has been its lack of emotional intensity, its failure to communicate an erotic yearning that might succeed in frustrating its own fictionality. Perhaps Góngora's lyric did not allow a post-Romantic readership to play the game, blocking any attempt to recognise in the semblance of his speaking subject anything other than the unreality of that semblance. Abandonment of mimetic or conventionally referential obligations in the longer works could be defended, at least by some, as fundamental to generic experimentation, necessarily underpinned by a revisionary, metaphorical, indeterminacy. But the absence of a referent in the more securely encoded love sonnet was felt as a void and its rhetoric inevitably diminished, as if hollowed out. Dissenting voices, significant but somewhat isolated, have arisen within a dominant discriminatory system to challenge aspects of this reading. It is now over thirty years since Calcraft, following Russell, took issue with Crawford,

---

[91] The subtitle is a deliberate play on Hemingway's short story 'A Clean, Well-lighted Place' (1933) where 'nada' is repeated twenty-two times when the old waiter inserts it as substitute into the prayers he recites: 'Our father who art in *nada, nada* be thy name', etc. See Jeffrey Meyer's brief consideration of Góngora as an influence on Hemingway: 'Hemingway, Góngora and the Concept of *Nada*', *Notes on Contemporary Literature*, 38.3 (2008), 2–4.

[92] The sonnets form a substantial part of Góngora's poetic output and date from 1582 to 1625–26. Of an accepted corpus of 167 poems (plus 50 of more dubious attribution), love sonnets account for approximately a quarter. Most were written before 1600, although Góngora revisited the genre at the end of his life. One of the earliest modern critics to refer to 'the apprentice years' was J.P.W. Crawford. See 'Italian Sources of Góngora's Poetry', *Romanic Review*, 20 (1929), 122–30 (130).

Ciplijauskaité and Jammes, among others, to argue that the sonnets also offered Góngora a creative space for fresh utterance.[93] Since then, the debate
has been noted, but with little sustained interest. More recently, Martín has
drawn our attention to the voyeuristic dimension of the love poetry and contested the tendency to deny the shorter 'straight' love poems the erotic energy of the burlesque and satirical compositions;[94] while Amann has made a
strong case for reconsidering the later love sonnets as metatextual vignettes
which demonstrate the 'vivifying function' of wit, thereby putting into practice what Gracián would later preach.[95]

My own approach to Góngora's shorter love poems draws together the strands
of these arguments in order to demonstrate how the erotic, the eristic and the
experimental lexical configurations interconnect and co-exist in these, as in the
major works, with a profoundly visualising poetics. More specifically, the aim
is to interrogate all of this around the contested notion of Góngora's compulsion
to nothingness. If Góngora's love poetry appears to have more head than heart,
this is because the unfolding of the insubstantial, which simultaneously reveals
and undercuts the illusion of the sonnet's fiction-making, is a deliberate textual
strategy. The poet's attention to the aesthetic structure of 'agudeza', his play
with paradox and his sensitivity to the sonnet's rhythmic contours and inherent
tensions of sound and sense require the reader's full co-operation with deceptive
appearance. It is a co-signifying response that can never be static, wherein reality, represented via an intricate weaving of allusion and false pretences, is experienced as a complex intersection of appearances. The foregrounding of the
act and form of expression reminds us that representation is constitutive of reality, but also that there is no representation without intention and interpretation.
Meaning is, therefore, related to crucial questions of practice and power. In this
dynamic process of signification, language does not acquire the illusion of
transparency, nor can it be easily 'suppressed' or 'overlooked' to accommodate
suspension of disbelief.[96] Perhaps, on occasions, we have taken this artistic

[93]   See Calcraft, *The Sonnets*, esp. pp. 18–19; Biruté Ciplijauskaité, ed., *Luis de Góngora,
Sonetos Completos* (Madrid: Castalia, 1969); Jammes, *Études*, esp. part 3, ch. 1; Crawford, 'Italian Sources'.

[94]   See Adrienne L. Martín, 'Góngora y la visualización del cuerpo erótico', in *Góngora Hoy,*
pp. 265–91.

[95]   See Elizabeth Amann, 'Pointed Poetry: Agudeza and Petrarchism in Góngora's Late Sonnets', *Hispanic Research Journal*, 12.4 (2011), 306–22.

[96]   Catherine Belsey, explaining the tenacity of the empiricist-idealist theory of language, in
terms of the relationship between language and thought, states: 'Language is *experienced* as a
nomenclature because its existence precedes our understanding of the world. Words seem to be
symbols for things because things are inconceivable outside the system of differences which
constitutes the language. Similarly, these very things seem to be represented in the mind, in an
autonomous realm of thought, because thought is in essence symbolic [...] And so language is
"overlooked", suppressed in favour of a quest for meaning in experience and/or in the mind'. See
Critical Practice (New York and London: Routledge, 1980), p. 46.

calculation in the love poetry for coldness, because we have tried, and not been permitted, to have faith in its intimacy. Judith Butler would have us ask, 'what does transparency keep obscure?'[97] Góngora's poetry, similarly scepti-cal of the interests served by the 'protocols of clarity', begs a differently formulated question: 'what does obscurity make apparent?' When we engage with that, Góngora's poetic world opens out into a broader realm of possi-bilities, but not without implications for the individual. This is demonstrated in the perverse openness of one of his earliest sonnets, 'Mientras por compe-tir con tu cabello' (1582), which, despite its signposting to *loci classici* such as Horace and Ausonius, and to the vernacular contributions of Bernardo Tasso and Garcilaso, cannot be said to reiterate the 'timeworn patterns of signification'.[98] The sonnet has been variously designated a love poem, a moral poem, a corrective rewriting of the *carpe diem* topos, and/or a *me-mento mori*.[99]

> Mientras por competir con tu cabello
> oro bruñido al sol relumbra en vano;
> mientras con menosprecio en medio el llano
> mira tu blanca frente el lilio bello;
>
> mientras a cada labio, por cogello,
> siguen más ojos que al clavel temprano,
> y mientras triunfa con desdén lozano
> del luciente cristal tu gentil cuello;

---

[97] See Judith Butler, *Gender Trouble. Feminism and the Subversion of Identity* (New York and London: Routledge, 1999). In the preface to this reissue of her 1990 work, Butler addressed those who had criticised the difficulty of her style, commenting on a general tendency both to underestimate the reading public's desire and capacity to engage with challenging texts and to forget, in our demand for clarity, 'the ruses that motor the ostensibly "clear" view'. She concludes: 'Who devises the protocols of "clarity" and whose interests do they serve? What is foreclosed by the insistence on parochial standards of transparency as a requisite for communication? What does transparency keep obscure?' (p. xix).

[98] For quote, see Belsey, *Critical Practice*, p. 45.

[99] Note that this poem and its companion piece, 'Ilustre y hermosísima María', were in-cluded in the *Sonetos amorosos* section of the 1627 Vicuña edition, but appear in the Chacón manuscript under *Sonetos varios*. Lore Terracini offers an insightful reading of temporality and perspective in the sonnet, but comes to a rather closed conclusion regarding the theme of 'nothing-ness', which results in the exclusive categorisation of the poem as a moral sonnet of 'desengaño'. See '"Cristal", no "marfil", en "Mientras por competir con tu cabello"', in *Homenaje a Ana María Berrenechea*, eds Lía Schwartz Lerner and Isías Lerner (Madrid: Castalia, 1984), pp. 341–53 (esp. pp. 344, 353). See also, Ricardo Senabre, 'La sombra alargada de un verso gongorino', in *Hom-mage à Robert Jammes*, pp. 1089–98, who demonstrates through a survey of imitations of the sonnet's final line (from the seventeenth century right up to Blas de Otero) that most readers engaged with it in terms of a 'meditatio mortis'.

> goza cuello, cabello, labio y frente,
> antes que lo que fue en tu edad dorada
> oro, lilio, clavel, cristal luciente,
>
> no sólo en plata o vïola troncada
> se vuelva, mas tú y ello juntamente
> en tierra, en humo, en polvo, en sombra, en nada. (p. 27)

[While your hair competes, the sun shines on burnished gold in vain; while in the midst of the plain your white brow beholds the lily with disdain; while more eyes attend each lip of yours to kiss, than to pluck the carnation in its prime; and while your slender neck triumphs over gleaming glass with scorn sublime. Enjoy your neck, hair, lip and brow, before what was in golden youth, gold, lily, carnation, gleaming glass, turns not just to silver or to wilting violet, but you and all of it as one, become earth, smoke, dust, shadow, nothing.]

Confrontation with the concept of a future nothingness in this poem works to negate stasis, compelling the construction of an alternative, imagined, reality which allows for choice and creativity in the seizing of opportunities. Several commentators have analysed the poem as a response to Garcilaso's Sonnet XXIII, 'En tanto que de rosa y azucena', noting how Góngora's re-elaboration lacks the ultimately comforting epistemology of his predecessor's.[100] Góngora's poem certainly forces a more aggressive confrontation between beauty and its opposite, but the implications of that are lost if we underestimate the unresolved tensions in the earlier poem's own representation and manipulation of time. Garcilaso's sonnet reads:

> En tanto que de rosa y azucena
> se muestra la color en vuestro gesto,
> y que vuestro mirar ardiente, honesto,
> enciende al corazón y lo refrena;
>
> y en tanto que el cabello, que en la vena
> del oro se escogió, con vuelo presto,
> por el hermoso cuello blanco, enhiesto,
> el viento mueve, esparce y desordena:

---

[100] The bibliography on these sonnets is extensive. For the moment, I note the following and will refer to others as relevant to my own reading: R.P. Calcraft, 'The *carpe diem* sonnets of Garcilaso and Góngora', *Modern Language Review*, 76. 2 (1981), 332–37; Eduardo Aznar Anglés, 'Clásico y Barroco (dos sonetos del clasicismo español)', in *Homenaje al profesor Antonio Vilanova*, 2 vols, ed. Marta C. Carbonell (Barcelona: Universidad de Barcelona, 1989), I, pp. 57–74; Michael E. Gerli, '"Más allá del carpe diem: el soneto "Mientras por competir con tu cabello" de Luis de Góngora', in *Estudios en homenaje a Enrique Ruíz-Fornells*, eds Teresa Valdivielso *et al.* (Pennsylvania: ALDEEU, 1990), pp. 255–58.

> coged de vuestra alegre primavera
> el dulce fruto, antes que el tiempo airado
> cubra de nieve la hermosa cumbre;
>
> marchitará la rosa el viento helado.
> Todo lo mudará la edad ligera
> por no hacer mudanza en su costumbre.

[As long as the colour of roses and lilies is seen on your face, and (as long as) your gaze, ardent and chaste, inflames and restrains my heart; and as long as your hair, singled out from veins of gold, is blown, scattered and swept awry by the wind over your beautiful, white and slender neck: gather the sweet fruit of your joyful spring before angry time covers your beautiful crown with snow. The icy wind will wither the rose, fleeting time will change everything so as not to change its own custom.]

We can identify in Garcilaso's poem an interest in imitating the processes rather than the products of nature. The quatrains especially convey a harmonious structure that is precariously dependent upon agonistic relationships, suggesting a world of flux in which only change is 'real' and stability an illusion, including, of course, the woman's resistance to the rhetorical charms of the speaker. The concept of time itself is also subject to this duality. It operates in linear mode as an irreversible agent of destruction, against whose force the human and natural world are powerless, but its cyclical dimension is enacted consistently in the pattern of changing seasons. García argues for the triumph of the cyclical over the linear in the final tercet, a resolution in which a pagan world view dominates and makes more effective the erotic charge of the *carpe diem* motif.[101] But there is more invested in Garcilaso's ultimate acclamation of time's inexorable essence. Herrera thought the verse weak, and lacking the spirit and energy of the quatrains.[102] His appreciation of the downbeat is interesting, because it captures the lack of challenge that is at its core. Rather than foregrounding death as a natural part of human life, Garcilaso embraces the analogical figuration that has underpinned the sonnet, thereby de-personalising the individual's relationship with time and distancing death from individual human experience. We are not permitted self-willed excursions into temporal domains beyond human

---

[101] See Gustavo V. García, 'El intertexto de la imitación en Garcilaso, Góngora y Balbuena', *Revista Iberoamericana*, LXIII (1997), 391–401 (esp. 395–96).

[102] Herrera's evaluation of this final verse in the *Anotaciones* reads: 'este es lánguido i casi muerto verso, i mui plebeyo modo de hablar; fue común falta en aquella edad no solo de los nuestros, pero de los Toscanos, acabar el soneto, no con la fuerza i espíritu de los cuarteles, sino floxa, desmayadamente'. Edward Stanton also finds the ending less than compelling (see 'Garcilaso's Sonnet XXIII', *Hispanic Review*, 40.2 [1972], 198–201 [201]).

control. The prevailing images linger on the threshold of the ultimate transformation, gold hair turning to white, blushing cheeks that will lose their bloom.
There is some imperfection in the metamorphosis, a persistence of essential
beauty in the wind's 'cover up', that retains the ambiguity generated by a gaze
that is at once passionate and pure. There are few clear boundaries in this sonnet,
and none effectively transgressed. But the outcome is darker than we have been
prepared to acknowledge. For by embedding individual life in the natural processes of the cosmos, Garcilaso's sonnet denies us the validation of the momen-
tary lived experience. In pulling back from a scene of human extinction, the
sonnet suppresses its own desires, both erotic and aesthetic, and marks out the
impossible limit of representation.

Góngora's text takes the correlative arrangement between idealised feminine
beauty and the natural world and drives a competitive wedge between them,
thereby widening the gap between his own contribution to the topos and those
of his Classical and Renaissance predecessors. Friedman's observations on the
implications of this competitive quality are worth quoting in full:

> Disjunction replaces equilibrium, in form and content. Góngora moves to
> obliterate the initial premise, challenging not only Garcilaso's poem, but the
> poet, the movement he represents, and the historical movement over which
> he presides. *Carpe diem* is the medium, not the message. Góngora's sonnet is
> about competition, about composition. Competition is a key to the structure
> of the text and is its principal conceit as well. Rhetoric merges with ideology,
> a conventional topos with a metapoetic macrostructure.[103]

This 'metapoetic macrostructure' becomes even more apparent, however, when
we attend to the chromatic intensity of the poem. Just as in the *Polifemo*, where
the resolution of metaphor reproduces pictorial effects that prioritise colour and
movement (especially the perspective that is active in vision),[104] the foregrounding of colour in the quatrains of this sonnet becomes a locus of anti-Platonism.
Colour celebrates the material dimension to representation, its power to bring
illusion into being, and thus threatens the hegemony of a metaphysical concep-

---

[103] See Friedman, 'Creative Space', 53. See also, by the same author, 'Realities and Poets:
Góngora, Cervantes and the Nature of Art', *Calíope*, 8.1 (2002), 55–68 (61–64), where he explores
the nature/art dichotomy at the centre of this poem and the sonnet 'De pura honestidad templo
sagrado'.

[104] See especially the arc formed between stanzas 32 and 34. I have discussed this passage
elsewhere and drawn attention to its relationship with the contemporary polemic on the doctrine
of imitation. Particularly significant is the alignment within that of writers who promoted an anti-
Aristotelian negation of the principle of verisimilitude and artists, ('colourists'), who promoted
the autonomy of pictorial representation. See Torres, *The Polyphemus Complex*, pp. 58–60, and
also pp. 84–85, where the pictorial qualities of Jáuregui's *Orfeo* are located within the contemporary *dibujo/color* debate. See also Darst, *Imitatio*, pp. 17–50.

tion of image. Colour serves also to charge images with effects, promoting pleasure and the seduction of the senses. The primacy of the idea, the *res*, in representation is subverted and discourses of rationality and truth are disturbed by emotional response. The woman is conveyed here through a sequence of separate images, united only in their luminosity, and all subject to the emanation of light. These images are affective, but they cannot, and do not, depict directly translatable form. As the vanishing point of the poem, the female addressee is deconstructed by the absence of a centrally located viewer who might hold her passive and transfixed, with uncontested mastery. She emerges rather, via an overlapping system of perspective, as the desired object of multiple gazing, fractured and fragmented accordingly. This visual 'disjunction' undermines any appearance of a coherent representational space that is created by means of the sonnet's precise mathematical schema. Much critical attention has been paid to the latter, little to the former, yet the final vision of a totalising metamorphosis ('tú y ello juntamente'; 13) calls us to recognise this dissonant interplay.[105]

Until the penultimate verse of the sonnet, the reader is a frustrated viewer, compelled to gaze into the poem as Narcissus into a constantly moving stream, implicated in the urgency of the temporal anaphora and yet controlled by the shifting reorganisation of figural correlatives, so that a complete picture remains elusive. The text, thus far, is all dynamic surface, evocatively captured in the 'cristal' at its centre, a mirror motif which renders and reconfigures the core questions of identity and representation. The mirror vision provides a single perspective for sight, an axis of vision that is premised around a self–other relation in which visualisation is constrained to comprehension of static poses. How can one ever see oneself move? By situating the woman in front of her own mirror, the speaker traps her as a reflected and incomplete object within an immediate, material world view. She is called upon to meld with herself, to pass beyond passive spectatorship towards complete immersion in the sexual dimension of being. From the point of view of the male speaker, this constitutes a recuperation of an aspect of identity that has been artificially alienated. In fact, it is this rhetorical perspective, the drive towards the speaker's own sexual gratification, that dominates the tercets, opening up an experiential temporal dimension that unhinges time from its actual conditioning and makes a linear life narrative incoherent. The preterite 'fue' in verse 11 extracts the present moment out of its own time, so that it not only incorporates present luminosity as already having been, but also experiences it in terms of the overwhelming darkness that it will become.[106] The threat

---

[105] Terracini's analysis of the sonnet's symmetrical patterns (the collapsing of an ordered '4' into a binary system, ultimately expanded and synthesised in 'nada') is notable for her astute consideration of the phonic patterns that convey semantic oppositions (SOLo [12] – SOL (2); sOLO [12] – sOL [2] –pOLvo [14] etc.). See '"Cristal", no "márfil"', pp. 348–49.

[106] Although violets are often depicted as pale in Latin poets and in the Petrarchan tradition, Góngora follows Virgil here (*Eclogue* X, v. 39) who calls them black ('nigrae violae sunt'). In the

that all possibilities will be annihilated forces a revelation that some, if grasped, might construct a reality of a different order, the experience of which could somehow suspend awareness of the body's inevitable extinction.

When we restore primacy to the strategies of erotic persuasion that inform the sonnet, the poem's confrontation with 'nothingness' produces an ironic distortion which is difficult to accommodate within a conventionally didactic paradigm of 'desengaño'[disillusion].[107] The sonnet's conflict between reality (as appearance) and desire (unrealised) is not resolved (as it would be in Quevedo's majestic 'Cerrar podrá mis ojos') via an affirmation of the power of human desire (realised) over death, but by an altogether more negative revelation: the power of death (made tangible and secure) over desire (secured *in potentia*). The traditional co-ordinates of *carpe diem* thus co-exist with a radical articulation of 'desengaño' that defends and yet extends their egotistical borders. Via an extremely self-conscious interlocutory system, the reader is implicated in a structure of address that is at once intimate and universal. Notwithstanding the poem's pretensions to self-expression, it succeeds, above all, as a shared act of, and an active, (re)making. The poet speaks as the fictional lover, but also from a specific place in history, and from a particular 'disillusioned' national consciousness. The absence of the explicit deictic pronoun, 'yo' (the 'I' of the poem), relative to the reiterated presence of 'tú' disguises (although does not diminish) the agency of the speaker, and foregrounds the poem's apostrophic utterance. The 'you' is conjured up to confirm the speaker's authority, but it also functions as a 'symbolic mediator' through which intimate communication can be translated into public speech.[108] Vocative gestures make the reader a proxy when the speaker goes to war with Time on behalf of love and, indeed, function as metatextual agents that call attention to the inadequacies of earlier modes of expression. But their reach is wider. The reader is also addressed as a contemporary citizen of a socio-political climate of disintegrating ideals, and as a fellow human being sharing the predicament of mortality.

By extending the limits of destruction beyond old age, Góngora offers a self-conscious revision of Garcilaso's poem ('no sólo ... mas'); a reimagining that announces its intention in the opening verses, when the eyes that would mirror

---

Polifemo, the presence of black violets on the bridal bed of Galatea and Acis (333–36) recalls the dark threat of Polyphemus and foreshadows the tragedy.

[107] See, for instance, Gerli, '"Más allá del carpe diem"', p. 256, who seeks for a 'hidden truth' in the sonnet, 'el inexorable y humillante proceso de ruina que existe potencialmente en todo, y que termina no sólo en la vejez, sino en la aniquilación total' [the inexorable and humiliating process of ruin which exists *in potentia* in everyone, and which ends, not in old age, but in complete annihilation']. More problematic, however, is Jones's view that the sonnet constitutes a 'personal cry of horror at the thought of ceasing to exist' (*Poems of Góngora*, p. 17).

[108] See W.R. Johnson, *The Idea of Lyric: Lyric Modes in Ancient and Modern Poetry* (Berkeley: University of California Press, 1982). The quotation is taken from his meditation on the use of pronouns in lyric, p. 3.

the soul are substituted by sensually provocative lips. Whereas Garcilaso's poem marks the limit of representation, death, in Góngora's sonnet, is its inevitability. It is the very fact of death that can lead human beings to recreate both in life and in art. 'Mientras por competir', like its predecessor, also celebrates beauty as it pertains to process, but it more overtly affirms values that negate any sense of static selfhood: choice, creativity and reinterpretation. All levels of discourse in the poem are permeated by a fusion of transformative vision and (re)making: this is embedded in the symbolic stratum of suggestion which underpins the surface level of pseudo-narrative; it is submerged in the poem's metaphorical markers of auto-referentiality (the 'metapoetic macrostructure'), and in the image fragments that are emblematic of intertextual composition. It is also a defining feature of the reader's participation in the immediate reality of the work in process. In this regard, the experience of temporal disequilibrium is key to the unlocking of new potentialities. The sequential, linear discourse that is feigned on the surface is thwarted both by the imperative ('goza'; 9), which injects a rupture and, as we have noted, by the grammatical disarticulation of the invasive preterite ('fue'; 10). An unstable platform is established upon which future nothingness, otherwise unattainable in time and space, can be brought into being. By breaking out of its arithmetic 'four by four' organisation to add the definitive 'nada', fleeting movement appears transformed into a final moment of fixity. But if 'nada' contains within it the full consciousness of human finitude, it also makes a statement about the infinite nature of the word, for 'nothing' cannot exist in any empirical sense and we relate to it as we would to any future event not actualised – that is, we imagine it.

The space of darkness in the poem is not, therefore, arrived at through a deliberate departure from the symbolic world.[109] Rather, the concept of nothingness is made attainable, not in a single word, but in the powerful analogical transfer that takes place between words in context. 'Nada' particularly gathers into itself the figurative and cultural connotations of its own evolving nature, 'tierra', 'humo', 'polvo', and 'sombra', but it draws also on broader lexical relations that are both synchronic (within the poem, counter-associations with the figurative category of light) and diachronic (the transformations that occur over time, reaching back, for instance, to Horace's 'pulvis et umbra sumus' [we are dust and shade; *Odes*, 4. 7. 16], but also embracing the 'absence' of the void in Garcilaso). Representation of the absolute, therefore, still harbours fragmentation and a certain degree of indeterminacy. Meaning can move backwards and forwards through the rhyming moments of the poetic microcosm, transforming oblivion back into a recuperated golden age, and even suggesting that the relishing of physical beauty might offer significant compensation for mortality. But

---

[109] See Terracini, "'Cristal", no "márfil"', who makes the case for the stark destruction of the metonymic system at verse 13, arguing that 'tú y ello juntamente' shatters the poem's figurative frame.

it can also expand limitlessly and ambiguously through semantic fields, awakening us to its complexities time and time over.

In fact, Góngora himself returns to the possibilities inherent in this sonnet, a year later, in 1583, refashioning its *carpe diem* medium so that the speaker's efforts appear to be even more directly aimed at the beloved's own narcissism. The poem reads:

> Ilustre y hermosísima María,
> mientras se dejan ver a cualquier hora
> en tus mejillas la rosada Aurora,
> Febo en tus ojos, y en tu frente el día,
>
> y mientras con gentil descortesía
> mueve el viento la hebra voladora
> que la Arabia en sus venas atesora
> y el rico Tajo en sus arenas cría;
>
> antes que de la edad Febo eclipsado
> y el claro día vuelto en noche obscura,
> huya la Aurora del mortal nublado;
>
> antes que lo que hoy es rubio tesoro
> venza a la blanca nieve su blancura:
> goza, goza el color, la luz, el oro. (pp. 41–2)

[Most beautiful and illustrious María, while at every moment the red of dawn is revealed in your cheeks; the sun (shining) in your eyes, daylight on your brow; and while with graceful discourtesy, the wind stirs the fleeing strands which Arabia treasures in its veins and the rich Tagus yields in its sands; before the dawn flees mortal shadows – when the sun is eclipsed by time and the bright day darkened into night; before what is today golden treasure surpasses the white snow with its own white: enjoy, enjoy, the colour, the light, the gold.]

The relationship between this poem and Garcilaso's *carpe diem* sonnet (XXIII) has been the subject of considerable attention.[110] The geometric arrangement in

---

[110] In addition to Calcraft's study referred to above (see p. 122, n. 93), see also John D. Smith, 'Metaphysical Descriptions of Women in the First Sonnets of Garcilaso', *Hispania*, 56 (1973), 244–48; and Lore Terracini, 'Entre la nada y el oro. Sistema y estructura en el soneto 235 de Góngora', in *Actas del VIII congreso de la asociación de hispanistas*, eds A. David Kossoff *et al.* (Madrid: Istmus, 1986), pp. 619–28. Terracini provides a concise history of bibliography on the topic and distances herself from those who have disputed the Chacón date of composition, based on the argument that this sonnet's more obvious engagement with Garcilaso suggests that it was produced prior to 'Mientras por competir'. I agree entirely with Terracini in terms of respecting the later date, although, as will become apparent, my argumentation is different.

Góngora's poem is at once similar to and different from the pattern established in the model. Góngora follows the series of parallels which emerge from a contemplation of the beloved's face, maintaining the focus on her complexion, eyes, brow and hair. But the temporal conjunction is doubled and the imperative delayed, so that the gaze is closer and held longer. A lifetime is captured symbolically in a single day, and time itself appears contracted into that urgent and intimate encounter. The poem unfolds in the reading as the 'day' that is being seized. The emulative spirit of 'Mientras por competir' also features here, but its signs are more subtly 'presenced'. On the surface of the text, 'vencer' [to conquer] is an auto-reflexive substitute for Garcilaso's 'cubrir' [to cover], while the art/nature dichotomy, rendered in *cultista* mode, gestures towards emulation, but also preservation. Words acquire allusive freedom, a movement across the landscape of literary context, but they are not denied their provenance, nor are their stories suppressed. Myth collides and colludes with feminine beauty. All that is or has been emblematised in Aurora, the Roman goddess of the dawn, or in Phoebus Apollo, the sun-god and dispenser of light, becomes, and is becoming to, the speaker's beloved. Transformation is (textually) the making of her, but it is also, as in 'Mientras por competir', thematised as Time's champion and, therefore, the ultimate nemesis of beauty. The figure of the eclipse converts the mirror motif of Góngora's earlier poem into an even more troubling exploration of anti-mimetic desire. Beauty's life story is imagined in a series of images which fast-forward to death, rewind and are stilled at the speculation of old age. In this reverse chronology, the present is not extracted from its own time ('lo que es hoy'), but represents the locus of the speaker's desire for the woman not to become the 'other', and to continue suspended in thrall to the materiality, luminosity and treasures of youth. The eclipse is central to the poem's resistance to temporal convention. It is a powerful, visual sign that something in the present is out of place. When the moon crosses the disk of the sun in a unique intersection of their respective paths, displacing the light, and giving day the appearance of night, time seems just to hold, until old patterns are dismantled and a new cycle can emerge. It is at once, therefore, a symbol of speculation and of distorted reflection – the shadow of a future death and the immediate promise of an altered course in life; a reflection which materialises in the altogether darker brilliance of gold whitened beyond recognition. [111]

The seamless light of the quatrains is lacerated by Time. The poem proposes to heal this by urging full commitment to the pleasures of present experience. The final proposition of pure, unmediated experience is undermined, however, by the fact of the poem's own allusive fabrication and by its position in an historical framework. To live in terms of absolute focus on the present involves

[111] Interestingly, the longest solar total eclipse of the sixteenth century (six minutes and twenty-three seconds) occurred on 19 June 1583. Whether or not this has any bearing on the composition of this sonnet would involve a different type of speculation.

negating memory on the one hand and denying entry to consequence on the other; in other words, turning away from history and tradition and taking no account of eternalising aesthetics. It is an untenable position and entirely at variance with Góngora's primary intertextual model, Garcilaso de la Vega. Modern editors have identified a broader engagement with Garcilaso's poetics in terms of 'sourcing' individual verses, but the ramifications of this have rarely been explored. The opening verse, taken directly from the second line of *Eclogue* III, also echoes the opening of Sonnet XXIV. María Osorio de Pimentel, wife of Pedro de Toledo, brother of the Duke of Alba, is the addressee of the Eclogue, while María de Cardona, the Marquess of Padua, is evoked in the sonnet. In both poems Garcilaso exploits the allegorical mythology of Apollo, the Muses and Parnassus to make claims for a new Castilian poetry, self-fashioned from a body of Classical and Renaissance precedents, and works to resolve the tensions between authority and autonomy in terms of Orphic transcendence. It is a 'new poetry' which Garcilaso sites on the resplendent banks of the River Tagus and it is, as we have seen previously in this study, a poetry in which patronage and politics are fundamentally interrelated. Garcilaso's poetics are best understood, therefore, within an evolving process of *traslatio studii*, a spatio-temporal movement of cultural transfer from ancient Greece and Rome to the Iberian peninsula, a politico-cultural phenomenon that underpinned the *traslatio imperii*, the transfer of authority over territories and peoples that was already well established under the Emperor Charles V. We have also referred to the exploitation of both tropes by Nebrija, whose project to regulate the Castilian language as an instrument of empire, depended on a cyclically oriented survey of great political and linguistic powers of the past.[112] The lessons of Nebrija's manipulated history for contemporary Spain and Castilian were clear: just as empire and language could rise and shine together, the fall of empire could herald linguistic oblivion.

The foregrounding of Garcilaso as intertext in Góngora's poem should alert us to the possibility of a more provocative, politicised encounter with the present, a collectively resonant experience of frustration which is given voice through the erotic medium of *carpe diem*. Additionally, the empowerment of the present in Góngora is in keeping with the dominant concern for the Spanish language which characterises the theory and practice of Fernando de Herrera (1580) and is especially aligned, in this poem, with Herrera's desire to secure a temporally unfettered linguistic self-determination. But whereas Herrera had built his project upon an allegorical solar system that struggled to accommodate the material specificity of language, Góngora at this very early stage of his poetic trajectory calls for colour and gives a darker substance to the light. The *traslatio studii* is respected, but differently conceptualised, and its relationship to empire

---

112 For much more detailed discussion, see Navarrete, *Orphans of Petrarch*, pp. 19–24.

is also reconceived. Góngora's poem breaks out of Nebrija's cyclical frame, thereby dismantling its correlative analogy. Moreover, the gleaming gold, whose origins in real time lie in the treasure mines of the New World, casts its own shadow. Until the latter stages of the sixteenth century, New World gold had brought undisputed economic benefit to the realm. But the enthusiastic defence of treasure acquisition by the early explorers began to collapse when the production of precious metals diminished, while inflation and recession increased. In this more negative socio-economic climate, empire became a problem to be scrutinised and solved. As Lía Schwartz has demonstrated, the moral and satirical poetry of the age re-elaborated the concerns of dominant ideological discourses (theological and political) and sourced the problems of empire in human error and transgression.[113] A semantic repertoire of motifs and topoi emerged within which human greed and ambition were subject to castigation. Hunger and thirst for gold became a recurrent metaphor for 'codicia' [greed], which, as we will see in Chapter 6, impacted beyond more conventionally didactic genres. In Góngora's own *Soledad Primera*, the *serrano* who grieves a son lost to the sea will denounce greed as the helmsman that steers the ships of conquest and colonisation (403). 'Oro', then, is a multivalent sign of moral corruption, national unproductivity and erotic acts of trespass. As such, it captures in this early sonnet that coincidence of luminosity and shadow that characterises Góngora's lyric production.

The sonnet's rhetoric of seduction urges the beloved to withdraw from connections to the world and to enjoy the self in the here and now, a present in which the desires of the speaker will emerge triumphant. It is a persuasive and reader-compromising 'smokescreen' behind which Góngora locates other narratives: an ironic repudiation of contemporary society's indulgent attachment to appearance, as well as advocacy of a reimagined vernacular eloquence. In the *Soledad Primera*, the latter will effect the subjugation of the sun to greed (405–12), remaking 'the most brilliant Neoplatonic symbol', in terms of limited reach and wisdom.[114] In the *Polifemo* it will make of the sun the mirror of a monstrous soul and dare to go where no poetic voice had gone before.

113 See Lía Schwartz, '"Novus orbis victus vos vicit": El oro de las Indias en la sátira y en la literatura moral áureas', in *Actas del III congreso argentino de hispanistas "España en América y América en España"*, eds Luís Martínez Cuitiño and Élida Lois (Argentina: Universidad de Buenos Aires, 1992). We will return to the motif of greed for gold as exploited in the transgressive context of Quevedo's love poetry in Chapter 6.
114 See Johnson, *Hyperboles*, p. 180.

5

Luis de Góngora y Argote:
Out of the Dark – Emulative Poetry in Motion

Introduction

Neoplatonic love had been presented by Castiglione as the perfect antidote to the darker emotions associated with human passion – jealousy being prominent among the transgressive desires that required suppression.[1] It is not wholly surprising, therefore, that the dismantling of the Neoplatonic aesthetic in Góngora would liberate a revisionary play upon that most illicit, appetitive drive whose cultural history allowed for the interconnection of erotic and emulative poetics. This chapter will explore how motifs of envy and jealousy are interwoven in Góngora's love poetry and forge a metaphoric merger between two complementary attitudes: the will to usurp the forbidden feminine object of desire and the will to trespass beyond established poetic norms. The result is a persistent erotic colouration of the principles of *aemulatio*,[2] a rhetorical reshaping which includes contingently within it something of the ambiguous moral properties of envy that, as we will see, had infected the literature of both *eros* and *eris* from the pre-Hellenistic tradition through to the Renaissance.

Fundamental to Góngora's metatextual schema is the shared, illicit movement of erotic and emulative desire towards appropriation. This enterprise, self-consciously undertaken at the expense of order, is often figured in the

---

[1]   The context is Pietro Bembo's discussion of Neoplatonic love in *Il libro del Cortegiano* where jealousy is cited along with 'a thousand other types of frenzy' that can lead mad and desperate lovers to take their own lives. See Baldassare Castiglione, *El Cortesano*, trans. Juan Boscán, ed. Mario Pozzi (Madrid: Cátedra, 1994), p. 527.

[2]   Wayne A. Rebhorn's understanding of emulation as an extreme form of imitation in its depiction of a dyadic relationship between *amor* [love] and *invidia* [envy] echoes Cicero's *De Oratore* 2. 205–10: 'In Renaissance rhetorical and educational theory, emulation is classified as a form of imitation, an identification with one's model at the same time that one attempts to surpass it […] emulation means identification with another person, a model, or an ideal; it can indicate a form of brotherhood or comradeship or even love. On the other hand, it simultaneously means rivalry; it is a competitive urge that […] can also, when taken to an extreme, entail feelings of hatred and envy.' See 'The Crisis of the Aristocracy in Julius Caesar', *Renaissance Quarterly*, 43 (1990), 75–111 (77).

texts as an invidious gaze within which, and/or against which, the poetic persona writes and is written, both as active subject (seeking completion and transcendent definition) and passive object (incomplete and limited by dependency). The envious 'eye' of Góngora's poetry, always operating under the sign of *eros*, confronts these ethical and identity crises in myriad configurations: viscerally anti-Petrarchan in the shape-changing analogies of 'O niebla del estado más sereno' [Oh fog of the most serene state; 1582]; apostrophised as the erotic dreamer's solar nemesis in 'Ya besando unas manos cristalinas' [Now kissing crystalline hands; 1582]; personified as hubristic thought, soaring in Icarian flight towards forbidden erotic and aesthetic goals in 'Qué de invidiosos montes levantados' [What of the tall, envious mountains; 1600]; subtly interventionist as the apian force that prevents violation in 'Al tronco Filis' [Filis reclining against the trunk; 1621]; and overwhelmingly destructive as the force that violates the bridal bed of lovers in *Angelica y Medoro*, 1602 and the *Fábula de Polifemo y Galatea* (1613). Throughout the emulative fabric of all these texts a dynamic process of reverse valorisation compels us to think through time in flexible and correlative ways, so that in the reactivation of the past in the present the negative paradigm of envy can be mobilised as a potent catalyst for artistic creativity.

Envy has long been a subject of debate in various disciplines: philosophy, anthropology, political science and economics. It has enjoyed a particularly prominent role in psychoanalytical theory, thanks in no small part to Freud's conceptualisation of 'penis envy' as a primary motivating factor of women's development, an interpretation of envy's relationship to a perceived lack in the self which inextricably bound envy and competition to gender. When Steven Wagschal addresses the question of why representations of jealousy abound in the literature of Spain's Golden Age, he provides arguments from the fields of psychology and from contemporary philosophies of mind to illustrate the phenomenon's non unitary nature.[3] Freudian displacement theory (the idea that jealousy of the beloved can come from a projection of the lover's own illicit desire for another) offers Wagschal useful points of reference for his analysis of jealousy in the drama of Lope de Vega. When he turns to Góngora to account for the poet's foregrounding of jealousy in the expression of a Baroque 'new age poetics', he also prefers to look forward from the text's moment of origin – in this case, to the Kantian phenomenology of the sublime.[4] It is Wagschal's contention that the mathematical sublime is anticipated in the sonnet 'O niebla del estado más sereno' and that 'early stirrings' of the dynamic sublime are represented in the *Polifemo*. Wagschal offers an insightful study that is sensitive both to the flux that characterises the literary treatment of jealousy, and to how

3   Wagschal, *The Literature of Jealousy*, 'Introduction' pp. 1–21.
4   Wagschal, *The Literature of Jealousy*, ch. 7: 'Góngora on the Beautiful and the Sublime', pp. 157–87.

its multiple functions operate as a textual tool for 'working through a range of contemporary political and cultural issues', especially those involving relations of power.[5] Wagschal also draws our attention to what he sees as a complicating factor – that is, when jealousy operates as part of a rhetorical strategy that displays the creativity of the poet while simultaneously interrogating the poetic process itself: 'all of the authors [...] refer not only to jealousy that obtains in actual human minds, but also to literary traditions of jealousy, sometimes as a self-conscious, allusive, literary device, while at other times in an intertextual competition'.[6] There is a clear connection here with Wagschal's broader premise, for power is often related to the negotiation and reinterpretation of precedent and its acquisition is dependent upon the fulfilment of a mimetic desire to impose one's own will. Indeed, the mechanics of a polemical *aemulatio* are tacitly acknowledged in Wagschal's articulation of a jealousy-driven poetics as a mimetic practice that embraces difference and potential rivalry. But this conflicted understanding of *aemulatio* is not easily accommodated within the Kantian frame of Wagschal's textual readings of Góngora and, somewhat sacrificed to that, slips to the background. My own preference is to respect the direction of Góngora's envious gazing, to begin by looking back to the poetic legacies of envy's relationship to emulation and to *eros*, and then to look inwards to the poetry itself, focusing on two sonnets (one early, one late), with reference to the *Polifemo*, as representative sites of critical reflection and of the aggressively innovative attitude to poetic legacy that pervades Góngora's lyric.

Harold Bloom's work has made us keenly sensitive to the apprehensions that can haunt the individual poet's relationship to antecedents and to the poetic past, even if we do not always buy into the Bloomian concept of an anxiety that is rooted in universal psychic phenomena.[7] But the anxieties of writers, like Góngora, who strive for distinction (as discussed in the previous chapter), centre as much on the future as on the past. This is not just because authorial status, authority and posthumous life are dependent on readers, as Newlyn has observed,[8] but because writing exists in a dialogue whose historicity is tripled: materially executed in the present, the text exists in relation to a diachronic chain of previous texts (its temporal relationship to them often

---

5   Wagschal, *The Literature of Jealousy*, 'Introduction', p. 2.
6   Wagschal, *The Literature of Jealousy*, 'Introduction', p. 8.
7   Although Bloom exempts poets prior to the mid seventeenth century from his theory, Bloomian readings of early modern texts abound. See *The Anxiety of Influence: A Theory of Poetry* (New York: Oxford University Press, 1973), pp. 11 and 27. Friedman, for instance, reads Góngora's reconstruction of pastoral as part of his strategy for overcoming and confronting the burden of literary predecessors, with Garcilaso emerging as the most overwhelming among them. See 'Realities and Poets' (esp. 57).
8   This has been acutely observed by Lucy Newlyn in her study of an 'anxiety of reception' in the Romantic period, although it is not a phenomenon restricted to that period. See *Reading, Writing, and Romanticism: The Anxiety of Reception* (Oxford: Oxford University Press, 2000).

complicated by reinstantiated and/or substitutional impulses) and in relation to an imagined context of future writers and readers. The relationship writers have with the future is indicated, therefore, by their relationship, as readers, to the past. It is a temporal configuration in which distinct points in the temporal system are pulled together until they meet. But the emulative text's linguistic signing into the past (through mythological allusion, translation, citation, intertextual resonance) and into the future (through dedications, invocations to the Muses, symbolic manifestations of apotheosis) risks a 'falling away' from the event of the poem itself, a dissolution of immediacy that might undermine aesthetic impact and, indeed, the whole emulative enterprise. Yet Góngora's highly mediated, allusive poetry manages to reconcile intellectual depth with instantaneous pleasure, exploiting intense visuality to bend the poetic narrative back in on itself, as if 'pulling on time'.[9] Joseph Addison famously defended the imagination as the mental capacity that is 'furnished' by our sight. But whereas Addison suggested some privileging of the visual over the intellectual,[10] Góngora aspires to have the best of both the Sister Arts. In the *Polifemo*, for instance, words and images are coloured in and shimmer on the surface of the page, in overlapping tonal patterns that extend sensuously and ingeniously as if pushing against their own materiality, testing the limits of textuality itself, just as they challenge conventional notions of decorum, form and genre. The visual aesthetic absorbs the darkest iconographies of envy and *eros* and paints a poetry of a shifting, uncertain world; its monstrous, hybrid origins capturing the upheaval of the writer's and receivers' own historical moment. In Góngora's lyric a new poetic subjectivity disrupts and extends the normative nature of the Petrarchan poetic persona, raising questions about self-identity and the early modern subject's ambiguous relationship with his world. It emerges from the shadows of cultural memory, from Ovid's cavern of Envy, Enceladus's tomb, Vulcan's subterranean forge, even from Hell itself. It is marked by jealousy's 'evil eye' and infected by love's serpentine poison. But it sings a more powerfully dialectical song for all that, one whose dissonance and ironic reflection on limits connects the poem's *res* to *respublica*, and conveys the broader conflicting discourses of

---

9   My thinking here is informed by Nagel and Wood's research on clashing temporalities in fifteenth-century painting, especially their arguments around the relationship of visual artefacts to time, which I have adapted in accordance with the very different context of how visual imagery works within written (self-consciously allusive) texts. See Alexander Nagel and Christopher S. Wood, 'Interventions: Towards a New Model of Renaissance Anachronism', *Art Bulletin*, 87.3 (2005), 403–32 (409).

10   See Joseph Addison, 'The Pleasures of the Imagination' (first published in *The Spectator*, no. 411, 21 June 1712): 'Besides, the Pleasures of the Imagination have this Advantage, above those of the Understanding, that they are more obvious, and more easie to be acquired. It is but opening the Eye, and the Scene enters. The Colours paint themselves on the Fancy, with very little Attention of Thought or Application of Mind in the Beholder'.

its moment of origin, a gazing inwards (in the etymological spirit of 'videre'
– 'intus') that ventures out. As we will see, invention in Góngora's love poetry connects to violent desire,[11] and owes much to 'envidia'. Envy is not
demystified in the emulative process, nor separated from its moral connotations. On the contrary, at the core of Góngora's progressive poetics, the self-
consuming paralysis of traditional envy narratives, with their pointless plots
of destruction and predictions of social disintegration, are encouraged to rear
their ugliest heads.

Envy, eris and eros: looking back ...

The existence of *aemulatio* as a technical term among Renaissance theorists has
been called into question. As I have discussed briefly elsewhere, this was not the
case in the ancient world, where the extant rhetorical writings of Dionysus and
Longinus point to subtle differences of attitude between *mimesis* (*imitatio*) and
zelosis (*aemulatio*): the former an active reproduction of a model based on theoretical principles; the latter an activity of the mind, stimulated by admiration of
something beautiful.[12] Russell has concluded that evidence from these texts tends
to suggest a complex idea of 'mimesis-zelosis' as complementary aspects of the
same process,[13] and that even where the notion of competition between imitator
and model is recommended, it is integral to the whole project and not assigned to
a component part. This would assume an element of misreading, therefore, in the
interpretation of Classical antecedents both by Renaissance theorists and by
creative practitioners. A seminal study by G.W. Pigman sheds significant light on
the problem. Through a detailed, analytical survey of the analogies, images and
metaphors used by Renaissance humanists in their theoretical discussions of
imitation, Pigman provides evidence of the following: no explicit *imitatio/aemu-
latio* distinction is made in any of the works examined; nonetheless, an identifiable concept of *aemulatio* which aims for the re-creation and surpassing of the
prior text is implied in many; key images can be grouped within three dominant
categories, which Pigman labels transformative, dissimulative and eristic; the third
category (with its emphasis on conflict and conquest) is associated with *aemulatio*; despite some theoretical reticence, this emulative (eristic) approach was en-

---

[11]   See a recent study by Emilie L. Bergmann which connects the erotic violence of the *Soledades* and *Polifemo* ('a narration of jealous desire') with philosophies of visual perception: 'Violencia, voyeurismo y genética: versiones de la sexualidad en Góngora y Sor Juana', in *Venus
venerada*, pp. 89–106.
[12]   See Torres, *The Polyphemus Complex*, pp. 10–12.
[13]   See D.A. Russell, 'De Imitatio', in *Creative Imitation and Latin Literature*, eds David West
and Tony Woodman (Cambridge: Cambridge University Press, 1979), pp. 1–16 (p. 10). Victoria
Pineda's review of extant ancient writings comes to similar conclusions. See *La imitación como
arte literario en el siglo XVI español (con una edición y traducción del diálogo 'De Imitatione'
de Sebastián Fox Morcillo)* (Seville: Diputación Provincial de Sevilla, 1994), esp. p. 17.

thusiastically embraced in creative practice where it is inextricably bound up with transformation, but necessarily excludes dissimulation.[14]

In an attempt to account for the reluctance of theorists to embrace *aemulatio* as a technical term, Pigman points to its 'ambiguous moral significances'. He finds a source for this in Longinus who, rather defensively, refers to Hesiod to support the eristic analogy he exploits to convey Plato's relationship with Homer:

> Nor does it seem to me that he [Plato] would have excelled so much in his philosophical doctrines or would have so often hit on poetical subject matter and expression, had he not, by God, with all his heart struggled with Homer for pre-eminence, like a young competitor against an already admired one, perhaps too contentiously and, as it were, breaking a lance with him, but nevertheless not without profit. For according to Hesiod, 'This strife [eris] is good for mortals', and truly this contest for the crown of glory is noble and worth winning, in which even to be defeated by one's elders is not inglorious.[15]

Hesiod explores the disparate genealogies of Eris in two works: the *Theogony* and the *Works and Days*. The characterisation of Eris in the *Theogony* (generally considered the earlier work) is consistent with that of the Homeric epics, where, as the daughter of Nyx and sister of all manner of destructive forces, she fosters war among men and operates beyond the control of Olympian order.[16] She reappears in this negative guise in the *Works and Days*, but then seems to be contradicted and supplanted by a second 'good' Eris, one that shares the dark origins of her counterpart, but stimulates a jealous competitiveness in mortals that brings benefits both to the individual and to society. It is this new account of the productive Eris, associated with labour and toil, that is referred to in the passage partly cited by Longinus:

> So, after all, there was not one kind of Eris (Strife) alone, but all over the earth there are two. As for the one, a man would praise her when he came to understand her; but the other is blameworthy: and they are wholly different in nature. For one fosters evil war and battle, being cruel: her no man loves; but perforce, through the will of the deathless gods, men pay harsh Eris her honour due. But the other is the elder daughter of dark Nyx (Night), and the son of Cronos who sits above and dwells in the ether, set her in the roots of the earth: and she is far kinder to men. She stirs up even the shiftless to toil; for a man grows eager to work when he considers his neighbour, a rich man who hastens to plough and plant and put his house in good order;

---

14   See G.W. Pigman, 'Versions of Imitation in the Renaissance', *Renaissance Quarterly*, 33 (1980), 1–32.

15   Longinus, 13. 4–5, as cited in Pigman, 'Versions of Imitation', 16.

16   See, for instance, *Illiad* 4.439–45; 5.5.18; 11.3–4 and 14.259–61.

and neighbour vies with his neighbour as he hurries after wealth. This Eris is wholesome for men. And potter is angry with potter, and craftsman with craftsman, and beggar is jealous of beggar, and minstrel of minstrel.[17]

Pigman argues that Hesiod (unlike Longinus) reveals a certain ambivalence about the distinction which he draws, that he subsequently explores the more negative motivations behind emulation and makes little attempt to disassociate it from malicious envy. It is Pigman's contention that this darker aspect of *ae-mulatio*, which is evident also in Cicero, Nonnius and Pliny, undermines its effectiveness as a descriptive term in the Renaissance. Although Pigman's reading of the representation of the *Erites* in the *Works and Days* is by no means conclusive (critics are divided on the question of Hesiod's ambivalence),[18] the relationship between emulation and envy that is established here would come to be compromised in any case by the time of its encounter with Renaissance humanism.[19] Once envy had attached itself to emulation, the portrayal of the former across a range of influential texts and traditions (rhetorical, literary and didactic) would inevitably inform the reception of the latter, for better (for example, Pindaric envy as the agent of success in athletic contest)[20] or worse (Ciceronian envy as the dominant value of an aristocratic elite that had to be sublimated).[21] The paradox is patent. Any possibility of formulating a coherent theory of *aemulatio* in the Renaissance was complicated by, and in, the emulative procedures of humanism itself.

Moreover, taking into account the variability that underpins the conceptualisation of morality from culture to culture, the 'moral ambiguity' of Renaissance

[17]   Hesiod, *Works and Days, 11–24, trans. Hugh G. Evelyn-White [1914] (Gloucester: Dodo Press, 2008).

[18]   For diverging views on Eris in Hesiod see, for instance: B. Mezzadri, 'La double Eris initiale', *Métis*, 4 (1989), 51–60; M. Gagarin, 'The Ambiguity of Eris in the "Works and Days"', in *The Cabinet of the Muses: Essays on Classical and Comparative Literature in Honour of Thomas G. Rosenmeyer*, eds M. Griffith and D. Mastronarde (Atlanta: Scholars Press, 1990), pp. 173–83; M.N. Nagler, 'Discourse and Conflict in Hesiod: Eris and the Erides', *Ramus*, 21 (1992), 79–96.

[19]   Giorgio Vasari's *Lives of the Most Excellent Painters, Sculptors and Architects* (1550 and 1568) offers the first sustained use of artistic rivalry for rhetorical purposes. Vasari promotes healthy competition, rejecting envy as its opposite, 'as a means not only of developing the individual's skill but also of improving art itself in a communal endeavor'. Quoted in James Clifton, 'Vasari on Competition', *Sixteenth Century Journal*, XXVII.1 (1996), 23–41 (23). Clifton (28) offers a brief consideration of Vasari's own debt to the artist's anecdotes contained in Pliny's *Natural History* (e.g. competitions between Apelles and Protogenes, Zeuxis and Parrhasius).

[20]   There are several instances in Pinder's *Odes* where the exaltation of victory is informed by human envy as motivated by the success of others in athletic competition. See, for instance: O. 6.7 and 74; O. 8. 55; O. 11.7.

[21]   For a very thoughtful discussion of the envy passages in the *De oratore*, see Michelle Zerba, 'Love, Envy and Pantomimic Morality in Cicero's *De oratore*', *Classical Philology*, 97.4 (2002), 299–321. Zerba's observations on how envy can be positively harnessed in rhetorical performance are of particular relevance to Góngora's poetics.

aemulatio no doubt owed something to the certainty with which envy was vili-
fied as one of the seven deadly sins in the Judeo-Christian traditions: the sin that
caused the first murder; that festers in families, in hierarchies, and in structured
societies of all kinds. Patristic writings, for instance, cite the biblical story of
Cain and Abel as the *locus classicus* of the evil of envy;[22] Saint Augustine mag-
nifies envy as the source of the fratricide that lies at the mythic origins of Rome,
exploiting the Genesis narrative as an interpretive lens;[23] Aquinas makes envy
contrary to charity; while Dante, who situates Envy in the *Purgatorio* between
Pride and Anger, has the eyelids of the envious sewn shut with metal thread and,
in the *Inferno*, engages with a complex range of significations to posit envy's
consequence as the negation of identity and creativity.[24] Emblem books, one of
the most popular and widespread art forms of the period, featured symbolic
pictures and texts with veiled moral messages that suggested a homogeneous
set of Christian cultural values. The potential for a more subversive decoding,
however, was accessible via the multifarious range of Classical and humanist
sources which informed the written epigrams (Virgil, Ovid, Aesop, Erasmus, to
name but a few). Emblem books provided, therefore, a significant intermediary
and disseminating function in the literary system of Renaissance culture. The
first book of emblems was introduced into Germany by the Italian, Andrea
Alciato, in 1531, containing epigrammatic verses in Latin and illustrated with
woodcut figures. The text entry on 'Invidia' first appeared in the second collection, published in Venice by Aldus Manutius in 1546, and was accompanied by
the image of a naked woman feeding on a snake.[25] It reads as follows:

> Squallida vipereas manducans foemina carnes,
> Cuique dolent oculi quaeque suum cor edit,
> Quam macies, & pallor habent, spinosaque gestat
> Tela manu. Talis pingitur invidia
> (Alciato, *Emblematum libellus*, CXLI, 1546, 35v)

---

22   Angela Kim argues that this was a deliberate strategy on the part of early Church translators and interpreters as a means of diverting attention from the capricious portrayal of God in the
story. Kim points out that envy is not explicitly referred to in the Hebrew text. See 'Cain and Abel
in the Light of Envy: A Study in the History of the Interpretation of Envy in Genesis 4.1–16',
Journal for the Study of Pseudepigrapha, 12.1 (2001), 65–84.

23   See Augustine, 'The City of God' in *Writings of Saint Augustine*, trans. G.G. Walsh and
G. Monahan, Fathers of the Church, 14, 17 vols (New York: Fathers of the Church, 1952), VII,
(p. 420).

24   See Robert J. Elrich's analysis of the poetic processes deployed by Dante in the exploration
and representation of envy and its destructive consequences: 'Envy, Identity, Creativity: Inferno
XXIV–XXV', *Dante Studies*, 102 (1984), 61–84.

25   Illustrations in subsequent editions vary and include Envy as an old woman walking along
a road, carrying a stick, with snakes emerging from her mouth (as in *Les Emblemes*, Lyon, 1549,
and *Emblematica*, Lyon, 1550).

[A filthy woman chewing the flesh of vipers, whose eyes are painful, who gnaws her own heart, emaciated & deathly pale, carrying prickly sticks in her hand. Thus is Envy depicted.]

Alciato's gruesome feminine personification is consistent with the features of *phthonos* that pervaded ancient texts: repulsive self-consumption, symptoms of terminal disease (emaciation, pallor), association with venomous creatures and squalor. This envious creature, consumed by the act of looking, was thought to have been afflicted by the 'evil eye', a condition given a 'scientific' treatment by Plutarch in a passage that exposes the deviant forces that threaten the Platonic 'optics of love':

> *For the sight, being very vigorous and active*, together with the spirit upon which it depends, *sends forth a strange fiery power*; so that by it men act and suffer very much, and are always proportionally pleased or displeased, according as the visible objects are agreeable or not. *Love, that greatest and most violent passion of the soul, takes its beginning from the eye;* so that a lover, when he looks upon the fair, flows out, as it were, and seems to mix with them. And therefore why should any one, that believes men can be affected and prejudiced by the sight, imagine that they cannot act and hurt as well? For the mutual looks of mature beauties, and that which comes from the eye, whether light or a stream of spirits, melt and dissolve the lovers with a pleasing pain, which they call the bittersweet of love. For neither by touching or hearing the voice of their beloved are they so much wounded and wrought upon, as by looking and being looked upon again. [...] *And of all diseases, soreness of the eyes is the most infectious; so strong and vigorous is the sight, and so easily does it cause infirmities in another.* [...] *Thoughts of love excite lust*, and rage often blinds dogs as they fight with wild beasts. Sorrow, covetousness, or *jealousy makes us change colour, and destroys the habit of the body; and envy more than any passion, when fixed in the soul, fills the body full of ill humours, and makes it pale and ugly; which deformities good painters in their pictures of envy endeavour to represent. Now, when men thus perverted by envy fix their eyes upon another, and these, being nearest to the soul, easily draw the venom from it, and send out as it were poisoned darts* [26] (*Quaestiones Convivales*, 5.7 680ff; emphasis added)

Ovid's personification of 'Invidia' in the *Metamorphoses* (II, 708–36), with its emphasis on destructive acts of vision, has much in common with Plutarch's disquisition on *Ophthalmia*, and is the most sustained graphic treatment of the emotion in extant Classical literature. The gaunt and wasted Ovidian figure is depicted in terms of an excessive and relentless malignancy that is both en-

---

[26] Plutarch, *Quaestiones Convivales*, translated from the Greek by several hands. Corrected and revised by William W. Goodwin (Boston: Little, Brown, and Company; Cambridge: Press of John Wilson and Son, 1874).

acted and afflicted upon others. As a distinctly dehumanised and dissocialised 'embodiment' (Virgil's mythological fury, Alecto, is its closest epic relation), Ovid's envy inspired a host of Medieval and Renaissance allegorical imitations. Notable among these are Spenser's *Faerie Queen* (where envy, one of the six counsellors of Pride, rides on a wolf chewing a venomous toad) and, of course, the Alciato emblem cited above. Of most relevance to Gongorist poetics, however, is Ovid's interest in conflating the properties of envy and *eros*. In the *Metamorphoses*, these are intrinsically connected on both thematic and structural levels, operating as migratory, intertexual motifs that stimulate fluid strands of a highly visual imaginary and propel narrative action. Two further innovations are worth noting. Ovid is the first writer to provide envy with a fixed abode, a physical setting that manages to complement the characteristics of the emotion, without negating the sense of a contagious identity that is formed 'on the move'; and the first to accommodate an eroticised envy within a metatextual frame. This is realised, in part, through the text's combined processes of visualisation and personification, although it also owes something to the episode's intertextual resonances, Callimachean and elegiac but, more significantly, epic.[27] Envy's attack on Aglauros recalls Cupid's assault on Queen Dido in Virgil's *Aeneid*. A poison flows through her bones, enflaming beyond measure and yet concealing the source of the pain. A summary of the Ovidian story, incorporating excerpts from the translated text, is included below:

> The god Mercury, in flight over the Festival of Pallas, sees the virgin Herse and is inflamed. He approaches her sister, Aglauros, and begs her to help him gain access. Aglauros looks upon him with the same 'greedy eyes' with which she had looked into the secrets of Minerva and demands gold for her services. Recalling Aglauros's earlier profane action, Minerva turns 'angry eyes' upon her. Resentful of the gold which the girl will receive and of the relationship she will forge with the god, Minerva makes for Envy's house:

> *Her cave was hidden deep among valleys, sunless and inaccessible to the winds, a melancholy place and filled with a numbing cold. Fire is always absent, and fog always fills it. When the feared war goddess came there, she stood outside the cave, since she had no right to enter the place, and struck the doors with the butt of her spear. With the blow they flew open. Envy could be seen, eating vipers' meat that fed her venom, and at the sight the goddess*

---

27   The personification of Envy in the epilogue of Callimachus's *Hymn to Apollo* (vv. 105–13) is generally interpreted as metatextual commentary: as the Greek poet's contribution to contemporary polemics and read as a statement of his poetic principles. Envy whispers into the ear of Apollo, criticising poetry which seems not to correspond to the characteristics of Homeric epic, but the god is not amused and pushes Envy aside. The most pertinent elegiac dimension in Ovid's narrative is the depiction of Mercury as an 'exclusus amator' and engagement with the 'paraclausithyron' motif. Allusions to the *Aeneid* correspond primarily to Book 4 (e.g. 1–2; 67–68).

averted her eyes. But the other got up slowly from the ground, leaving the half-eaten snake flesh, and came forward with sluggish steps. When she saw the goddess dressed in her armour and her beauty, she moaned and frowned as she sighed. Pallor spreads over her face, and all her body shrivels. Her sight is skewed, her teeth are livid with decay, her breast is green with bile, and her tongue is suffused with venom. She only smiles at the sight of suffering. She never sleeps, excited by watchful cares. She finds men's successes disagreeable, and pines away at the sight. She gnaws and being gnawed is also her own punishment.

Envy obeys Minerva's commands and poisons Aglauros:

[…] she carried out her command and touched her breast with a hand tinted with darkness and filled her heart with sharp thorns. Then she breathed poisonous, destructive breath into her and spread black venom through her bones and the inside of her lungs. And so that the cause for pain might never be far away she placed Aglauros's sister before her eyes, in imagination, her sister's fortunate marriage, and the beauty of the god, magnifying it all. Cecrops's daughter, tormented by this, is eaten by secret agony, and troubled by night and troubled by light, she moans and wastes away in slow, wretched decay, like ice eroded by the fitful sun.

In revenge Mercury turns Aglauros to stone:

[…] so a lethal chill gradually filled her breast sealing the vital paths and airways. She no longer tried to speak, and if she had tried, her voice had no means of exit. Already stone had gripped her neck, her features hardened, and she sat there, a bloodless statue. Nor was she white stone: her mind had stained it.[28]

Tissol has pointed out how the visual components of the story engage the reader in the power of the narrative, while permitting us to witness its operations: 'our experience as readers mirrors that of Aglauros, in that we have, just before, witnessed the personification of "Invidia" as a really detailed *imago* before our eyes, so to speak'.[29] In fact, personification, as a rhetorical figure, gestures towards its own fictiveness, 'exposing the absence of the real at the same time as it constructs a fantastic, textual, presence'.[30] Moreover, in the Ovidian text, Envy's mode of action, the reproduction of her victims as versions of herself,

---

[28]   *Metamorphoses* II, 708–36, prose translation by A.S. Kline.

[29]   See G. Tissol, *The Face of Nature. Wit, Narrative and Cosmic Origins in Ovid's Metamorphoses* (Princeton NJ and Chichester: Princeton University Press, 1997), p. 67.

[30]   See Philip Hardie's discussion of how Ovidian personifications deconstruct their own presence: *Ovid's Poetics of Illusion* (Cambridge: Cambridge University Press, 2002), ch. 7: 'About Presences of Language', pp. 227–57 (p. 234).

schematised as a foul 'breathing into', reflects positively on the transforming poet's own activity in language that brings the dynamic, emulative, text into being. Ultimately, the poet escapes the boundaries of finite, sterile, reproduction. Envy, subtly distanced from *aemulatio*, is reconceptualised by Ovid as *mimesis* and thematised in the solidification of Aglauros, who is forever silenced and eternally frozen in an attitude of self-erosion. Mercury, in 'true' Ovidian fashion, lives on to desire (and to transform) another day.

Envy, eris and eros: looking to excess …

Góngora's earliest poem on the topic of jealousy ('¡Oh niebla del estado más sereno…') conceptualises the emotion through a mercurial, metaphorical system in which familiarisation and defamiliarisation operate as mutually inclusive principles. The sonnet reads:

> ¡Oh niebla del estado más sereno,
> furia infernal, serpiente mal nacida!
> ¡Oh ponzoñosa víbora escondida
> de verde prado en oloroso seno!
>
> ¡Oh entre el néctar de Amor mortal veneno,
> que en vaso de cristal quitas la vida!
> ¡Oh espada sobre mí de un pelo asida,
> de la amorosa espuela duro freno!
>
> Oh celo, del favor verdugo eterno,
> vuélvete al lugar triste donde estabas,
> o al reino (si allá cabes) del espanto;
>
> mas no cabrás allá, que pues ha tanto
> que comes de ti mesmo y no te acabas,
> mayor debes de ser que el mismo infierno. (p. 26)

[Oh fog of the most serene state, infernal fury, loathsome serpent! Oh venomous viper, hiding in the fragrant hollow of a green meadow! Oh lethal poison in Love's nectar, life-eliding in a crystal glass! Oh sword, hanging by a hair above me, harsh rein to love's spur. Oh jealousy, favour's eternal hangman! Go back to your dismal dwelling place or to the realm (if you fit there) of fear; but you will not fit there, because for so long you have been consuming yourself and are never consumed, you must be greater than hell itself.

Pervasive motifs of traditional pagan and Christian envy narratives (serpentine poison, infernal origins, self-consumption), as well as specific allusions to identifiable poetic models (Sannazaro's Sonnet XXIII, and Garcilaso's Sonnet

XXXIX, an elegant translation of the Italian poem), are integrated into the son-net's analogical infrastructure.[31] Familiar modes of expression function as a dynamic *captatio benevolentiae*, but the limitations inherent in habitual modes of perception are circumvented through strategies of estrangement that operate across all levels of the text: phonetic (the circular, confining, rhyme scheme of the tercets), grammatical (syntactical disruption via parenthesis in v. 11) and semantic (the imaginative reach of the metaphors and extreme hyperbole). Imitating the liquid venom of jealousy itself, familiar propositions slither and seep out beyond their categorical boundaries, never quite shedding the cultural norms inscribed within them, but compelling new modes of perception that challenge their stability. The primary proposition of Sannazaro's poem, retained by Garcilaso, connects ideal love to a hierarchically ordered world view, where-in jealousy emerges as a grotesque manifestation of the darker forces which undermine universal harmony. Góngora's poem opens up this scheme via a subjective thematising of time and space that articulates the sonnet's central psychological and historical commitments, thereby exposing the insufficiency of inherited designations for revealing the contemporary nature of things. Within the unpredictable turns of the text, conventional connotations are ex-tended into alternative figural domains, so that jealousy can be 'seen' for all that it is, and for what it does, in new socio-cultural surroundings, and not simply 'recognised' as a shadow version of former literary selves.[32]

Previous incarnations throb beneath a maelstrom of abstract, exclamatory images that surge through the quatrains towards postponed acknowledgement of any relationship to a speaker (v. 7) and any sense of an identifiable subject in which they might find coherent origin (v. 9). The poem pays its figurative significances forward so that retrospection, quite literally, makes sense. When fog becomes the Fury that is serpent, viper, venom, sword and rein, the meta-phorical premise of the 'most serene state' evolves through a process of imagi-native, metonymic remapping. The catalyst in the opening conceit is implicit. Blocked by the fog, 'cielo' [both sky and heaven] is the locus of psychological 'fall-out', a trauma whose topography finds congruent co-ordinates in the lost paradises, pagan and Christian, of an expanding intertextual landscape. Adam, Eve, Eurydice, Psyche and Damocles emerge in ironised apposition, their own

---

[31] The quatrains of Garcilaso's Sonnet XXXIX read: ¡Oh celos, de amor terrible freno / qu'en un punto me vuelve y tiene fuerte; / hermanos de crüel amarga muerte / que vista, turbas el cielo sereno!; / ¡Oh serpiente nacida en dulce seno / de hermosas flores, mi esperanza es muerte: / tras próspero comienzo, adversa suerte, / tras süave manjar, recio veneno!

[32] My argument here is informed by and adapts Viktor Shklovsky, who drew a distinction between recognition ('automatised perception') and seeing in his essay 'Iskusstvo kak priem' ('Art as Device', 1917); a ground-breaking vindication of disorder in literary style. According to Shk-lovsky, 'seeing' comes about when we are compelled to look at something again as if for the first time. See 'Art as Technique', in *Russian Formalist Criticism: Four Essays*, eds and trans. Lee T. Lemon and Marion J. Reiss (Lincoln: University of Nebraska Press, 1965), pp. 3–24.

exilic conditioning (from Eden, Elysium, the ecstasy of *eros*, the summit of Parnassus, the consciousness of true virtue) marking the self's dark detours through the fluctuating experience of jealous love. The sonnet yields to what John Olson has termed 'extreme reading' – the reader's mind encouraged to go 'as deep as it wants in a word or string of words'.[33] So the 'Furia infernal', the single echo from Garcilaso that finds no correspondence in Sannazaro, takes us down into the depths of Tartarus, the netherworld of the three avenging goddesses, spawn of the Night, winged-avengers of crimes against the natural order, whose wrath manifests itself as tormenting madness.[34] Usually depicted as gorgon-like, garbed in black, blood dripping from their eyes and their waists, arms and hair entwined with poisonous serpents, they were also attributed abhorrent shape-changing powers.

The evil unleashed by the infernal fury lurks firstly as the viper of sacred and profane *loci amoeni*, those idyllic spaces of upper worlds, made fragile and precarious by the concealed, demonic presence.[35] Then it is released as venom, lacing Love's liquid nectar with the bitter taste of death. Ambrosia and nectar were the food and drink of the Olympian gods, and could confer immortality on mortals fortunate enough to be invited to the feast. Only one mortal was granted divine status in this manner. Her name was Psyche and her ultimate divination, through the intervention of Jupiter, legitimised her love for Cupid and recognised her as his wife. But eternal life with the god of love was hard earned. Apuleius recounts the trials of Psyche as a narration of jealousy and desire. Before the 'happy ever

---

33 'Extreme Reading' (May–June 2009) is an essay by the poet John Olson, posted online in *The Glade of Theoric Ornithic Hermetica*: <http://stevenfama.blogspot.co.uk/2009/06/adventures-in-pharmakon.html> [last accessed 8 September 2012].

34 The Furies were first named by Virgil as Tisiphone, Megaera and Alecto (*Aeneid* XII, 845). Their origins in Hades, serpentine appearance and association with firebrands are a standard feature of Classical accounts (e.g. Ovid, *Met*. 4. 451; *Met*. 10. 41ff; Virgil, *Aen*. VI, 268, *Georgic* IV, 471 and *Georgic* III, 37, where even 'Invidia' cowers before them; Statius, *Thebaid*, 1. 46 ff; and 11. 47). The following passage from Nonnus captures the spirit of these accounts with a particular emphasis on shape-changing: 'The *Erinys* of many shapes [...] loudly cracking her snaky whip; she shook her head, and a deadly hiss issued from her quivering serpent-hair, terrible, and fountains of poison drenched the rocky wilderness [...] At times, again, she showed a face like some wild beast; a mad and awful lion with thick bristles upon his neck, threatening Dionysos with bloody gape [...] Now Megaira black in her infernal robe went back into the darkness, and sent many spectral visions to Lyaios. Showers of poison-drops were shot upon the head of Bromios and big fat sparks; ever in his ears was the whistling sound of the hellish whip which robbed him of his senses.' (Nonnus, *Dionysiaca* 32. 100 ff).

35 Lucifer's invasion of Eden in the form of the snake in *Genesis* is the model for subsequent Christian allegorical writings. The pastoral *locus classicus* is Virgil, *Georgic* III, 93 ('latet anguis in herbis'), a premonition that is tragically realised in the Orphic epyllion of *Georgic* IV when Eurydice, in flight from Aristaeus, is bitten by a snake and must descend into Hades. Ariosto exploits the 'snake in the grass' simile on three occasions in the *Orlando furioso*: at the beginning at 1. 11, 5–8; in 39. 32, 3–8, and, most relevantly, at Canto 23.123, 6–8, when Orlando cannot sleep in the bed given to him by the shepherd because of his tremendous jealousy.

after' resolution, Psyche has to overcome sibling rivalry, the envy of Venus and her own human failings.[36] Along the way Venus imposes four potentially impossible punitive tasks, the third of which involves braving the guardian snakes and dragons of the underworld to collect the black water of the River Styx in a crystal goblet. Góngora's 'vaso de cristal' illuminates the darkest, most invidious dimensions of the Psyche myth, in alignment with the symbolism that dominates the quatrains. But the allusion also points to the apotheosis of the outcome and thus anticipates the apertures in space and time that will open up in the tercets.

The explicit identification of the speaker with Damocles is a startling deviation from the precursor poems which reconfigures the self-pitying persona of Sannazaro and Garcilaso into an exemplar of the dangers of envying to excess. There has been a tendency in recent times to misread references to Damocles's sword as a metaphor for 'impending doom'; John F. Kennedy's 'Every man, woman and child lives under a nuclear sword of Damocles hanging by the slenderest of threads' is a famous case in point[37]. But the moral parable as evoked by Cicero in the *Tusculan Disputations* (5. 61–62) is an intensely politicised observation on the sycophantic practices that undermined the public life of his day. Damocles, envious of the power and wealth of Dionysus of Syracuse, flatters the tyrant excessively in the hope of securing a greater position for himself at court. Allowed to switch places with the tyrant for a day, Damocles is made to recognise the peril of power. Fear and disillusionment are the price he pays for his illicit desire. The original extract reads:

> Quamquam hic quidem tyrannus ipse iudicavit, quam esset beatus. Nam cum quidam ex eius adsentatoribus, Damocles, commemoraret in sermone copias eius, opes, maiestatem dominatus, rerum abundantiam, magnificentiam aedium regiarum negaretque umquam beatiorem quemquam fuisse, 'Visne igitur' inquit, 'o Damocle, quoniam te haec vita delectat, ipse eam degustare et fortunam experiri meam?' Cum se ille cupere dixisset, conlocari iussit hominem in aureo lecto strato pulcherrimo textili stragulo, magnificis operibus picto, abacosque compluris ornavit argento auroque caelato. Tum ad mensam eximia forma pueros delectos iussit consistere eosque nutum illius

---

[36]   The myth of Cupid and Psyche is embedded as the centrepiece (books 4–6) of Apuleius's work *The Metamorphosis* (also known as *The Golden Ass*) as a story told by the robbers' housekeeper. The allegorical dimensions of the story are well established and most prominent in the names of the protagonists, which suggest the human soul (Psyche) and the divine love that is prominent in Platonic philosophy. Fulgentius's Christian allegorical interpretation retains the idea of Psyche as the soul, but reads Cupid as both good and evil desire. Additionally, Venus represents the lust which envies the soul and sends desire to ruin her. Psyche's search for Cupid and the sequence of perilous tasks all follow from the soul having capitulated to desire. Fulgentius opts not to resolve the allegory once the components have been set up. The issue of the soul's redemption through a reconciliation with desire is, therefore, left open.

[37]   The reference was made in a speech to the General Assembly of the United Nations on 25 September 1961.

intuentis diligenter ministrare. Aderant unguenta coronae, incendebantur odores, mensae conquisitissimis epulis extruebantur. Fortunatus sibi Damocles videbatur. *In hoc medio apparatu fulgentem gladium e lacunari saeta equina aptum demitti iussit, ut impenderet illius beati cervicibus.* Itaque nec pulchros illos ministratores aspiciebat nec plenum artis argentum nec manum porrigebat in mensam; iam ipsae defluebant coronae; denique exoravit tyrannum, ut abire liceret, quod iam beatus nollet esse.

[Indeed this tyrant himself gave his judgement as to how fortunate he was. For when one of his flatterers, Damocles, mentioned in conversation the wealth (of Dionysius), the majesty of his rule, the abundance of his possessions, the magnificence of the royal palace and denied that there had ever been anyone more fortunate, he said, 'So, Damocles, since this life delights you, do you wish to taste it yourself and to try out my fortune?' When Damocles said that he did desire this, Dionysius gave orders that he be placed on a golden couch covered with a beautiful woven rug, embroidered with splendid works; he adorned many sideboards with silver and gold; then he gave orders that boys, chosen for their outstanding beauty, should stand by his table and, watching for a sign from Damocles, should attentively wait on him; there were fragrances and garlands; perfumes were burning; tables were piled high with the most delicious foods. Damocles deemed himself fortunate. *In the middle of this, Dionysius ordered that a shining sword, fastened from the ceiling by a horse-hair, be let down so that it hung over the neck of that fortunate man.* And so he no longer looked at those handsome waiters or at the wonderful silver work, nor did he stretch his hand to the table. Now the very garlands slipped off. Finally he begged the tyrant to allow him to depart because he no longer wanted to be fortunate.]

The self that so dramatically reveals itself in Góngora's poem as the pretentious flatterer, Damocles, stripped of vain human desires, is a self 'desengañado'. It suggests 'being' in two places at once: the interiorised, fictional world of the unrequited lover, reined in by jealousy; and the reality of envy's public role in a master narrative, authorising an ideological script whose illusory value set pulls society back in upon itself (and can also create a problematic environment for the ambitious artist, as the *cultista* polemic would come to demonstrate). The extra space provided by this doubleness also accommodates 'favor', refer- ring to the beloved's favour withheld from the speaker, but also suggesting favour that is curried socially, that is bestowed or denied through prejudice, partiality and political persuasion.[38] Likewise, 'verdugo eterno' operates as a

---

38 Political favouritism would become overtly systemised under Philip III, under whose rule (from 1598) the 'privanza' of the Duke of Lerma was firmly established. For a survey of 'privan- zas' in early modern Spain as compared to the rest of Europe, see J.H. Elliott, 'Unas reflexiones acerca de la privanza española en el contexto europeo', *Anuario de la historia del derecho español*, 67.2 (1997), 885–99.

satanic figure within the symbolic frame of the sonnet, but it also evokes the ritual festivity of early modern Spain's public executions, spectacles of suppression that entertained mass audiences on a regular basis.

The innovative processes, therefore, that drive metaphoric conceptualisation throughout the sonnet create a graphic depiction of 'jealousy' as a transgressive force that breaches both private and public spheres. Moreover, the dynamic effects of this direct the reader's attention to the underlying procedure of meaning-making, and in particular towards the systematic deviances that replace archetypal representations. Thus the poem becomes a performative experience, an instance (to adapt Linda Hutcheon) of 'process *zelosis*', in which the text, as it unravels, foregrounds the emulative process of its own production,[39] articulating a discourse of power that speaks of itself and of its anxious relationship with origins. The speaker tries to rewrite the rules of traditional envy narratives and to send jealousy back to its dismal dwelling place. But this is a duplicated image (both Sannazaro and Garcilaso are models) and the poetic voice undergoes a radical differentiation (a self-questioning self) in order to stage a subversive intervention. In a departure from the precursor texts, Góngora interrogates the delimiting attributes of parenthesis in tension with the 'stretch' that is inevitably involved in the incorporation of supplementary material.[40] As in the Herrera sonnet discussed above (Chapter 3), parenthesis draws the reader to a fixed point of interruption, foregrounding subject intervention as an act of creative interruption. Additionally, the self-reflexive insight interrupts the speaker's singular version of Garcilaso's periphrasis of hell ('reino del espanto'), a leitmotif of peninsular lyric since its coinage.[41] There is much at play here. By marking out the vocative mode, the relationship between speaker and addressee (jealousy) is made more uncomfortably intimate. Moreover, the plurality of voice flirts with the limits of self-making and introduces an epistemological uncertainty that undermines the stability of representation. But it is the symbolic manipulation of the spatial elements of language as material that makes Góngora's '(si allá cabes)' [if you fit there] so compelling. The parenthetical text exists in isolation and interaction with the mimetic text; they make sense separately, but are thematically interwoven. The dependency that is engendered through this the-

---

[39]   'Process mimesis' is the broad critical context within which Linda Hutcheon analyses modern metafiction. See *Narcissistic Narrative: The Metafictional Paradox* (Waterloo, Ontario: Wilfrid Laurier University Press, 1980).

[40]   Williams observes that parenthesis can signal 'dead text'; that it can operate as 'an intrusive adjunct which readers quickly skim over to return to the live text'. There is, therefore, a strong element of reversing reader expectation when parenthesis is exploited as a symbolic poetic device and as an object of interpretation. See Robert Grant Williams, 'Reading the Parenthesis.' *SubStance*, 70 (1993): 53–64 (57).

[41]   For discussion of Garcilaso's motif in context, see Chapter 1 above. For analysis of its re-elaboration in Quevedo, see Chapter 6 below.

matic interrelation suggests a creative claustrophobia within which the re-creating poet struggles to draw breath. We might contrast the confident open-endedness of the penultimate verse of the *Angélica y Medoro* ballad ('el cielo os guarde si puede' [may Heaven preserve you, if it can]), but nonetheless there is a confident poetic voice in the making here, twenty years earlier. The fragmentation of Garcilaso's text interrupts the precursor's symbolic flow, thereby challenging its Orphic credentials and questioning its claims to completeness. The spatial dynamics also produce the impression of simultaneity,[42] a sense of encounter in the present that the poetic voice will surpass in the final tercet, when the interrupting voice becomes dominant. Jealousy is indeed, as Wagschal has pointed out, 'a magnitude that cannot be captured'.[43] Well, certainly not 'there' ('allá'), within the confining strictures of archetypal image systems. But can it be conveyed in the here and now of Góngora's new text? The final verses open up to limitless possibilities. The poetic voice marvels before his own monstrously regenerative image, a creature that has outgrown the limits of its previous incarnations but which, with the imaginative complicity of the reader, as Góngora's subsequent lyric demonstrates, will not outlive its usefulness.

Fascination with the imagination's power to create (and to suppress) the unprecedented lies at the heart of the 'Canción', 'Qué de invidiosos montes levantados' (1602).[44] The speaker, exiled from 'the sweet, beautiful eyes' of the beloved, and tormented by jealous suspicions, allows his mind to don wings and to fly above and beyond the limits of rational consciousness. The use of the word 'pluma', simultaneously meaning feather and pen, reinforces the correlation between the will of the subjective imagination, given a freer field of erotic expression through envy, and an intensely penetrative creative process. The unrequited subject perceives and experiences his world in bolder, more meaningful terms, interiorising and transcending time and space. But ambiguity complicates the performative conditions of the text, fracturing our appreciation, both intellectual and sensual,

---

[42] See E.A. Levensten, *The Stuff of Literature: Physical Aspects of Texts and Their Relation to Literary Meaning* (Albany: SUNY Press, 1992): 'simultaneity of perception in time can best be represented by interpenetration in space' (p. 26).

[43] See *The Literature of Jealousy*, p. 174. The context is as follows: 'For Góngora jealousy is not simply worse than hell. Its horror is inconceivable and can only be represented by what it is not, by a "negative representation", thus exemplifying the mathematical sublime in kantian terms'. However, hell is not evoked in Góngora's text as a point of comparison, rather in terms of symbolic origins, and ultimately as a locus that has become too overly conventionalised to contain Baroque experience.

[44] See Ignacio Navarrete's article which develops the work of Javier García Gilbert to point up Góngora's belief in the relationship between the erotic imagination and the creative process: 'La poesía erótica y la imaginación visual', in *Venus venerada*, pp. 73–87. Góngora's 1602 *canción* is cited as an example on p. 75.

of a complete and consistent subjectivity. Traces of Icarus and Vulcan inscribe illegitimacy. Both are loosely assimilated intertextual identities that expose the unresolved tensions and distortions at the core of an invidious self-consciousness.[45] The role of jealous husband is exposed as particularly precarious when the imagination invades the beloved's bridal chamber. But it arrives too late to witness the lovemaking itself. Temporality lies outside full control, appearing to forge its own fallible terms. The absence of the sexual encounter opens up a dynamic space at the threshold between seeing/knowing and feeling/imagining. In an inventive reconfiguration of the 'exclusus amator',[46] the mind, reactivated, lingers on the representational limits of the imagined post-coital embrace, fixated on, and seduced by, the signs of desire accomplished outside the self. The elision, the lack in language, affirms discovery and doubt (the rival can be strength or beauty, victim or vanquished, heroism humiliated or youth extinguished), and is generative for the creation of meaning in the poem.

> Tarde batiste la invidiosa pluma,
>   que en sabrosa fatiga
> vieras (muerta la voz, suelto el cabello)
> la blanca hija de la blanca espuma,
>   no sé si en brazos diga
> de un fiero Marte, o de un Adonis bello;
>   ya anudada a su cuello
>   podrás verla dormida,
> y a él casi trasladado a nueva vida.
>
> Desnuda el brazo, el pecho descubierta,
>   entre templada nieve
> evaporar contempla un fuego helado,
> y al esposo, en figura casi muerta,
>   que el silencio le bebe
> del sueño con sudor solicitado.
>   (Qué de invidiosos montes levantados pp. 182–83)

[Too late you beat your envious plumage, otherwise you might have seen the white daughter of the white foam, pleasurably exhausted (her voice dead, her

45   See R.P. Calcraft, 'The Lover as Icarus: Góngora's "Que de invidiosos montes levantados"', in *What's Past is Prologue. A Collection of Essays in Honour of L.J. Woodward*, ed. Salvador Bacarisse (Edinburgh: Scottish Academic Press, 1984), pp. 10–28 . See also Steven Wagschal, 'Myth and the Fractured "I" in Góngora', in *The Literature of Jealousy*, pp. 136–56. Wagschal identifies two opposing traditions of the myth of Venus and Mars at the core of the poem, according to which the poetic voice is figured as Vulcan. Wagschal does not attend to the illusory nature of this. He reads the conflicted subject in Freudian terms.
46   See Giulia Poggi's study of elegiac resonance in the poem: 'Exclusus amator e poeta ausente: alcune note ad una canzone gongorina', *Linguistica e Letteratura*, VII (1983), 189–222.

hair loose) in the arms of, I'm not sure whether to call him a fierce Mars or handsome Adonis; but now wrapped around his neck, you will see her asleep and see him transported almost to the next life. Her arm naked, her breast uncovered, observe how fire freezes and melts on temperate snow, and the husband, as if figured in death, who drinks in the silence of her sleeping, with solicitous sweat.]

Likewise, apostrophic instability, the dyadic fluidity of subject–object relations, embraces an amplified sense of self, but also challenges coherency: the addressee oscillates between the beloved, the imaginative mind separated from the self, and the song itself as ultimate interlocutor. The 'I' sees itself in a multiple, mobile 'you': as a disembodied, rhetorical figure, carrying erotic traces of its material terrain; then refigured as an embodied verse form, with the power not only to cohere and unify, but to carry forward:

> Canción, di al pensamiento
> que corra la cortina,
> y vuelva al desdichado que camina. (p. 183)

[Song, tell thought to close the curtain and to come back to the unhappy one who walks.]

In the ironic epithalamic ventriloquising that ends the song, the speaker appears to close the text down literally and figuratively. The lyric voice, created beyond normative modes,[47] deviates from the conventional marriage blessing to emphasise its own isolation. Estrangement from the beloved is no longer the cause of unhappiness, but rather the despair that has dichotomised and 'grounded' the self since the imagination took flight. The final verse subverts the illusion of a stable 'I' and a roaming imagination (the way one might experience the relationship between earth and sun), but reveals an unexpected contrary 'reality': the fact that both are equally inclined to motion. Roland Barthes's understanding of the 'text of pleasure', and his foregrounding of the intersection of desire and undecidability, can be usefully adapted to illuminate these final verses, which have become a contentious interpretive site in modern criticism.[48] The concep-

---

47   José María Micó's very detailed study of the poem ultimately prioritises the text's agonistic relationship with Petrarchan lyric. See 'La superación del petrarquismo', in *La fragua de las Soledades* (Barcelona: Sirmio, 1990), pp. 59–102.

48   Critics have tended to associate the 'problem' of the ending with the issue of generic classification, especially on whether the poem is or is not an epithalamium. Wagschal offers a useful summary of the opposing schools ('Myth and the Fractured "I" in Góngora', in *The Literature of Jealousy*, pp. 144–45) before offering his own 'unified reading' as a development of Micó's anti-epithalamium stance. More recently, Ponce Cárdenas has designated the text marvellously 'hybrid'. See *El tapiz narrativo*, pp. 72–76.

tual framing of Barthes's theory is introduced as follows: 'The pleasure of the text: like Bacon's simulator, it can say: *never apologize, never explain*. It never denies anything: "I shall look away, that will henceforth be my sole negotiation"'.[49] In Góngora's poem, the speaker is the author and reader of the erotic text, fashioned in and by his own envious imagination. Drawn into its ambiguous spaces, where loss is sited and productive, where the impossible is held out and denied, he wields anxious and defensive control. In the end, however, reading against the grain of Barthes's post-structuralist paradigm, it is Góngora's envious subject/reader that gestures towards control, who leaves the tensions of the text unresolved and negotiates by 'looking (and walking) away'.

One of Góngora's latest sonnets, 'Al tronco Filis de un laurel sagrado' (1621), is a text of unrestrained and dangerous desire. Its erotic envy is channelled through a complex symbolic system of *chiaroscuro* and a revisionary re-creation of literary traditions and poetic models (a sonnet by Tasso is a key precursor text).[50] Rather than 'looking away', the poetic voice asserts ambivalent authority in the guise of deviant alter-egos (a satyr and a bee), whose lascivious gazing upon the body of the sleeping shepherdess, Filis, looks past the familiar points of pastoral, and places the poetic persona of the Petrarchan tradition under ironic erasure. Thus the poem asserts a strong subjective presence without ever saying 'I';[51] proclaiming the power of subjectivity to shape a new poetics of risk and dissonance, while acknowledging the role of history and tradition in the shaping of new subjects. The sonnet reads:

> Al tronco Filis de un laurel sagrado
> reclinada, el convexo de su cuello
> lamía en ondas rubias el cabello,
> lascivamente al aire encomendado.
>
> Las hojas del clavel, que había juntado
> el silencio en un labio y otro bello,
> violar intentaba, y pudo hacello,
> sátiro mal de hiedras coronado;

---

[49] See Roland Barthes, *The Pleasure of the Text*, trans. R. Miller (New York: Hill and Wang, 1975), p. 3.

[50] Amann explores the connections and divergences between Tasso's poem and the Góngora sonnet, arguing, very persuasively, that a scene from the Aminta is also in the background of Góngora's poem. See her detailed treatment in 'Pointed Poetry', esp. 307–11.

[51] In a journal entry of May 1921 André Gide relates that Proust once remarked to him: 'You can tell anything as long as you never say "I"' as discussed by Michael Lucey in *Never Say I. Sexuality and the First Person in Colette, Gide and Proust* (Durham: Duke University Press, 2006), pp. 4–5. The implications of this, while clearly contextually distinct, are worth bearing in mind for early modern lyric poems, which are often too readily dismissed as objective and descriptive. See, for instance, a recent article that contrasts Góngora's objectivity with the subjective tone of a sonnet by Juan Bautista de Mesa. See Juan Bautista Martínez Bennecker, 'La poesía de senectud de Juan Bautista de Mesa', *Lemir*, 12 (2008), 235–54 (241).

mas la invidia interpuesta de una abeja,
dulce libando púrpura, al instante
previno la dormida zagaleja.

El semidiós, burlado, petulante,
en atenciones tímidas la deja
de cuanto bella tanto vigilante. (p. 559)

[(Picture this:) Filis, reclining against the trunk of a sacred laurel tree, the golden waves of her hair, lasciviously entrusted to the breeze, lapping at the curve of her neck. Carnation petals, the lips that silence had joined together, a satyr, ill-wreathed in ivy, tried to violate, and could have done it; but the intervention of an envious bee, sucking the sweet purple nectar, immediately alerted the sleeping shepherdess. The demigod, tricked, shameless, leaves her cautious and fearful, as beautiful as she is vigilant.]

Adrienne Martín has drawn attention to the relationship between the visual and the verbal in the communication of the sonnet's dominant erotic stimulus: the image of the female body, asleep in an attitude of wanton abandonment. Martín reminds us how Classical mythology, as in painting, offered poetry an ambiguous space where the naked body could be depicted in passive mode, as an object of contemplation, and yet, also, actively provocative.[52] We might say that Góngora's sensuously vivid image is ekphastic, in the earliest rhetorical definition of the term, where ekphrasis refers to 'writerly procedé', oriented towards eliciting affective response, rather than to a specific relationship between a written text and an *objet d'art*.[53] As Scholz observes, *enargeia* was the ekphrastic text's most distinctive feature, identified in the difference between an emphatic 'showing itself' of the represented object and an unemphatic 'letting itself be seen'. It is through the illusion of movement, in particular, that Góngora's opening image 'shows itself', transforming readers into viewing participants of transformation in, and as, process. Repeating patterns of alliteration ('c', 'l' and 's'), onomatopoeia (hair that 'licks' the naked skin of the neck; silence that sounds itself out), colour that pushes metaphor boldly forward (the gold hair that is sun, sea and sun on sea; lips that are blood-red, nectar-filled carnations, open in bloom, but closed in sleep) – all of these interact tightly along the loose lines that connect the image's component parts.

---

52   See Adrienne Martín,'Góngora y la visualización del cuerpo erótico', esp. pp. 271–75. See also Navarrete, 'La poesía erótica', where this sonnet is cited as an example of how Góngora's poetry demonstrates a clear relationship with the erotic tradition, 'en el sentido específico de la enargeia' (p. 84). The sonnet 'ya besando unas manos cristalinas' also falls into this category.

53   See Bernhardt F. Scholz, 'Ekphrasis and Enargeia in Quintilian's *Institutionis oratoriae libri xii*', in *Rhetorica Movet: Studies in Historical and Modern Rhetoric in Honour of Heinrich F. Plett*, eds Peter L. Osterreich and Thomas O. Sloane (Leiden: Brill, 1999), pp. 3–24 (pp. 6–8).

The sonnet directs our gaze into a defamiliarised pastoral *mise en scène*; the *locus classicus* of creative composition. From the Hellenistic period onwards, to write poetry while reclining under a tree (usually a beech tree in honour of Virgil's Tityrus)[54] came to rank as a poetical topos in itself, accommodating within it the vast majority of erotic motifs available.[55] Within a constantly evolving Arcadia, the *locus amoenus* – a site of shaded natural beauty – acquired 'an independent rhetorico-poetical existence', based on certain stable ingredients: a tree, a meadow, a stream or pond, with more elaborate examples (such as the Sicilian bower where Acis finds the sleeping Galatea) also including birdsong, a gentle breeze and flowers. In Góngora's sonnet, Filis occupies the place of the shepherd-poet, but also embodies this creative site to erotic excess: the sun glints in her hair, the breeze moves through waves that stream across her neck, its curving provides the requisite shade, and flowers bloom in her lips. The poetic word emerges as a matter to be moved and re-situates inscription with respect to time and space. This re-enactment of nature in process, rendered through the reader's participatory agency, evokes the kinetic energy of *aemulatio* against the fixity of *mimesis*, while the creative impulse that gives it shape derives not from rational philosophy, but from envy and desire. Creativity is thus connected to the body, but thematised conceptually. It can only be brought into being via the imaginative functioning of the intellect – that is, through the operations of 'ingenio' [wit]. Wit is central to Góngora's poetry, therefore, not only because it 'transforms straightforward ideas into different thinking',[56] and captures the synthesising quality of mind that allows for ethical and political 'desengaño',[57] but also because, at the highest level of human creativity, through the medium of language, the operation of wit 'discovers' alternative significance in the reality of 'self'-contradiction.[58] Gracián's theory identifies the artistry of wit in a harmonious correlation between objects, regardless of their inherent disparity. Góngora's poetry demonstrates the inherent precariousness in practice when the corporeal converges upon the spiritual.

Although the nostalgia of pastoral has already been violated before the satyr's assault is frustrated by the bee,[59] the ivy-wreathed creature concretises the sonnet's

---

[54]   See Virgil, *Eclogue* 1, vv. 1–5, where Tityrus, in repose beneath a beech tree, wooing the Muses with his reed pipe, teaches the woods to echo 'beautiful Amarylis'.

[55]   See Curtius, *European Literature*, p. 187.

[56]   See Parker, *Polyphemus and Galatea*, p. 26.

[57]   See Beverley, *Essays on the Literary Baroque*, pp. 11–12.

[58]   Parker sums up the nature of discovery in wit: the revelation of a 'relationship between objects and ideas that has always existed but not previously been shown' (*Polyphemus and Galatea*, p. 26)

[59]   Beverley speaks of a 'radically new aesthetics', announced in Cervantes's prologue to *Don Quijote*, but also manifest in Góngora, in which idealised modes, such as the pastoral and the chivalric, are given a more contemporary, ironic treatment. Within this new schema, conventional principles of beauty are subverted and replaced by principles of 'novelty and invention'.

opposition to decorum. Within this antagonistic schema, the significance of the laurel tree as sacred to Apollo has been noted by Amann. She identifies a number of iconic gestures towards the Petrarchist mode that are demystified in Góngora's reconfiguration of key tropes (Daphne-laurel-Laura).[60] Amann reads this in terms of amorous lyric's agonistic relationship with the more profane literary form of satire, as represented in the sonnet by the 'sátiro'. It is not impossible, of course, that Góngora shared a long-held mistaken notion that satire derives from a relationship with Greek satyr plays. But it is more probable that the symbolic axis corresponds to the narrative's antithetical binaries; that just as the satyr threatens Filis, the ivy confronts the laurel to evoke polarisation in broader aesthetic terms. Long before Nietzsche gave theoretical credence to the duality of the Apollonian and Dionysian in the development of art, lyric poets apprehended the tensions of being in terms of these instinctual, oppositional realms. The insistence on the laurel at the centre of Góngora's erotic image creates a fragile Apollonian illusion of light, harmony and order, even of apotheosis, and suspends it on the verge of chaotic collapse. The ivy wreath connects the satyr to the retinue of Dionysus (Bacchus),[61] to the sensual pleasures associated with worship of that darker deity, and to the ecstatic, unrestraint of Dionysian song.[62] The imposition of the ivy upon the laurel may also have politico-generic connotations. Virgil called on Pollio, the military conqueror, to let ivy creep among the laurels on his brow, while Horace initiated a tradition of associating ivy with the highest achievements of a learned art (of the *poeta doctus*), leaving it to the laurel and other plants to recognise the glories of war.[63] The metaphorical dimensions of ivy and bay may have provided Góngora, therefore, with a means of positioning linguistic advance at a further remove from the instability of imperial ambition.

The failure of the satyr to impose the luxuriant powers of Dionysian consciousness is frustrated, however, by the usurping action of the envious bee. The

See *Essays on the Literary Baroque,* pp. 9–10. See also Arthur Terry, *Seventeenth-Century Poetry*, pp. 72–75, for a reading of the 1602 ballad *Angélica y Medoro*, which is relevant to this discussion. Terry emphasises how the transformation of pastoral conventions points to the precariousness of the text itself and how this very self-reflexiveness questions the ways in which language creates meaning. There may also be an echo of the penultimate verse of the ballad ('el cielo os guarde si puede') [may Heaven preserve you, if it can] in the 'pudo hacello' (v. 7) of 'Al tronco Filis'.

60 See 'Pointed Poetry', 312. For a more detailed discussion of the centrality of the Apollo/ Daphne myth in Petrarch and its re-elaboration in Garcilaso, see Chapter 1 above.

61 The satyr's association with the worship of Dionysus is a constant of ancient literature. See, for instance, Ovid, *Fasti* III, 732; *Ars Amatoria* 1, 542; III, 157; *Met.* 1, 692; Horace, *Odes* II, 19. 3. The god himself is often depicted as ivy crowned (e.g. in one of the *Homeric Hymns*). The lascivious connotations of the plant are expressed in ancient and Renaissance texts (see, for instance, Catullus, 61. 33–35; Spenser, *Faerie Queene* 2, 5. 29 and 2, 12. 61).

62 The representation of Orpheus as a flawed, but redeemable, tragic hero is achieved in Jáuregui's *Orfeo* through the ultimate triumph of Apollonian impulse over Dionysian. See Torres, 'Painting it Safe – Juan de Jáuregui's Orfeo', in the *Polyphemus Complex*, pp. 81–101.

63 See Virgil, *Eclogue* 8, 11–13; Horace, *Odes* 1.1. 29–30

bee's protagonism in amorous literature has been well established, as has its
lascivious presence throughout Góngora's lyric.[64] In this poem, as Amann's
analysis indicates, Góngora pays only intertextual 'lip' service to the conventional motif of the *ape ingannata*.[65] More provocative is the emblematic agency
of the bee as embodiment of erotic envy, what has been referred to above as a
metatextual role within the sonnet's performance of 'process *zelosis*'. The intervention of the bee effects a regenerative awakening, a transformation in the
text – one that allows the vital energies of the Dionysian to persist and pulsate
in its substratum, without cancelling out the possibilities of Apollonian beauty.
The verb associated with the activity of the bee, 'libando', indicates productiv-
ity, while also pointing towards the (sweet) substantiveness of artistic labour. It
draws us back to the most graphic demonstration of transformative imitation in
Góngora's *Polifemo*, to the jealous Cyclops's exquisite song of love to Galatea:

> Sudando néctar, lambicando olores,
> senos que ignora aun la golosa cabra
> corchos me guardan, más que abeja flores
> *liba inquïeta, ingenïosa labra*;
> troncos me ofrecen árboles mayores,
> cuyos enjambres, o el abril los abra
> o los desate el mayo, ámbar distilan
> y en ruecas de oro rayos del sol hilan. (*Polifemo*, 393–400; emphasis
> added)

> [In nooks where greediest goats forbear to stray,
> To every flower my hives send many a bee,
> The fragrant nectar of whose petals they
> Restlessly sip, liquefy skilfully.
> To house my swarms, when April wakes or May
> Release them for flight, the tallest tree

[64] For a survey of the bee conceit in Spanish literature, see María Rosa Lida de Malkiel, 'La abeja: la historia de un motivo poético', *Romance Philology*, 17 (1963), 75–86. Ponce Cárdenas applies Blanco's paradigm theory to his discussion of the bee motif as a topos of the epithalamium; working back from the metaphor used by Góngora to convey the audacity of Acis's action in kiss-ing Galatea and the intensity of the kiss itself, he charts how this obsessive constant in Góngora operates within the ambit of Salcedo Coronel's 'honesta oscuridad' and prefigures an (elided) sexual intercourse. See 'La abeja y la flor: paradigma para un pequeño escorzo', in *El tapiz nar-rativo*, pp. 94–111.

[65] Amann highlights, in particular, how Góngora distances his treatment of the erotic bee from that of Tasso (where the bee stings the mouth because he mistakes it for a flower); 'Pointed Poetry', 312–13. For Amann, the bee represents 'agudeza' and introduces dissonance: 'Góngora's poem critiques a self-absorbed and unselfconscious lyricism, which has let down its guard and opened itself to satire' (13). This reading, however, depends upon accepting a shift in the sonnet from voyeurism (the beloved as a passive object) to dialogue (the beloved as 'other'), which, I would argue, is not reflected in the intertextual activity or ekphrastic movement of the quatrains.

> Offers its trunk, and threads of amber run
> Like sunlight from their golden distaff spun.][66]

I have addressed this passage in some detail elsewhere, noting in particular how its allusive depth and competitive stimulus crystallise the poem's engagement with the contradictory mechanics of *aemulatio*.[67] But the conceptualisation of the bee as an intruder, interrupting the sonnet *in medias res*, offers a more dynamic representation of emulative empowerment that feeds on and surpasses its composite origins. The intertextual nectar is substantial: Pliny's eloquent bee on the lips of Plato, Colmela's bee that was once Melissa, Horace's emulative bee challenging the Pindaric swan, Seneca's transforming bee, Petrarch's 'Senecan' bee, and Virgil's entire bee community – connecting Carthaginians to Cyclops – all swept up in the torrential transfigurations of the magnificent *Polifemo*.[68] In this world of shifting contexts, apian immersion suggests the triumph of a self defined by intervention and inclusion, acting upon dominant discourses as an initiating force, interfering in conventional cultural spaces, and utimately undermining traditional hierarchies.[69] The reactivated image of the final tercet is a wholly subjective remediation of poetic and perceptual norms. The seductive outer beauty is retained, but darker inner realities have been unleashed upon the surface.

---

[66]   The verse translation is by Gilbert F. Cunningham and included in Parker, *Polyphemus and Galatea*, p. 133.

[67]   See Torres, '"Sudando néctar": (re)constructing *aemulatio* in Góngora's *Fábula de Polifemo y Galatea*', in *The Polyphemus Complex*, pp. 23–78, esp. pp. 69–71. See also the analysis of the metatextual implications of the bee motif in Soto de Rojas's *Fragmentos de Adonis*, offered within the same study (*The Polyphemus Complex*, p. 113)

[68]   See *The Polyphemus Complex*, pp. 23–78, where these references are provided in full and discussed in context. Beyond the allegorical interpretation of the bees as representative of the perfectly organised state, a great part of its metaphorical function as poetic symbol in subsequent literature has its roots in Virgil's depiction of the bee community in *Georgic* IV. For instance, the link between honey and the gods is prioritised in the first verse ('mellis … caelestia dona') and reiterated in the references to 'purissima mella', 'liquido nectare' (164–65); the association of bees with immortality (the individual bee will die but the race is immortal – 'at genus immortale manet' 208) is reinforced in the Aristaeus epyllion where the miracle of the regeneration of the race from the rotting flesh of the oxen establishes the bee as an ambiguous symbol of resurrection (554–58). For a discussion of the apian analogies that pervaded ancient and Renaissance writings on *imitatio*, see Pigman, 'Versions of Imitation', 4–7.

[69]   In the metaphor of the bee, poets throughout the ages have refined and modulated their art. In the last century, Machado was a prominent 'bee' poet in the Spanish-speaking world; Sylvia Plath in the English. The current poet laureate, Carol Ann Duffy, has recently published her latest anthology. Its title – *The Bees* (London: Picador, 2011). The apian spirit clearly still presides over the private voice of public poetry.

6

Francisco de Quevedo Villegas (1580–1645):
Metaphor, Materiality and Metaphysics

Introduction: *'Nada menos que ... toda una literatura'*

Francisco de Quevedo's remarkable love poetry has finally begun to speak to us on its own terms: as poetry. For too long its voice struggled to be heard under the considerable weight of alternative critical displacement activity; that is, engagement with the still unresolved issues of chronology, dating, and corpus definition that are inevitably dominant when a poet does not publish his work in his own lifetime. However, there are some things that we do know for certain: the first posthumous edition of Quevedo's poetry was compiled and edited by his friend, José Antonio González de Salas, in 1648, under the title *El Parnaso español, monte en dos cumbres dividido, con las nueve Musas castellanas* [The Spanish Parnassus, a mountain divided into two summits, with nine Castilian Muses]; six 'Muses' were completed before Salas's death and the task of editing the remaining three fell to Quevedo's nephew, Pedro Aldrete Quevedo. *Las tres Musas últimas* [The final three Muses], a work of more dubious scholarship, was published over two decades later, in 1670. The love poetry, totalling more than 200 poems in Blecua's canonical edition (if we eliminate some of doubtful attribution), appeared originally in Salas's Muse *Erato* and in Aldrete's *Euterpe*.[1] Salas divided the 132 love poems of the Muse *Erato* into two sections: the first, *Poesías a varios sujetos*, contains poems that are either addressed to women with conventional names (Aminta, Amarylis, Flora, Floralba), some simply to 'una dama', others to no-one at all; the second section, *Poesías singularmente a un sujeto*, contains a mini-anthology addressed either to Lisi or, again, not specified. Notwithstanding the first editor's separation and explicit identification of the Lisi poems as a self-conscious imitation of Petrarch's *canzoniere* (*Parnassus* 257), a debate still smouldering, if no

[1] José Manuel Blecua's first edition of Quevedo's *Obra poética* was published by Planeta in 1963, revised in 1968. Subsequent editions by Blecua were published by Castalia, in four volumes, 1969–81. Poems will be cited in this chapter according to the following edition: Francisco de Quevedo, *Obra poética* (Barcelona: Planeta, 1981).

longer raging,[2] it is my intention to respect the unreliability of chronological data (despite the exceptional efforts of Crosby and others, only about a quarter of the poems can be dated with any accuracy)[3] and, for the purposes of this brief study, to treat the love poetry as a relatively coherent unit. Both sections of *Erato* share a similar linguistic landscape; both derive singular invention from corresponding contradictory impulses, and from a plurality of conventional perspectives. Moreover, the notion of female protagonism is equally false across all the poems of *Erato*. There is, however, in this latter Lisi cycle, a sustained lack of fulfilment for a more consistently named beloved, a cumulative sense of absence and silence, which is felt so intensely by the poetic subject that it amounts to a presence that drowns out all but desire. As Fernández Mosquera has argued, Quevedo's debt to Petrarch is most notable in the Lisi cycle (the inclusion of anniversary sonnets, for instance, that convey temporal progression in milestones of six, ten and twenty-two years), but these are blatant generic markers designed to draw attention to distance and to a very deliberate and emulative reconfiguration.[4] Quevedo may not have lived to see his poetry in print, but his involvement in preparing the texts for publication and his intervention in the creative process is incontrovertible.[5]

The amorous sonnets, in particular, are exquisitely crafted, with an ice-sharp wit that is calculated to blow uncomfortably hot. Their extravagant rhetorical energy produces such an aggressively passionate sentiment, so timelessly close to the bone, that many have been tempted, following Dámaso Alonso, to disen-

---

2   The issue of whether the Lisi poems constitute an authentic *canzoniere*, and what the criteria for such a definition should be, is still very much alive. Santiago Fernández Mosquera offers an excellent synthesis of the various schools of thought (from Salas through the speculative biographical arguments of Astrana Marín, 1930, and Montesinos, 1972, to the more recent deconstructive arguments of Cabello Porras, 1981, and Walters' view of a *canzoniere* that is incomplete, defended in various publications from 1984 to 1994.) See *La poesía amorosa de Quevedo: Disposición y estilo desde Canta sola a Lisi* (Madrid: Editorial Gredos, 1999), pp. 16–23.

3   See James O. Crosby, *En torno a la poesía de Quevedo* (Madrid: Castalia, 1967). The more recent edition by Arellano and Schwartz also indicates variant versions of 43 of the 290 texts included and edits 17 of these: Francisco de Quevedo, *Un Heráclito cristiano, Canta sola a Lisi y otros poemas*, ed. and preliminary study by Lía Schwartz e Ignacio Arellano (Barcelona: Crítica, 1998).

4   Fernández Mosquera's view can be summarised as follows: Quevedo's Lisi cycle, like all his love poetry, cannot be explained in terms of a single literary tradition. However, there are indications of a will to imitate Petrarch in the Lisi poems which González de Salas, as a contemporary reader, identified and which he sought to realise *a posteriori* in the organisation of the *editio princeps*. Date of composition and biographical data are, therefore, irrelevant. Quevedo's Lisi cycle has to be interpreted not in terms of a direct comparison with Petrarch's anthology, but in terms of how the *cancionero* genre had evolved over the intervening centuries and was understood in seventeenth-century Spain (*La poesía amorosa de Quevedo*, pp. 23–31). See also Santiago Fernández Mosquera, 'La poesía amorosa de Quevedo', *Insula*, 648 (2000), 20–22.

5   See, for instance, Isabel Pérez Cuenca and Mariano de la Campa Gutiérrez, 'Creación y recreación en la poesía de Quevedo: el caso de los sonetos', in *Studies in Honor of James O. Crosby*, ed. Lía Schwartz (Newark, Delaware: Juan de la Cuesta, 2004), pp. 281–310.

gage their 'desgarrón afectivo' [affective rending] from the conditions of its own time.[6] In fact, the surface contradictions of Quevedo's love poetry have often been reduced to a set of problems to be solved, not just outside the poetry and its relevant socio-historical contexts, but, inevitably, outside our own engagement with them. Love, as theme and complex signifying system, has everything to do with how we relate Quevedo's amorous verse to literary traditions (Classical elegy, Courtly Love, Petrarchism) and to its own contemporary politico-cultural circumstances (in particular, the rise of literary academies and the interdependence of artists and aristocracy), but it has little to do with the underlying driving premises of Quevedo's love poetry.[7] It is certainly not an expression of the author's profound philosophical convictions. Although Quevedo had a keen interest in Neostoicism, evidenced by his correspondence with the Belgian scholar Justus Lipsius and his engagement with Seneca and Epictetus (expressed most explicitly in his treatise, *La cuna y la sepultura*), the lyric speaker of the love poetry is a poor advocate of Stoic apathy and is far from immune to the irrational passions (avarice, envy, fear, love) which a rationalist, ascetic attitude would ensure. Nor are we dealing with the lyric articulation of an overly morbid personality. Quevedo's rhetorical formation ensures that he worked from the outside in and was, therefore, unlikely to let ego intrude upon lyric voice. This concern with voice brings us back to the poetry. If we accept Halliwell's contention that the guiding notion of Aristotelian *mimesis* is enactment,[8] then love in Quevedo's 'love' poetry can be understood quite literally as the dramatic protagonist of a complex signifying system. Operating as a performative master metaphor, love is the familiar touchstone of a new expansionist poetics, which releases the reader into charged, defamiliarised, terrain. And therein lies the root of Quevedesque paradox – how individual metaphors, whose meanings appear not to be predetermined by logic or experience, interconnect within this metaphorical frame and ultimately make sense within a broadened landscape of meaning and feeling.

Pre-metaphorically speaking, as Thomas Hobbes reminds us, the word 'person' meant 'mask'; 'persona' in Latin signifying:

---

6   Dámaso Alonso's reading of Quevedo in terms of modern, existential anguish succeeded in mediating the distance between twentieth-century sensibilities and the poetry of the earlier period, but in so doing his approach detached Quevedo's poetry not only from other poetry of its time, but also from other expressions of early modern constructions of identity that are pertinent to it (*Poesía española*).

7   Carlos M.G. Gutiérrez addresses this issue in terms of identifying the place of the love poetry in Quevedo's literary strategy. His conclusion, however – that Quevedo writes for the future and not for his own time – is quite different from my own view. See 'La poesía amorosa de Quevedo como estrategia literaria', *La Perinola*, 9 (2005), 79–97 (esp. 90–91).

8   See Stephen Halliwell, *Aristotle's Poetics* (Chicago: University of Chicago Press, 1986), esp. p. 128.

the disguise or outward appearance of a man, counterfeited on the stage; and sometimes more particularly that part of it, which disguiseth the face, as a Mask [...] And from the stage hath been translated to any represeter of speech and action [...] So that a person, is the same that an actor is, both on the Stage and in common conversation.[9]

The idea that 'person' should now be considered a 'dead metaphor' (a word that through overuse has lost its figurative value) is hardly an endorsement of the human being's creative potential in the realm of language. But it is from this starting point, the analogy between linguistic self-expression and role playing, that Tronstadt explores the similarities between the concept of metaphor and theatricality; specifically, how grasping the former allows us to understand the latter.[10] And it is from this same starting point, informed by Tronstadt's observations regarding the relational rather than the qualitative nature of both, that I would suggest we explore the rhetorical reformulations of the lyric persona in the post-Petrarchan (early Baroque) love poetry of Francisco de Quevedo.[11] Bakhtin's dialogism is a useful theoretical platform (despite its underestimation of lyric poetry) from which to consider how subjectivity is performed in these texts through multiple, dynamic self–other voices that compete for primacy and/ or ideological control even within a single poem. The relationship between agency and identity in this context must, therefore, be understood as fluid, negotiable and interactive, and is often investigated around this differential relationship, or dialogue, between self and other. But in the context of the 'inaccessibility crisis' that characterised Petrarchan subjectivity and, as Bloom would have it, 'burdened' belated or post-Petrarchan poetry, identifying the 'other' is as complex as defining the 'self'[12].

Indeed, as we have already established, from Garcilaso through to Góngora, the site of Petrarchan lyric is a matrix of incongruities (an unattainable beloved, an unspeakable desire, elusive allusions, decentred authority) and of outright contradictions (public against private, body opposing soul, nature subsumed by art). Only the presence of the reader in the text, bringing contex-

---

9   Thomas Hobbes, *Leviathan* (1651) (Harmondsworth: Penguin Books, 1985), p. 217, as cited in Ragnhild Tronstad, 'Could the World become a Stage? Theatricality and Metaphorical Structures', *SubStance*, 31.2 (2002), 216–24.

10   See Trondstadt, 'Could the World become a Stage?'

11   Paul Julian Smith's book, *Quevedo on Parnassus: Allusive Context and Literary Theory in the Love Lyric* (London: MHRA, 1987), offers the most detailed study to date of the rhetorical and intertextual basis of Quevedo's verse. See also Marie Roig Miranda's complementary study of style in the sonnets: *Les sonnets de Quevedo, variations, constances, evolution* (Nancy: PUN, 1989). Distinct from these, Fernández Mosquera's discussion of metaphor is organised thematically, in terms of the links between recurrent metaphors and traditional motifs: *La poesía amorosa de Quevedo*, pp. 57–165.

12   Bloom, *The Anxiety of Influence.*

tual resonance alive, can prompt a process of reconciliation that moves towards, or indeed, deliberately away from, resolution. The most effective lyric poetry facilitates this by projecting a human subject voice along axes that integrate erudition and artifice (the *sine qua non* of literary creation according to Gracián),[13] but which also combine affective power, thereby passing beyond reader identification to appropriation. Consequently, provisional identities made in and through and by language are fixed and meaningful momentarily, universality comes into being via skilfully constructed introspection, and a genre that seems so apparently remote from all political considerations can become the hotly contested ground upon which to establish the vernacular as the flag bearer of national culture or to reshape it in collaboration with emergent discourses of national decline. Fernando de Herrera's poetry, for instance, as we have seen, offers a prime example of the former. In *Algunas obras*, metaphor, as one of the most reader-compromising and yet enabling features of language, has a key role to play in the early modern Spanish project of politico-aesthetic advantage. Francisco de Quevedo's poetry of *desengaño*, still resonant with contemporary artistic and political controversies, is more appropriately positioned in the context of the latter.[14]

The reach of Quevedo's erudition has been well substantiated. José Luis Borges commented that Quevedo 'es menos un hombre que una dilatada y compleja literatura' [less a man, more a vast, complex literature]. Lía Schwartz, perhaps more persuasively than any other Quevedo scholar, has substantiated the latter part of this assertion, emphasising how diverse rhetorical contexts and poetic traditions interact in the love poetry to secure the success of a single communicative act.[15] The result is often a polyphonic power of eloquence which, as Mercedes Blanco points out, is structured to resist reader fragmentation or disruption at the level of *res*.[16] Prioritisation of *res* over *verba*, metalinguistics operating in the service of metaphysics, involves the reader in an emotional endgame

[13] See Baltasar Gracián, *Agudeza y arte de ingenio*, ed. E. Correa Calderón, 2 vols (Madrid: Castalia, 1969), the most celebrated treatise of the period on the aesthetics of the conceit.

[14] See Lía Schwartz's scholarly study of metaphor in Quevedo's satire: *Metáfora y sátira en la obra de Quevedo* (Madrid: Taurus, 1984).

[15] José Luis Borges, *Otras inquisiciones* (Buenos Aires: Seix Barral, 1993), p. 70. Lía Schwartz's work on Quevedo is substantial. The following studies, among many others, are relevant and merely illustrative: *Quevedo: discurso y representación* (Pamplona: Universidad de Zaragoza, 1986); 'La transmisión renacentista de la poesía grecolatina y dos sonetos de Quevedo', *Edad de Oro*, 12 (1993), 303–20; 'Las voces del poeta amante en la poesía quevediana', in *Quevedo a nueva luz: escritura y política*, eds A. Carreira and L. Schwartz (Malaga: Universidad de Málaga, 1997), pp. 271–95; Francisco de Quevedo, *Un Heráclito cristiano*; 'Entre Propercio y Persio: Quevedo, poeta erudito', *La Perinola*, 7 (2003), 367–95; 'Notas sobre dos conceptos del discurso amoroso de Quevedo y sus fuentes: la *amada fiera* y la *amada pétrea*', *La Perinola*, 9 (2005), 215–26.

[16] See Mercedes Blanco, *Introducción al comentario de la poesía amorosa de Quevedo* (Madrid: Arco libros, 1998), esp. pp. 16–17.

that distinguishes Quevedo from Góngora. It is now generally accepted that locking Quevedo and Góngora into unstable silos, such as *conceptismo* and *culteranismo*, has proven wholly unsatisfactory, with overlapping exceptions threatening the rules of enforced categorisation at every turn. Both poets satisfy a broadly similar set of aesthetic criteria: ultimately producing conceptually sophisticated verse that pushes linguistic figuration to unconventional limits and gives the reader enhanced agency within the interpretative arena of the poem. However, whereas Góngora's reader engages with the analogies of his intricate verse head-first, always intellectually invigorated, but never quite owning the poem emotionally, the reader of Quevedo's love poetry almost always has it both ways.[17] Artifice generates affect and both are equally determining factors of reader response, so that correspondences that appear illogically conceived can be received as real. Across the love poetry, Quevedo's reader plots conventional connections between recurring objective conditions and the defamiliarised, subjective disposition of individual sonnets. Complex metaphorical structures interact and open out into a universally significant symbolic system in which the reader can claim intimate ownership of the poetic 'I'.

Words used metaphorically do not, as Black once suggested, undergo a shift in meaning.[18] Rather, in the interaction of vehicle and tenor, a new meaning emerges which suspends and transcends the literality of language. The shift from designation to connotation expands the verbal repertoire, admits unpredictability and allows for change that has the potential to be significantly radical. In fact, despite Aristotelian confidence in the association of metaphor and mimesis, this operation of metaphor is at its most effective when the new world it creates trespasses across the boundaries of logical categories in order to challenge universal truths. This takes us far beyond the issue of poetry as a creative imitation of reality, and connects generic redefinition and renewal to broader politico-existential concerns.[19] For instance, in both Herrera and Quevedo, the lyric space of enunciation interrogates the universal trauma of

17   Mary Malcolm Gaylord makes a case for the dual claims of artifice and affective power in a very convincing reading of the sonnet 'En breve cárcel traigo aprisionado' [In a compact cell I bear captive]. See 'Intimacy and Allegory in a Quevedo Sonnet (En breve cárcel traigo aprisionado)', in *Studies in Honor of Denah Lida*, eds Mary G. Berg and Lanin A. Gyurko (Potomac, Maryland: Scripta Humanistica, 2005), pp. 103–12.

18   See Max Black, *Models and Metaphors* (London: Cornell University Press, 1962). The bibliography on metaphor is simply too vast to include here. A recent study by Kathryn Allan offers a useful review and reveals how little consensus there still is around what actually constitutes metaphor: *Metaphor and Metonymy: A Diachronic Approach*, Publications of the Philological Society, 42 (Oxford: Wiley-Blackwell, 2008), esp. pp. 1–10.

19   Generic deviation was characteristic of many poets of the period but, as Roig Miranda has noted, it is much more striking in Quevedo. She identifies the integration of indecorous language and tone as two more obvious manifestations, as well as the creation of original conceits. See 'La poesía amorosa de Quevedo y su originalidad', *La Perinola*, 9 (2005), 172–81.

transience in and through metaphor. But whereas Herrera's poetic subject exhibits a will to idealisation, paying metaphorical lip service to Neoplatonic values of contemplation and transcendental knowing, Quevedo's speaker struggles to accommodate an emerging imperative to materialism within a linguistic system that confronts the figurative limits of Neoplatonism with a less than convincing performance of Neostoic paradoxes. Metaphor is manipulated along with its more 'dangerous' manifestation, the metaphysical conceit, to achieve the deliberate embedding of linguistic failure, thereby creating paradoxical counterpoints that challenge Renaissance epistemological and ontological principles. Quevedo inherits the Neoplatonist view of man's place in the cosmos as *discordia concors* and *coincidentia oppositorum* but, as many have argued, throughout the body of his work (straight, sacred and parodic) he tends to stress discord in terms of a conflict between the ideal and, in some cases, the grotesquely real. There is little to be gained from further review or debate over the meaning of contradiction in Quevedo's poetry,[20] a debate not disconnected from the polemic over the poet's 'modernity' – which is, after all, a misguided attempt by the 'modern' mind to recuperate an earlier tradition on our own terms. More relevant is the why and wherefore of this prioritisation of collision. Analysis of the operations of metaphorical performance offers some insights. The joining of dissimilars is not (as Harries points out) about perceiving something that was previously hidden, but rather about making the reader complicitous in the creation of something altogether new; an 'as if' world that is 'other', not just different.[21] In terms of Renaissance poetic practices, the power of metaphor in this action might also be considered integral to the move from *imitatio* to *inventio*, a move underpinned by aspirations of autonomy. The transgression or even dissolution of boundaries in Quevedo's persistent hyperboles, hypothesis and dream poems, and unrivalled 'mas allá de la muerte' [beyond death] sonnets, might even be considered a more radical 'liberation of the word' than Góngora's, freeing both poet and reader from the world of universal truths and, following Ricoeur, compelling us to treat the imagination as a dimension of language.[22] But the scepticism behind the new vision is counter-intuitive to the establish-

---

[20]   Among those many critics who have identified and addressed the issue of 'contradiction' in Quevedo's poetry, George Mariscal's study of multiple and conflicting subjectivities is, to my mind, the most perceptive in its awareness of how Quevedo's poetic speakers 'are implicated in a variety of assemblies ranging from the *gremio* of courtly poets to the power of the literary tradition itself' (*Contradictory Subjects: Quevedo, Cervantes and Seventeenth-Century Spanish Poetry* [Ithaca: Cornell University Press, 1991]), p. 36. Mariscal's analysis takes particular account of how the construct of the individual, emerging from competing discourses, was being constituted within writing itself.

[21]   See Karsten Harries, 'Metaphor and Transcendence', *Critical Enquiry*, 5.1 (1978), 73–90.

[22]   See Paul Ricoeur, 'Metaphor and the Main Problem of Hermeneutics', *New Literary History*, 6 (1974), 95–110.

ment of new certainties. Quevedo's attempts to interpret time according to human desire, to place the subject, poetry and mortality beyond time, only serve to expose that all of this is temporally conditioned.

Just as Herrera's Platonism is allegory, thinly disguised, the 'new face' of Baroque poetry, as performed by Quevedo's amorous persona, is masked in metaphor. With all due respect to the position taken by scholars such as Alexander Parker,[23] Quevedo's sonnets, in particular, suggest that it is time we stopped talking about the philosophy of love in Spanish poetry – at least in any real terms. As we shall see, outside the abstractions of the philosophical treatise, and given the nature of the problems, the solutions of Neostoicim are simply untenable.

As if ...

Transgression in the context of the poetic artefact, if we follow Edward Said's argument, is always relative to a conventional platform of interpretation and should be viewed, therefore, in terms of deliberate deviation.[24] If we take this argument further, following Ricoeur's theory of denotation, linguistic transgression should also be considered in terms of shifting alternatives whose elements of common discourse are already metaphors, made ambiguous and meaningful as a result of fluid interactions within poetic tradition.[25] However, when meaning is anchored in a Petrarchan love lyric whose metaphorical field of love and loss has become subject to an inevitable de-semanticisation over time (for instance, when the ice/fire antithesis has become ornamentally 'dead'), a radical recharging is required. Quevedo responds, in Sonnet 337, in terms that are at once transgressive and transcendent.

> ¡Ay Floralba! Soñé que te ... ¿Dirélo?
> Sí, pues que sueño fue: que te gozaba.
> ¿Y quién, sino un amante que soñaba,
> juntara tanto infierno a tanto cielo?
>
> Mis llamas con tu nieve y con tu yelo,
> cual suele opuestas flechas de su aljaba,

---

[23]   Parker ends his discussion of Quevedo's love poetry as follows: 'we are forced to conclude that this Christian stoicism of Quevedo was a profound conviction' (*Philosophy of Love*, p. 158).

[24]   See Edward Said, 'On the Transgressive Elements in Music', in *Musical Elaborations* (New York: Columbia University Press, 1991), Part Two. This is a collection of the *Welleck Library Lectures in Critical Theory*, given by the author at Columbia University in 1989.

[25]   See Paul Ricoeur, *The Rule of Metaphor: The Creation of Meaning in Language*, trans. Robert Czerny with Kathleen McLaughlin and John Costello (London and New York: Routledge, 1978), esp. pp. 161–68 ('Deviation and Rhetoric Degree Zero') and pp. 255–302 ('Metaphor and Reference').

mezclaba Amor, y honesto las mezclaba,
como mi adoración en su desvelo.

Y dije: «Quiera Amor, quiera mi suerte,
que nunca duerma yo, si estoy despierto,
y que si duermo, que jamás despierte».

Mas desperté del dulce desconcierto;
y vi que estuve vivo con la muerte,
y vi que con la vida estaba muerto.[26]

[Oh, Floralba!, I dreamt that ... Shall I say it? Yes, for it was a dream: that I
made love to you. And who, if not a lover who was dreaming, could merge
such a hell with such a heaven? My flames mixed with your snow and with
your ice, just as Cupid often mixed the different darts of his quiver, and
mixed them honestly, just as I (honestly) adore you when awake. And I said:
"May Love, may destiny decree that I should never sleep, if I'm awake, and
if I am sleeping now, that I never wake again." But I awoke from this sweet
discord; and found that I was alive with death, and found that with living I
was dead.]

The dream texts of the Western canon, from Homer, Plato, Socrates, Cicero and
Virgil in the ancient world, through to Dante and the visionary literature of
Renaissance mystics, were well known to Quevedo who contributed to the
tradition most provocatively with the publication of his satirical *Sueños* in 1627.[27]
Often associated with the paintings of Hieronymus Bosch, Quevedo's *Sueños*
blend doctrinal moralising and scathing social satire within 'an overriding impression of grotesqueness', an unsettled and unsettling environment which Iffland associates with the actual experience of nightmare.[28] Within the love poetry, the fictional framework of the dream mode offers Quevedo similar licence
to create powerful nightmarish images in which the speaker delves into his
erotic subconscious – a dangerous descent that resonates metaphorically with

---

[26]   Ricardo Senabre identifies this sonnet as the final stage in a complex rhetorical design that
he traces from Sonnet 365 through Silva 398, various Sonnets 356, 358 and 366, and a group of
poems known as the Floris cycle (dated between 1624 and 1628) which includes the burlesque
Sonnet 528. See 'Sobre el proceso creador en la poesía de Quevedo', in *Estudios sobre el Siglo de
Oro: Homenaje al profesor Francisco Ynduráin* (Madrid: Editorial Nacional, 1984), pp. 463–78
(esp. 461–71).

[27]   The *Sueños* had done the rounds for years in manuscript and the version that appeared in
1627 was considerably toned down by censorship. More stringent ecclesiastical censorship in 1631
resulted in an even more deformed text entitled *Juguetes de la niñez*.

[28]   See James Iffland's study *Quevedo and the Grotesque: The Grotesque Image*, 2 vols (London: Tamesis, 1978), I, Part I, p. 19. As Iffland notes, only two of the 'dreams' are presented fully
within the dream frame; hell is the setting of the majority.

the ancient mythical *katabasis*. The hallucinatory dream narratives of a series of sonnets (for example, 356, 357, 358, 366 and 368) are dynamic intertextual sites of temporal dislocation, where characters interweave (Aeneas, Orpheus, Palinurus), conflicting perspectives (e)merge, and the voices and stories of the past are reconceived by/in a new voice for a traumatic present.[29] As one might expect, confrontation with the full horror of sexual repression in these nightmare poems lacks the restorative closure of Classic *katabasis*. Rather, the fantasy functions as an aesthetic site of projection, wherein physical exhaustion and spiritual dissolution are concretised. The general rule of these poems, that 'imagined intercourse gives [the speaker] no consolation',[30] is qualified to some extent by Sonnet 337, addressed to Floralba. This is Quevedo's indecorous contribution to a more decorous tradition of dream sonnets that reaches back to Boscán's 'Dulce soñar' [Sweet dreaming]. In Quevedo's sonnet, the poetic imagination gives voice to desire in a breaching of boundaries that unsettles the silencing mechanisms of traditional concepts of authority and representation. This illegitimate crossing is, at least temporarily, liberating, transforming the moment of ecstasy into the ecstasy of a poetic moment.

The poetic subject recalls and articulates an erotic dream, not as a 'thinner silhouette of two dimensions', but in terms of a material and metaphysical encounter that challenges the 'ab-sence(s)' of his waking world,[31] the non-presence of the named beloved, Floralba, and the realisation that perception of reality occurs at unsettling degrees of detachment from it. The very substance of the dream is metaphorical, seeming to offer the speaker the opportunity to make sense of his world on the basis of its difference from the erotic fantasy. Nonetheless, the temporality of the dream state is complex: the past is filtered via internally generated stimuli into a present experience that is recalled, and to some extent reimagined by the dreamer, who is enchanted by the memory of the dream, yet ensnared by it within a waking moment that is both present (to him) and future (to the dream). This conflation of temporalities impinges upon the retelling, promoting a cognitive dissonance between the speaker's sense of self and his ability to comprehend and to decipher the difference between reality and illusion. The poem lives on these fluctuating boundaries: appearing to articulate sexual satisfaction, but pivoting on prolonged, unsatisfied, desire; seeming to conform to what Greene has identified

---

[29]   I have discussed the Classical intertexts of these and other amorous sonnets elsewhere. See Isabel Torres, 'Shades of Significance in Quevedo's Internal Hades: Orphic Resonance and Latin Intertexts in the Love Poetry', *Caliope*, 2.1 (1996), 5–35.

[30]   See Julián Olivares, *The Love Poetry of Francisco de Quevedo: An Existential and Aesthetic Approach*, Cambridge Iberian and Latin American Studies (Cambridge: Cambridge University Press, 1983), p. 74.

[31]   The quote is from James Hillman's discussion of Plato on dreams, in particular, Plato's comparison of dream images and shadows (*The Dream and the Underworld* [New York: Harper and Row, 1979], p. 54), as explored by David Punter in his recent study *Metaphor* (London and New York: Routledge, 2007), ch. 5: 'Metaphor and Psychoanalysis', pp. 72–87.

as a logical chronology of lyric,[32] a binary system of 'then' and 'now' (in this case playing the dream off against the world into which the speaker awakes), while establishing a deviant type of time that is at once linear and circular – opening and re-opening the dream after it has been closed down.[33]

The sonnet itself opens in an illusory 'here and now'. The exclamatory apostrophe that calls Floralba forth into the world of the poem effects an impression of immediacy that is qualified on a formal level by the self-reflexive, rhetorical shifts of the first quatrain (unsettling reminders of generic conditions). It is also compromised because the basic premise of the evocation – that the dayworld might acquire the dimensions of the dream and become like night, a place where reality is reversed – is doomed to failure. Apostrophe in Quevedo's lyric, as Sepúlveda has observed, has a function analogous to that of Latin elegy, with all the contingent I/you structural implications of a direct address that is manipulated in an indirect, fictionalised, manner.[34] In this sonnet, however, the amplifications of the opening 'Ay' (grammatical, I/you; figurative, hell/heaven, flames/ice) reject the animation that is implicit in the figure of apostrophe, while also resisting the conventional abstraction of amorous dichotomies (antitheses that are a pervasive presence throughout Quevedo's love poetry).[35] The poem's erotic presencing of the subject and object, which blends within the speaker's initial sigh what Jakobson has referred to as conative and emotive functions, is reinforced by the intrusion of the euphemistic 'gozar'. But beyond this, Floralba, as animated interlocutor, drops out of the poem. Mute responsiveness is all that is demanded from her, both in the lover's dream and in its subsequent expression, but even this passive role comes under erasure. Self-interrupting questions (vv. 1; 3–4) turn the dialogue back upon the consciousness of a conflicted speaker, who stops and shivers on the brink of articulation, but also back

[32]   See Greene, *Origins and Innovations*, p. 33.

[33]   Most commentators take a linear temporal sequence (from initial ecstasy to despair) for granted. For instance, Olivares's comments on the tercets begin: 'Reality undermines his *dulce desconcierto* and he is shaken from his ecstasy' (*The Love Poetry*, p. 75). Francisco Ayala makes similar assumptions in an otherwise penetrating analysis. See 'Sueño y realidad en el barroco', *Insula*, 184 (1962), 1.

[34]   See Jesús Sepúlveda, 'Con un soneto de Quevedo: léxico erótico y niveles de interpretación', *La Perinola*, 5 (2001), 285–319 (293 and 297). The focus of Sepúlveda's study is the burlesque poem 528, whose opening echoes that of 337, even repeating '¿dírelo?' There is similar self-referencing in poem 440, vv. 9–13, addressed to Floris. It is impossible to determine with certainty the order in which these three texts were written. We do know that the Floralba poem passed through several versions, that Floralba was originally 'Zafira'. For a detailed survey of the apostrophe in Quevedo's amorous lyric, see Fernández Mosquera, *La poesía amorosa de Quevedo*, pp. 234–43.

[35]   The Petrarchan fire/ice paradox finds conventional expression in Quevedo's love poetry in three ways: the beloved as the embodiment of both ice and fire (e.g. 305, 313, 348, 443, 462, 465, 484 and 500); the icy beloved in conflict with an enflamed poetic subject (e.g. 350, 387, 446, 496 and 503); fire as the most destructive weapon of the beloved's icy beauty (e.g. 306, 317, 327, 431 and 464).

upon the poem whose frame and its inherited ideology are broken by these interventions and by their defiance of discretion.

Throughout Quevedo's amorous poetry the poetic subject reacts violently against the imposition of abstract poetic codes. But it is the concept of forced silence and its dehumanising consequences that weighs most heavily. In Sonnet 360, for instance, again via an apostrophe that is ambiguously directed, the subject voice enacts an aggressive withdrawal from the conditions and procedures of Courtly Love, pleading for permission to yield to the dementia of frustrated desire:

> Dejad que a voces diga el bien que pierdo,
> si con mi llanto a lástima os provoco;
> y permitidme hacer cosas de loco:
> que parezco muy mal amante y cuerdo. (1–4)

[Let me shout aloud the good I lose, if I can move you to pity with my grief; and let me play the part of the madman: for I'm unconvincing as a sane lover.]

The speaker's unwillingness to participate in the ritual silence of chaste martyrdom transforms a repertoire of commonplaces into extreme and destructive speech-acts:

> La red que rompo y la prisión que muerdo,
> y el tirano rigor que adoro y toco,
> para mostrar mi pena son muy poco,
> si por mi mal de lo que fui me acuerdo. (5–8)

[The net I tear and the prison bonds I bite, and the tyrannical cruelty that I adore and endure, aren't enough to reveal my pain when, to my sorrow, I remember who I was.]

Even the most concrete images, as Iser reminds us, cannot evoke any empirical reality within the fictional utterance of a poetic text.[36] Of course, this is not to deny them a representational function, but if the 'net' and 'prison' do not exist in relation to existing objects, then what is represented here is language itself, and more specifically a referential literary system with a set of operational norms that provides the basis for the reader's expectations. The recodification of Courtly Love abstraction into material hyperboles in Sonnet 360 can be viewed, in this context, as a failed attempt to repel the boundaries between the expressed

---

[36] See Wolfgang Iser, *The Act of Reading. A Theory of Aesthetic Response* (Baltimore: John Hopkins University Press, 1978), esp. ch. 3: 'The Repertoire'.

and the not expressed. As such, this 'show' without 'tell' does more than call
the validity of amorous conventions into question; it thematises the ultimate
failure of language itself. The implications of this for the 'speaking' subject are
negotiated with greater urgency in the Floralba poem. Insofar as Sonnet 337
foregrounds the dream as a safe space for free speech, the subject is decentred
by his own impulse to construct creatively in language a realm of imagined
possibilities, where hell and heaven, fire and ice, might come together as natu-
rally as Cupid's arrows. In other words, the speaker, as dreamer, defamiliarises
perspectives to propose an alternative world where the most novel connections
are forged: where Hebreo's intellectualised love ('el amor de lo honesto')[37] is
given an *Ero*tic stamp of approval and where hedonism might co-exist alongside
a metaphysically oriented spirituality. ¿Dirélo? ['Shall I say it?'] The questions
opened up here are weighted and daring. The poetic persona is really asking
whether words might actualise the imagined and the possible. But the poem
speaks to us on another level, questioning whether its own rhetorical strategies
can stretch beyond the permissible, and in so doing restore to wholeness a human consciousness in crisis and, on a broader scale, seal the fundamental schisms
of the Spanish Baroque world view.

Using the erotic dream as a mechanism to reconcile worldly and transcendental perspectives is, however, a far cry from the reconfigured Christian allegory which Sofie Kluge identifies in other writing of the period, principally
Calderón's drama *La vida es sueño* [Life is a Dream], and Quevedo's own prose
satires (*Los sueños* [Visions]).[38] These literary texts, analytical rather than dog-
matic, offer paradoxical interpretations of very precarious historical circumstances, oscillating between the material and the moral, the secular and the
spiritual, the realistic and the figurative, but always establishing an underlying,
albeit ambiguous, connection between epistemological uncertainty and ethics.
Dream symbolism in the Floralba sonnet, similar to the discourse of allegory,
operates on a dual register of significations and, especially in the tercets, subjects
the very concept of reality to intense critical scrutiny. However, the 'reality'
explored here, in the guise of a summons to the twin authorities of love and fate,
has its origins in the self-conscious solitary confinement of unrequited love and
in the dilemma of a frustrated lover who is caught in two (troublingly interdependent) states of mind. The invocation outwards is challenged by this very

37 León Hebreo, *Diálogos de amor* (Sevilla: Padilla libros, 1989). The perfection of 'el amor
de lo honesto' is set out by Filón to Sofía in the first dialogue.

38 Kluge designates these texts 'meta-allegories'; texts that exhibit the conflicts characteristic not only of Baroque allegory, but of Baroque culture on a broad scale – that is, the tension
between the more progressive aspects of the Renaissance and those elements of Medieval culture
that were reinforced by Counter-Reformation ideology. See Sofie Kluge, *Baroque · Allegory ·
Comedia: The Transfiguration of Tragedy in Seventeenth-Century Spain* (Kassel: Edition Reichenberger, 2010), and also 'The Dialectics of Redemption: Fiction, Heresy and Divine Truth in
Francisco de Quevedo's *Dream of Hell*', *Orbis Litterarum*, 59.6 (2004), 416–38.

subjective conditioning, conveyed in a collision of temporal modes – a precariously 'real' present mirrored in a virtual subjunctive. To sleep, perchance to
wake. To wake, perchance to sleep. There is something of Hamlet's musings on
the surface of the speaker's intervention, but nothing of Shakespeare's more
profound agonies of moral choice or Calderón's schemes of redemption. In the
dream environment of the lover, the connection between uncertainty and ethics
rests not on the universal value of virtue, but on an entirely different, more
perverse, proposition. A creative process initiated by dreaming, remembering
and retelling has allowed the speaker to overcome the reality of stasis behind
love's appearance of flux and to reach from a temporal prison to a metaphysical
realm without abandoning the human, physical world. In short, the dreamer has
taken action in language to sever truth from its traditional trappings and to rea-
lign it with illusion. But the fallibility at the core of the transgression is exposed
in the final tercet when the sonnet falls into the degenerate, even superfluous,
*syn*tax of an extended *vida/muerte* antithesis. 'Morir', one of the most recurrent
metaphors for 'gozar' in the poetry of the period, holds the poem's bass note
like a suspended pedal point. The counterpuntal movement of the poem, a sweet
falsification by the speaker's senses (a 'dulce desconcierto'), is paralysed in this
closing cadence which combines a distressing certainty of self-loss with the
tragic pathos of a broader *desengaño*.

The subterfuge of the dream allows Quevedo to test the abstract semantic
field of conventional amorous lyric against the unrequited lover's experience
of the world – and to find it wanting. However, its alternative proposition is
precariously poised and involves a provisional displacement of the self from
the empirical world to an imaginative realm that is constituted out of, and in,
language. The result is a blurring of the boundaries between the two which cor-
rodes the contours of both. Stabilising the imagined world requires the deployment of a volatile rhetorical figure that can operate in perverse defiance of imagination's lack of fixity. Hypothesis, more precisely the hypothetical conceit,
not only permits the impossible to be said, but shapes an alternative poetic
universe in which the focus is entirely on the ideation of the individual. As such,
it becomes something of a habit in Quevedo's love poetry and, not surprisingly,
a fertile breeding ground for hyperbole.[39] A notable example is Sonnet 460, 'Si
hija de mi amor mi muerte fuese' [If my death were the daughter of my love],
wherein the hypothetical mode, communicating the inherent subjectivity of
human perception, mediates between the present and forever, and sacrifices in
the process any autonomous realia against which to measure selfhood ('y el no

---

[39]   As Christopher Johnson notes: 'Comparing himself [*sic*] to a speck of dust or a mountain,
to Tantalus, Orpheus, or Hercules, his beloved to Venus, the sky, a sepulcher [...] Quevedo, as is
the Petrarchist's wont, involves the entire macrocosm in his passion'. See *Hyperboles*, p. 201. See
also Aurora Egido, 'La *Hidra bocal*: sobre la palabra poética en el Barroco', *Edad de Oro*, VI,
(1987), 79–113 (esp. 90).

ser, por amar, será mi gloria' [and non being, caused by love, will be my glory; v. 14].[40] The 'exchange' that takes place in the poem (love for death that will be love eternal) is aggressively and ambivalently triumphant. The switch out of the subjunctive in the tercets is an attempt to make the proposition less conditional, more universally resonant, more absolute. However, the necessary integration of antitheses (the speaker imagines love in all its spiritual purity and its infernal desire surviving infinitely in a heaven that is Hades) undermines the feasibility of the resolution.

There are similar unresolved tensions in the illicit transactions of Sonnet 448, 'Si mis párpados, Lisi, labios fueren' [If my eyelids, Lisi, were lips], although the poem's sustained subjunctive embraces its antagonistic core in a more ironic vein. Exploring similar erotic territory as the Floralba dream poem, although more radically experimental, Quevedo transfers the self out of the empirical world so entirely that the borders between the real and the imagined are eradicated rather than blurred. The result is an act of exaggerated self-validation and self-deceit that depends on the successful substitution of conjecture for assertion, of false for true, of eyelids for lips, of light beams for kisses. The power of the poem does not reside in its imagining of sexual intercourse in public, but in its imagining of that imagining; in how it uses its conditional mode to create expectations of the unexpected that are actually not far from the reader's horizon. Negotiating *inventio* through the poem is not a journey to distant topoi, nor are the conceits affectively remote. Rather, the seeing but not speaking of 'discreción' [discretion], the seeing but not touching of 'ausencia' [absence] – these are the courtly/Petrarchan premises that are under attack from Quevedo's 'new' optics of love, metaphysics made material.

> Si mis párpados, Lisi, labios fueran,
> besos fueran los rayos visuales
> de mis ojos, que al sol miran caudales
> águilas, y besaran más que vieran.
>
> Tus bellezas, hidrópicos, bebieran,
> y cristales, sedientos de cristales;
> de luces y de incendios celestiales,
> alimentando su morir, vivieran.

40   For more detailed discussion of this sonnet, see, among others, Olivares, *The Love Poetry*, pp. 123–27; Parker, *Philosophy of Love*, pp. 168–70; Emilia Navarro de Kelley, *La poesía metafísica de Quevedo* (Madrid: Ediciones Guadarrama, 1973), pp. 119–23. A more recent reading by Guillermo Serés returns to Navarro de Kelley's rather one-dimensional interpretation. Serés recognises the various models (*Cancionero*, Petrarchist, latent eroticism of Classical elegy) operating upon the poet and poem, but argues that the tensions generated by all of these are subsumed into a 'single', harmoniously syncretised Christocentric Neoplatonic affirmation. See '"Si hija de mi amor mi muerte fuese". Tradiciones y Sentido', *La Perinola*, 8 (2004), 463–83.

De invisible comercio mantenidos,
y desnudos de cuerpo, los favores
gozaran mis potencias y sentidos;

mudos se requebraron los ardores,
Pudieran, apartados, verse unidos
y en público, secretos, los amores.   [Sonnet 448]

[If my eyelids, Lisi, were lips, the visual rays of my eyes would surely be kisses which, gazing eagle-like into the sun, would kiss more than they would see. They would drink in your beauty insatiably, and as crystals, thirsting for crystal, for light and for heavenly fire, thus nourishing their death, they would live. Sustained by invisible commerce, stripped of the body, my powers and senses would enjoy your favours; our passions would erupt in silent wooing; apart we would see ourselves entwined and in public possess a secret love.]

The protagonist of this poem, the dominant 'I', feeds on conventional centres of authority in the service of an all-consuming desire for self-gratification. From the opening conceit, cut loose from any rules of rationality, the poetic voice 'runs amok', to the point of transgressing the limits of the initial hypothetical premise. The gaze is the catalyst for an ocular 'touch' that is realised in the demystifying, extreme closure of the space separating lover and beloved. There is errancy in this movement across forbidden spaces, but this is not the haptic eye of Quevedo's moral poems, the eye that happens upon the 'muros de la patria' [walls of my homeland] in a 'process of perception in which subjectivication and objectivication are quasi-simultaneous'.[41] The speaker of Sonnet 448 is circumscribed so dynamically within the field of the beloved who is gazed upon that the epistemological distinction between subject and object no longer pertains. The incorporation of the subject as eagle into the solar image that is seen suggests, at the very least, a shared majesty that dissolves former divisions in a new reciprocated double mirroring. The imaginative flight soars on powerfully symbolic wings, harnessing the emblematic force of supreme powers both divine (Jupiter) and earthly (the Caesars) to transform the gaze itself into a victorious, pre-naming, colonial moment. Ultimately the eloquent enactment of imaginative seeing in Quevedo's sonnet, with appropriation at its core, overturns the phenomenology of vision as conceptualised by Merleau-Ponty, suggesting another more subversive way of understanding the 'crystallisation of the impossible'.[42]

---

41   See Tom Conley, *An Errant Eye: Poetry and Topography in Early Modern France* (Minneapolis: University of Minnesota Press, 2011), p. 16. I am grateful to Professor Anne Cruz whose perceptive paper on the relationship between Quevedo's lyric and early modern cartography (*SRBHP* conference, Belfast, 2011) drew my attention to Conley's study.

42   Maurice Merleau-Ponty's description of the phenomenology of vision as a transcendent non-merging represents a move in his thinking towards a constitutive invisibility at the heart of

It would be wrong, however, to consider this an unproblematic totalitarian text. The poem's heightened vanity makes it no less polyvocal than the other Lisi poems. Its voice is similarly mortgaged in counter-distinction to other voices (the *locus classicus* of the topos is Ovid, *Amores*, i, iv) and its sexual direction (to an abstract Lisi, addressed and undressed) is an anxious redirection, a pulling away from spiritual contemplation. Smith has paid due regard to the former, while Parker has focused his attention on the latter.[43] Most pertinent to this reading is how the linguistic quality of desire, which is forged in these reciprocities, draws attention to the precarious ambiguity of its own rhetoric. The strong sexual overtones of the tercets exchange the more ideologically fluid space of the quatrains, for a poetic procedure whose rhyme and sound patterns close down to different histories. Ambivalent words and phrases (*comercio, desnudos de cuerpo, favores, gozaran, potencias, sentidos, ardores*; 9–12) become collectively, strongly, univocal – a reticence ultimately overthrown by repression. The paradox of silent rhetoric has rarely been more illegitimately proclaimed. Gracián, writing in 1648, three years after Quevedo's death, praises human *oratio* and inherent *agudeza* in terms of an expansive hyperbole of ascent: 'Si el percibir la agudeza acredita el águila, el producirla empeñará el ángel'.[44] To perceive wit is to have the acuity of the eagle; to produce it is to be like an angel. Quevedo's eagle, however, alters the course of divine *ratio*, denigrating its fundamental principles with the powers of a dark Orpheus.[45] 'Si fueras tu mi Eurídice' [If you were my Eurydice], the speaker hypothesises in another poem (407), my gaze would be your undoing ('tanto el poder mirarte en mí pudiera; / que sólo por mirarte te perdiera').[46] The relational analogies,

the visible and is contained in his last work, *The Visible and the Invisible: Studies in Phenomenology and Existential Philosophy*, ed. Claude Lefort and trans. Alphonso Lingis (Evanston, Illinois: Northwestern University Press, 1968). One of the many provocative statements of this complex work, 'Vision is tele-vision, trancendence, crystallization of the impossible', is the focal point of a study by Jenny Slatman that testifies to the persistent resonance of Merleau-Ponty's thinking: 'Tele-vision: Between Blind Trust and Perceptual Faith', in *Religion and Media*, eds Hent de Vries and Samuel Weber (Stanford: Stanford University Press, 2001), pp. 216–27.

[43] See Smith, *Quevedo on Parnassus*, p. 168; and Parker, for whom the whole poem is a metaphysical conceit: 'with a pair of opposites that support and complete each other while at the same time denying each other: eye lids both are, and are not, lips'; 'the furtive betrayal of the soul by an imagination that turns the mind's aspirations into an illicit sensuality', *Philosophy of Love*, pp. 162 and 163 respectively.

[44] The second edition and final form of Gracián's *Agudeza y arte de ingenio* appeared in Huesca in 1648; this was a revised and amplified version of the *Arte de ingenio* of 1642.

[45] Throughout the love poems, there is a sustained dissolution of the figure of Orpheus as a credible authoritative model, although this is interrogated with inevitable paradox. Intertextual allusion is the norm, although where the myth is explicitly evoked, as in Sonnet 297, it is Orphic failure that is stressed. For more detailed discussion, see Torres, *Shades of Significance*, esp. 8–22.

[46] Beyond identification of a madrigal by Grotti as the poem's model, no. 407 has received scant attention.

which operate in an environment of conspicuous *cancionero* ambiguity, lend a chromatic harmony to the madrigal, but the contrasting pitch of sensual energy modifies, but never disrupts, the melancholic Orphic song. As we have seen, the erotic impulse of the gaze in Sonnet 448 is less subtly 'presenced'. The hypothetical structure provides a semblance of containment within a controlled linguistic system, and there is clearly a balanced complementarity of *inventio* and technical expertise that keeps the poem just under mimetic control. But the creative imagination, thematised as a willed and conscious activity, dispenses with decorum to transform formless desire out of all acceptable proportion. Ultimately, the transgressive model of intimate vision that is performed in and through the conceits of Sonnet 448 invites materialisation in the mind of an uneasy, but collaborating, public.

Metaphor as mask

[handwritten marginalia: unrequired love]

The singular pretension of erotic desire, that human experience is not limited to the domain of materiality, nor bound by the intransigence of time, raises the stakes of Quevedo's love poetry and makes death its thematic centre. The speaker as unrequited lover characterises a being that is incomplete or, in broader ontological terms, 'fallen', conscious always of what has been lost, and occupying a plane of reality wherein recuperation or self-completion is a desire infinitely deferred. The anxieties of Quevedo's poetic voice are not those of the existentialist before death; rather, they reflect the frustrated sense of an inauthentic self – conditioned both by its relation to death and by a somewhat imperceptible futurity promised by the very meaninglessness of human life. These fundamental antagonisms (expertly analysed by Mariscal[47]) find expression across a range of mythical narratives (for example, Tantalus, Midas, Enceladus) which grant language a secure point of anchorage while also allowing it to slip its temporal moorings. Indeed, myth as intertext tears the temporal order apart and facilitates a 'beyondness' that (even in the darkest poems) suggests artistic transcendence.

In the celebrated sonnet 'Cerrar podrá mis ojos', contradictions become connections, seduced into conformity by the unifying functions of language. The materiality of language mediates between the immediate and the ephemeral, brings the ineffable into being and, to some extent, negates the thing (death) that is its object. However, this very moment of negation brings the poetic subject into material and substantial contact with the moment of death which it would presume to defy.

---

[47] See Mariscal, *Contradictory Subjects*, ch. 3.

The sonnet reads:

> Cerrar podrá mis ojos la postrera
> sombra que me llevare el blanco día,
> y podrá desatar esta alma mía
> hora a su afán ansioso lisonjera;
>
> mas no, de esotra parte, en la ribera,
> dejará la memoria, en donde ardía:
> nadar sabe mi llama el agua fría,
> y perder el respeto a ley severa.
>
> Alma a quien todo un dios prisión ha sido,
> venas que humor a tanto fuego han dado,
> medulas que han gloriosamente ardido,
>
> su cuerpo dejará, no su cuidado;
> serán ceniza, mas tendrá sentido;
> polvo serán, mas polvo enamorado.

[The final shadow, that will take from me white day, will close my eyes, and a single hour in time, indulging anxious longing, will set free this soul of mine; but it will not leave behind, on that further river bank, the memory in which it used to burn: my flame knows how to swim across the cold water and lose respect for a law that is stern. A soul for which a god, no less, has been a prison, veins which have fed moisture to so great a fire, marrows which have so gloriously burned, it will abandon its body, but not its love; they will be ash, but the ash will be sentient still; dust they will be, but dust that is in love.]

Some years ago I read this sonnet from the perspective of its Classical intertexts, particularly Propertian resonance (*Elegy* I.19 as identified initially by Borges, but also II.13[b]), and as an externalisation of a recurrent motif in Quevedo, namely the 'Internal Hades'.[48] It is not my intention here to retrace those steps through Quevedo's amorous hell, but rather to explore briefly, and in relation to similar motifs in other poems, how, and to what effect, the operation of metaphor in the sonnet enables a fundamental rebellion of reason and reality.

Rebellion is not explicitly evident in the first quatrain where the reiterated future 'podrá' anticipates and facilitates an imagined smooth transition between the oppositional realms of life and death, a passing over from light to dark, from day to night, that is rationally presented, although sonorously seductive and emphatically subject specific. The breakdown of reason is signalled by the

---

48   See Torres, 'Shades of Significance', 22–26.

disjunctive 'mas no' of verse 5. The fact, and the presence, of love as desire ('ardía'; 'llama') is the catalyst for an assertion of immortality that undermines all linguistic principles of order, that resists any Neoplatonic conception of love, and which contradicts entirely any Christian comprehension of life. Reason is redefined here through a metaphysical inversion, whereby transgressing the bounds of ordinary language use (going linguistically beyond, 'mas allá') permits a disconnecting from community and the laws that bind it collectively. Thus the universal law of death is undone by a particular and subjective passion. In the process, and similar to John Donne's 'well wrought urne' [*The Canonization*], the poem becomes, through excessive figuration, a material memorial. But this memorial is not without its inherent tensions. The underside of love is fear (as verse 8 implies) and the conceit that would have fire navigate water, physical love survive death, corporeal matter retain sentiment, carries within it a matrix of forbidden feelings and guilt regarding the metaphysical trespass.

The conceit, as encapsulated in verse 7, has received various critical responses, but these are unanimous in identifying an obsessive core metaphor of Quevedo's love poetry which is here given a radical treatment. Olivares's attention to 'nadar' is worth quoting: 'the traditional fire/water antithesis is invigorated through presentation and context. The poet does not use the infinitive "cruzar" [...] but "nadar", which is concrete and emphasises the soul's contact with powerless oblivion.'[49] But we could take this further. Sea-faring as a motif in Quevedo's poetry, as emblematic of an exaggerated and negatively audacious 'codicia' [greed], often has metapoetic, political, as well as ethical implications. As Robert Ter Horst reminded us some years ago, we can reach back from Quevedo to Catullus and Horace, via the 'Vida retirada' [Ode to Retirement] of Fray Luis de León: 'It takes almost no effort to read the risks of seafaring morally.'[50] Quevedo's *Silva* XVIII, for instance, entitled *El escarmiento* [Warning], exploits a framing conceit of the body as prison/tomb, within which the Classical motif of the shipwrecked sailor, envisaged hanging his clothes in a temple as an offering of thanks (Horace, *Odes* 1.5), is a central organising principle.[51] Johnson identifies this poem as one of a series of navigation poems, located mostly in the *Calíope* section of *Las tres últimas musas*, in which geographical space, exploited as an extension of individual, ethical space, allows Quevedo to conflate personal and imperial concerns.[52] The poem is ostensibly

49 See Olivares, *The Love Poetry*, p. 130.

50 Robert Ter Horst, 'Death and Resurrection in the Quevedo Sonnet: "En crespa tempestad"', *Journal of Hispanic Philology*, 5 (1980), 41–49 (42). It is worth remembering that Quevedo published an edition of Fray Luis's poems in 1631.

51 The metaphor of shipwreck in Golden Age poetry, with particular emphasis on the motif of the sailor hanging *ex-votos* in a temple, is explored by Elizabeth B. Davis in her article 'La promesa del naúfrago: el motivo marinero del ex-voto, de Garcilaso a Quevedo', in *Studies in Honor of James O. Crosby*, pp. 109–23.

52 See Johnson, *Hyperboles*, pp. 209–21.

a Neostoic celebration of the speaker's victory over the Adam within ('el primer hombre' [the first man; 63], a didactic rejection of worldly wealth, power, military glory and love ('mentidos placeres' [deceptive pleasures; 121]. Quevedo's speaker-survivor hangs up the 'spoils' of allegorical storms (remnants of frustrated worldly ambitions and amorous liaisons, 33–42), thereby undermining Herrera's call in the *Anotaciones* for Spanish poets to plunder the 'spoils' of Classical and Italian literary traditions, while doing precisely that. The trajectory of existential solitude traced in the poem, which culminates in a nihilistic reduction of the human being to 'polvo soberbio y presumida, ambiciosa ceniza' [proud, presumptious dust, ambitious ash; 107–08], is infused with such a tragic individual awareness of the inescapable fact of mortality that any broader mitigating membership of a collective humanity is negated. The poem's 'warning' is extended outwards, via apostrophe to an imagined passing traveller, to an implied 'other', but the realisation that all human beings are, as Wordsworth has stated so eloquently, ultimately 'disowned by memory' (*Prelude*, I. 643) is experienced uniquely by Quevedo's speaker and articulated within these subjective experiential parameters.

Within an amorous context, this early modern ontotheological understanding of being, as 'being toward death', is explored by Quevedo in intensely subjective terms that are often most effective when contingent upon the dialectical energy that is generated by motifs of drowning and/or shipwreck, operating both as a potent symbol of the risks and rigours of uncontrollable desire, and as emblematic of artistic over-reaching. Leander, whose arrested poetic present epitomises the human being's struggle against his own implied future absence, is the perfect prototype and the catalyst for an interconnected series of mythical allusions in Sonnet 449: *Afectos varios de su corazón fluctuando en las ondas de los cabellos de Lisi* [The varied passions of his heart tossed in the waves of Lisi's hair].[53] The sonnet is based on a conventional topos of lyric poetry which depicts the beloved in the act of combing her hair (here simply untying it) and analyses the impact of this action on the male speaker.[54] The poem reads:

> En crespa tempestad del oro undoso,
> *nada* golfos de luz ardiente y pura
> *mi corazón*, sediento de hermosura,
> si el cabello deslazas generoso.

---

[53] I have translated *afectos* as 'passions' rather than 'emotions' in recognition of the early modern understanding of 'passions' as bodily phenomena that entered the body from without (in this case the stimulus is the beloved's beauty) and were, therefore, 'suffered' – passion not constituting the individual's 'true nature'. See Teresa Brennan's study, *The Transmission of Affect* (Ithaca: Cornell University Press, 2004), esp. p. 16.

[54] See César Nicolás, 'Al sol Nise surcaba golfos bellos ... Culteranismo, conceptismo y culminación de un diseño retórico', *Anuario de estudios filológicos*, 10 (1987), 265–94.

Leandro, en mar de fuego proceloso,
su amor ostenta, su vivir apura;
Ícaro, en senda de oro mal segura,
arde sus alas por morir glorioso.

Con pretensión de *fénix*, encendidas
sus esperanzas, que difuntas lloro,
intenta que su muerte engendre vidas.

Ávaro y rico y pobre, en el tesoro,
el castigo y la hambre imita a *Midas*,
Tántalo en fugitiva fuente de oro. [Sonnet 449, emphasis added]

[In a storm of raging waves and rippling gold, thirsting for beauty, *my heart swims* through gulf streams of pure, burning light – when you unbind your abundant hair. *Leander*, in a stormy sea of fire, shows off his love, refines his life; *Icarus*, on a precarious path of gold, burns his wings for a glorious death. As an aspiring *Phoenix*, its hopes on fire – a death I mourn – my heart attempts to make its death engender lives. Mean and rich and poor in its treasure, *Midas*-like in punishment and hunger, aping *Tantalus* in a fleeting fountain of gold.]

I have discussed this sonnet elsewhere focusing primarily on the rhetorical function of mythological allusion.[55] The wonderfully compressed opening metaphor operates on the basis of deferred and evolving signification. Its meaning(s) are realised through reader engagement with the motifs and images which constitute the standard rhetorical design of the topos. Predominant among these are the nautical analogy replete with fatal connotations of shipwreck and drowning, and the golden, fiery radiance of a beloved whose powerful beauty outshines the sun and who attracts and captivates, but ultimately destroys. Underlying these, and antithetically expressed within the frame of allusions to Leander and Icarus, is the lover's inability to resist the allure of such dangerous attraction. 'Nada', in this imaginative context of transgressive sea-faring, connotes both heroic action and its annihilating consequences, opening out to relate (via the juxtaposition of Tantalus and Midas) the individual lover's insatiable desire for an elusive beloved with the unresolved collective crisis that was early modern Spain's grasping greed for American gold.

The conventional formal structures of the sonnet form are further tightened in Quevedo's poem by this system of ana*logical* interconnections whose relationship

---

55   See 'Con Pretensión de Fenix', in *Rewriting Classical Mythology in the Hispanic Baroque*, ed. Isabel Torres (Woodbridge: Tamesis, 2007), pp. 1–16, esp. pp. 12–16, where reference is made to the many excellent readings of this sonnet (such as, for instance, by A.A. Parker ('La agudeza en algunos sonetos de Quevedo', in *Estudios dedicados a D. Ramón Menéndez Pidal*, III [Madrid: Consejo Superior de Investigaciones Científicas, 1952], pp. 345–60), and P.J. Smith (Quevedo on Parnassus, pp. 78–84).

to the same point of departure belies the metaphorical expansion. The sonnet's technical performance is, therefore, a perfect corollary of its key thematic tensions: timelessness struggling with time; the pretensions of the living confronting the examples of the dead. The essence of this sonnet, its simulated world of emotional flux, is conditioned and constrained paradoxically by the weight of mutable metaphors and narrative expectations. By compelling the reader to recognise and remember the fates of Leander, Icarus, Midas and Tantalus (as ideas virtually occurring in timeless relation to one another), Quevedo entangles metaphor and mnemonics, connecting and challenging both with death. A problematic model of selfhood emerges. The poetic subject is simultaneously centred through binary oppositions that presume the existence of finite terms and yet suspended through an experience of relationality that presumes the reality of infinitude. The 'centrality' of the Phoenix myth within this contradictory matrix is deliberate.

Sonnet 313, 'Enriquecerse quiso, no vengarse, la llama' [Wealth, not vengeance, drove the flame], treads similar, though less complex, metaphorical territory – the speaker observing how a candle flame catches and sets alight Aminta's hair. The navigational context of contemporary 'codicia' is an informing, though not explicit, imperative of the sonnet's destructive impulses (the 'vela' suggested by the 'llama' of the title, as both candle and sale, anticipates the subtext). Generally, the poem is dismissed as a less interesting, occasional piece, but Walters has recognised in its contradictory energy and in the speaker's identification with the flame a railing against repressive norms of conventional concepts of love, particularly 'discreción'.[56] The quatrains read:

> Enriquecerse quiso, no vengarse,
> la llama que encendió vuestro cabello;
> que de no codiciarle, y poder vello,
> ni el tesoro del sol podrá librarse.
>
> Codicia fue, que puede mal culparse,
> robarle quien no pudo merecello;
> milagro fue pasar por vuestro cuello
> y en tanta nieve no temer helarse.

[Wealth, not vengeance, drove the flame that lit your hair; for even the sun, with all its treasure, were it to see, wouldn't escape a desire to covet. Greed was behind it, for the otherwise unworthy can't be blamed for theft; it was a miraculous flame that flowed along your neck without fear of freezing amidst so much snow.]

---

56   See D. Gareth Walters, 'Convention and Contradiction in a Quevedo Sonnet: An Analysis of "Enriquecerse quiso, no vengarse"', in *Readings in Spanish and Portuguese Poetry for Geoffrey Connell*, eds Nicholas G. Round and D. Gareth Walters (Glasgow: University of Glasgow, 1985), pp. 259–73.

The dominant metaphor of flame as plunderer, passing through the golden waves of the beloved's hair, and surviving the icy straits of her neck in pursuit of desired spoils, contests the constraints of conventional Petrarchan antithesis with the compromising avarice and concupiscence of 'codicia'. The acquisition of wealth as an ethical alternative to vengeance, so confidently asserted in line 1, is developed, at best, in terms of ironic relativity. There is some elision of the subject voice in the abstraction of the extended allegory, but this is balanced by a veneer of self-promotion inherent in the very act of personification. Any possibility of self-control, gratification or resolution of tensions, however, vanishes in the tercets:

> O quiso introducir en sol su llama,
> y aprender a ser día, a ser aurora,
> en las ondosas minas que derrama,
>
> o la hazaña de Eróstrato traidora
> repite, y busca por delitos fama,
> quemando al sol el templo que él adora.

[Or it sought to sink its flame in sun and learn to be daylight, to be dawn, in mines of rippling, overflowing gold; or it repeats Eratostratus' treacherous deed, and seeks infamy in crime, burning beneath the sun the temple that he adores.]

Reopening the question of motive, this first tercet negotiates a fine line between self-fulfilment and dissolution of identity. Extreme positions are expressed: a suggested Neoplatonic hyperbole (the lover's flame transformed in supreme solar fire) and the grounding of this in a fantasy of erotic intimacy (penetration in mines flowing with liquid gold). However, both emerge from a similar narcissistic aggression and both depend upon an illusion of reciprocity. The second tercet, structured as alternative reasoning and based upon the more likely prospect of the beloved's persistent rejection, takes the sonnet's interrogation of inherited lyric models to radical ends. In the role of Eratostratus (whose lust for fame was so great that he set fire to one of the seven Wonders of the World, the Temple of Diana), the speaking subject confronts the darkest dimensions of 'codicia' and lays claim to a perverse notoriety. Quevedo's poem reconstructs the Eratostratus story from the ruins of conventional amorous lyric ideologies. Negation of desire transforms the symbolic flame into a conflagration that, in this rewritten context, might raze a temple sacred to Apollo, laying waste in the process to the aesthetic principles of beauty and art that are enshrined within it. The hypothetical guise of a mythical anti-hero, who sought infamy when fame through conventional means seemed futile,[57] permits the lyric speaker to propose

---

57   This was a move rendered equally futile, in the short term at least, when mention of Eratostratus's name was outlawed. A longer-term legacy was, however, assured. Closer to our own

a new sacrilegious set of values, a non-ethical system of self-commemoration
founded on a deliberate act of trespass and treachery. The switch from preterite
to present in these final verses triggers a moment of conceptual and experiential
integration, distinct from the more calculated displacement activity that had
structured the sonnet's reasoning thus far. Quevedo may not achieve here the
emotional depth charge of other sonnets, but we see something of how metaphor
motivated experientially can involve significant referential shifts; in this case,
how a radical transaction between contexts (unconventional mythical and conventional amorous), when accessed by readers, can produce a semantic flexibility that transcends the demarcation of the individual domains.

Sonnet 311, *Describe a Leandro fluctuante en el mar* [Describes Leander
tossed in the sea] involves a more sustained metaphorical mapping:

> Flota de cuantos rayos y centellas,
> en puntas de oro, el ciego Amor derrama,
> nada Leandro; y cuanto el Ponto brama
> con olas, tanto gime por vencellas.
>
> Maligna luz multiplicó en estrellas
> y grande incendio sigue pobre llama:
> en la cuna de Venus, quien bien ama,
> no debió recelarse de perdellas.
>
> Vela y remeros es, nave sedienta;
> mas no le aprovechó, pues, desatado,
> Noto los campos líquidos violenta.
>
> Ni volver puede, ni pasar a nado;
> si llora, crece el mar y la tormenta:
> que hasta poder llorar le fue vedado.   [Sonnet 311]

[A fleet made of every ray and spark, which blind Love scatters, in points of
gold, Leander swims; and as the Pontus roars in waves, so he groans to beat
them back. The malignant light multiplied in stars and a great blaze follows a
feeble flame: in Venus's cradle, none whose love is fine, should ever fear the
stars decline. Sail and oarsman, he is both, and thirsting ship; but all of this
in vain, for Notus, unleashed, wreaks havoc on the liquid plain. He cannot
turn, nor swim ahead; if he cries out, he swells both sea and storm; so even
tears had to stay unshed.]

---

time, for instance, Jean Paul Sartre turned Eratostratus into an existential anti-hero, Erostratus,
while in Don Levy's controversial film of 1967, *Herostratus*, he becomes the young poet Max who
hires a marketing company to turn his suicide into a mass media spectacle. Sartre's short story,
written in 1936, was first published in 1939 in the collection *Le mur*. See *The Wall [Intimacy]:
And Other Stories*, 3rd edn, trans Lloyd Alexander (New York: New Directions, 1969).

There is a primary tension in the poem between a predominantly present-tense temporal development at the level of action (that is, the experience of the mythical subject Leander), and how this experience is mediated by the narrator and articulated through a series of disruptive preterites (5, 8, 10, 14). The teleological shape of the narrative, as well as any sense of objective perspective, is deliberately undermined. The ending of the sonnet, in particular, casts historical chronology aside through an alternative, belated, generation of 'suspense', which maximises the reader's awareness of the contingency of the speaker–mythical-subject relationship. The problem of the poem's internal conclusiveness (the 'condition of not knowing' is, after all, as impossible for myth as it is for epic) is neutralised by presenting time as a subjective phenomenon, which takes place in the speaker's mind, and is conditioned by the interaction of memory, representation and, ultimately, the inscription of meaning upon the other. The performance of lyric selfhood which emerges from such a representative perspective is inevitably less assertive, less strongly centred, for in the speaker's connectedness to Leander he is already outside the self. But this more permeable 'I' boundary, rather than weakening the force of the sonnet, opens it up to a more collective, contextually resonant, category of response.

In the final tercet, Quevedo's rewriting of Garcilaso's Apollo and Daphne sonnet (XIII), itself a revisionist correction of the Petrarchan model, is not without the backward-looking anxieties that accompany the dispersal of authority in 'third-person' lyric. However, these are balanced by the capacity of the static image to capture the broader disillusionment that has informed the sonnet's reflective doubling throughout and, therefore, to push Spanish poetics more authentically forward. Leander, stranded mid sea, in a state of imposed linguistic paralysis, denied even the conventional comfort of self-perpetuating misery, crystallises a sense of arrested development that is as meaningful to the individual Baroque poet as it is to the crisis culture that characterised contemporary Spain itself. Quevedo's Leander is figured along a very ambiguous Neostoic faultline. On the one hand, he is the self-sacrificing hero epitomising the determination and willpower of the individual in extreme adversity; against this, his excessive passion and lack of co-operation with the whole cosmological system threatens chaos. Ultimately, Quevedo's engagement with the myth, in common with his vernacular predecessors, shuns the specific dark dénouement, but not its wider tragic connotations. The ending does not close down, nor does it promote a status quo, rather it keeps us looking in different directions at the same time. But this surprising sting in the Leander 'tale' depends for its effectiveness upon the reader experiencing the poem throughout in full cognaisance of how its doubling dynamics are designed to stress the restraints of the human condition.

Critics who have approached this poem, and there are not many, generally limit its significance to a body of Quevedo's love poems which engage with the Courtly traditions of unfulfilled sexual desires; Leander's last fatal cross-

ing of the Hellespont to reach Hero is read as a rewriting of Classical and
Renaissance models (predominantly Ovid, Martial, Musaeus, Boscán, and
Garcilaso), which allegorises in extreme and ambiguously heroic terms the
frustrated desire of the lover.[58] Most recently, Bentley draws attention to linguistic ambiguities in the poem which compel the reader to reread the sonnet
even as it is being read.[59] Among these are: the verb 'flota', reread as noun;
the deflationary tactics of 'pobre llama' which is opposed to the lightning, the
stars and even Hero's misguided lamp; and the 'vela', both candle and ship's
sail. For Bentley, the sonnet's ambivalence suggests two coexisting registers
– we can opt to read it in serious allegorical vein or as a parodic deflation of
the mythical hero.

I would suggest that we add '*nada* Leandro' to Bentley's list; a verb, but which,
in light of its emphatic and alienated positioning, surely (as in 'En crespa tempestad') can also be reread as the indefinite pronoun 'nothing' – a thing or matter
of no importance or a condition of non-existence?[60] By representing Leander 'as
if' he were 'nothing', Quevedo dramatises the rupture between the two realms of
the poem – that is, the external universe (subject to the laws of nature), and the
inner world of the self, in the more provocative metaphysical terms that characterise his moral poetry and, especially, his treatise of Neostoic resonance, *La cuna
y la sepultura*. Even Leander's futile struggle is vocalised in terms of the individual's participation in a broader folly: 'La vida es toda muerte o locura; y
pasamos la mayor parte de la muerte, que es la vida, riendo, y *gimiendo a un instante della*, que es la postrera boqueada' [*La cuna y la sepultura*, 909].[61] Within
these parameters Leander, as *amante/caminante/navegante* [*lover/traveller/sea-
farer*], concretises the entrapment of the human being within a sepulchral body,
struggling through a linear existential trajectory, but caught in the circular currents
of time,[62] a context in which authentic self-articulation contributes to self-annihi-

58   See Torres, 'A Small Boat over an Open Sea? Gabriel Bocángel's Fábula de Leandro y
Hero and Epic Aspirations', in *The Polyphemus Complex,* pp. 131–63.

59   P.E. Bentley, 'Reading and Contextualising Quevedo: The Case of "Flota de cuantos
rayos y centellas"', *Caliope,* 6.1–2 (2000), 251–61.

60   According to the *Diccionario de Autoridades*, 'nada' means 'El no ser, o la carencia abso-
luta de todo ser' [Non-being, or the absolute lack of being]; but 'vale también la negación abso-
luta de las cosas' [it also means the absolute negation of anything].

61   [Life is all death or madness; and we spend the greater part of death, which is life, laugh-
ing and *moan only at one moment,* which is our last breath]. Emphasis added. Throughout the
moral and religious poetry 'gemir' is the leitmotif for the articulation of human anguish. See, for
instance, Poem 47, v. 1, no. 170, v. 4.

62   See Marie Roig Miranda's article which addresses the individual's relationship with temporality in Quevedo's sonnets, especially the question of whether the present actually exists as a
moment in/of time: '¿Existe el presente en los sonetos metafísicos de Quevedo?', in *Studia Aurea:
Actas del III congreso de la AISO (Toulouse, 1993)*, eds I. Arellano *et al.* (Navarra: Eurograf, 1996),
pp. 487–94.

lation.[63] Perhaps there is something of an ironic nod to the reader in verses 7–8, a devaluation of the Neostoic *cuna/sepultura* metaphor as applied to the erotic domain of Venus. But the import of this – the lover's misguided faith in his special relationship with the erotic deity – has implications for the human value system of seventeenth-century Spain which are tragic rather than parodic.

Taking into account the ambiguities of 'nada' as contextualised both in Sonnet 449 and in Sonnet 311 and the broader ramifications of Quevedo's engagement with motifs of navigation, exemplified in both his moral and amorous poetry, we turn again to the central conceit of Sonnet 472. The triumphant horizontal journey of the 'llama' across the waters of Lethe is clearly much more than a subversive redirecting of metaphors of Neoplatonic ascent (which Quevedo himself exploits to designate exemplary failure in Sonnet 473, 'Estas son y serán ya las postreras lágrimas' [These are and already will be the final tears]); but rather is a radical reimagining of the *homo viator*,[64] a defiant *anti-Leander* declaration that negates human perceptions of time and anticipates the shocking images of self-communion which dominate the tercets.[65] The final lines of the poem make the most of the constrained and determined nature of rhyme, metre, repetition and tense-shifting to re-make logic and meaning in material form.[66] Indeed, in its symbolic fusing of body and soul, the poem manages to elide the tension between strict lyric conventions and passionate experience. The solipsistic, or profoundly inward, shift, which Pando Cantelli has identified as the transformation of Petrarchan anguish into an ontological problem in the poetry of both Quevedo and John Donne,[67] is here stripped of its conventional figurative trappings (gone is the Phoenix, for instance) in order to present the impossible as a literal truth. And the stakes are higher than in conventional amorous lyric. The speaker aspires not to unite 'I' with 'you', lover with beloved, but to integrate, and for all eternity, the conflicting principles of human selfhood. This sonnet does not shy away from confronting the physical disintegration of the human body but, unlike Góngora's

[63] The topos *cotidie morimur* is a constant in Quevedo's moral poetry and the metaphor of the sepulchral body is integral to its exposition. See Olga Rivera, 'El sepulcro como metáfora del cuerpo en algunos poemas de Quevedo', *Symposium*, 57.4 (2004), 231–40.

[64] Contrast Herrera's engagement with the topos as discussed above, Chapter 4. Fernández Mosquera's discussion of the motif in Quevedo recognises the fluid terms of its metaphorical expression (especially the interaction with motifs of sea-faring and drowning), but generally resists any sense of contamination between the religious and amorous verse: *La poesía amorosa de Quevedo*, pp. 66–74.

[65] Robert Ter Horst identified Leander as the 'latent form' behind these verses, but differentiates the speaker (as 'resurrected hero') from the prototype in starker, more positive terms. See 'Death and Resurrection', 46, n. 12.

[66] See J.M. Pozuelo's very pertinent analysis of how the spiritual and corporeal are connected in these closing verses: *El lenguaje poético de la lírica amorosa de Quevedo* (Murcia: Universidad de Murcia, 1979), pp. 224–28.

[67] See María J. Pando Cantelli, 'John Donne, Francisco de Quevedo, and the Construction of Subjectivity in Early Modern Poetry', in *Spanish Studies in Shakespeare and his Contemporaries*, ed. José Manuel González (Newark: University of Delaware Press, 2006), pp. 89–113.

memento mori which ultimately reduces everything to 'nada', Quevedo draws contradictory meaning out of the ambivalent, cyclical connotations of 'ceniza' [ash] and 'polvo' [dust] *pulvis es, et in pulverem reverteris.*[68] The signs of transience are recalled, but linguistically reconfigured 'as if' permanent.

In a recent article on the mechanics of memory in Quevedo's *silva* 'Roma antigua y moderna', Rodrigo Cacho Casal comments on the *res/verba* rupture which distinguishes Baroque *conceptismo* from a Renaissance poetics of memory (and metaphor) that had confirmed cosmic cohesion via a deep structure of discoverable analogies.[69] Memory remains 'the master key' of Baroque poetics, but, rather than unlocking true knowledge, it operates to make new perceptions of knowledge accessible. Such multiperspectivism is paradoxically liberating and limiting. A lack of confidence in Renaissance connectedness frees the Baroque poet to connect all possible signifieds and signifiers in his own imagined vision of the world, but in the end, as a creative mnemonic device, human language falls short. Self-conscious attempts to violate boundaries make those boundaries all the more present to the reader. Ultimately, the linguistic coherence of a poem like 'Cerrar podrá mis ojos' is an illusion born of scepticism, a marvellous mask which can disguise but not dispel epistemological uncertainty.

About time

> Exegi monumentum aere perennius
> regalique situ pyramidum altius,
> quod non imber edax, non Aquilo inpotens
> possit diruere aut innumerabilis
> annorum series et fuga temporum (Horace, *Odes*, 3, 30)

[I have wrought a monument more lasting than bronze and higher than the regal Pyramids, which neither the ravenous rain, nor the fierce north wind can destroy, nor countless, succeeding years and fleeting time]

Horace's claim to poetic immortality stages within it an internal polemic, a rivalry between the sculptural and written memorial. The written triumphs over the sculptural precisely because of the latter's fixed materiality and capacity for decay. It is this logical, subordinate positioning of the material which is overturned by the speaker of Quevedo's sonnet 'Cerrar podrá mis ojos', when he crafts an im-

---

68   Peter Frohlicher explores the function of these figures in Quevedo's love poetry in 'Muerte y escritura en la poesía amorosa de Quevedo', in *Fictio poetica. Studi italiani e ispanici in onore di Georges Güntert*, eds Katherina Maier-Troxler, Costantino Maeder and Jacques Geninasca (Florence: Cesati Editore, 1998), pp. 169–86.

69   See 'The Memory of Ruins: Quevedo's *Silva* to "Roma antigua y moderna"', *Renaissance Quarterly*, 62 (2009), 1167–203.

aginatively open song of survival in signs of bodily disintegration. The textual memorial moves beyond the poem's own call to order (the attention to rhyme and rhythm; the pseudo-intuitive syntactical pattern-seeking), reconceptualising not just the Horatian topos, but the time-bound nature of the body's chronic condition. The eristic dimension of the sonnet is evident in the push and pull of its intertextual undertow, the struggle with 'other' elegiac and vernacular voices tugging at the sonnet's subjective core across expanses of time and cultural divisions. But it is *eros*, experienced as an endlessly aspirational state, which drives together the poem's more extreme polarised positions, charging its immortalising rhetoric with the magnitude of a single moment, and of that moment's relationship to the speaker. It is, therefore, as many have noted, a 'precarious kind of triumph',[70] the implications of which are confronted in a number of poems that are positioned, somewhat appropriately, towards the end of the Lisi sequence: 'Cargado voy de mí' [Weighed down by myself]; 'En los claustros del alma' [In the cloisters of the soul]; 'Amor me ocupa el seso y los sentidos' [Love besieges my sense and senses]; 'Ya que pasó mi verde primavera' [Now that my verdant spring has passed]; 'Mejor vida es morir que vivir muerto' [Dying is a better life]; 'Pierdes el tiempo, Muerte, en mi herida' [Death, you're wasting time on my wound]. Of all of these poems, Sonnet 485, 'En los claustros del alma', offers the most harrowing response to the radical idealism of Sonnet 472, conveying both the absolute situating of the human body in time and the problematic representation of poetry itself as an embodied time-situated process:

> En los claustros de l'alma la herida
> yace callada; mas consume, hambrienta,
> la vida, que en mis venas alimenta
> llama por las medulas extendida.
>
> Bebe el ardor, hidrópica, mi vida,
> que ya, ceniza amante y macilenta,
> cadáver del incendio hermoso, ostenta
> su luz en humo y noche fallecida.
>
> La gente esquivo y me es horror el día;
> dilato en largas voces negro llanto,
> que a sordo mar mi ardiente pena envía.
>
> A los suspiros di la voz del canto;
> la confusión inunda l'alma mía;
> mi corazón es reino del espanto.

70 See Terry, *Seventeenth-Century Spanish Poetry*, p. 173, where he engages with Lorna Close's similar reading of Sonnet 472: 'Petrarchism and the *Cancioneros*: The Problem of Discrimination', *Modern Language Review*, 74 (1979), 836–55 (854).

[In the cloisters of the soul the wound lies silenced; but it consumes, ravenously, the life that is fed in my veins by a flame that spreads through my marrow. My life, thirsting insatiably, drinks in the heat that now, as emaciated and enamoured ash, a corpse of a once glorious conflagration, displays its light expired in smoke and night. I shun everyone and find fright in the day; my black weeping flows in an endless wail, sending my burning sorrow to a deaf sea. I surrendered the voice of song to sighs; confusion floods my soul; my heart is a realm of fear.]

The poem's 'borrowed voices' have been discussed and disputed at some length.[71] Virgilian epic, Petrarchan lyric and Garcilasian pastoral are all identifiable to a greater or lesser extent.[72] The point here, however, is not to prove a fixed intentional connection, nor to establish a critical narrative of unified progression. Rather, by recognising and retrieving some sense of the conditioning, fluid, horizon of contemporary reading expectations, we can begin to tease out the broader ideological implications of the transformed text's central paradox – that is, an embedded contradiction between stasis and movement. Within this schema, the permanency of art is interrogated through an ongoing encounter with the ephemerality of human life; creative emancipation (the demarcation of an autonomous 'owned' space) relies on encounters with other texts, contexts and voices; meaning is expanded and figural language tested to its limits through metaphorical manoeuvres that convey the static experience of temporal reality. Ultimately, the poem builds its memorial in and against time through a display of radical self-consciousness which identifies with death as the limit of embodied language.

It is through the poem's allusive frame particularly that the speaker's body, mediated by language, is brought into the realm of literature where the exploration of poetry as an act of authorisation or, indeed, of self-negation can be sited upon it. Intertextual fractures of genre and gender are physically enacted in the metaphorical representation of erotic and aesthetic failure as corporeal disintegration. In fact, the sonnet's dominant, controlling, image works out from the elegiac motif of 'eros-as-wound', thereby initiating a complex negotiation with a range of models, including three stanzas by Sappho (poem 31), Catullus (poem

---

[71]   Mary Gaylord Randel has explored the paradox of the poetic 'I' constructed through the 'borrowed words' of others in an insightful analysis of the tensions of authority and ownership in the lyric poetry of Lope de Vega. See 'Proper Language and Language as Property: The Personal Poetics of Lope's *Rimas*', *Modern Language Notes*, 101.2 (1986), 220–46.

[72]   Possible models in Virgil, *Aeneid* IV, Petrarchan lyric, Garcilaso, *Eclogue* III, etc. are discussed by, among others, Gonzalo Sobejano, '"En los claustros del alma": Apuntaciones sobre la lengua poética de Quevedo', in *Sprache und Geschichte: Festschrift für Harri Meier zum 65. Geburtstag*, eds Eugenio Coseriu and Wolf-Dieter Stempel (Munich: Fink, 1971), pp. 459–92; Lía Schwartz, 'Figuras del orco y el infierno interior en Quevedo', in *Hommage à Robert Jammes III*, pp. 1079-88 (pp. 1081-83); Torres, 'Shades of Significance', 29–30.

51) and Horace's exaggerated troping of both these in Odes 1.13.[73] Quevedo's stripped-back inscription of suffering, sustained upon the lover's inner being, is notably different from the tensions of inner turmoil and displays of external affect which tend to characterise the Classical poems, but there are some interesting points of contact and contrast with the Horatian Ode. The speaker's performance, for instance, could be said to assimilate the anti-heroism of Horace's persona, and Horace's depiction of a self that is physically collapsing in crisis is forged in oppositional patterns of fixity and mobility that include symbolic fire/water interactions. In fact, as Elizabeth Sutherland has argued, only Horace's re-versioning of the *eros*-[as-]wound motif can be read as an attack from the inside out, and as a violation of boundaries beyond the lover's control. Steeped in fire and excessively bloated with liquid, there is nothing about the Horatian body that is 'stable, bounded, or appropriately contained'.[74] The demonstrable differences from Quevedo's sonnet are also worth noting. Meaning in Horace's Ode is compromised in internally relative terms, for the speaker's is not the only body written upon and read in the poem. Systemic breakdown is occasioned when the subject hears his beloved Lydia praise the body of a younger man, Telephus, and is exacerbated by the picture of Lydia's body marked by the signs of lovemaking with the rival. Quevedo's poem, conversely, exposes the body as a narcissistic object, creating the illusion of self observing self, a strategy that is anchored in the absence of the other (the beloved), in imposed silence and in a prolonged absorption in suffering. Insofar as the sonnet valorises this inner world of its own making, its key thematic concern, lack of reception from the outside world, is upheld. But the idea of the speaker as his own viewing subject lends an unsettling ekphrastic dimension to the body. For the very act of '*being* on display' transforms it into a work of art, with the potential to verbalise meanings its owner/creator would apparently repress. It is, therefore, a truly eloquent poem which allows its audience to have it both ways: to be moved, and to be moved to thinking.

The relationship between ekphrasis and rhetorical performance goes back as far as the earliest manuals of oratory which encouraged the use of the ekphrastic *logos* as a key exercise in the training programme of young orators.[75] Defined consistently as a descriptive speech that brings the object shown vividly before the eyes, ekphrasis connects with *enargeia*, the most powerful weapon of persuasion in the orator's arsenal. By describing the wounded body so vividly, the

---

73   For a detailed analysis of the play of differences in the ancient texts (including earlier modifications of Sappho by Valerius Aedituus and Lucretius), see Christina A. Clark, 'The Poetics of Manhood? Nonverbal Behavior in Catullus 51', *Classical Philology*, 103.3 (2008), 257–81.

74   See Elizabeth H. Sutherland, 'Writing (On) Bodies: Lyric Discourse and the Production of Gender in Horace Odes 1. 13', *Classical Philology*, 100.1 (2005), 52–82 (65).

75   See Simon Goldhill, 'What is Ekphrasis For?', *Classical Philology*, 102.1 (2007), 1–19 (esp. 3–8).

speaker compels us to share the critical gaze of the creator and draws us uncomfortably into the poem's dark, enclosed, spaces. This is a corporeal 'locus horribilis', within which the soul is materialised as a repressive cloister, the self-devouring core of an infernal wasteland whose rivers of burning blood flow in confused circles, and whose volcanic ash vomits its black smoke back inwards. A nexus of these volcanic metaphors expresses the violent and constraining nature of the speaker's passion throughout the love poetry, positing silence over articulation, while capturing an always imminent explosion of consciousness: 'pues yo en el corazón, y tú en las cuevas / callamos los volcanes florecidos' [since I, in my heart, and you, in your caves, both silence the flowering volcanoes; 302, 13–14)].[76] The speaker's point of identification here is with Vesuvius; elsewhere it is with Mount Etna. In Sonnet 293, for instance (an analogy that is reiterated in the idyll 390), he longs to cast off an Enceladic condition and to rival Etna through exaggerated linguistic displays of emotion.[77] These emulative aspirations appear to be realised in 'En los claustros del alma', erupting out of enforced silence with devastating images that remake the poetic landscape. But instead of swallowing up an exterior that would seek to contain it, the poetic voice materialises only in an imagined inner space, where conventional motifs of regeneration (fire, ash/phoenix, water) are stripped of credibility and where a tone of tragic immanence replaces Sonnet 472's faith in imminent transcendence.[78]

Subjectivity is the architect of the sonnet's interior spatial metaphors, whose prominence in the poem has been acknowledged. They clearly signpost Quevedo's reliance on, and distance from, more traditional tropings of absence and discretion, but also, as Pando Cantelli has argued, they separate Quevedo's text from the more extensive Petrarchan geographies, and thus intensify the expression of ontological conflict.[79] In addition, the topographical infrastructure functions as an integral component of a complex intertextual system, wherein the subject voice is constructed in terms of its relation to the infernal spaces and condemned mythological inhabitants of Tartarus. As Schwartz has demonstrated, this repertoire of topoi and images, transmitted via the rhetorical culture of the period, pervades the amorous corpus and, indeed, extends beyond it to the *Sueños*.[80] Less often noted, although of equal significance, is the impact of the sonnet's spatial orientation on its temporal reasoning. Individual metaphorical expressions are sanctioned in the

[76]   Antonio Gargano reads the fire/ice antithesis of sonnet 306 'Lo que me quita en fuego' within this metaphorical context. See 'Lectura del soneto "Lo que me quita en fuego me da en nieve" de Quevedo: entre tradición y contextos', *La Perinola*, 6 (2002), 117–36 (esp. 130–33).

[77]   Johnson sees a figuring of the belated Petrarchan poet in this image of Etna vomiting forth its own transformed body ('Quevedo's Poetics of Disillusion', in *Hyperboles*, p. 230).

[78]   The motif of fire as a transforming agent in Quevedo's poetry, which finds its most sustained expression in the phoenix poems (esp. 308, 449, 450), is discussed by Fernández Mosquera, *La poesía amorosa de Quevedo*, pp. 113–114.

[79]   See Pando Cantelli, 'John Donne, Francisco de Quevedo', p. 104.

[80]   See Lía Schwartz, 'Figuras del orco y el infierno interior'.

poem by a broader conceptual mapping, within which the abstract domain of time is shaped by the more concrete representation of the body as an experiential space.[81] Metaphorising time in terms of space permits the poet to exploit a three-dimensional topology which empowers temporal notions with new meanings. Present suffering is thus communicated as a prolonged and endlessly progressing state in which the sense of death having already occurred (yet simultaneously occurring), before death itself, yields to the inevitability of a foreclosed future. At the very centre of the poem lie the signs of love's demise, displayed in the charred remains of an already extinguished fire. As in much of Quevedo's moral and amorous poetry, time flows through these inner cloisters via a highly subjective point of reference, cracking the time line at its seam. But the eternal now (the *nunc stans*) conceived by the poetic 'I' is different here, conveyed ultimately in terms of a stationary self in whom past and future 'deaths' collide.

Once again movement operates within stasis and, as elsewhere, the fire/ water antithesis is a dominant hard-core metaphor animating the process – inventively reimagined in this poem according to a perverse logic in which inherent dualities can be reconciled within a coherently negative context. This symbolic fusion of opposites is also the organising principle of the sonnet 'Los que ciego me ven de haber llorado', [Those who see me blind from weeping], wherein union, as Arellano has shown, emerges out of a dynamic process of counter-positioning:[82]

> Los que ciego me ven de haber llorado
> y las lágrimas saben que he vertido,
> admiran de que, en fuentes dividido
> o en lluvias, ya no corra derramado.
>
> Pero mi corazón arde admirado
> (porque en tus llamas, Lisi, está encendido)
> de no verme en centellas repartido,
> y en humo negro y llamas desatado.
>
> En mí no vencen largos y altos ríos
> a incendios, que animosos me maltratan,
> ni el llanto se defiende de sus bríos.

---

81   This argument is informed by Lakoff's conceptual metaphor theory according to which the comprehension of abstract time via space is biologically determined. See George Lakoff, 'The Contemporary Theory of Metaphor', in *Metaphor and Thought*, ed. Andrew Ordony (Cambridge: Cambridge University Press, 1993).

82   See Ignacio Arellano, 'Comentario de un soneto amoroso de Quevedo: "Los que ciego me ven de haber llorado" y el arte de la ingeniosa contraposición', *La Perinola*, 6 (2002), 15–27 (esp. 21–22 and 25). As the title of the article suggests, Arellano's analysis situates Quevedo's poetic practice, as represented by this sonnet, within the model of *conceptismo* elaborated by Gracián in his *Agudeza y arte de ingenio*.

La agua y el fuego en mí de paces tratan;
y amigos son, por ser contrarios míos;
y los dos, por matarme, no se matan.   [Sonnet 444]

[Those who see me blind from weeping and know the tears that I have shed,
are surprised that, spilling over into floods or fountains, I have not yet flowed
away. But my heart burns in wonder (ignited, Lisi, in your flames), that I
have not yet been scattered in sparks, and in black smoke and flames undone.
In me long, high rivers do not defeat the hostile fires set against me, nor is
weeping a defence against their force. Water and fire make peace in me and
become friends, united against me; two as one, to kill me, they do not kill
each other.]

The subject's submission to the combined force of suffering love, as 'fuego',
and its overwhelming manifestation in 'llanto', is reflected in the shift from
active protagonism in the quatrains to passive in the tercets. Arellano sums up
the speaker's loss of agency and control in spatial terms, drawing our attention
to the hyperbolic personification of the contrary elements whose transformation
into autonomous actors is balanced by the reductive self-representation of the
speaker as setting, as a 'mere battle ground' upon which his own disintegration
will be enacted. A similar interiorised topography governs the metaphorical
processes of Sonnet 486, lending weight to otherwise abstract encounters. The
quatrains read:

Amor me ocupa el seso y los sentidos;
absorto estoy en éxtasi amoroso;
no me concede tregua ni reposo
esta guerra civil de los nacidos.

Explayóse el raudal de mis gemidos
por el grande distrito y doloroso
del corazón, en su penar dichoso,
y mis memorias anegó en olvidos.   [486, 1–8]

[Love besieges my sense and senses; I have surrendered entirely to the ecstasy
of Love; this civil war common to all human beings, brings me neither rest
nor respite. Torrential moaning flooded the vast region of my aching heart, so
blessed in its suffering, and drowned my memory in oblivion.]

In this poem the mind-body tensions of unrequited love, stretched to signify
the inherent paradoxes of human existence, find a perverse resolution in a
combined attack in, and on, the poet's inner being. The speaker infiltrates the
mystical mode only to subvert its basic premises. Meditation, which aims at
the voluntary surrender of self-control, here results from extreme acts of aggression. The numinous is not reached through transcendence, but through a

painful psychological process. Ecstasy in love does not offer intimations of the ineffable, nor does its altered state promise the experience of a reality that lies beyond human limits. Rather, its drastic intervention seems to move down and close in, across a spatial template that conveys the dark consequences of human temporal limitations. Fire/light is absent from the poem. Water is the implacable natural force, relentless over time, acting upon the material of memory and endangering the self. For if the past is an assemblage of experiences that can be carried forward, reassembled in the present and stabilised subjectively in the future, then the erosion of memory calls a halt to the potency of the individual in time.

Self-dissolution, set against a graphic canvas of civil war, takes place within the individual, but it also takes shape within a larger cultural matrix of martial strife and national *desengaño*. This is not, as Pando Cantelli would have it, a 'displacement of interest' from the external to the internal,[83] a move inwards where meaning is limited to subjective microcosmic confines. Rather, the material (re)metaphorising of the lover's emotional torment as an occupied war zone, razed and flooded, defamiliarises the conventional fire/water dialectic within a signifying system that has collective resonance. Sonnet 486 demonstrates just how misguided it is to read the 'yo gigantesco' [gigantic I] of Quevedo's love poetry as metaphysical solipsism,[84] a stance that not only misses the point of metaphor, but that also shuts the door on active, creative, reading. In fact, meaning explicitly transcends the limits of the subject's destroyed body in the tercets, opening out to acquire metapoetic and macrocosmic dimensions:

> Todo soy ruinas, todo soy destrozos,
> escándalo funesto a los amantes,
> que fabrican de lástimas sus gozos.
>
> Los que han de ser, y los que fueron antes,
> estudien su salud en mis sollozos,
> y envidien mi dolor, si son constantes.   [486, 9–14]

[I am all ruins, I am all ravages, a scandalous, morbid, example for lovers who fashion their joy from sorrow. Let lovers of the future and those of the past learn of their own wellbeing from my tears and envy my suffering, if they are constant.]

---

83   See María J. Pando Cantelli, '"… and often Absences / Withdrew our Soules and made us Carcasses". The destructive power of the female figure in Donne's *Nocturnall* and Quevedo's love poetry', *SEDERI*, 13 (2003), 155–62 (158).

84   The expression was coined by Raimundo Lida in a study of Quevedo's prose work and applied to the poetry by Pando Cantelli. See Raimundo Lida, *Prosas de Quevedo* (Barcelona: Crítica, 1981), pp. 39–40; Pando Cantelli, '"And often Absences"', p. 161.

The speaker gazes upon his own body, now in ruins, imagining how it might be visualised and interpreted by others. In the moment of vision, the past and the future are the horizons of the speaker's present, while the present itself becomes part of the past by construing it as ruined. These temporal disjunctures are accommodated within a symbolic, anti-heroic, figuration of the self that posits a new model of exemplarity that challenges traditional authorities. Ruin gazing always reflects on the impact of history on the living and on the nature of history itself as an eternal cycle. The personal history of the speaker writ large in this poem upon a fragmented body that is scattered across a scarred, internal, landscape traps the viewer in the complicity of failed ideals, thereby resuscitating memory that exceeds its own domain, slipping into other more collective sites of experience and representation. The story these ruins tell, of personal sacrifice and silence, surely must also carry, in the imagination of the reader, some reminder that whole cultures, like individuals, are transient, some trace of the future past of present imperial grandeur? Of course, the aestheticisation of ruins is incontrovertible. When temporal distance between genesis and gaze is stretched, there is often a compelling, coherent beauty, even in the most traumatised form. The epitaph upon which the sonnet ends expresses a tentative hope in aesthetic durability, giving material substance and greater funereal weight to Horace's marble headstone.

The awkward question of literary potency and erotic impotency is also confronted in the tercets of Sonnet 485, 'En los claustros del alma'. A problematic protagonism marks the subject's surrender to definitive 'ausencia', while acceptance of failure undermines ownership of a poetic voice that is identified uncompromisingly as an alternative to traditional Petrarchan lyric. Autonomous creativity is connected to Satan's kingdom of dark negation, the lowest state of being within the Renaissance's vertical hierarchy, here conveyed through the mythic geography of Hades, the lover's internal underworld. Hell is not rendered horrific through threat of punishment (the 'culpa', or sin, of the lover's figuration as a failed Orpheus in Sonnet 297), nor via traditional demonic representations. Rather, the speaker endures the suspension of self-control, intelligibility and articulation that would be afforded by 'complete' consciousness. Moreover, for the eloquent poet, eternal damnation is constituted by the failure to elicit response. The Phlegethon-like lament flowing into the 'sordo mar' [deaf sea] transforms the 'morir cotidiano' [daily dying] metaphor of the *Heráclito cristiano* into an 'infierno cotidiano' that encapsulates existential disillusionment in the idea of Lisi's indifference.[85] There is also, as I have noted elsewhere, an echo of Aeneas reaching out for Dido in *Aeneid* VI and meeting only rejection and silence.[86]

[85] See, for instance, Psalm 18, in which life is depicted as a 'turbio' [cloudy] river swallowed up in a dark sea of 'altas ondas' [high waves].

[86] Torres, 'Shades of Significance', 29. The Aeneas/Dido scene of *Aeneid* VI also informs the final lines of Sonnet 358 where the frustrated speaker pursues the elusive image of his be-

The encounter, in the *campi lugenti*, the grieving fields, where the shades of those consumed by love dwell, is a poignant presencing of a past that cannot be talked away. Right at the centre of the imperial epic, in the context of Herculean *katabasis*, Virgil renders his hero impotent. For T.S. Eliot, 'Dido's behaviour appears almost as a projection of Aeneas's own conscience'.[87] Insofar as we can accept the emulation of anti-heroic paradigms in the construction of Quevedo's poetic subject, this particular allusion is an emotive resonance in Sonnet 485's environment of wilful self-destruction. The degradation of the Orphic as a credible model for contemporary poetics, implicit in the tercets and particularly resonant in the final verse's corrective call and echo of Garcilaso's *Eclogue* III,[88] should also be viewed in terms of this transvaluation of an heroic ethos that was central to Renaissance humanism.

Conclusion

Some years ago, Timothy Hampton argued that narrative texts of the late Renaissance registered a crisis in the representation of exemplarity, as they assimilated the rhetorical and epistemological paradoxes of humanist discourse, especially around the practical application of the past in the present.[89] Hampton's broader context also holds true for the representation of archetypal mythological *exempla* in the poetry of the period – that is, how ideological anxieties, evolving epistemological scepticism and shifting socio-political circumstances led to an erosion of the authority of inherited exemplary figures. From these transformations of authority in Quevedo's love poetry emerges a new depiction of the self in language that reflects the changes in the individual's relationship with the world, communicating a growing tension between private and public spaces and an intense performance of lyric sensibility that is riven by the experience of embeddedness in a specific larger geo-historical site. Despite the best efforts of the Alonso School who deem Quevedo 'modern', or more recent attempts to pin down his 'postmodernity',[90] the poetic

---

loved with the river of his tears: 'y como de alcanzarla tengo gana, / hago correr tras ella el llanto en ríos' [and as I want to reach her, I follow her in a river-flood of tears; 358, 13–14].

87 See T.S. Eliot, *What is a Classic?* (London: Faber, 1945), p. 20.

88 The presence of a Garcilasian subtext has been acknowledged by almost all commentators of this poem. The seminal study of the intermediary versions of the 'reino del espanto' motif between Garcilaso and Quevedo is Gonzalo Sobejano's 'Reinos del espanto: Garcilaso, Góngora y otros', in *Busquemos otros montes y otros ríos,* pp. 253–67.

89 See Timothy Hampton, *Writing for History: The Rhetoric of Exemplarity in Renaissance Literature* (New York: Cornell University Press, 1990). The study includes a chapter analysis of Cervantes's *Don Quijote*.

90 See, for instance, Giulia Poggi, 'Quevedo con / sin Petrarca: apuntes para un debate', *La Perinola*, 8 (2004), 359–74, esp. 367–68, where she associates fragmented argument with postmodernist practise. This is a very problematic enterprise, not just because the term 'postmodernism'

voice of Quevedo's love poetry drags its historicity with it. For the subject that is heard as the speaking voice of the love poetry is constituted out of, and in, the linguistic materials of inherited textual and intellectual traditions and articulates them as what articulates it. Moreover, this lyric 'I' is a metaleptic figure, an illusion of an individual voice projected upon, and projecting, an emotionally charged individual amorous history that self-consciously violates its first-person poetic posture. The speaker's insistence on individual 'being' here and now sounds the whole of Quevedo's time–space surroundings, making audible a communal being that coheres around the mechanics of a radically subjective metaphorical performance and enhanced reader intervention. As we have seen, the reader plays a creatively determinant role in the poetry's complex border transgressions: suspended at the crossroads between the rational and the irrational, mediating the distance between memory and oblivion, always negotiating the broader tensions between the ideal and the real. For unlike the contained idealised spaces of poetic pastoral, where the 'nightmare' of history threatens, but is held temporarily at bay, looming on the horizons of a nostalgic timelessness, the aesthetic inner realm that is embodied in Quevedo's amorous lyric denies even 'a purely formal resolution' to the contradictions of the day.[91] The sonnet space that is subjectively and irrationally reimagined in excess of language's referential functions is ultimately invaded by disturbing extra-textual realities, by the uncompromising fact of the human condition and by the abject failure of the poetic enterprise. But this failure is also rhetorically constructed. Produced within an atmosphere of national disillusionment, Quevedo's 'failed' poetic project attends to language as a material aspect of his world and its power structures. By positing the voice of the unrequited lover, an incomplete and anti-heroic self, as the primary organising feature of a metaphorically expansive vernacular, Quevedo appears to figure the fractured, central consciousness of a 'precarious', imperial identity, which seeks consolidation through overseas conquest.[92] By

itself is overused and ill-defined, but because the evidential base is flimsy. *Res* may be constructed in ruins, but meaning (as noted above) is resistant to reader fragmentation.

[91] I am indebted here to Rosilie Hernández Pecoraro's recent study of the pastoral novel, which applies the Jamesonian model of pastoral as a 'symbolic act' where 'real, social contradictions, insurmountable in their own terms, find a purely formal resolution in the aesthetic realm'. See *Bucolic Metaphors: History, Subjectivity and Gender in the Early Modern Spanish Pastoral*, North Carolina Studies in the Romance Languages and Literatures, no. 287 (Chapel Hill: University of North Carolina Press, 2006). James is cited on p. 39.

[92] Barbara Fuchs reminds us that early modern Spain was not an achieved whole but a precarious construct; that the idea of the Spanish nation as a continuous unitary subject is a myth. See *Passing for Spain*, p. 78. See also the recent study by David Rojinsky, *Companion to Empire: A Genealogy of the Written Word in Spain and New Spain, c.550–1550* (Amsterdam and New York: Rodopi, 2010), whose analysis of *imperium* as an historically variable concept in Hispanic written cultures 'responds to the notion that maritime expansion combined the striving for an early modern state with the struggle to formulate modern conceptions of empire' (p. 20).

means of metaphor, Quevedo gives to his comprehension of the human community the figure of an individual body, disintegrating from within. To his conception of Spain's imperial aspirations, he gives its most appropriate, commemorating, companion.

Bibliography

Addison, Joseph, 'The Pleasures of the Imagination', *The Spectator*, no. 411, 21 June 1712, no pagination

Alatorre, Antonio, 'Garcilaso, Herrera, Prete Jacopín y Don Tomás Tamayo de Vargas', *MLN*, 78 (1963), 126–51

Alciato, Andrea, *Emblematum Libellus* (Venice: Aldus, 1546)

Allan, Kathryn, *Metaphor and Metonymy: A Diachronic Approach*, Publications of the Philological Society, 42 (Oxford: Wiley-Blackwell, 2008)

Alonso, Dámaso, *Cuatro poetas españoles* (Madrid: Gredos, 1962)

——, *Góngora y El Polifemo*, I (Madrid: Gredos, 1961)

——, *Poesía española: ensayo de métodos y límites estilísticos* (Madrid: Gredos, 1956)

Amann, Elizabeth, 'Pointed Poetry: Agudeza and Petrarchism in Góngora's Late Sonnets', *Hispanic Research Journal*, 12.4 (2011), 306–22

Ancell, Matthew, 'Este....Cíclope: Góngora's *Polifemo* and the Poetics of Disfiguration', *Hispanic Review*, 79.4 (2011), 547–72

Anderson, Benedict, *Imagined Communities: Reflections on the Origin and Spread of Nationalism* (London and New York: Verso, 1983)

Apuleius, *Cupid and Psyche*, ed. E. J. Kenney (Cambridge: Cambridge University Press, 1990)

Arce de Vázquez, Margot, 'Cerca el Danubio una isla', *Studia Philologica*, 1 (1960), 91–100

——, 'La Égloga Primera de Garcilaso', *La Torre*, L (1953), 31–68

Arellano, Ignacio, 'Comentario de un soneto amoroso de Quevedo: "Los que ciego me ven de haber llorado" y el arte de la ingeniosa contraposición', *La Perinola*, 6 (2002), 15–27

Armas, Frederick A. de, ed., *Ekphrasis in the Age of Cervantes* (Lewisberg: Bucknell University Press, 2005)

Arnheim, Rudolph, *Art and Visual Perception: A Psychology of the Creative Eye* (Berkeley: University of California Press, 1954)

Arredondo, María Soledad, 'El exceso de guerras, de peligros y destierro: de Garcilaso a Quevedo', in *Garcilaso y su época: del amor y la guerra*, eds José María Díez Borque and Luís Ribot García Morros (Madrid: Sociedad Estatal de Conmemoraciones Culturales, 2003), pp. 265–73

Asensio, Eugenio, 'El Brocense contra Fernando de Herrera y sus Anotaciones a Garcilaso', *El Crótalon. Anuario de Filología Española*, I (1984), 13–24

Asensio, José María, *Controversia sobre sus Anotaciones a las obras de Garcilaso de la Vega* (Seville: [n.p.], 1870)

Augustine, 'The City of God', in *Writings of Saint Augustine*, trans. G.G.Walsh and G. Monahan, Fathers of the Church, 14, 17 vols (New York: Fathers of the Church, 1952), VII

Austen, R.G., 'Ille qui quondam …', *The Classical Quarterly*, 18.1 (1968), 107–15

Ayala, Francisco, 'Sueño y realidad en el barroco', *Insula*, 184 (1962), 1

Azar, Inés, *Discurso retórico y mundo pastoral en la "Égloga segunda" de Garcilaso* (Amsterdam: Benjamins, 1981)

Aznar Anglés, Eduardo, 'Clásico y Barroco (dos sonetos del clasicismo español)', in *Homenaje al profesor Antonio Vilanova*, 2 vols, ed. Marta C. Carbonell (Barcelona: Universidad de Barcelona, 1989), I, pp. 57–74

Barnard, Mary E., 'The Mirror of Narcissus: Imaging the Self in Garcilaso's Second Eclogue', in *Ovid in the Age of Cervantes*, ed. Frederick A. de Armas (Toronto: University of Toronto Press, 2010), pp. 137–57

——, 'Myth, Rhetoric and the Failure of Language in Garcilaso's "Ode ad Florem Gnidi"', in *Brave New Words: Studies in Spanish Golden Age Literature*, eds Edward H. Friedman and Catherine Larson (New Orleans: University Press of the South, 1996), pp. 51–65

——, 'Garcilaso's Poetics of Subversion and the Orpheus Tapestry', *PMLA*, 102 (1987), 316–25

——, *The Myth of Apollo and Daphne from Ovid to Quevedo: Love, Agon, and the Grotesque*, Duke Monographs in Medieval and Renaissance Studies, 8 (Durham: Duke University Press, 1987)

Barthes, Roland, 'The Death of the Author', in *Image, Music, Text*, trans. Stephen Heath (London: Fontana Press, 1977), pp. 142–48

——, *The Pleasure of the Text*, trans. R. Miller (New York: Hill and Wang, 1975)

——, *S/Z*, trans. Richard Miller (Oxford: Basil Blackwell, 1974)

Bautista Martínez Bennecker, Juan, 'La poesía de senectud de Juan Bautista de Mesa', *Lemir*, 12 (2008), 235–54

Belsey, Catherine, *Critical Practice* (New York and London: Routledge, 1980)

Benjamin, Walter, 'On Language as Such and on the Language of Man (1916)', in *One-Way Street*, trans. Edmund Jephcott and Kingsley Shorter (London: Verso, 1997), pp. 107–23

Bentley, P.E., 'Reading and Contextualising Quevedo: The Case of "Flota de cuantos rayos y centellas"', *Calíope*, 6. 1–2 (2000), 251–62

Bergmann, Emilie L., *Art Inscribed: Essays on Ekphrasis in Spanish Golden Age Poetry* (Cambridge, MA: Harvard University Press, 1979)

——, 'Violencia, voyeurism y genética: versiones de la sexualidad en Góngora y Sor Juana', in *Venus venerada: tradiciones eróticas de la literatura española*, eds J. Ignacio Díez and Adrienne L. Martín (Madrid: Editorial Complutense, 2006), pp. 89–106

Beverley, John R., *Essays on the Literary Baroque in Spain and Spanish America* (Woodbridge: Tamesis, 2008)

——, *Against Literature* (Minneapolis and London: Univeristy of Minnesota Press, 1993)

——, *Aspects of Góngora's 'Soledades'*, Purdue University Monographs in Romance Languages, 1 (Amsterdam: John Benjamins, 1980)

Bianchini, Andreina, 'Herrera: Questions and Contradictions in the Critical Tradition', *Caliope*, 1 (1995), 58–71

——, 'Herrera and Prete Jacopín: The Consequences of the Controversy', *Hispanic Review*, 2 (1978), 221–34

Black, Max, *Models and Metaphors* (London: Cornell University Press, 1962)

Blanco, Mercedes, *Góngora o la invención de una lengua* (León: Universidad de León, 2012)

——, *Introducción al comentario de la poesía amorosa de Quevedo* (Madrid: Arco libros, 1998)

Bloom, Harold, *The Anxiety of Influence: A Theory of Poetry* (New York: Oxford University Press, 1973)

Boase, Roger, 'The Meaning of the Crow-Hunting Episode in Garcilaso's *Égloga Segunda* (ll. 260–95)', *Journal of Hispanic Philology*, 13 (1988), 41–48

Bocángel y Unzueta, Gabriel, *Obras completas*, ed. Trevor J. Dadson, Biblioteca Áurea Hispánica, 2 vols (Madrid: Iberoamericana and Frankfurt am Main: Vervuert, 2000)

Bongie, Chris, 'What's Literature Got To Do With It?', *Comparative Literature*, 54.3 (2002), 256–67

Bono, Barbara J., *Literary Transvaluation: From Vergilian Epic to Shakespearean Tragicomedy* (Berkeley: University of California Press, 1984)

Borges, José Luis, *Otras Inquisiciones* (Buenos Aires: Seix Barral, 1993)

Boscán, Juan, *Obras completas*, ed. Carlos Clavería (Madrid: Cátedra, 1999)

Brennan, Teresa, *The Transmission of Affect* (Ithaca: Cornell University Press, 2004)

Brown, Jonathan, and John H. Elliot, *A Palace for a King: The Buen Retiro and the Court of Phillip IV* (New Haven: Yale University Press, 1980)

Bruns, Gerald, *Hermeneutics: Ancient and Modern* (New Haven: Yale University Press, 1992)

Bultman, Dana, 'Góngora's Invocation of *Prudente consul*: Censorship and Humanist Doubts about his Lyric Language', *Hispanófila*, 142 (2004), 1–19

Butler, Judith, *Gender Trouble. Feminism and the Subversion of Identity* (New York and London: Routledge, 1999)

Cabañas Martínez, María Jesús, 'El mito de Apolo y Dafne: diferencias de tratamiento en Garcilaso y Quevedo a través de dos sonetos', in *La maravilla escrita. Antonio de Torquemada y el siglo de oro. Actas del Congreso Internacional Antonio de Torquemada y la literatura del Siglo de Oro, León-Astorga 7–9 de mayo de 2003*, eds Juan Matas Caballero, José Manuel Trabado Cabado and Juan José Alonso Perandones (León: Universidad de León, 2005), pp. 213–26

Cacho Casal, Rodrigo, 'The Memory of Ruins: Quevedo's *Silva* to "Roma antigua y moderna"', *Renaissance Quarterly*, 62 (2009), 1167–203

Calcraft, R.P., 'The Lover as Icarus: Góngora's "Que de invidiosos montes levantados"', in *What's Past is Prologue: A Collection of Essays in Honour of L.J. Woodward*, ed. Salvador Bacarisse (Edinburgh: Scottish Academic Press, 1984), pp. 10–28

——, 'The *carpe diem* sonnets of Garcilaso and Góngora', *Modern Language Review*, 76.2 (1981), 332–37

——, *The Sonnets of Luis de Góngora* (Durham: University of Durham, 1980)

Cancelliere, Enrica, *Góngora: itinerarios de la visión*, trans. Rafael Bonilla and Linda Garosi (Córdoba: Diputación de Córdoba, 2006)

Carreira, Antonio, 'La controversia en torno a las *Soledades*: un parecer desconocido, y edición crítica de las primeras cartas', in *Hommage à Robert Jammes (Anejos de Criticón)*, ed. Francis Cerdon, 3 vols (Toulouse: Presses Universitaires du Mirail, 1994), I, pp. 151–71

Carreño, Antonio, 'Of "Orders" and "Disorders": Analogy in the Spanish Baroque Poetry', in *The Image of the Baroque*, ed. Aldo Scaglione, with Gianni Eugenio Viola (New York: Peter Lang, 1995), pp. 139–56

Carrillo y Sotomayor, Luis, *Obras*, ed. Rosa Navarro Durán (Madrid: Castalia, 1990)

Carruthers, Mary, *The Craft of Thought: Meditation, Rhetoric and the Making of Images. 400–1200* (Cambridge: Cambridge University Press, 1998)

Cascales, Francisco, *Cartas filológicas*, ed. Justo García Soriano (Madrid: Espasa Calpe, 1959)

Cascardi, Anthony J., *Ideologies of History in the Spanish Golden Age* (University Park PA: Pennsylvania State University Press, 1997)

Castiglione, Baldassare, *El Cortesano*, trans. Juan Boscán, ed. Mario Pozzi (Madrid: Cátedra, 1994)

——, *Il libro del Cortegiano* (Venice: Aldo Manuzio and Andrea Asolo, 1528)

Cave, Terence, 'Locating the Early Modern', *Paragraph*, 29.1 (2006), 12–26

Celaya, Gabriel, *Exploración de la poesía* (Barcelona: Seix Barral, 1964)

Cerdan, Francis, ed., *Hommage à Robert Jammes (Anejos de Criticón)*, 3 vols (Toulouse: Presses Universitaires du Mirail, 1994)

Charnes, Linda, 'What's Love Got To Do With it? Reading the Liberal Humanist Romance in Antony and Cleopatra', in *Shakespearean Tragedy and Gender*, eds Shirley Nelson Garner and Madelon Springnether (Bloomington and Indianapolis: Indiana University Press, 1996), pp. 268–86

Chemris, Crystal Anne, *Góngora's 'Soledades' and the Problem of Modernity* (Woodbridge: Tamesis, 2008)

Clark, Christina A., 'The Poetics of Manhood? Nonverbal Behaviour in Catullus 51', *Classical Philology*, 103.3 (2008), 257–81

Clifton, James, 'Vasari on Competition', *Sixteenth Century Journal*, XXVII.1 (1996), 23–41

Close, Lorna, 'The Play of Difference: A Reading of Góngora's Soledades', in *Conflicts of Discourse: Spanish Literature in the Golden Age*, ed. Peter W. Evans (Manchester and New York: Manchester University Press, 1990), pp. 184–98

——, 'Petrarchism and the *Cancioneros*: The Problem of Discrimination', *Modern Language Review*, 74 (1979), 836–55

Cody, J.V., *Horace and Callimachean Aesthetics*, Collection Latomus, 147 (Brussels: Latomus Revue D'Etudes Latines, 1976)

Cohen, Murray, *Sensible Words: Linguistic Practice in England 1640–1785* (Baltimore and London: John Hopkins University Press, 1977)

Collard, Andrée, 'La "herejía" de Góngora', *Hispanic Review*, 36.4 (1968), 328–37

Collins, Marsha S., *Góngora's Masque of the Imagination* (Columbia: University of Missouri Press, 2002)

Conley, Tom, *An Errant Eye: Poetry and Topography in Early Modern France* (Minneapolis: University of Minnesota Press, 2011)

Conte, Gian Biagio, *The Rhetoric of Imitation: Genre and Poetic Memory in Virgil and Other Latin Poets*, ed. Charles Segal, Cornell Studies in Classical Philology, 44 (Ithaca and London: Cornell University Press, 1986)

Correa, Gustavo, 'Garcilaso y la mitología', *Hispanic Review*, 45.3 (1977), 269–81

Coster, Adolphe, *Algunas obras de Fernando de Herrera* (Paris: Champion, 1908)

Cravens, Sydney P., and Edward V. George, 'Garcilaso's Salicio and Vergil's Eighth Eclogue', *Hispania*, 64.2 (1981), 209–14

Crawford, J.P.W., 'Italian Sources of Góngora's Poetry', *Romanic Review*, 20 (1929), 122–30

Creel, Bryant, *The Voice of the Phoenix: Metaphors of Death and Rebirth in Classics of the Iberian Renaissance*, Medieval and Renaissance Texts and Studies, 272 (Tempe: Arizona Center for Medieval and Renaissance Studies, 2004)

Crosby, James O., *En torno a la poesía de Quevedo* (Madrid: Castalia, 1967)

Cruz, Anne J., Elias L. Rivers, 'Three Literary Manifestos of Early Modern Spain: Juan Boscán and Garcilaso de la Vega', *Publications of the Modern Language Association*, 126.1 (2011), 233–42

——, E.C. Graf, Elias L. Rivers, 'Forum', *Publications of the Modern Language Association of America*, 117.2 (2002), 324–28

——, 'Arms versus Letters: The Poetics of War and the Career of the Poet in Early Modern Spain', in *European Literary Careers: The Author from Antiquity to the Renaissance*, eds Patrick Cheney and Frederick A. de Armas (Toronto: University of Toronto Press, 2002), pp. 186–205

——, *Imitación y transformación: el petrarquismo en la poesía de Boscán y Garcilaso de la Vega* (Amsterdam: John Benjamins Publishing Co., 1988)

Cruz, Arnaldo, 'Exclusión y afirmación en Góngora', *Dispositio*, IX, 24–26 (1984), 167–82

Cuevas García, Cristóbal, 'Teoría del lenguaje poético en las anotaciones de Herrera', in *Las anotaciones de Fernando de Herrera: doce estudios* (Sevilla: Universidad de Sevilla, 1997), pp. 157–71

Cull, John T., '"Mas no lo saben todo los letrados/ni todos son ydiotas los soldados." Francisco de Guzmán's *Digresión de las armas y letras* (1565)', *Cervantes*, 29.2 (2009), 5–31

Curtius, Ernst Robert, *European Literature and the Latin Middle Ages*, trans. Willard R. Trask (New York: Pantheon Books, 1953)

Darst, David H., *Imitatio: polémicas sobre la imitación en el siglo de oro* (Madrid: Orígenes, 1985)

——, 'Garcilaso's Love For Isabel Freire: The Creation of a Myth', *Journal of Hispanic Philology*, 3 (1979), 261–68

Davis, Elizabeth B., 'La promesa del naúfrago: el motivo marinero del ex-voto, de Garcilaso a Quevedo', in *Studies in Honor of James O'Crosby*, ed. Lía Schwartz (Newark, Delaware: Juan de la Cuesta, 2004), pp. 109–23

DellaNeva, JoAnn, 'Poetry, Metamorphosis, and the Laurel: Ovid, Petrarch and Scève', *French Forum*, 7 (1982), 197–209

Díez Borque, José María, and Luís Ribot García Morros, eds, *Garcilaso y su época: del amor y la guerra* (Madrid: Sociedad Estatal de Conmemoraciones Culturales, 2003)

Díez, J. Ignacio, 'La inspirada poética del soneto "Al rey, nuestro señor", de Hernando de Acuña', *Hispanic Review*, 79.4 (2011), 527–46

——, and Adrienne L. Martín, eds, *Venus venerada: tradiciones eróticas de la literatura española* (Madrid: Editorial Complutense, 2006)

Dudley, Edward, 'The Lady is Out of this World: Erotic Conceits and Carnal Displacements in Three Protocols of Desire', in *Negotiating Past and Present: Studies in Spanish Literature for Javier Herrero*, ed. David Gies (Charlottesville, VA: Rookwood, 1997), pp. 176–93

Duffy, Carol Ann, *The Bees* (London: Picador, 2011)

Dunn, Peter N., 'La Oda de Garcilaso "A La Flor de Gnido"', in *La poesía de Garcilaso: ensayos críticos*, ed. Olga Rivera (Barcelona: Ediciones Ariel, 1974), pp. 129–62

Durling, Robert, *Petrarch's Lyric Poems: The 'Rime sparse' and Other Lyrics* (Cambridge, MA: Harvard University Press, 1976)

Dutton, Brian, 'Garcilaso's *sin duelo*', *MLN*, 80.2 (1965), 251–58

——, and Victoriano Roncero López, eds, *Busquemos otros montes y otros ríos: estudios de literatura española del Siglo de Oro dedicados a E.L. Rivers* (Madrid: Castalia, 1992)

Eco, Umberto, *Semiotics and the Philosophy of Language* (Bloomington: Indiana University Press, 1984)

Egido, Aurora, 'Garcilaso y la puerta cerrada', in *Al otro lado del espejo. Comentario lingüístico de textos literarios. Homenaje a José Manuel Blecua Perdices*, eds Gloria Clavería and Dolors Poch (Barcelona: Ariel, 2010), pp. 63–85

——, '"Dos soles de poesía": Lupercio y Bartolomé Leonardo de Argensola', in *Dos soles de poesía. 450 años. Lupercio y Bartolomé Leonardo de Argensola*, eds Aurora Egido and José Enrique Laplana, *Argensola*, special monograph issue, 119 (2009), pp. 15–39

——, *Fronteras de la poesía en el Barroco* (Barcelona: Crítica, 1990)

——, 'La *Hidra bocal:* sobre la palabra poética en el Barroco', *Edad de Oro*, VI, (1987), 79–113

——, 'Sin poética hay poetas: sobre la teoría de la égloga en el siglo de oro', *Criticón*, 30 (1985), 43–77

Eiland, Howard, and Michael W. Jennings, eds, *Walter Benjamin: Selected Writings*, vol. 4, trans. Edmund Jephcott *et al.* (Cambridge, MA: Harvard University Press, 2003)

Eliot, T.S., *What is a Classic?* (London: Faber, 1945)

Elliott, J.H., *Spain, Europe and the Wider World 1500–1800* (New Haven and London: Yale University Press, 2009)

——, 'Unas reflexiones acerca de la privanza española en el contexto europeo', *Anuario de la historia del derecho español*, 67.2 (1997), 885–99

Elrich, Robert J., 'Envy, Identity, Creativity: Inferno XXIV–XXV', *Dante Studies*, 102 (1984), 61–84

Enterline, Lynn, *The Rhetoric of the Body from Ovid to Shakespeare*, Cambridge
    Studies in Renaissance Literature and Culture, 35 (Cambridge: Cambridge Uni-
    versity Press, 2000)
——, *The Tears of Narcissus: Melancholy and Masculinity in Early Modern Writing*
    (Stanford: Stanford University Press, 1995)
Entwistle, William J., 'Garcilaso's Fourth Canzon and Other Matters', *Modern Lan-
    guage Review*, 45.2 (1950), 225–28
——, 'The Loves of Garci-Laso', *Hispania*, 13.5 (1930), 377–88
Entzminger, Robert L., *Divine Word: Milton and the Redemption of Language* (Pitts-
    burgh: Duquesne, 1985)
Fedeli, P., *Sesto Properzio: il terzo libro delle elegie* (Bari: [n.p.], 1985)
Fernández Mosquera, Santiago, 'La poesía amorosa de Quevedo', *Insula*, 648
    (2000), 20–22
——, *La poesía amorosa de Quevedo: disposición y estilo desde Canta sola a Lisi*
    (Madrid: Editorial Gredos, 1999)
——, 'De nuevo sobre la consideración de "Algunas obras de Herrera" como can-
    cionero petrarquista', *Insula-Revista de Letras y Ciencias Humanas*, 610 (1997),
    14–17
Fernández-Morera, Darío, *The Lyre and the Oaten Flute: Garcilaso and the Pastoral*
    (London: Tamesis, 1982)
——, 'Garcilaso's Second Eclogue and the Literary Tradition', *Hispanic Review*,
    47.1 (1979), 37–53
Fish, Stanley, *Is there a Text in this Class? The Authority of Interpretive Communities*
    (Cambridge, MA: Harvard University Press, 1980)
Foucault, Michel, 'What is an Author?', in *Michel Foucault Language, Counter-
    Memory, Practice: Selected Essays and Interviews*, ed. Donald F. Bouchard,
    trans. Donald F. Bouchard and Sherry Simon (Ithaca: Cornell University Press,
    1977), pp. 133–38
Fowler, D.P., 'Narrate and Describe: The Problem of Ekphrasis', *The Journal of Ro-
    man Studies*, 81 (1991), 25–35
Fox, Dian, Harry Sieber, and Robert Ter Horst, eds, *Studies in Honour of Bruce W.
    Wardropper* (Delaware: Juan de la Cuesta, 1989)
Freccero, Carla, 'Ovidian Subjectivities in Early Modern Lyric: Identification and
    Desire in Petrarch and Louise Labé', in *Ovid and the Body in the Renaissance*, ed.
    Goran V. Stanivukovic (Toronto: University of Toronto Press, 2001), pp. 21–37
Freccero, John, 'The Fig Tree and the Laurel: Petrarch's Poetics,' *Diacritics*, 5
    (1975), 34–40
Friedman, Edward, 'Realities and Poets: Góngora, Cervantes and the Nature of Art',
    Caliope, 8.1 (2002), 55–68
——, 'Creative Space: Ideologies of Discourse in Góngora's *Polifemo*', in *Cultural
    Authority in Golden Age Spain*, eds Marina Scordilis Brownlee and Hans Ulrich
    Gumbrecht (Baltimore: John Hopkins University Press, 1995), pp. 51–78
Frohlicher, Peter, 'Muerte y escritura en la poesía amorosa de Quevedo', in *Fic-
    tio poética: studi italiani e ispanici in onore di Georges Güntert*, eds Katherina
    Maier-Troxler, Costantino Maeder and Jacques Geninasca (Florence: Cesati Edi-
    tore, 1998), pp. 169–86

Fuchs, Barbara, *Passing For Spain: Cervantes and the Fictions of Identity* (Chicago: University of Illinois Press, 2003)

Fucilla, Joseph, 'Etapas en el desarrollo del mito de Icaro en el renacimiento y en el siglo de oro', *Hispanófila*, 3 (1960), 1–34

Gaetano, Chiappini, ed., *Fernando de Herrera y la escuela sevillana* (Madrid: Taurus, 1985)

Gagarin, M., 'The Ambiguity of Eris in the "Works and Days"', in *The Cabinet of the Muses: Essays on Classical and Comparative Literature in Honour of Thomas G. Rosenmeyer*, eds M. Griffith and D. Mastronarde (Atlanta: Scholars Press, 1990), pp. 173–83

Gale, Glen Ross, 'Garcilaso's Sonnet XIII Metamorphosed', *Romanische Forschungen*, 80 (1969), 504–09

Gallagher, Patrick, 'Garcilaso's First Eclogue and the Lamentations of Love', *Forum for Modern Language Studies*, IX (1973), 192–99

Gallego Morell, Antonio, *Garcilaso de la Vega y sus comentaristas* (Madrid: Editorial Gredos, 1972)

Gallop, Jane, *Reading Lacan* (Ithaca: Cornell University Press, 1985)

García Aquilar, Ignacio, *Poesía y edición en el siglo de oro* (Madrid: Calambur Editorial, 2009)

García de Diego, Vicente, *Poesías* (Madrid: Espasa-Calpe, 1962)

García, Gustavo V., 'El intertexto de la imitación en Garcilaso, Góngora y Balbuena', *Revista Iberoamericana,* LXIII (1997), 391–401

Garcilaso de la Vega*, Poesía castellana completa*, ed. J. F. Alcina (Madrid: Espasa Calpe, 1998)

——, *Obra poética y textos en prosa*, ed. Bienvenido Morros, preliminary study by Rafael Lapesa, Biblioteca Clásica, 27 (Barcelona: Crítica, 1995)

——, *Cancionero*, ed. Antonio Prieto (Barcelona: Bruguera, 1982)

Gardner, F.C., *The Pilgrimage of Desire: A Study of Theme and Genre in Medieval Literature* (Leiden: Brill, 1971)

Gargano, Antonio, 'Lectura del soneto "Lo que me quita en fuego me da en nieve" de Quevedo: entre tradición y contextos', *La Perinola*, 6 (2002), 117–36

Gaylord, Mary Malcolm, 'Intimacy and Allegory in a Quevedo Sonnet (En breve cárcel traigo aprisionado)', in *Studies in Honor of Denah Lida*, eds Mary G. Berg and Lanin A. Gyurko (Potomac, Maryland: Scripta Humanistica, 2005), pp. 103–12

Gaylord Randel, Mary, 'Proper Language and Language as Property: The Personal Poetics of Lope's *Rimas*', *Modern Language Notes*, 101.2 (1986), 220–46

——, 'Metaphor and Fable in Góngora's *Soledad Primera*', *Revista Hispánica Moderna*, 40 (1978–79), 97–112

——, *The Historical Prose of Fernando de Herrera* (London: Tamesis, 1971)

Gerli, Michael E., '"Más allá del carpe diem: el soneto "Mientras por competir con tu cabello" de Luis de Góngora', in *Estudios en homenaje a Enrique Ruíz-Fornells*, eds Teresa Valdivielso *et al.* (Pennsylvania: ALDEEU, 1990), pp. 255–58

Ghertman, Sharon, *Petrarch and Garcilaso: A Linguistic Approach to Style* (London: Tamesis, 1975)

Gicovate, Bernard, *Garcilaso de la Vega* (Boston: Twayne Publishers, 1975)

Gilson, Simon, 'Historicism, Philology and the Text: An Interview with Teolinda Barolini', *Italian Studies*, 63.1 (2008), 141–52

Goldhill, Simon, 'What is Ekphrasis For?', *Classical Philology*, 102.1 (2007), 1–19

Góngora y Argote, Luis de, *Obras completas,* ed. Antonio Carreira, I (*Poemas de autoría segura. Poemas de autenticidad probable*) (Madrid: Biblioteca Castro, 2000)

——, *Soledades*, ed. John Beverley (Madrid: Cátedra, 1980)

——, *Sonetos completos*, ed. Biruté Ciplijauskaité (Madrid: Castalia, 1969)

——, *Obras completas,* eds Juan Millé y Giménez and Isabel Millé y Giménez (Madrid: Aguilar, 1961)

——, *Poesías completas*, ed. R. Foulché-Delbosc, 3 vols (New York: Hispanic Society of North America, 1921)

Goodwyn, Frank, 'New Light on the Historical Setting of Garcilaso's Poetry', *Hispanic Review*, 46 (1978), 1–22

Gracián, Baltasar, *Agudeza y arte de ingenio*, ed. E. Correa Calderón, 2 vols (Madrid: Castalia, 1969)

Graf, E.C., 'From Scipio to Nero to the Self: The Exemplary Politics of Stoicism in Garcilaso de la Vega's Elegies', *PMLA*, 116.5 (2001), 1316–33

——, 'Forcing the Poetic Voice: Garcilaso de la Vega's Sonnet XXIX as a Deconstruction of the Idea of Harmony', *Modern Language Notes*, 109 (1994), 163–85

Green, Otis H., 'The Abode of the Blest in Garcilaso's *Égloga Primera*', *Romance Philology*, VI (1953), 272–78

Greene, Roland, *Unrequited Conquests: Love and Empire in the Colonial Americas* (Chicago: University of Chicago Press, 2000)

——, *Post-Petrarchism: Origins and Innovations of the Western Lyric Sequence* (Princeton: Princeton University Press, 1991)

Greene, Thomas M., *The Light in Troy: Imitation and Discovery in Renaissance Poetry* (New Haven and London: Yale University Press, 1982)

Gutiérrez, Carlos M.G., 'La poesía amorosa de Quevedo como estrategia literaria', *La Perinola*, 9 (2005), 79–97

——, 'The Challenges of Freedom: Social Reflexivity in the Seventeenth-Century Spanish Literary Field', in *Hispanic Baroques. Reading Cultures in Context*, eds Nicholas Spadaccini and Luis Martín-Estudillo (Nashville: Vanderbilt University Press, 2005), pp. 137–62

——, 'Las *Soledades* y El *Polifemo* de Góngora: Distinción, capitalización simbólica y tomas de posición en el campo literario español de la primera mitad del siglo XVII', *Romance Languages Annual*, 10.2 (1998), 621–25

Halliwell, Stephen, *Aristotle's Poetics* (Chicago: University of Chicago Press, 1986)

Hampton, Timothy, *Writing for History: The Rhetoric of Exemplarity in Renaissance Literature* (New York: Cornell University Press, 1990)

Hardie, Philip, ed., *The Cambridge Companion to Ovid* (Cambridge: Cambridge University Press, 2002)

——, *Ovid's Poetics of Illusion* (Cambridge: Cambridge University Press, 2002)

Harries, Karsten, 'Metaphor and Transcendence', *Critical Enquiry*, 5.1 (1978), 73–90

Hebreo, León, *Diálogos de amor* (Sevilla: Padilla libros, 1989)

——, *Diálogos de amor*, trans. David Romano (Barcelona: José Jones, 1953)

Heffernan, James A.W., *Museum of Words: The Poetics of Ekphrasis from Homer to Ashbery* (Chicago: University of Chicago Press, 1993)

Heidegger, Martin, 'A Dialogue on Language: Between a Japanese and an Inquirer', in *On the Way to Language*, trans. Peter D. Hertz (New York: Harper and Row, 1971), pp. 1–54

Heiple, Daniel, *Garcilaso de la Vega and the Italian Renaissance* (University Park: Pennsylvania State University Press, 1994)

Helgerson, Richard, *A Sonnet from Carthage: Garcilaso de la Vega and the New Poetry of Sixteenth-Century Europe* (Philadelphia: University of Pennsylvania Press, 2007)

Hernández Pecoraro, Rosilie, *Bucolic Metaphors: History, Subjectivity and Gender in the Early Modern Spanish Pastoral*, North Carolina Studies in the Romance Languages and Literatures, no. 287 (Chapel Hill: University of North Carolina Press, 2006)

Herrera, Fernando de, *Anotaciones a la poesía de Garcilaso*, eds Inoria Pepe and José María Reyes (Madrid: Cátedra, 2001)

——, *Poesía castellana original completa*, ed. Cristóbal Cuevas (Madrid: Cátedra, 1985)

Hesiod, *Works and Days*, trans. Hugh G. Evelyn-White [1914] (Gloucester: Dodo Press, 2008)

——, *The Theogony*, trans. Hugh G. Evelyn-White [1914] (Gloucester: Dodo Press, 2008)

Hillman, James, *The Dream and the Underworld* (New York: Harper and Row, 1979)

Hoefmans, Marjorie, 'Myth into Reality: The Metamorphosis of Daedalus and Icarus (Ovid, *Metamorphoses* 8, 183–235)', *L'Antiquité Classique*, LXIII (1994), 137–60

Homer, *The Iliad*, trans. Robert Fagles (New York: Penguin, 1990)

——, *The Odyssey*, trans. E. V. Rieu (Middlesex: Penguin, 1987)

Honig, Edwin, *Dark Conceit: The Making of Allegory* (London: Faber and Faber, 1959)

Horace [Quintus Horatius Flaccus], *Satires, Epistles and Ars Poética*, trans. H. R. Fairclough, Loeb Classical Library (London: Heineman; Cambridge Mass.: Harvard University Press, 1978)

Hutcheon, Linda, *Narcissistic Narrative: The Metafictional Paradox* (Waterloo, Ontario: Wilfrid Laurier University Press, 1980)

Iffland, James, *Quevedo and the Grotesque*: *The Grotesque Image*, 2 vols (London: Tamesis, 1978)

Iglesias Feijóo, Luís, 'Lectura de la Egloga 1', in *Academia Literaria Renacentista IV, Garcilaso de la Vega*, ed. Víctor García de la Concha (Salamanca: Ediciones Universidad de Salamanca, 1983), pp. 61–82

Ilie, Paul, 'Purifying Poetry: The Ineffable and the Dehumanized', in *Studies in Honour of Bruce W. Wardropper*, eds Dian Fox, Harry Sieber and Robert ter Horst (Delaware: Juan de la Cuesta, 1989), pp. 163–79

Iser, Wolfgang, *The Act of Reading: A Theory of Aesthetic Response* (Baltimore: John Hopkins University Press, 1978)

Jammes, Robert, *Études sur l'oeuvre poetique de Don Luis de Góngora* (Bordeaux: Institut d'études ibériques et ibéro-américaines de l'Université de Bordeaux, 1967)

Jauralde Pou, Pablo, 'El público y la realidad histórica de la literatura española de los siglos XVI y XVII', *Edad de Oro*, I (1982), 55–64

Jáuregui, Juan de, *Antídoto contra la pestilente poesía de las Soledades por Juan de Jáuregui*, ed. José Manuel Rico García (Sevilla: Universidad de Sevilla, 2002)

Johnson, Carroll B., 'Personal Involvement and Poetic Tradition in the Spanish Renaissance: Some Thoughts on Reading Garcilaso', *Romanic Review*, 80 (1989), 288–304

Johnson, Christopher D., *Hyperboles: The Rhetoric of Excess in Baroque Literature and Thought* (Cambridge, MA, and London: Harvard University Press, 2010)

Johnson, W.R., *The Idea of Lyric: Lyric Modes in Ancient and Modern Poetry* (Berkeley: University of California Press, 1982)

Joiner Gates, Eunice, ed., *Documentos gongorinos* (Mexico: Colegio de México, 1960)

Jones, R.O., ed., *Poems of Góngora* (Cambridge: Cambridge University Press, 1966)

——, 'The Idea of Love in Garcilaso's Second Eclogue', *Modern Language Review*, 46.3/4 (1951), 388–95

Keniston, Hayward, *Garcilaso de la Vega: A Critical Study of His Life and Works* (New York: Hispanic Society of America, 1922)

Kepler, Johannes, *The Harmony of the World by Johannes Kepler*, translated into English with an Introduction and Notes by E.J. Aiton, A.M. Duncan and J.V. Field (Philadelphia: American Philosophical Society, 1997)

——, *Mysterium Cosmographicum: The Secret of the Universe*, trans. A.M. Duncan, introduction and commentary by E.J. Aiton (New York: Abaris Books, 1981)

Kerrigan, William, and Gordon Braden, *The Idea of the Renaissance* (Baltimore: John Hopkins University Press, 1989)

Kim, Angela, 'Cain and Abel in the Light of Envy: A Study in the History of the Interpretation of Envy in Genesis 4.1–16', *Journal for the Study of Pseudepigrapha*, 12.1 (2001), 65–84

Kluge, Sofie, *Baroque · Allegory · Comedia: The Transfiguration of Tragedy in Seventeenth-Century Spain* (Kassel: Edition Reichenberger, 2010)

——, 'Góngora's Heresy: Literary Theory and Criticism in the Golden Age', *Modern Language Notes*, 122.2 (2007), 251–71

——, 'The Dialectics of Redemption: Fiction, Heresy and Divine Truth in Francisco de Quevedo's *Dream of Hell*', *Orbis Litterarum*, 59.6 (2004), 416–38

Knox, Peter E., 'In Pursuit of Daphne', *Transactions of the American Philological Association,* 120 (1990), 183–202

Komanecky, Peter M., 'Epic and Pastoral in Garcilaso's Eclogues', *Modern Language Notes*, 86.2 (1971), 154–66

Lacher, Gerhart B., '*Homo viator*: Medieval Ideas on Alienation and Order', *Speculum,* 42 (1967), 233–59

Lakoff, George, 'The Contemporary Theory of Metaphor', in *Metaphor and Thought*, ed. Andrew Ordony (Cambridge: Cambridge University Press, 1993)

Lapesa, Rafael, *La trayectoria poética de Garcilaso de la Vega* (Madrid: Revista de Occidente, 1948)

Lázaro Carreter, Fernando, 'La *Ode ad Florem Gnidi* de Garcilaso de la Vega', in *Garcilaso: Actas de la IV Academia Literaria Renacentista, Universidad de Salamanca, 2–4 de marzo de 1983*, ed. Víctor García de la Concha (Salamanca: Universidad de Salamanca, 1986), pp. 109–26

Lehrer, Melinda Eve, *Classical Myth and the 'Polifemo' of Góngora* (Potomac, Maryland: Scripta Humanistica, 1989)

Levensten, E.A., *The Stuff of Literature: Physical Aspects of Texts and Their Relation to Literary Meaning* (Albany: SUNY Press, 1992)

Lida de Malkiel, María Rosa, 'La abeja: la historia de un motivo poético', *Romance Philology*, 17 (1963), 75–86

Lida, Raimundo, *Prosas de Quevedo* (Barcelona: Crítica, 1981)

Lipmann, Stephen, 'On the Significance of the "Trance de Lucina" in Garcilaso's First Eclogue', *Neophilologus*, 67 (1983), 65–70

Llosa Sanz, Álvaro, 'El tacto invisible. Relectura erótica del soneto VIII de Garcilaso: del eros fantástico a la fantasía erótica', *Hispanic Review*, 77.4 (2009), 413–25

López Bueno, Begoña, ed., *Las anotaciones de Fernando de Herrera: doce estudios* (Sevilla: Universidad de Sevilla, 1997)

——, *La poética cultista de Herrera a Góngora* (Sevilla: Alfar, 1987)

Low, Anthony, *The Reinvention of Love: Poetry, Politics and Culture from Sidney to Milton* (Cambridge: Cambridge University Press, 1993)

Lucey, Michael, *Never Say I. Sexuality and the First Person in Colette, Gide and Proust* (Durham: Duke University Press, 2006)

Lumsden Kouvel, Audrey, 'Nature and Time in Garcilaso de la Vega', *Kentucky Romance Quarterly*, 19 (1972), 199–209

——, 'Problems Connected with the Second Eclogue of Garcilaso de la Vega', *Hispanic Review*, 15.2 (1947), 251–71

Macrí, Oreste, 'Autenticidad y estructura de la edición póstuma de *Versos de Fernando de Herrera*', *FR*, VI (1959), 1–26 and 151–84

Maglione, Sabatino, 'Fernando de Herrera and Neoplatonism', *Hispanófila*, 69 (1980), 45–71

Mariscal, George, *Contradictory Subjects: Quevedo, Cervantes and Seventeenth-Century Spanish Poetry* (Ithaca: Cornell University Press, 1991)

Martín, Adrienne, 'Góngora y la visualización del cuerpo erótico', in *Góngora Hoy, IX, Actas del Foro de Debate Góngora Hoy celebrado en la Diputación de Córdoba*, ed. Joaquín Roses Lozano (Córdoba: Diputación de Córdoba, 2007), pp. 265–91

Martínez Arancón, Ana, *La batalla en torno a Góngora (selección de textos)* (Barcelona: Antoni Bosch, 1978)

Martínez Góngora, Mar, 'Relaciones homosociales, discurso antibelicista y ansiedades masculinas en Garcilaso de la Vega', *Calíope*, 10.1 (2004), 123–40

Martínez-López, Enrique, 'Sobre aquella bestialidad de Garcilaso (égl. III, 230)', *Publications of the Modern Language Association*, 87 (1972), 12–25

Martínez Ruíz, Francisco Javier, 'Fernando de Herrera ante la crítica', in *Las anotaciones de Fernando de Herrera: doce estudios*, ed. Begoña López Bueno (Sevilla: Universidad de Sevilla, 1997), pp. 280–81.

McCaw, R. John, 'Turning a Blind Eye: Sexual Competition, Self-Contradiction and the Impotence of Pastoral in Góngora's *Fábula de Polifemo y Galatea*', *His-*

panófila, 127 (1999), 27–35

McGann, Jerome, *A Critique of Modern Textual Criticism* (Chicago: University of Chicago Press, 1983)

——, *The Romantic Ideology: A Critical Investigation* (Chicago: University of Chicago Press, 1983)

McNair, Alexander J., 'Re-evaluating Herrera's Sonnet XXXVIII: Notes on Sense and Intellect in the Lyric Persona of Algunas Obras', *Hispanic Review*, 71 (2003), 565–84

Melchoir-Bonnet, Sabine, *The Mirror: A History*, trans. Katherine H. Jewett (New York: Routledge, 2001)

Menocal, María Rosa, *Writing in Dante's Cult of Truth: From Borges to Boccaccio* (Durham: Duke University Press, 1991)

Merleau-Ponty, Maurice, *The Visible and the Invisible: Studies in Phenomenology and Existential Philosophy*, ed. Claude Lefort, trans. Alphonso Lingis (Evanston, Illinois: Northwestern University Press, 1968)

Meyer, Jeffrey, 'Hemingway, Góngora and the Concept of *Nada*', *Notes on Contemporary Literature*, 38.3 (2008), 2–4

Mezzadri, B., 'La double Eris initiale', *Métis*, 4 (1989), 51–60

Micó, José María, *El 'Polifemo' de Luis de Góngora: ensayo de crítica e historia literaria* (Barcelona, Península, 2001)

——, *La fragua de las Soledades* (Barcelona: Sirmio, 1990)

Middlebrook, Leah, *Imperial Lyric: New Poetry and New Subjects in Early Modern Spain* (University Park, PA: Pennsylvania University Press, 2009)

Mitchell, Juliette and Jacqueline Rose, eds, *Feminine Sexuality; Jacques Lacan and the Ecole Freudienne* (New York: Norton, 1982)

Molho, Maurice, *Semántica y poética (Góngora, Quevedo)* (Barcelona: Crítica, 1997)

Montero, Juan, 'Las anotaciones, del texto al lector', in *Las anotaciones de Fernando de Herrera: doce estudios*, ed. Begoña López Bueno (Sevilla: Universidad de Sevilla, 1997), pp. 91–105

Moriarty, Michael, and John O'Brien, eds, *Theory and the Early Modern*, special issue, *Paragraph*, 29.1 (2006)

Morros, Bienvenido, 'Idea de la lírica en las anotaciones a Garcilaso de Fernando de Herrera', in *Idea de la lírica en el Renacimiento (entre Italia y España)*, eds María José Vega and Cesc Esteve (Barcelona: Mirabel Editorial, 2004), pp. 211–29

——, *Las polémicas literarias en la España del siglo XVI: a propósito de Fernando de Herrera y Garcilaso de la Vega* (Barcelona: QC, 1998)

Nagel, Alexander, and Christopher S. Wood, 'Interventions: Towards a New Model of Renaissance Anachronism', *Art Bulletin*, 87.3 (2005), 403–32

Nagler, M.N., 'Discourse and Conflict in Hesiod: Eris and the Erides', *Ramus*, 21 (1992), 79–96

Navarrete, Ignacio, *Orphans of Petrarch, Poetry and Theory in the Spanish Renaissance* (Los Angeles: University of California Press, 1994)

——, 'La poesía erótica y la imaginación visual', in *Venus venerada: tradiciones eróticas de la literatura española*, eds. J. Ignacio Díez and Adrienne L. Martín

(Madrid: Editorial Complutense, 2006), pp. 73–87

Navarro de Kelley, Emilia, *La poesía metafísica de Quevedo* (Madrid: Ediciones Guadarrama, 1973)

Navarro, M. Romera, *Historia de la literatura española*, 2nd edn (Boston: D.C. Heath, 1966)

Nebrija, Antonio de, *Gramática de la lengua española,* eds. Pascual Galindo Romeo and Luís Ortiz Muñoz, 2 vols (Madrid: CSIC, 1946)

Newlyn, Lucy, *Reading, Writing, and Romanticism: The Anxiety of Reception* (Oxford: Oxford University Press, 2000)

Nicolás, César, 'Al sol Nise surcaba golfos bellos … Culteranismo, conceptismo y culminación de un diseño retórico', *Anuario de estudios filológicos*, 10 (1987), 265–94

Nicoll, W.S.M., 'Cupid, Apollo, and Daphne (Ovid, *Met.* 1, 452ff)', *Classical Quarterly*, N.S., 30 (1980), 174–82

Nightingale, Jeanne, 'From Mirror to Metamorphosis: Echoes of Ovid's Narcissus in Chrétien's *Eric et Enide*', in *The Mythographic Art*, ed. Jane Chance (Gainesville: University of Florida Press, 1990), pp. 47–82

Nitsch, Wolfram, 'Prisiones textuales. Artificio y violencia en la poesía española del barroco', *Olivar*, 5 (2004), 31–47 <http://wwwfuentesmemoria.fahce.unlp.edu.ar/art_revistas/pr.3259/pr.3259.pdf> [last accessed 1 September 2012]

Nonnus, *Dionysiaca,* trans. W. H. D. Rouse, introduction and notes by H. J. Rose, 3 vols (Cambridge, Mass: Harvard University Press, 1940–42)

O'Reilly, Terence, 'The Figure of Elisa in the Eclogues of Garcilaso', in *Spanish Poetry of the Golden Age*, eds Stephen Boyd and Jo Richardson (Manchester: Manchester Spanish and Portuguese Studies, 2002), pp. 85–96

——, ed., *The Philosophy of Love in Spanish Literature: 1480–1680* (Edinburgh: Edinburgh University Press, 1985)

Olivares, Julián, *The Love Poetry of Francisco de Quevedo: An Existential and Aesthetic Approach*, Cambridge Iberian and Latin American Studies (Cambridge: Cambridge University Press, 1983)

Olson, John, 'Extreme Reading', <http://stevenfama.blogspot.co.uk/2009/06/adventures-in-pharmakon.html> [last accessed 8 September 2012]

Ormiston, Gayle L., and Alan D. Schrift, eds, *The Hermeneutic Tradition: From Ast to Ricoer* (New York: State University of New York Press, 1990)

Orozco Díaz, Emilio, *Lope y Góngora frente a frente* (Madrid: Gredos, 1973)

Otto, Walter F., *The Homeric Gods: The Spiritual Significance of Greek Religion*, trans. Moses Hadas (New York: Thames and Hudson, 1979)

Ovid, *Metamorphoses*, with an English translation by Frank Justus Miller, revised by G.P. Goold, 3rd edn, Loeb Classical Library (Cambridge, MA: Harvard University Press, 1977)

Pabst, W., *La creación gongorina en los poemas Polifemo y Soledades*, trans. Nicolás Marín (Madrid: C.S.I.C., 1966)

Padrón, Ricardo, 'Exile and Empire: The Spaces of the Subject in Fernando de Herrera', *Hispanic Review*, 70 (2002), 497–520

Pagden, Anthony, *The Fall of Natural Man: The American Indian and the Origins of Comparative Ethnography* (Cambridge: Cambridge University Press, 1987)

Palmer, Patricia, *Language and Conquest in Early Modern England* (Cambridge: Cambridge University Press, 2001)

Palomo, María del Pilar, *La poesía de la edad barroca* (Barcelona: SGEL, 1975)

Pando Cantelli, María J., 'John Donne, Francisco de Quevedo, and the Construction of Subjectivity in Early Modern Poetry', in *Spanish Studies in Shakespeare and his Contemporaries*, ed. José Manuel González (Newark: University of Delaware Press, 2006), pp. 89–113

——, '"… and often Absences / Withdrew our Soules and made us Carcasses". The Destructive Power of the Female Figure in Donne's *Nocturnall* and Quevedo's Love Poetry', *SEDERI*, 13 (2003), 155–62

Parker, Alexander A., *The Philosophy of Love in Spanish Literature*, ed. Terence O'Reilly (Edinburgh: Edinburgh University Press, 1985)

——, 'La agudeza en algunos sonetos de Quevedo', in *Estudios dedicados a D. Ramón Menéndez Pidal,* III (Madrid: Consejo Superior de Investigaciones Científicas, 1952), pp. 345–60

——, *Polyphemus and Galatea: A Study in the Interpretation of a Baroque Poem* (Edinburgh: Edinburgh University Press, 1977)

——, 'Theme and Imagery in Garcilaso's First Eclogue', *Bulletin of Spanish Studies*, 25 (1948), 222–27

Parker, Patricia, 'Virile Style', in *Premodern Sexualities*, eds Louise Fradenburg and Carla Freccero (New York: Routledge, 1996), pp. 199–222

Parkinson Zamora, Lois, and Monika Kaup, eds, *Baroque New Worlds: Representation, Transculturation, Counterconquest* (Durham and London: Duke University Press, 2010)

Paterson, Alan K.G., 'Ekphrasis in Garcilaso's "Egloga Tercera"', *Modern Language Review*, 72 (1977), 73–92

Penny, Ralph, *A History of the Spanish Language* (Cambridge: Cambridge University Press, 1971)

Pepe Sarno, Inoria, 'Fernando de Herrera creador del Petrarca español: *Las anotaciones a la obra de Garcilaso*', *Calíope*, 10 (2004), 69–86

——, and Jose María Reyes, eds, *Fernando de Herrera, Anotaciones a la poesía de Garcilaso* (Madrid: Cátedra, 2001)

Pérez Cuenca, Isabel, and Mariano de la Campa Gutiérrez, 'Creación y recreación en la poesía de Quevedo: el caso de los sonetos', in *Studies in Honor of James O'Crosby*, ed. Lía Schwartz (Newark, Delaware: Juan de la Cuesta, 2004), pp. 281–310

Pérez López, Manuel M., *Pedro de Valencia: Primer Crítico Gongorino* (Salamanca: Ediciones Universidad de Salamanca, 1988)

Persin, Margaret H., *Getting the Picture: The Ekphrastic Principle in Twentieth-Century Spanish Poetry* (Lewisberg: Bucknell University Press, 1997)

Pigman, G.W., 'Versions of Imitation in the Renaissance', *Renaissance Quarterly*, 33 (1980), 1–32

Pineda, Victoria, *La imitación como arte literario en el siglo XVI español (con una edición y traducción del diálogo 'De Imitatione' de Sebastián Fox Morcillo)* (Seville: Diputación Provincial de Sevilla, 1994)

Plutarch, *Quaestiones Convivales*, translated from the Greek by several hands. Corrected and revised by William W. Goodwin (Boston: Little, Brown, and Company; Cambridge: Press of John Wilson and Son, 1874)

Poggi, Giulia, 'Quevedo con / sin Petrarca: apuntes para un debate', *La Perinola*, 8 (2004), 359–74

——, 'Exclusus amator e poeta ausente: alcune note ad una canzone gongorina', *Linguistica e Letteratura*, VII (1983), 189–222

Ponce Cárdenas, Jesús, 'Taceat superata vetustas: poesía y oratoria clásicas en el *Panegírico al duque de Lerma*', in *El Duque de Lerma: Poder y literatura en el siglo de oro*, eds Juan Matas Caballero, José María Micó y Jesús Ponce Cárdenas (Madrid: Centro de Estudios Europa Hispánica, 2011), pp. 57–103

——, *El tapiz narrativo del Polifemo: eros y elipsis* (Barcelona: Universitat Pompeu Fabra, 2010)

Pozuelo, J.M., *El lenguaje poético de la lírica amorosa de Quevedo* (Murcia: Universidad de Murcia, 1979)

Prieto, Antonio, *Imago Vitae: Garcilaso y otros acercamientos al siglo XVI* (Málaga: Universidad de Málaga, 2002)

——, *Garcilaso de la Vega* (Madrid: S.G.E.L., 1975)

Ptolemy, *Almagest*, trans. and ed. G.J. Toomer (London: Duckworth, 1984)

Punter, David, *Metaphor* (London and New York: Routledge, 2007)

Putnam, Michael C.J., *Virgil's Epic Designs: Ekphrasis in the Aeneid* (New Haven and London: Yale University Press, 1998)

Quevedo, Francisco de, *Un Heráclito cristiano, Canta sola a Lisi y otros poemas*, ed. and preliminary study by Lía Schwartz and Ignacio Arellano (Barcelona: Crítica, 1998)

——, *Obra poética*, ed. José Manuel Blecua (Barcelona: Planeta, 1981)

——, *Los Suenos*, ed. Julio Cejador y Franca, 2 vols (Madrid: Espasa Calpe, 1972)

Quinn, David, 'Garcilaso's Égloga Primera: Autobiography or Art?', *Symposium*, 37.2 (1983), 147–64

Rapport, Andrew, and Nigel Dawson, 'Home and Movement: A Polemic,' in *Migrants of Identity: Perceptions of Home in a World of Movement*, eds Andrew Rapport and Nigel Dawson (Oxford and New York: Berg, 1998), pp. 3–38

Read, Malcolm K., *Visions in Exile: The Body in Spanish Literature and Linguistics 1500–1800*, Purdue University Monographs in Romance Linguistics, 30 (Amsterdam and Philadelphia: John Benjamins, 1990)

Rebhorn, Wayne A., 'The Crisis of the Aristocracy in Julius Caesar', *Renaissance Quarterly*, 43 (1990), 75–111

Rendall, Steven F., and Miriam D. Sugarmon, 'Imitation, Theme and Structure in Garcilaso's First Elegy', *Modern Language Notes*, 82 (1967), 230–37

Ricoeur, Paul, *The Rule of Metaphor: The Creation of Meaning in Language*, trans. Robert Czerny with Kathleen McLaughlin and John Costello (London and New York: Routledge, 1978)

——, 'Metaphor and the Main Problem of Hermeneutics', *New Literary History*, 6 (1974), 95–110

Riordan, Maurice, and Jocelyn Bell Burnell, eds, *Dark Matter: Poems of Space* (London: Calouste Gulbenkian Foundation, 2008)

Rivera, Olga, 'El sepulcro como metáfora del cuerpo en algunos poemas de Quevedo', *Symposium*, 57.4 (2004), 231–40

Rivers, Elías L., 'Góngora and his Readers' in *The Image of the Baroque*, ed. Aldo Scaglione, with Gianni Eugenio Viola (New York: Peter Lang, 1995), pp. 109–21

——, *Garcilaso de la Vega: Obras completas con comentario* (Madrid: Castalia, 1974)

——, ed., *La poesía de Garcilaso: ensayos críticos* (Barcelona: Ediciones Ariel, 1974)

——, 'Albanio as Narcissus in Garcilaso's Second Eclogue', *Hispanic Review*, 41.1 (1973), 297–304

Robbins, Jeremy, *Arts of Perception: The Epistemological Mentality of the Spanish Baroque 1580–1720* (Abington: Routledge, 2007)

Rodríguez García, José María, 'Epos delendum est: The Subject of Carthage in Garcilaso's "A Boscán desde La Goleta"', *Hispanic Review*, 66.2 (1998), 151–70

Roig Miranda, Marie, 'La poesía amorosa de Quevedo y su originalidad', *La Perinola*, 9 (2005), 172–81

——, '¿Existe el presente en los sonetos metafísicos de Quevedo?', in *Studia Aurea: Actas del III congreso de la AISO (Toulouse, 1993)*, eds I. Arellano *et al.* (Navarra: Eurograf, 1996), pp. 487–94

——, *Les sonnets de Quevedo, variations, constance, évolution* (Nancy: PUN, 1989)

Rojinsky, David, *Companion to Empire: A Genealogy of the Written Word in Spain and New Spain, c.550–1550* (Amsterdam and New York: Rodopi, 2010)

Romanos, Melchora, 'Los "tan nuevos y peregrinos modos" del Polifemo: ponderación de la poética gongorina en los comentaristas del sigo XVII', in *Góngora Hoy VII: El Polifemo. Actas del Foro del Debate Góngora Hoy celebrado en la Diputación de Córdoba del 22 al 23 de abril de 2004*, ed. Joaquín Roses (Córdoba: Diputación de Córdoba, 2006), pp. 215–31

Roses Lozano, Joaquín, ed., *Góngora Hoy, IX, Actas del Foro de Debate Góngora Hoy celebrado en la Diputación de Córdoba* (Córdoba: Diputación de Córdoba, 2007)

——, *Una Poética de la Oscuridad: la recepción crítica de las 'Soledades' en el siglo XVII* (London: Tamesis, 1994)

Ruíz Pérez, Pedro, 'Mitología del ascenso en los sonetos herrerianos', *Insula*, 610 (1997), 6–9

——, 'De la teoría a la práctica: modelos y modelización en "Algunas obras"', in *Las anotaciones de Fernando de Herrera: doce estudios*, ed. Begoña López Bueno (Sevilla: Universidad de Sevilla, 1997), pp. 239–61

Russell, D.A., 'De Imitatio', in *Creative Imitation and Latin Literature*, eds David West and Tony Woodman (Cambridge: Cambridge University Press, 1979), pp. 1–16

Rutledge, Harry C., 'The Opening of *Aeneid* 6', *The Classical Journal*, 67.2 (1971), 110–15

Said, Edward, 'On the Transgressive Elements in Music', in *Musical Elaborations* (New York: Columbia University Press, 1991), pp. 35–72

Sanders Regan, Mariann, *Love Words: The Self and the Text in Medieval and Renaissance Poetry* (Ithaca: Cornell University Press, 1982)

Sannazaro, Jacopo, *Arcadia*, ed. Francesco Tateo, trans. Julia Martínez Mesanza (Madrid: Cátedra, 1993)

Sarduy, Severo, 'Baroque Cosmology: Kepler', in *Baroque New Worlds: Representation, Transculturation, Counterconquest*, eds Lois Parkinson Zamora and Monika Kaup (Durham and London: Duke University Press, 2010), pp. 292–315

——, *Barroco* (Buenos Aires: Editorial Sudamericana, 1974)

Sartre, Jean Paul, *The Wall [Intimacy]: And Other Stories*, 3rd edn, trans. Lloyd Alexander (New York: New Directions, 1969)

Scaglione, Aldo, ed., with Gianni Eugenio Viola, *The Image of the Baroque* (New York: Peter Lang, 1995)

Schlig, Michael, *The Mirror Metaphor in Modern Spanish Literary Aesthetics* (Lewiston: The Edwin Mellen Press, 2004)

Schmidt, Rachel, 'Herrera's Concept of Imitation as the Taking of Italian Spoils', *Calíope*, 1 (1995), 12–26

Scholz, Bernhardt F., 'Ekphrasis and Enargeia in Quintilian's Institutionis oratoriae libri xii', in *Rhetorica Movet: Studies in Historical and Modern Rhetoric in Honour of Heinrich F. Plett*, eds Peter L. Osterreich and Thomas O. Sloane (Leiden: Brill, 1999), pp. 3–24

Schwartz, Lía, 'Notas sobre dos conceptos del discurso amoroso de Quevedo y sus fuentes: la *amada fiera* y la *amada pétrea*', *La Perinola*, 9 (2005), 215–26

——, ed., *Studies in Honor of James O. Crosby* (Delaware: Juan de la Cuesta, 2004)

——, 'Entre Propercio y Persio: Quevedo, poeta erudito', *La Perinola*, 7 (2003), 367–95

——, 'Herrera, poeta bucólico, y sus predecesores italianos', in *Spagna e Italia attraverso la letteratura del secondo cinquecento*, eds E. Sánchez García, A. Cerbo and C. Borrelli (Napoli: Instituto Universitario Orientale, 2001), pp. 475–500

——, 'Las voces del poeta amante en la poesía quevediana', in *Quevedo a nueva luz: escritura y política*, eds A. Carreira and L. Schwartz (Malaga: Universidad de Málaga, 1997), pp. 271–95

——, 'Figuras del orco y el infierno interior en Quevedo', in *Hommage à Robert Jammes (Anejos de Criticón)*, ed. Francis Cerdon, 3 vols (Toulouse: Presses Universitaires du Mirail, 1994), pp. 1079–88

——, 'La transmisión renacentista de la poesía grecolatina y dos sonetos de Quevedo', *Edad de Oro*, 12 (1993), 303–20

——, '"Novus orbis victus vos vicit": El oro de las Indias en la sátira y en la literatura moral áureas', in *Actas del III congreso argentino de hispanistas "España en América y América en España"*, eds Luís Martínez Cuitiño and Élida Lois (Argentina: Universidad de Buenos Aires, 1992)

——, 'Prisión y desengaño de amor: dos topoi de la retórica amorosa en Quevedo y en Soto de Rojas', *Criticón*, 56 (1992), 21–39

——, *Quevedo: discurso y representación* (Pamplona: Universidad de Zaragoza, 1986)

——, *Metáfora y sátira en la obra de Quevedo* (Madrid: Taurus, 1984)

Scordilis Brownlee, Marina, and Hans Ulrich Gumbrecht, eds *Cultural Authority in Golden Age Spain* (Baltimore: John Hopkins University Press, 1995)

Scorpioni, Valeria, ed. 'Discurso sobre la lengua castellana', *Studi ispanici*, 3 (1977), 177–94

Segal, Charles, *Orpheus: The Myth of the Poet* (Baltimore: John Hopkins University Press, 1989)

Senabre, Ricardo, 'Sobre el proceso creador en la poesía de Quevedo', in *Estudios sobre el Siglo de Oro: homenaje al profesor Francisco Ynduraín*, ed. Francisco Ynduraín (Madrid: Editorial Nacional, 1984), pp. 463–78

——, 'La sombra alargada de un verso gongorino', in *Hommage à Robert Jammes (Anejos de Criticón)*, ed. Francis Cerdan, 3 vols (Toulouse: Presses Universitaires du Mirail, 1994), pp. 1089–98

Sepúlveda, Jesús, 'Con un soneto de Quevedo: léxico erótico y niveles de interpretación', *La Perinola*, 5 (2001), 285–319

Serés, Guillermo, '"Si hija de mi amor mi muerte fuese". Tradiciones y Sentido', *La Perinola*, 8 (2004), 463–83

Sharrock, Alison, 'Gender and Sexuality', in *The Cambridge Companion to Ovid*, ed. Philip Hardie (Cambridge: Cambridge University Press, 2002) pp. 95–107

Sheppard, Anne, D. R., *Studies on the 5th and 6th Essays of Proclus' Commentary on the Republic* (Goettingen: Vandenhoeck & Ruprecht, 1980)

Shklovsky, Viktor, 'Art as Technique', in *Russian Formalist Criticism: Four Essays*, eds and trans. Lee T. Lemon and Marion J. Reiss (Lincoln: University of Nebraska Press, 1965), pp. 3–24

Sigel, Scott, *The Baroque Poetry of Fernando de Herrera, 1534–1597: Decoro in the Spanish Poetry of the Sixteenth and Seventeenth Centuries* (Lewiston: Edwin Mellen Press, 2007)

Slatman, Jenny, 'Tele-vision: Between Blind Trust and Perceptual Faith', in *Religion and Media*, eds Hent de Vries and Samuel Weber (Stanford: Stanford University Press, 2001), pp. 216–27

Smith, John D., 'Metaphysical Descriptions of Women in the First Sonnets of Garcilaso', *Hispania*, 56 (1973), 244–48

Smith, Paul Julian, *Writing in the Margin: Spanish Literature of the Golden Age* (Oxford: Oxford University Press, 1988)

——, *Quevedo on Parnassus: Allusive Context and Literary Theory in the Love Lyric* (London: MHRA, 1987)

——, 'Homographesis in Salicio's Song', in *Busquemos otros montes y otros ríos: estudios de literatura española del Siglo del Oro dedicados a E.L. Rivers*, eds Brian Dutton and Victoriano Roncero López (Madrid: Castilia, 1992), pp. 243–51

Sobejano, Gonzalo, '"En los claustros del alma": Apuntaciones sobre la lengua poética de Quevedo', in *Sprache und Geschichte: Festschrift für Harri Meier zum 65. Geburtstag,* eds Eugenio Coseriu and Wolf-Dieter Stempel (Munich: Fink, 1971), pp. 459–92

——, 'Reinos del espanto: Garcilaso, Góngora y otros', in *Busquemos otros montes y otros ríos: estudios de literatura española del Siglo de Oro dedicados a E.L. Rivers*, eds Brian Dutton and Victoriano Roncero López (Madrid: Castalia, 1992), pp. 253–67

Stanton, Edward, 'Garcilaso's Sonnet XXIII', *Hispanic Review*, 40.2 (1972), 198–201

Stirrup, Barbara E., 'Techniques of Rape: Variety of Wit in Ovid's *Metamorphoses*', *Greece and Rome*, 2nd Series, 24 (1977), 170–84

Sutherland, Elizabeth H., 'Writing (On) Bodies: Lyric Discourse and The Production of Gender in Horace Odes 1. 13', *Classical Philology*, 100.1 (2005),
52–82

ter Horst, Robert, 'In an Echoing Grove: Quijote II and a Sonnet of Garcilaso',
in *Studies in Honour of Bruce W. Wardropper*, eds Dian Fox, Harry Sieber and
Robert ter Horst, (Delaware: Juan de la Cuesta, 1989)

——, 'Poetry and Power in Garcilaso's *Égloga Primera*', *Revista de Estudios
Hispánicos*, 21 (1987), 1–10

——, 'Death and Resurrection in the Quevedo Sonnet: "En crespa tempestad"',
Journal of Hispanic Philology, 5 (1980), 41–49

——, 'Time and the Tactics of Suspense in Garcilaso's *Egloga Primera*', *MLA*,
83.2 (1968), 145–63

Terracini, Lore, 'Entre la nada y el oro. Sistema y estructura en el soneto 235 de
Góngora', in *Actas del VIII congreso de la asociación de hispanistas*, eds A.
David Kossoff *et al*. (Madrid: Istmus, 1986), pp. 619–28

——, '"Cristal", no "marfil", en "Mientras por competir con tu cabello"', in
Homenaje a Ana María Berrenechea, eds Lía Schwartz Lerner and Isías Lerner (Madrid: Castalia, 1984), pp. 341–53

Terry, Arthur, *Seventeenth-Century Spanish Poetry: The Power of Artifice* (Cambridge: Cambridge University Press, 1993)

——, 'Review of *The Philosophy of Love*', *Bulletin of Hispanic Studies*, 65
(1988), 169–74

Tissol, G., *The Face of Nature. Wit, Narrative and Cosmic Origins in Ovid's Metamorphoses* (Princeton NJ and Chichester: Princeton University Press, 1997)

Todorov, Tzvetan, 'Les Catégories du récit littéraire', *Communications*, 8 (1966),
125–51

Torres, Isabel, 'Broaching the Void: Reconsidering Góngora's Indeterminate Poetics', *Bulletin of Spanish Studies*, 90.1 (2013), 107–29

——, 'Sites of Speculation: Water / Mirror Poetics in Garcilaso de la Vega, Eclogue II', *Bulletin of Hispanic Studies*, 86.6 (2009), 877–92

——, 'Neo-Parkerism: An Approach to Reading Garcilaso de la Vega, Eclogue
I', *Bulletin of Spanish Studies*, LXXXV:6 (2008), 93–105

——, 'Lope de Vega's *La Gatomaquia* and positive parody', *Caliope*, 14.1
(2008), 5–22

——, 'Con Pretensión de Fenix', in *Rewriting Classical Mythology in the Hispanic Baroque*, ed. Isabel Torres (Woodbridge: Tamesis, 2007), pp. 1–16

——, *The Polyphemus Complex: Rereading the Baroque Mythological Fable*,
Bulletin of Hispanic Studies, monograph issue, 83.2 (2006)

——, 'Shades of Significance in Quevedo's Internal Hades: Orphic Resonance
and Latin Intertexts in the Love Poetry', *Caliope*, 2.1 (1996), 5–35

Tronstad, Ragnhild, 'Could the World become a Stage? Theatricality and Metaphorical Structures', *SubStance*, 31.2 (2002), 216–24

Tuve, Rosemond, *Elizabethan and Metaphysical Imagery: Renaissance Poetic
and Twentieth-Century Critics* (Chicago: Chicago University Press, 1947)

Vanhoozer, Kevin J., *Is There a Meaning in This Text? The Bible, the Reader, and the
Morality of Literary Knowledge* (Grand Rapids: Zondervan, 1998)

Vaquero Serrano, María del Carmen, 'Dos sonetos para dos Sás: Garcilaso y Góngora', *Lemir*, 11 (2007), 37–44

——, 'Doña Beatriz de Sá, La Elisa posible de Garcilaso. Su genealogía', *Lemir,* 7 (2003), 1–48

Vilanova, Antonio, 'Fernando de Herrera', in *Historia general de las literaturas hispánicas*, ed. Guillermo Díaz-Plaja (Barcelona: Vergara, 1968), pp. 687–751

Virgilius, Maro P., *Opera*, ed. R. A. B. Mynors (Oxford: Clarendon Press, 1986)

Vitulli, Juan M., 'Polifemo reformado: imitación, comentario y diferencia en la poética de Góngora', *Revista de estudios hispánicos*, 41.1 (2007), 3–26

Wagschal, Steven, *The Literature of Jealousy in the Age of Cervantes* (Columbia and London: University of Missouri Press, 2006)

Waley, Pamela, 'Garcilaso, Isabel and Elena: The growth of a legend', *Bulletin of Hispanic Studies*, LVI (1979), 11–15

——, 'Garcilaso's Second Eclogue is a Play', *Modern Language Review*, 72 (1977), 585–96

Walker, Steven F., 'The Wrong Word at the Right Time: Verbal Dissonance and the Social Function of Mannerist Hermeticism', in *Proceedings of the Xth Congress of the International Comparative Literature Association*, eds Anna Balakian, James J. Wilhelm *et al.* (New York: Garland, 1985), pp. 582–86

Waller, Gary F., 'Struggling into Discourse: The Emergence of Renaissance Women's Writing', in *Silent But for the Word: Tudor Women as Patrons, Translators and Writers of Religious Works*, ed. Margaret Patterson Hannay (Kent: Kent State University Press, 1985), pp. 238–56

Walters, D. Gareth, 'Convention and Contradiction in a Quevedo Sonnet: An Analysis of "Enriquecerse quiso, no vengarse"', in *Readings in Spanish and Portuguese Poetry for Geoffrey Connell*, eds Nicholas G. Round and D. Gareth Walters (Glasgow: University of Glasgow, 1985), pp. 259–73

Waswo, Richard, *Language and Meaning in the Renaissance* (Princeton: Princeton University Press, 1987)

Westcott, Howard B., 'Garcilaso's Eclogues: Artifice, Metafiction, Self-Representation', *Calíope*, 3.1 (1997), 71–85

Williams, Robert Grant, 'Reading the Parenthesis', *SubStance*, 70 (1993), 53–64

Williams, Wes, '"Being in the Middle": Translation, Transition and the "Early Modern"', in *Theory and the Early Modern*, eds Michael Moriarty and John O'Brien, special issue, *Paragraph*, 29.1 (2006)

Woods, M.J., 'Herrera's Voices', in *Medieval and Renaissance Studies on Spain and Portugal in Honour of P.E. Russell*, eds F.W. Hodcroft, D.G. Pattison, R.D.F. Pring-Mill and R. Truman (Oxford: The Society for the Study of Medieval Languages and Literatures, 1981), pp. 121–32

——, 'Rhetoric in Garcilaso's First Eclogue', *Modern Language Notes*, 84 (1969), 143–56

Zerba, Michelle, 'Love, Envy and Pantomimic Morality in Cicero's *De oratore*', *Classical Philology*, 97.4 (2002), 299–321

Index